KU-700-942

Education, Globalisation and New Times

The late 1970s and early 1980s was a period of crisis within the education sector, out of which came an extensive, ongoing and global project of reform. Policies proliferated and education was no longer a policy backwater. The *Journal of Education Policy* offered, and continues to offer, a forum for debate, informed analysis and policy theorisation, with its central focus on critical policy analysis which seeks to explore and interrogate the ways in which policy engages with practice.

Education, Globalisation and New Times comprises a selection of the most influential papers published over the 21 years of the journal's history. Written by many of the leading scholars in the field, these seminal papers cover a variety of subjects, sectors and levels of education, focussed around the following major themes:

- Education, globalisation and new times
- Policy theory and method
- Policy and equity.

Compiled by the journal's editors, Stephen Ball, Ivor Goodson and Meg Maguire, the book illustrates the development of the field of education policy studies, and the specially written Introduction contextualises the selection, whilst introducing students to the main issues and current thinking in the field. This volume is part of the Education Heritage series. For details of other books in the series, please go to www.routledge.com/education

Stephen J. Ball is Karl Mannheim Professor of Sociology at the Institute of Education, University of London, UK.

Ivor F. Goodson is Professor of Learning Theory at the University of Brighton, UK.

Meg Maguire is Professor of Sociology of Education at King's College London, UK.

Education Heritage series

Other titles in the series:

From Adult Education to the Learning Society
21 years from the International Journal of Lifelong Education
Peter Jarvis

A Feminist Critique of Education
Christine Skelton and Becky Francis

Overcoming Disabling Barriers
18 years of disability & society
Len Barton

Tracing Education Policy
Selections from the Oxford Review of Education
David Phillips and Geoffrey Walford

Making Curriculum Strange
Essays from the Journal of Curriculum Studies
Ian Westbury and Geoff Milburn

Readings from the Journal of Education Policy
Stephen J. Ball, Ivor F. Goodson and Meg Maguire

Forty Years of Comparative Education
Changing contexts, issues and identifies
Michael Crossley, Patricia Broadfoot and Michele Schweisfurth

Education and Society
25 years of the British Journal of Education
Len Barton

Education, Globalisation and New Times

Edited by

Stephen J. Ball,
Ivor F. Goodson and
Meg Maguire

LONDON AND NEW YORK

First published 2007
by Routledge
2 Park Square, Milton Park, Abingdon, Oxon OX14 4RN

Simultaneously published in the USA and Canada
by Roultedge
270 Madison Ave, New York, NY 10016

Routledge is an imprint of the Taylor & Francis Group, an informa business

Selection and editorial matter © 2007 Stephen J. Ball, Ivor F. Goodson and Meg Maguire

Typeset in Times New Roman by
Newgen Imaging Systems (P) Ltd, Chennai, India
Printed and bound in Great Britain by
MPG Books Ltd, Bodmin

All rights reserved. No part of this book may be reprinted or reproduced or utilised in any form or by any electronic, mechanical, or other means, now known or hereafter invented, including photocopying and recording, or in any information storage or retrieval system, without permission in writing from the publishers.

British Library Cataloguing in Publication Data
A catalogue record for this book is available from the British Library

Library of Congress Cataloging in Publication Data
Education, globalisation, and new times / edited by Stephen J. Ball, Ivor F. Goodson, and Meg Maguire.
p. cm.
Includes bibliographical references and index.
1. Education and globalization. 2. Education and state. 3. International education. 4. Educational change. I. Ball, Stephen J. II. Goodson, Ivor. III. Maguire, Meg, 1949–

LC71.E298 2007
379–dc22 2006029029

ISBN10: 0–415–42598–0 (hbk)
ISBN10: 0–203–96399–7 (ebk)

ISBN13: 978–0–415–42598–8 (hbk)
ISBN13: 978–0–203–96399–9 (ebk)

Contents

Introduction

The seething and swirling of education policy

The *Journal of Education Policy* is now in its twenty-first year, a kind of coming of age. The main actors in founding the journal were Ivor Goodson and Stephen Ball, then colleagues at the University of Sussex and working closely on a range of projects and publications. The journal was founded to fill a gap, and to respond to changes in the way education was being thought about and talked about. The late 1970s and early 1980s was a decade of education crisis, real or manufactured. Policies began to proliferate and seethe around education in this period to control, delineate, specify or require of education and educators that they 'reform'. Educational institutions were made more autonomous and more accountable, some decisions were devolved and others centralised – forms of controlled de-control. Countries without systems of National Curricula began to design them, while other countries with long traditions of National Curricula began to loosen central controls and new kinds of academic 'subjects' appeared in both. New forms of testing and qualification systems were introduced. Parental choice began its inexorable spread. Market forces were let loose in the relationships between institutions and their clients. Teachers were subject to new forms of training and evaluation. New actors made their appearance within education policy and new discourses developed to reconstruct the ways in which education could be discussed and practised.

Early papers in the journal reflected this frenzy of policy activity: citizenship education (Ranson); pupil-profiling (Fairbairn); education for enterprise (Rees); business leaders and the politics of school reform (Ray and Mickelson); Private Higher Education (Walker); policy analysis as practical reason (Rizvi); school improvement (Hargreaves); IT and education (Beynon and MacKay); the New Right and the National Curriculum (Whitty); political literacy (Carrington and Short); multicultural education (Ball and Troyna). Education was no longer a policy backwater, rather educational issues were to the fore of national politics around the globe as the new demands of the global economy began to re-work the way in which the role of education within national societies was constructed.

The journal set out to be a forum for debate and an outlet for policy theorisation, theoretically informed analysis and careful empirical research on policy from a whole range of relevant disciplines – sociology, political science, economics, history, linguistics, philosophy, etc. The central focus has always been with critical policy analysis. The idea was to offer readers ways of thinking about and responding to policy that put policy into political, ideological and cultural context – and to use theoretical ideas to do so. Thus, in the pages of the journal it has been possible to air issues and consequences arising in and from policies which are systematically neglected in many of the main arenas of policy formation and implementation.

The journal also sought to influence and interrogate media coverage of educational policy issues. For instance, in the early issues Peter Wilby, later to become editor of the *New Statesman*, organised a 'document and debates' section.

Selecting a small sample of the best of the papers published over 21 years was never going to be easy. Many very good papers missed the final cut. There were arguments and compromises along the way, and undoubtedly mistakes have been made. Nineteen were eventually selected (given the word limit within which we were required to work) from a short-list of thirty-seven. The papers included here meet three basic criteria. They are well written and presented. They are theoretically informed and substantively original. They have a general rather than specific or simply national relevance to policy analysis. There is a range of papers from different countries of origin (Australia, Canada, England, France, New Zealand, Portugal, Scotland, the US and Wales), but with a strong Anglo-Saxon and Western bias; seven of the lead authors are women, 12 are men. They cover a variety of topics and sectors and levels of education but are focused around three major themes that we discuss here.

Education, globalisation and new times

Education policy of the past 25 years can sensibly be read as a 'political response to the challenges *and opportunities*' which arise from the decomposition of Fordism and the 'economic and extra economic' (Jessop 2002: 124) tendencies of 'globalisations'.[1] Jessop sees globalisation(s) not as 'being a unitary causal mechanism' but rather 'as the complex emergent product of many different forces operating on many scales' (p. 114). Globalisation is a heterogeneous process. It has economic, cultural and political dimensions, and is made up of erratic flows of capital, goods, services, labour and ideas (including policy ideas (Ball 1998)) which all contribute to an increasing synchronicity of demands, the weakening of traditional structures of meaning, and increasing but varying degrees of difficulty for nation states in the management of their economies – of the world's 100 largest 'economies' 47 are multinational corporations. The term is used and the processes it refers to take place both in a transitive sense, something which is made to happen, and in an intransitive sense, as something that happens. And it is not just 'an "out there" phenomenon. It refers not only to the emergence of large scale world systems, but to transformations in the very texture of everyday life' (Giddens 1996: 367–8). But 'to a large extent, globalization represents the triumph of the economy over politics and culture' (Burbules and Torres 2003). For Western developed economies globalisation is a threat to traditional forms of production and accumulation and the opportunity for new forms. As Brown and Lauder explain: 'The significance of globalisation to questions of national educational and economic development can be summarised in terms of a change in the rules of eligibility, engagement and wealth creation' (Brown and Lauder 1996). Education has become differently and specifically tied to the necessities of competition. The role of the state has changed, the requirements and training of workers have altered dramatically, and education is increasingly a site of production as well as reproduction in relation to the emerging, if sometimes over-hyped, 'knowledge economy'. The demand for highly skilled, flexible workers in fields like ICT has increased alongside the massive growth in employment in low-paid, low-skill service jobs (see Ball *et al.* 2000).

One of the strengths of the JEP is its capacity to provide an arena in which key policy turns can be debated, critiqued, refined, reworked and their specificities teased out forensically. The selected papers that explore education, globalisation and new times do exactly this. They mark up the distinction between economic, political and cultural forms. This is possible in a policy journal that is alive to nuances of critique and wants to stimulate disagreement and recognise contradictions.

In general terms two complexly interrelated policy agendas are discernible in all the heat and noise of education reform of the past 25 years. Both agendas directly connect with the economic discourses of globalisation and the 'responses' to globalisation which they mobilise. The first aims to tie education more closely to national economic interests, while the second involves a de-coupling of education from direct state control. The first rests on a clear articulation and assertion by the state of its requirements of education, while the second gives at least the appearance of greater autonomy to educational institutions in the delivery of those requirements. The first involves a reaffirmation of the state functions of education as a 'public good' and economic necessity. The second subjects education to the disciplines of the market and the methods and values of business and redefines it as a competitive private good. In many respects, educational institutions are now being expected to take on the qualities and characteristics of 'fast capitalism' (Gee and Lankshear 1995) and this involves not only changes in organisational practices and methods but also the adoption of new social relationships, values and ethical principles.

We can see these two political agendas being played out in terms of an ensemble of generic policies – parental choice and institutional competition, site-based autonomy, managerialism, performative steering, curricula fundamentalism – which nonetheless have local variations, twists and nuances – *hybridity* – and different degrees of application – *intensity*. The purest and most intense versions of this ensemble are evident in places like England, New Zealand and Alberta (Canada). Mixed and low intensity versions are evident in places like France, Colombia and many US and Australian states. Places like Portugal and Sweden display hybrid but low intensity versions.

One of the tensions which runs through all varieties of policy analysis is that between the need to attend to the local particularities of policy making and policy-enactment and the need to be aware of general patterns and apparent commonalities or convergences across localities. Policy ideas are also received and interpreted differently within different political architectures (Cerny 1990), national infrastructures (Hall 1986) and national ideologies. The new orthodoxies of education policy are grafted onto and realised within very different national and cultural contexts and are affected, inflected and deflected by them. They enter rather than simply change existing power relations and cultural practices (see, for example, Lingard *et al.* (1997) on OECD education policies), a process Robertson (1995) calls 'glocalisation'. This is the terrain over which the first set of papers in the collection range.

In a special edition that concentrates on globalisation and education policy (14/1/1999) Dale rejects any easy constructions or processes of convergence. Instead, he claims that globalisation 'does require one to consider anew how (those) policies are formed, shaped and directed'. The process of globalisation takes many forms and in the case study of France produced by Van Zanten in this collection, the role of national state policies are carefully traced. 'Cleavages' between key educational stakeholders, here head teachers, teachers and parents, are explored in order to reveal the ways in which global pressures can be 'twisted and transformed' to fit the purposes of the national state. Stoer and Cortesao's paper goes even further and suggests that in a semi-peripheral country (within Europe) 'state schooling may be the last refuge of resistance to the transnationalization process'. But the paper by Blackmore in this collection raises a key issue in relation to globalisation, an issue that still has salience. She writes, 'gender is notably absent from mainstream discussion of globalization, either as an organizing principle or a category of analysis.'

This section of the collection also includes a paper by Hartley that concentrates on theoretical and cultural influences on understanding and interpreting education changes in new times. The argument in this paper is that greater insights could be gained into aspects of school management if the 'ideas from post modern theory and chaos theory and the culture of postmodernism were incorporated into policy analysis'. Going further, Kenway *et al.* highlight the 'intellectual and psychic numbing and emotional shallowness' of much that passes for policy making (with a focus on the Australian setting). This paper asks two questions that in many ways frame the first section:

> The questions for educators are: 'where do we think new times and new educational forms leaves us?' and 'what do we intend to do about it?'

Policy theory and method

One of the strengths, we believe, of the *Journal of Education Policy* is the opportunity it offers to publish new theoretical ideas and applications and new forms of research practice in the general field of education policy. Theory can be both exciting and appropriately dangerous. It is constructive and invigorating, and violent and destructive. It challenges cherished orthodoxies and taken-for-granted practices and methods and allows us to begin to think 'otherwise'. Social theory, rather than being an indulgence or irrelevance to research, is a necessity. It plays a key role in forming and re-forming key research questions, invigorating the interpretation of research and ensuring reflexivity in relation to research practice and the social production of research.

In the social sciences generally, post-structural and postmodern disruptions of various kinds have been a major feature of the scholarship of the final decades of the twentieth century. Not all of these disruptions have been equally helpful or useful but the postmodern turn has brought new life and new rigour into many facets of social science practice. As a result, 'Over the last two decades "post-modernism" has become a concept to be wrestled with, and such a battleground of conflicting opinions and political forces that it can no longer be ignored' (Harvey 1989: 39). It is 'the end' of social science and a new beginning. Postmodern theory presents a challenge to a whole raft of fundamental, often dearly cherished but sometimes unexamined, assumptions in the social sciences; most obviously and profoundly the deployment of totalising 'grand narratives'. Large, all-encompassing and systemic 'explanations' of 'the social' are disrupted and eschewed by postmodernism. Lyotard quite simply defines the postmodern as 'incredulity towards meta-narratives' or as Lather (1988: 7) explains: 'What is destroyed by the post-structuralist suspicion of the lust for authoritative accounts is not meaning, but claims to the unequivocal dominance of any one meaning.'

In the modernist fightback against the postmodern onslaught, this suspicion of authoritative meaning is subjected to the charge of 'relativism', which is 'everywhere abominated' (Barnes and Bloor 1991: 21). Relativism is often taken to require the removal of any possibility for certainty, especially the ability to make rational and moral judgements but more accurately it is a refusal to accept foundational truth claims; instead, all ontologies and epistemologies are viewed as historically contextual and socially conditioned. Postmodernism eschews the idea of an 'originary position' outside of the social or outside the discourse from which authoritative judgements can be made. Rather, *authority* is viewed as 'the prize for which the competing vocabularies vie with one another' (Fish 1994: 10–11). Truth rests on the workings of power and material interests. All of this requires the rigorous scrutiny of the assumptions that shape the meaning of research itself. Taking postmodernism very seriously also means a careful re-examination of structuralism, realism and agency and that keystone of the Western 'enlightenment legacy', the pursuit of better futures – the relationships between knowledge and progress/social criticism and political liberation.

In Pillow's paper she explores the 'implications of paying attention to the body, literally and figuratively, in policy analysis and policy theory'. Drawing on a Foucauldian analysis, and illuminating her argument through an exploration of 'teen pregnant female bodies', Pillow opens up new questions about what is meant by policy studies and policy work. Gale's paper argues that Foucault's work on historiography and genealogy also needs to be applied to policy analysis if it is to consider 'modalities of power' and the specificities of 'temporary policy settlements'. Taken together, these papers offer an account of policy analysis that draws, differently and contrastively, on the work of a very influential (and fashionable) theorist. In more practical terms Codd looks at what policy analysts can do with the texts of policy and outlines an approach to the deconstruction of policy languages focusing on how language works to manufacture consent. In a complimentary fashion, but from a philosophical perspective, Rizvi employs a Wittgensteinian understanding of language to criticise the 'technological conception of policy analysis and to argue that questions of moral value lie at the heart of policy and should be integral to the analysis of policy'.

Fielding's paper appears in another special edition of the JEP that explores the relationship between philosophy and policy analysis entitled 'Education Policy and the Challenge of Living Philosophy'. His primary aim is to establish the 'centrality of community in human affairs' (p. 397). Drawing on the work by Scottish philosopher Macmurray, Fielding rejects managerialism and its attendant discourses of effectiveness and performance and asserts the power of personal relations in policy enactments.

Policy and equity

One simple condensate of critical concerns in education policy is the question of equity. A very high proportion of papers received and published in the journal are concerned with the consequences for equity of new or functioning education policies, both the first order consequences in terms of new practices and structures and the second order consequences in terms of outcomes for identities, recognition, well-being and the distribution of material benefits.

Paquette argues that 'equity remains at the heart of the *raison d'etre* of publicly funded education.' His paper explores the way in which the contested concept of equity (which Paquette takes as fairness) has been 'assaulted' as a policy imperative. Economism is now the main focus of education policies. He also deals with the post-positivist critique of equity as a grand narrative. The paper asks whether equity is a 'policy priority in peril' (p. 57). Kovachs' paper deals with poverty in the US, and what he calls the 'larger problem of inequality'. His view is that education policy needs to take 'larger social and economic contexts seriously' if they are to respond effectively and equitably in educational settings. In some ways, Kovach's paper echoes the concerns expressed by Paquette: in contexts that are increasingly shaped by market imperatives, equity is much harder to bring off. One distinction made by Kovach is that what is needed is a politics of social justice and this is perhaps harder to pursue and achieve within the current framework of policy thinking.

This is an issue that Seddon picks up and critiques in her paper. She believes that much contemporary policy analysis positions social justice as displaced by post-welfarist discourses. In contrast, she argues for a reconceptualisation of social justice that recognises the importance of structural and material constraints but that works to 'document, interrogate, and critique historicized social practices' in order to reveal the ways in which justice and injustice are (re)produced in different times and in different places. Her approach towards social justice brings back a historicity and specificity that helps ground work in this area and offers a way beyond any deterministic approaches in the work on social justice or the lack of it. And in talking of social justice, rather than equity or fairness, what is being included is a wider range of justice imperatives including issues of redistribution but also cultural and associational forms of justice.

Reed's paper has a similar project. She argues that policy analysis needs to deal with the 'emotional and psychic landscapes' that are produced in schools in response to policy shifts. Even more strongly, she believes that distributive forms of justice marginalise these concerns and that there is a need to articulate the emotional consequences of policy in relation to two key concepts: oppression and domination. Nash's paper also reaches into the emotional/affect domain and he suggests that policy studies that engage with what he calls 'non-cognitive' dispositions such as attitudes towards schooling need to be incorporated into what we know about policy issues, such as school effectiveness and progress.

Other papers that have been included in this collection take a more grounded approach towards social justice issues in educational provision. For example, Morley's gendered exploration of a quality audit into UK Higher Education exposes the way in which women's labour was appropriated and 'often unrecognised and unacknowledged'. Although this paper concentrates on a piece of public policy – the need for transparency and accountability in Higher Education – the consequences of participation in this process for women, both 'bad' and 'good', highlight the situatedness and complexities in achieving social justice in the micro-context of an institution.

Gulson's paper relates back to the issue of globalisation and explores the inter-relationships of the global and the local in the specifics of education policy and in the lives of schools and children in marginalised communities in two 'global cities' – London and Sydney. The paper works across space and place and with the concept of space, and demonstrates the synergies of theorising across sociology, educational research and geography. It ably demonstrates the scope and reach of the *Journal of Education Policy* in terms of the theorising and critical analysis of policy.

Conclusion

In this collection from 21 years of the *Journal of Educational Policy* we have put together a set of papers that have contributed in different ways to important shifts in the theoretical and empirical landscapes of policy analysis. Some of these papers have been able to disrupt the 'common-sense' of and in policy thinking; others have focused substantively on international and transnational developments such as the impact of forms of globalisation, privatisation and market-driven changes; they also provide new 'methods' for policy work. The papers were chosen for their usefulness and transposability – they constitute a valuable toolbox of ideas, methods and concepts for the policy researcher. The very best policy work contains within it the potential to demonstrate the complexity of progress, change and reform (good and bad or both) and to reveal how and why policies are thought and made, as well as showing how they are struggled over and contested in their various enactments and what fairer and more just policies might look like and might be achieved in the future.

Note

1 'A supercomplex series of multicentric, *multiscale*, multitemporal, multiform and multicausal processes' (p. 113).

References

Ball, S. J. (1998). 'Big Policies/Small World: an introduction to international perspectives in education policy'. *Comparative Education* **34**(2): 119–129.

Ball, S. J., M. M. Maguire and S. Macrae (2000). 'Space, Work and the "New Urban Economies"'. *Journal of Youth Studies* **3**(3): 279–300.

Barnes, B. and D. Bloor (1991). 'Relativism, rationalism and the sociology of knowledge'. In M. Hollis and S. Lukes (Eds.) *Rationality and Relativism*. Cambridge: MA, MIT Press.

Brown, P. and H. Lauder (1996). 'Education, Globalisation and Economic Development'. *Journal of Education Policy* **11**(1): 1–25.

Burbules, N. and C.-A. Torres, Eds. (2003). *Globalisation and Education*. New York, Routledge.

Fish, S. (1994). *There's No Such Thing as Free Speech ... and it's a Good Thing Too*. Oxford, Oxford University Press.

Gee, J. and C. Lankshear (1995). 'The new work order: critical language awareness and "fast capitalism" texts'. *Discourse* **16**(1): 5–20.

Giddens, A. (1996). *Introduction to Sociology*. New York, W. W. Norton.

Hall, P. (1986). *Governing the Economy*. Cambridge, Polity Press.

Harvey, D. (1989). *The Condition of Postmodernity*. Oxford, Basil Blackwell.

Jessop, B. (2002). *The Future of the Capitalist State*. Cambridge, Polity.

Lather, P. (1988). *Ideology and Methodological Attitude*. American Educational Research Association Annual Meeting, New Orleans.

Lewin, K. M. (1997). *Knowledge Matters for Development*. Unpublished paper. University of Sussex.

Lingard, B., M. Henry and S. Taylor (1997). *Educational Policy and the Politics of Change*. London, Routledge.

Robertson, R. (1995). 'Glocalization: Time-space and Homogeneity – Heterogeneity'. In M. Feathersone, S. Lash and R. Robertson (Eds.) *Global Modernities*. London, Sage.

1 New education in new times

Jane Kenway,[1] *Chris Bigum*[2] *and Lindsay Fitzclarence*[1] *with Janine Collier and Karen Tregenza*

[1] Monash University, [2] Deakin University, Victoria, Australia

Source: *Journal of Education Policy*, 9 (4): 317–33, 1994.

Introduction

As the title implies, this paper is concerned with the new: with the new times we are going through; the new education policies and new and pseudo-new education forms that both reflect and help to effect such times; and with the new issues for education that arise as a result of the new. We will begin with a brief overview of the current education policies that are seeking to effect 'new' education and will point to one particular consequence of such policies. We will then briefly identify some of the key features of 'new times' and some of the debates about this concept. The rest of the paper will focus on the new educational forms which have emerged as a result of the heady mix of new policies and new times. It will identify their key features, put them into historical context, and identify a framework which helps to conceptualize the structural shifts which these new forms represent. We will conclude by raising a number of issues about new education in new times.

The research project from which this paper arises is called 'Marketing Education in the Information Age'. The project began in 1992, during which time we: identified the many ways in which Australian education is assuming a market identity; examined the different national and international literatures in education that have promoted the marketization process; explored the different ways in which this marketization process has been conceptualized and explained; examined the arguments of those who have been critical about marketing education and identified the political, education and ethical grounds on which such critiques have been developed; and identified and critically examined the empirical research and theorizing which has been conducted in Australia, the UK, New Zealand, the USA and Canada (Kenway 1993b).

All of this was, in a sense, background work for current documentary, empirical and theoretical work being conducted on a number of case and cameo studies of different examples of market forms in education. The focus is particularly on those education markets within which information technology plays a role and it is our contention that this is the site at which new forms of education are emerging. Our intention in this project is partly to explore the origins of a market-based culture (Fitzclarence *et al.* 1993), the ways in which the conditions of postmodernity have further contribution to the development of this market form (Kenway, with Bigum and Fitzclarence 1993), the ways in which it helps to sustain the conditions of postmodernity and the ways in which markets may work within and against the more oppressive dimensions of postmodernity. And, finally, our ultimate intention is to identify and explore the implications of these various market forms for policy, curriculum, teachers and pedagogy and more particularly to ask 'what new notions of teachers, pedagogy, curriculum and policy do these new forms generate?'.

New education policies and new times

Since the mid-1980s, Australia has experienced rapid and extensive changes in education at the Commonwealth, national and state levels. Such changes have impinged to varying degrees on almost every sector and aspect of education. Observers of education politics tend to agree that, at all levels of education, economic restructuring is the master discourse which informs all policy decisions (see further Lingard *et al.* 1993). In broad terms policy makers have decided (1) that education's prime purpose is to enhance the economy, (2) that if the economy is to change in response to international economic and technological trends, then education must also change in line with these trends, and (3) that despite education's central role in reshaping the economic future of Australia, its costs to the state must be kept down.

According to this logic, the 'education industry' is to 'get smart and get real'. And, to help it do both, two dominant restructuring tendencies have emerged – one centralizing, the other decentralizing. The centralizing agenda is largely concerned with curriculum and professional development. It is made possible by the imperatives of consensus, corporate federalism and new nationalism.[1] It is guided by two principles: one is vocationalism and the other is scientific rationality. As a result of the vocationalist logic, worthwhile knowledge is defined as that which prepares students for paid work. More specifically, the most worthwhile knowledge is defined as that which can assist Australia to 'gear up' economically and technologically; hence the stress on mathematics, science, technology, Asian languages and commerce. Alongside this, principles of technical/scientific rationality increasingly inform curriculum design and professional development; hence the somewhat behaviourist, reductionist and instrumentalist emphasis on competencies (Collins, C. 1993) and, perhaps to a lesser extent, profiles. Given these emphases it could be argued that the current centralizing agenda is, in many ways, offering old forms of education disguised as new education for new times. The decentralizing agenda is largely concerned with money, management and industrial relations. It is organized according to principles of deregulation, devolution, privatization, commercialization and commodification. Educational institutions are encouraged into the market by anorexic funding policies and the principles and morals of the market are increasingly driving the decentralizing agenda.

These two strategies come together in the sense that the state produces the frameworks within which decentralization and marketization are supposed to happen; it promotes certain values to guide these processes and undertakes certain ideological work in an attempt to ensure they are publicly accepted. For instance, the Australian Education Council (AEC), consisting of Commonwealth, state and territory Ministers of Education, has recently developed a policy statement and set of guidelines for the relationships between schools and industry, with particular reference to sponsorship (AEC 1993). Social justice is included on the planned decentralization agenda in an important way. While it is subordinate and marginal to these dominant logics, it is used as a form of legitimation to help reinforce the main agenda (see Fitzclarence and Kenway 1993). What we have, then, is a system of planned decentralization.

Planned decentralization arises from the values, aspirations, fears and fantasies of the Captains of Educational Consciousness – an affectionate title we have drawn from Ewen (1976) and given to senior policy makers from the Commonwealth Department of Employment Education and Training (DEET), the AEC, state and territory education ministries/directorates/ departments and peak business, industry and union bodies.[2] These people's constant fear during the 1980s and 1990s has been that education is insufficiently responsive to new economic times; that is, to the changed conditions of the emerging global economic village, and so is unable to play a role in shaping these new conditions in ways favourable to Australia's economic interests. Their ambitious aspirations for education are played out in the welter of policy documents which have emerged from DEET, the AEC and state education ministries since the mid-1980s. One of the fantasies of the Captains of Educational Consciousness is that Australia will soon have a perfect match between education and new economic times; each fulfilling the needs of the other and both contributing to Australia's success on the global economy. Another fantasy is that this can be achieved through the system of planned decentralization outlined above. However, this system depends very much on the stability and continuity of consensus politics, on the obedience of all the respective parties 'down the line' and on the expectation that neither side of the restructuring agenda will subvert the other. Wishful thinking aside, there clearly can be no guarantees on any of these matters – particularly when the national interest seems to be defined so narrowly and when certain interests seem so constantly to be privileged over others.

The extent to which the system will work in the ways prescribed is indeed another story, one we will begin to explore in this paper which is concerned with the decentralizing side of the policy agenda. In this regard, our focus is on one particular aspect of its privatization, commercialization and commodification dimensions.[3] It is our contention that in exposing education to various market forces – global, national and local, state policy makers have both placed themselves in a paradoxical position and contributed to the development of new and somewhat problematic forms of education which are potentially outside their control.

As we see it, not only have they put at risk the vulnerable steering capacity of the state with regard to education, economics and, we might add, social justice, they have encouraged on to centre stage a range of relatively new 'players' in education. In effect, it is these new players who are currently developing new educational forms which, while apparently supporting governments' agendas, also take education into the zone of the unknown. The likely long-term consequences of these new directions are not at all clear, although we can make some informed guesses. They suggest that now that the market genie is out of the bottle, policy makers' fantasies about consensus, about rational, goal-directed change 'in the national interest', and about symmetry and control are likely to be unfulfilled. At the same time some of these new forms also suggest that some loss of control on the part of policy makers may not necessarily be a bad thing. We will elaborate on these points shortly. Meanwhile, the broad points to be made here are (1) that policy – on many educational fronts – is claiming and seeking to effect educational forms which will both reflect and effect new economic times; and (2) that as a result, new educational forms are emerging which both support but also have the potential to subvert policy agendas. It is these new forms which reflect and effect new times.

But what are these new times that have led to such dramatic policy shifts and why is it that the development of a market mode in education has shaped so quickly and had such rapid acceptance? Without going into detail, such changes are usually seen as arising from economic changes and imperatives overlain by the political and social values and orientations of powerful political groupings. The term often used to describe these changes is post-Fordism[4] which commonly, although not unproblematically, refers to an unevenly emerging movement away from the mass manufacturing base and assembly line practices of the Fordist era towards 'flexible' and decentralized labour processes and patterns of work organization brought about by the rapid growth, development and application of new information and communications technologies. This is accompanied by:

> the hiving off and contracting out of functions and services; a greater emphasis on choice and product differentiation, on marketing packaging and design, on the 'targeting' of consumers by lifestyle, taste and culture...a decline in the proportion of the skilled, male, manual working class, the rise of the service and white collar classes and the 'feminisation' of the work force.
>
> (Hall 1988: 24)

The economic imperatives which are having such an impact on education policy are associated with significant changes in international economies too. These changes include the growth of world trading blocks and super-national corporations, the internationalization of the labour market and the money market and the rapid growth, and extensive application of new information and communications technologies which have facilitated the development of this global economic village (Mahony 1990; Probert 1993). These changes are said to have resulted in crises both for the nation-state, which loses much of its capacity to control the economy, and for certain segments of capital, which seek out new and often very exploitative ways to survive in times which threaten their annihilation. Needless to say, as the unemployment figures and the attack on unions indicate, these changes have in many instances been disastrous for workers (Levidow 1990). Governments' particular approaches to addressing these crises are seen to arise from the profoundly successful discursive and inter-discursive work of disparate but powerful social and political groupings which have reshaped public and political opinion in favour of economic rationalism (Pusey 1991), corporate managerialism (Yeatman 1990) and market forms in public services (Marginson 1986). While we have some considerable sympathy with the lines of argument which focus on the economic and on the politics of discourse, we do not believe that they are fully able to explain either such dramatic shifts in policy or why such policy imperatives seem to have gained such ready and rapid acceptance 'down the line' and in popular consciousness. In our view, these sea changes are better explained by theories of postmodernity.

It is necessary that we begin our discussion of postmodernity with two qualifications. First, when we talk of postmodernity, we are focusing on broad material, social and cultural shifts and conditions. We are not focusing on the philosophical/intellectual shifts[5] often defined as postmodernism or the artistic/cultural products defined as postmodernist. Second, we acknowledge that as a descriptor of current times this is a highly contentious and contested term,[6] particularly when it is used to imply a sharp distinction between the historical periods of modernity and postmodernity, a global applicability without different implications for different regions, and when it suggests that all its defining characteristics are necessarily historically unique. As Featherstone (1991: 3) points out, 'the post-modern is a relatively ill-defined term as we are only on the threshold of the alleged shift, and not in the position to regard the post-modern as a fully fledged positivity which can be defined comprehensively in its own right'. In this sense then, postmodernity emerges from or 'feeds off' (1991: 6) rather than dramatically breaking with modernity. While we acknowledge a certain discomfort in using the concept, we none the less find it useful as a shorthand which points to the 'cultural logic' or 'cultural dominant' (Jameson 1984) or key features of contemporary times in the First World countries of the West – features which clearly also have an impact on Third World countries.

How, then, do we regard postmodernity? There is clearly not the space here for any detailed discussion on this point, so let us, first, refer readers to Hinkson (1991) for an elaboration of the ideas which help to inform this paper and, second, simply list what we consider its key features and then elaborate a little on its implications for education markets.

The key 'logics' or features of postmodernity include the techno-scientific and communications revolutions, the production of what can be called techno or media culture, the development of a form of techno-worship, the collapse of space and time brought about by the application of new technologies, the cultural dominance of the commodity and the image, the internationalization and post-industrial technologization of the economy, and an identity crisis for nation-states accompanied by the decline of the welfare state and the intensification of state-inspired nationalism. And, of course, all of this has implications for human relationships and subjectivities and for cultural 'sensibilities' or 'moods', as do the new social movements and philosophical and artistic/cultural trends which are part of postmodernity.

As we have argued in a previous article in this journal (Kenway *et al.* 1993) the rise of markets and the cultural dominance of commodity forms are amongst the defining features of postmodernity. The dramatic expansion of capitalist commodity production and of, 'material culture in the form of consumer goods and sites for purchase and consumption' (Featherstone 1991: 13) have produced what is called 'consumer culture' – a culture which owes much of its force to the techno-scientific and communications revolutions. Within consumer culture people's lives are saturated with a plethora of seductive commodities and images which generate various dreams, desires and aesthetic pleasures. As a result, people are dispersed across an ever-changing flow of commodities and images, often in strange juxtapositions. Jameson (1984) calls these decentred human subjects of postmodernity 'desiring machines' who are perfect subjects for the endless array of new images and identities offered by the advertising industry, which extends its reach into more and more aspects of social life as non-market relationships become increasingly redefined according to the logic of the market. Indeed, in this context, consumption becomes a primary source of identity. And, as stated earlier, drawing on Ranson (1990):

> markets require a shift in focus from the collective and the community to the individual, from public service to private service and from other people to the self. Markets redefined the meaning of such terms as rights, citizenship and democracy. Civil and welfare rights and civic responsibility give way to market rights in consumer democracy.
>
> (Kenway, with Bigum and Fitzclarence 1993: 116)

In promoting the marketization of education 'in the national interest', it would seem that the Captains of Educational Consciousness seek not only to redefine education as a commodity and to promote and tap into a cult of educational selfishness but also to produce in Australia's young people a consumer identity. As we will later suggest, other and new 'players' in the educational market-place also have a strong investment in the production of consumer identities but appear more interested in sectional rather than national interests. Overall, educational democracy is redefined as consumer democracy in the education 'industry'. Investors are encouraged to see education as a site worth cultivating for various sorts of profit, and consumers are encouraged to seek the competitive edge at the expense of others and to look for what is increasingly called 'value-added education'. Information technology is often seen by 'investors', consumers and producers of educational 'goods' as the best value to add. It is seen as a form of cultural and symbolic capital well worth institutional and individual expenditure. There is no doubt that information and communications technologies have become positional goods used to help define the status of educational institutions and the employability of workers. They are also becoming integral to the targeting and marketing projects of those who wish to cultivate consumers through schools. This has led to one particular manifestation of the market – a relatively new triad consisting of education, markets and information tecnology. It is this triad that we will focus on in the remainder of this paper.

New forms of education

There is no doubt that various media, information and communications technologies, in particular broadcasting, publishing and modern computing and telecommunications, are converging to become increasingly integral to the operations of many education (and other) markets. This education/markets/information technology triad has many different manifestations and shortly we shall elaborate on some of these. It is our view that this triad has the capacity significantly to alter the ways in which education is produced, conducted and consumed – that indeed it has the capacity to recast education in ways as yet unimaginable.

Even though many people in many current educational settings are grappling with the complexities of these new forms, and despite the considerable impact that their development is likely to have, educational researchers and others in education have been rather slow to cast a quizzical and critical eye in their direction. This paper is based on the premises that we must both develop a thorough understanding of what is happening as education is increasingly marketized and technologized and also explore the likely implications for education and for students.

We shall now put the development of the triad in a brief historical context and at the same time point to some of the unsettling effects it is already having on the conventional order of education, which is structured around such binary oppositions as formal and informal, institutional and non-institutional and public and private. In passing, we will mention a number of examples of the triad.

A brief history

State education policy in Australia has long had an orientation to labour and commodity markets. As far as policy makers are concerned, preparing students for the labour market and for the economy have always been amongst its purposes. And certain commodity markets, the textbook industry for instance, have long seen education as a source of consumers. Various private forms of educational provision have always operated along more direct market lines – although, increasingly in the case of private schools, these have been heavily subsidized and directed by the state as a 'protected education industry'. However, despite this history of associations with market forms, state education in Australia has primarily had a non-market identity. But, as we have indicated, over the last seven years or so, education has undergone something of an identity transformation. As the state has aligned itself more closely and directly with the corporate economy, as it has decreased its commitment to the social wage, state education has not only increased its market orientations but has adopted a variety of market or quasi-market forms. Privatization and commercialization are the key words here.

As education has turned to market forms, so too commercial markets in search of new consumers in times of economic down-turn have increasingly turned to education. Some examples here are the School Sample Bag Co., the Mars Sports Equipment Program, the Meadow Lea/HarperCollins Barcodes for Books promotion and the Pizza Hut's Book It and Sport It! Incentive Programs. For example, the School Sample Bag Co. provides schools with 'show bags' containing a small selection of 'nutritious products', various 'educational' competitions, some advertising brochures and a marketing questionnaire for parents. Bags are provided free of charge to schools which receive a commission for each bag that a child takes home and which use the bags in a variety of ways, for example, as rewards for students. Manufacturers pay for the opportunity to have their product(s) included in the bag. What we are seeing, then, is educational institutions increasingly becoming targets for commercial markets and thus for the values that these particular markets represent. Of course this has long been the case with textbooks, stationery and the like (Wilson 1992) and there is no doubt that cultural markets will increasingly overlap with educational markets in the future; witness the growth of joint educational, trade and cultural 'Expos'. However, it is now the case that commercial enterprises without any educational dimensions to them (and, indeed, certain charitable organizations) are 'targeting' schools, often by involving students in competitions which encourage their families to purchase certain commodities in large quantities and which result in rewards for the school.

If Australia follows the example of the USA then this sort of targeting is likely to increase. Alex Molnar (1993: 43) tells of the development in the USA of marketing firms which specialize in 'pitching' products at students in classrooms: and of the increasing recognition by corporations that 'young spenders', their teachers and parents are a very lucrative market. Hence many companies such as McDonald's now develop custom-made learning materials with a brand name attached. The purposes here are to produce consumers, to 'build brand and product loyalties' and in so doing to counter the bad public relations which arise when a company's negative work, employment or environmental practices are exposed or when its product is seen to have negative implications for people's health. Hence it is not at all unusual for companies to produce curriculum materials which address these problems or practices by offering students the positive alternative. McDonald's, for instance, has attractive materials on the environment to try to counter the bad publicity it received over its role in the destruction of rain forests. Such contradictions aside, in hard times with school budgets strained to the limit, 'cash hungry' (Giroux 1994: 53) schools and education systems are often very willing participants in such marketing efforts. In Australia, politicians and senior bureaucrats from certain state education systems have done deals with McDonalds, Mars and so on and in the process have delivered all schools within the state to the market. In return for the right to promote the company in schools, schools are offered 'free' equipment. In Toronto,

Canada, the 'cash strapped' Toronto Board of Education has gone further and for a million dollars has given Pepsi Cola exclusive pop and juice vending rights in 115 Toronto schools teaching 87000 students. Pepsi will also throw in student-of-the-month plaques and prizes for students – Pepsi T-shirts and hats. As Lantz (1994: 87) wryly observes, 'Obviously, this has taken the concept of educational fund raising to new level'. Clearly free materials are only one part of the story and companies now offer schools incentive deals in exchange for capturing their custom. As 'Education Special Report' in *Fortune* (21 October 1991: 91–108) entitled 'How business helps the schools', lists 133 major American companies and outlines their 'contributions' to education. Calvert and Kuehn (1993: 62) quote a study which indicates that nearly two-thirds of America's largest corporations provide schools with free curriculum materials. Molnar's (1993) close analysis of these materials points to their increasing pedagogical sophistication and suggests that the application of educational ideas from education experts is becoming a natural part of the process. It is worth noting that some such contributions may well be labelled educational philanthropy which has quite a significant history in the USA (Leonard 1992; Lobman 1992) in contrast with Australia which is strikingly parsimonious. One example of philanthropy in Australia worth noting here is The Body Shop's and Esprit's support of a homeless youth programme pioneered at Ardoch Windsor Secondary College. However, the line between philanthropy and marketing is often blurred, particularly given the increasing recognition in the business community of the market value of being seen as a good corporate citizen with a social conscience (Collins, M. 1993). And, as Calvert and Kuehn (1993: 58) point out, 'Charity from business rather than taxation of business puts power in the hands of business to set the agenda for education.' Giroux (1994: 48, 49) takes this line of argument further when he points to the extent to which donations to education can not only put businesses in the position to influence development of the curriculum, they can also save business substantial amounts of money in training programmes. He goes on to say:

> Corporations play a double role here. On the one hand they aggressively support tax cutting measures.... On the other, they then offer the financially strapped schools 'crumbs' that allow private business interests to turn the schools into market niches. Of course if public schools were adequately funded in the first place such bribes wouldn't be necessary. At risk is both the traditionally civic democratic function of public schooling and the very nature of how we define democratic community, critical citizenship, and the most basic premises of teaching and learning.
>
> (Giroux 1994: 51)

Overall the main imperative, then, is to commercialize the classroom (and other aspects of the school such as the canteen, the sports field, the front office), to establish schools as legitimate sites for profit and savings, and to produce future citizens who are dedicated and uncritical consumers and dedicated and docile workers.

Broadcasting, publishing, computing and telecommunications are becoming integral to this process of marketization. They have become part of more traditional market and quasi-market forms and orientations and they have made possible a multiplicity of new market genres. More traditionally, for example, because of their increasing use of 'new' technologies, state and private educational institutions are regarded by commercial marketeers as an expanding market. Computer vendors have always clamoured and continue to do so for school markets and schools continue to clamour for computers. The rich pickings here were recognized by Coles in its Apples for the Students campaign. In this instance Coles supermarkets encouraged schools to collect Coles shopping dockets and once certain targets were reached schools were awarded Apple soft- and hardware. Also, educational institutions are using their relationships to information technologies in their own promotional activities. Some are seeking to promote themselves on the basis of their use of such technologies in the curriculum. Methodist Ladies College, Melbourne, with its lap-top computers, is the best publicized example, but many schools highlight their 'state of the art' technology centres in their publicity materials. Interestingly, a number of girls' private schools have been quick to tie such developments to feminist discourses about girls' empowerment through their use and control of technology. Other institutions are reshaping their identities in order to concentrate on preparing their students for employment in 'high-tech' labour markets. Former public technical high schools and specialist technology high schools are the most obvious examples here. However, some private schools have also sought to move to the front of the pack in this new educational race. For example, in 1993, Ormiston College in Brisbane was promoting itself on the basis of its ambition to 'move to the forefront of computer/technology education' in the context of its development of a corporate culture which involves strong links with 'highly prominent entrepreneurs, marketeers and successful small business operators', a school foyer which is 'more akin to that experienced in the corporate world', an annual Trade and Commerce Fair and 'annual trips for groups of students to South East Asia to examine innovative business and technological practices' (Holmes n.d.).

Some educational institutions are using such technologies to enhance old pedagogies and to give an impression of cutting-edge curriculum innovation. For example, schools in Victoria have responded eagerly to SOLAS, the new on-line, home-based electronic information service. For a substantial fee per hour, this service assists the Victorian Certificate of Education students in the senior levels of their schooling to respond easily to the demands of research-based pedagogy. Schools are provided with various levels of incentive to sign up as many students as they can. Other educational institutions are using such technologies to increase their national and international market reach. In this respect, distance on and offshore fee-paying education is a key example.

The other side of this particular coin is the growth of a number of private tutoring services which assist students to develop their computer skills. '*Futurehids*' is one instance here. This is a US franchise which has been purchased in Australia and which sets up computer learning centres.

More broadly, many governmental and non-governmental agencies are currently exploring a range of ways in which education, markets and information technology can come together efficiently and profitably. The Open Learning Agency of Australia is a case in point here, with its new fee-charging degrees sold on public television (see further, Bigum, Fitzclarence and Kenway, with Collier and Croker 1993). Another example is the CD ROM disk for primary school science produced jointly by the NSW Board of Studies and IBM (Bigum *et al.* 1993). Successmaker, a multimedia integrated learning system, developed in the USA by Computer Curriculum Corporation, now owned by Paramount Communications, is currently establishing itself in a number of schools (at A$250000 a time) with the support of the government education systems of the eastern states of Australia. Science and technology parks and centres are further examples.

In the USA, we see perhaps the most developed instance of this new triad. Chris Whittle, an educational and publishing entrepreneur, has developed Channel One, which offers students 12 minutes of daily news and two minutes of commercials. In exchange for the students' viewing time, the school gets a satellite dish and video equipment. As Durie (1992: 13) notes, 'so far 11861 schools with six million children watch the program together with advertisements supplied by such consumer giants as Pepsi-Cola, Mars, Procter and Gamble, and others at $US200000 per 30-second spot'.[7] In Canada in 1992, Youth News Network (YNN), modelled largely on Channel One, was introduced. Like Channel One, YNN is legitimized, in part, by its capacity to help bring schools into the information age but with YNN there is an interesting twist. According to Duncan (1992), YNN will teach media teachers their media literacy skills in order that they can teach media literacy to students. Indeed some media teachers have been recruited to the board of YNN; a rather different pattern of recruitment from that of Whittle whose corporate pals include such free-market liberals as Chester Finn and John Chubb. However, as Duncan points out, this not only seeks to co-opt the critical language and purpose of media literacy and media teachers: the primary goal of YNN is still 'to sell young people to commercial sponsors' (p. 20). He makes the further case that YNN is yet another example of the corporate sector's take-over of public space and expression. He argues:

> Today the corporate presence is global and pervasive; establishing the rules for behaviour in shopping malls; promoting primarily those television programs which can attract advertising; sponsoring uncontroversial big ticket shows at museums and art galleries . . . and PBS documentaries that don't rock the boat; and controlling the transnational data banks that keep our information society humming.
>
> All of this has infringed on and reduced our social and cultural space, eroded our democratic institutions and, in time of lessened expectations and environmental awareness, legitimized rampant consumerism.
>
> (Duncan 1992: 18)

At stake for Duncan is 'the notion of maintaining a critical democracy through education' (p. 20).

As new information technologies have emerged as significant players in the marketization of the education process in Australia and elsewhere, we are beginning to witness the breaking down of a number of institutional boundaries. As Giroux observes, the intrusion of business into schools and the predictable increased dependency of poorer schools upon 'the support and priorities of the business community' is likely to further reinforce educational and social inequalities, threatens to undermine significantly schools' capacity to work towards the production of advocates for a more just world and by and large calls into question the identity of school as a public institution. But of course the matter does not stop there. There are some signs which suggest that, in part, education is being de-institutionalized and de-territorialized. Clearly TV open learning is one example here. Another example is a CD ROM which combines a comprehensive atlas, encyclopaedia and dictionary and is now available for students to use at home. Similarly, as noted above, students can access from home, via modem, SOLAS (Student On Line Academic Service) which provides 24-hour-a-day access to data from companies, professional and industry associations and special-interest groups, daily up-dated newspaper articles, subject and course information and study timetables and advice. A less obvious example is the Australian Broadcasting Commission's highly successful children's programme 'Lift Off'. This programme so prides itself on its educational qualities (based on Howard Gardner's theory of seven intelligences) that it markets itself to schools as well as overseas. Also, much public education is now taking place via the small screen. Religious organizations have been running *edverts* on TV for some time, and in recent years governments have also come to recognize the educational potency of the medium. The Commonwealth government, for example, used TV extensively in its AIDS campaign, developing a form of *info-vertisement.* The Victorian Traffic Accident Commission also runs a highly successful series of safe driving 'ed-verts' on commercial television (Davidson 1993: 7). In contrast many apparently non-education bodies are now seeing schools as useful sites for getting their message across via computer programs. The Victorian Traffic Accident Commission has also recently launched a project called 'Motorvation' which employs sporting and rock music heroes and simulated traffic situations on computer to teach young people about road safety.

Such examples suggest that the public/private binary is further being undermined at the level of educational policy and politics and at the level of education itself, as the home increasingly becomes a site for formal and informal learning mediated by information technologies. Indeed, it is possible that the examples cited above are early indicators that the state's monopoly over education in Australia is being challenged by this new triad and that new technologies are bringing into effect new modes of de-institutionalized education guided either entirely or partly by marketing logics. It is possible that informal technologically and commercially mediated learning will ultimately contribute more to decentring and destabilizing state education than the devolution and marketization of public educational services. Certainly these forms of 'education' mount a serious challenge to the role of institutionalized, formal and face-to-face learning in students' lives. This is not just because they offer education in alternative, more comfortable and possibly more attractive settings. It is also because they promote alternative expectations about both worthwhile knowledge and acceptable pedagogy. Either way, the home is increasingly becoming the focus for the delivery of information and 'education'. Digitalization and fibre-optic cables now provide the infrastructure for the bulk delivery of communication to the home and for the integration of a variety of forms of media within the home. Indeed, it will soon be possible to link the home to a vast network of educational, library and other services. And when virtual reality systems become commonplace the abstract will take on many dimensions of the concrete – the 'absent' will become 'present' (Sherman and Judkins 1992). This scenario clearly challenges many current notions of curriculum and pedagogy and notions of students and teachers. And, as we have said, it challenges some conventional educational binary distinctions.

The 'Rock Eisteddfod' points to another way in which the distinction between the formal and the informal, the public and the private becomes increasingly blurred.[8] Popular culture becomes popular pedagogy underwritten in different ways by the school, the state and commercial markets. Broadly, the school is in some senses de-schooled and re-schooled by different aspects of different markets. As formal institutional school education moves away from the 'crowded curriculum' and narrows its functions to skilling and credentialing for labour and commodity markets, and as it enhances its economic authority, it lets much of its moral, aesthetic and affective authority transfer to commercially mediated education markets. In our view the new, informal 'education' market genres *info-tainment* and *edu-tainment* step into the lacunae. And both induct students into what Stewart Brand (1987) has called the global 'media lab'. At the same time, the state seeks to extend its educational arm yet further through the use of television, radio, computers and print, that is, through multimedia educational packages sold nationally and internationally. What we see here is a further breaking down of conventional barriers. Not only does the state's educational arm 'invade' the home very directly, it also transcends the boundaries of the national state. In its search for niche education markets in the global media lab, it participates in a postmodern form of educational imperialism.

Some classifications of the markets/education/technology triad

As this brief and selective history of education markets indicates, there are many examples of the triad, some of them quite familiar, some quite new and some blending features of the old and the new. It is worth trying to identify the key features of these old, new and in-between forms of the triad because through doing so one can gain a sense of the directions that developments in this area seem to be taking. So let us consider particular examples of the triad according to certain criteria, under three headings: *modern* forms, *postmodern* forms and *mixed* or *hybrid* forms.

Modern forms can be identified as those which are primarily state funded, identified also as public, institutionalized, formal, largely print-based, mass-orientated, steered and serviced largely by education professionals and informed mainly by educational values. In contrast, postmodern forms can be categorized as those being produced and consumed outside the institutions of the state; identified as private, market funded, national and international, de-institutionalized, de-territorialized, informal, largely image-based, nicheorientated, steered and serviced mainly by commercial, cultural and technology professionals and informed mainly by market values. Hybrid forms are those which combine features of both.

While most forms do not fit exactly under a modern or a postmodern heading and combine features of each, some do tend to have more features from one side than from the other and can therefore be identified with that particular genre. Let us take some examples. Technology high schools are probably the best example of the modernist form. So is Methodist Ladies College with its lap-tops, except that in this case the public/private boundary is rather blurred given that MLC is a private school. Neither, in the first instance at least, appears to challenge the main conventions of schooling except to the extent that new technologies alter the culture of the schools themselves. The Coles/Apples project also tends towards the modernist side of the divide, although it invades the private sphere of the home as a site of motivation (parents are implicitly expected to shop at Coles), culture professionals are employed in order to overlay commercial values with educational values, and American popular culture is deployed as a form of extra motivation for students to collect dockets.[9] Further, the unpaid labour of mothers is put to work in the service of both commercial and state interests. The more school communities demonstrate that they can raise resources for the school, the easier it is for the state to reduce funding, that is, costs are transferred from the public to the private sector. Coles and Apple symbolically encourage this form of privatization.

The 'Rock Eisteddfod' could probably be regarded as an archetypical hybrid form. It is sponsored by the state, by various commercial interests and by individual schools, and it performs a marketing function for all. It draws on the full range of expertise and privatized parental support. It is intra-national, national and international. It is ultimately orientated towards the screen but until then it is certainly no abstraction. It is territorialized and de-territorialized, institutional and non-institutional and, again, it taps into the desires and fantasies produced by popular youth-cultural forms and maps these onto the performing arts. But it is also about teamwork, creativity, commitment and social issues, some raised by the schools themselves and others by the National Drug Offensive – a state-sponsored advertising or edvertising campaign against drug abuse.

These 'edverts' are best understood as a postmodern form of education. In a series of Baudrelardian collagic fractured image narratives, they show various down-sides of alcohol abuse. Both the 'Rock Eisteddfod' and these 'edverts' implicitly acknowledge that youthful identities are formed, in part, at the intersection of the commodity and the image and that, given this, education may well be most effective if it recognizes that this is so.

TV open learning and full-fee, multimedia offshore education are other examples of hybrid forms but ones which lean towards the postmodern. Both have their roots in state educational institutions, in educational expertise, in some continuing use of print and in formal approaches to learning, but in most other senses they become postmodern. In offshore distance education, the phone, the fax, E-mail and the satellite have brought space and time into realignment. Relationships in this educational mode are abstract and fleeting, mediated by the market and the technology. The global and the local are brought together in new forms of association. Learning packages can be produced in one country, sold to a tertiary institution in another and consumed in yet another. Other aspects of TV open learning also suggest that it can be categorized as leaning towards a postmodern educational form. It draws heavily on the expertise of professionals associated with media industries. Conventional educational practices do not screen well and there is an increasing recognition that 'edu-tainment' is the most appropriate way to proceed. Hence popular science shows and TV documentaries become vital teaching aids, and the centrality of the teacher is challenged by cultural workers, such as Mary Delahunty, a newsreader from ABC, who are deemed more appropriate to do the abstract 'face-to-face' work, not because of their teaching skills but because of their image/presentation skills. In some cases here and in distance education, teachers are exiled from their own curiculum developments.

Science and technology parks and centres are another hybrid form supported by both the state and the market. They provide a form of pleasurable 'hands on' edu-tainment relying for its effect, in many cases, on a carnivalesque disordered order, futuristic settings and spectacular effects. People's engagement with these centres is often similar to their engagement with TV – moving quickly from stand to stand – flicking quickly from channel to channel. Science parks and, to a lesser extent, education/trade/cultural Expos are somewhat reminiscent of the festive atmosphere of fairgrounds: conventional boundaries are often confounded, the juxtapositions are often bizarre and 'consumers' are immersed in a confusion of sounds, motions and images with the possible effect of intense sensory overload and disorientation.

It seems to us that info- and edu-tainment and info- and ed-verts are the clearest examples of postmodern educational forms. Many children's shows, and science and nature shows, fit into this category. Televised safe sex and safe driving ed-vertisements are other examples – leaving the crowded curriculum of schools to join the crowded curriculum of TV. But of course when one turns to matters of style, many such programmes follow very modernist narrative, pedagogic and filmic conventions. 'Lift Off', however, is another story. While clearly seeking to convey a set of educational messages, it relies for its effects on a thoroughly postmodern set of kaleidoscopic fragments, pastiche, an eclectic mixing of codes and a profusion of images and sensations, while at the same time 'chaining its signifiers' from programme to programme.

A difficulty with this postmodern category is: where do we draw the line and on what grounds? There is clearly a very fine line between what is educational and what is entertainment. How, for instance, does one classify a show like 'Beverly Hills 90210' which runs a clear moral agenda on a range of issues such as substance abuse, date rape, sexuality, racism, sexism, parent/child relationships, disability, violence, honesty and social responsibility? This particular mode of popular culture is very clearly a form of popular pedagogy. In a sense the show becomes the lecture and subsequent discussions amongst friends become the tutorial. Of course the messages delivered are multiple and contradictory but this is also the case with many conventional educational texts. Answers to the question of where to draw the line depends very much on how one defines education. But of course the meanings of education have always changed according to the times and the contexts. New times will undoubtedly mobilize new meanings and this is, in a sense, why it is difficult to draw any line, particularly if the market and new information and communications technologies play an increasing role in making meaning on this topic.

Some concluding thoughts

At the beginning of this paper we offered an interpretation of the implications of new times for the current Captains of Educational Consciousness in DEET, the AEC and so forth. From what we have subsequently said, two points should be clear. The first point is that they are only one set of players in an intensifying struggle to define new education; that there are many corporate and not-so-corporate citizens on the scene ready to capture both meaning and custom. Sometimes their intentions seem honourable enough but even when this is the case educators need to be wary that their market values do not over-determine the school's educational values. Certainly some corporate citizens 'down the line' seem more committed to their own enterprises than to the AEC's agenda for the development of a post-Fordist enterprise culture through Fordist curriculum reform.

The second point is that the trajectories of the Captains of Consciousness and the 'corporate citizens' are, in many ways, a highly restricted response to the educational and other challenges of new times. In vocationalizing and/or commodifying the curriculum in the way that they do, they do not attend seriously to what could be called the down-side of postmodernity. We have already implied that consumption and commodification work to produce a selfish, individualistic culture where the main moral imperative is gratification and that the marketization of education taps into this psyche. In hard times this does not make for much compassion and neither does it augur well for the humanity of future Australia. Other aspects of the 'down-side' of postmodernity include environmental destruction, planned obsolescence, waste and artificial scarcity, depersonalization, symbolic and other forms of violence, social dislocation and isolation, ideological bombardment and its associated intellectual and psychic numbing and emotional shallowness. The ultimate point here is that education policy makers (and many other new players) seem to have accepted unproblematically the dominant values of the postmodern age and have translated these values into education policy at every step along the way. In such policies they show little evidence of any serious attempt to come to grips with the problems associated with the environmental, social, cultural, corporeal, psychic and ethical consequences and costs of the unconstrained celebration and promotion of the market and of technology.

In our view, current government policies rest on fantasies of control and depend on fear of the future as a form of motivation. While educators may disagree on many things, we can probably all agree that control and fear are not sound pedagogical principles. Of course educators' views are rather marginal in the current corporate consensus about new educational directions. And, as we have implied, it is possible that the trend towards postmodern educational forms will further marginalize educational expertise and educational values. But it is not necessarily so. The questions for educators are: 'Where do we think new times and new educational forms leave us?' and 'What do we intend to do about it?'

Clearly new times and new educational forms leave us with many well-warranted uncertainties and anxieties. There exists a very grave danger that eventually schools will be expected primarily to produce workers and consumers and that their socially critical, creative, moral, cultural and aesthetic agendas will become marginal. As we have suggested, the market and the media are already moving into this potential vacuum and, ironically, in certain instances they are giving educators and policy makers a few lessons on pedagogy and curriculum development. 'Lift Off' and 'Rock Eisteddfod' and science and technology parks and centres demonstrate a certain understanding about the subjectivities of today's students; those who have grown up in new times and whose identities, as mentioned earlier, have been formed, to some extent, at the intersection of the commodity and the image. It may well be worth exploring what these lessons mean for our own teaching and, indeed, for our own, often rather heavy-handed, socially critical agendas.[10] This suggests that there are also some new opportunities in new times: opportunities to ask new questions, to work in new ways, with different people and different ideas. New times encourage us to look at old ground differently and to break new ground with a view to ensuring: (1) that education is not reduced to vocationalism, information exchange or entertainment; (2) that it is not totally absorbed into the 'vortex of the commodity' (Sharp 1985); and (3) that it makes real and holistic connections with the young people of today and with their concerns about their current lives and their futures. New times also encourage new forms of educational expertise, new, not *pseudo-new*, ways of thinking about policy, curriculum and pedagogy, and new educational values. It needs to be said, and said often, that in Australia today there is an urgent need for a comprehensive, balanced *and critical* understanding of the complex characteristics of the postmodern age and its implications for education. While we have some understanding of the role that certain forms of education play in constituting the postmodern condition, we are not at all sure of the sorts of education which may constitute it in a more wise, humane, just and balanced manner. In our view the primary questions of today are these: how can education deal with the full complexity of the postmodern age rather than with its economic needs? How can it help to produce people who are not simply clever workers and committed consumers, but cultured, compassionate, creative, critical and courageous human beings?

Notes

1 For discussions of consensus see Fitzclarence and Kenway (1993); of corporate federalism see Lingard (1993) and of new nationalism see Hinkson (1991).

2 See Hutnyk (1991) for a powerfully critical and entertaining discussion of the ways in which the values of the corporate world have come to dominate education.
3 For a discussion of a range of types of marketization in education in Australia, the UK, USA and New Zealand, see Kenway (1993a).
4 For an extensive discussion both of post-Fordism in its different variations, and of its implications for education see Kenway (1993a).
5 For a helpful introductory discussion of these see Rosenau (1992).
6 See Skeggs (1991) for an essay-review of four recent edited collections which employ and criticize theories of postmodernism with regard to culture, philosophy and the social. While her review is rather hostile and should not necessarily be taken at face value, it nevertheless provides a useful sense of the complexity of that which goes under the rubric 'postmodernism' and of the range and intensity of the associated debates.
7 For an extended analysis of Whittle's news 'service' and his Edison project (a series of private schools he is in the process of seeking to establish) see Giroux (1994). Giroux points to the ways in which these two projects relate to each other in class and racial terms, to the connections between Whittle and some of the USA's most outspoken free-market liberal educators and to the politics of representation and the implications for the learning of different groups of students of Whittle's intrusion into public education.
8 The 'Rock Eisteddfod' is a national performing arts competition between schools. Students choreograph a dance routine to recorded, usually popular, music which they select themselves. They also design costumes and the set. Schools proceed through a series of heats at the local and state levels. Those who win the state finals are televised and compete in the national final which is judged on the basis of the screen performance. Winners are awarded music equipment. Participants also have an opportunity to take a self-funded trip to the USA were they also perform. It is sponsored by The National Drug Offensive and its state counterparts, DEET and, to a lesser extent, by commercial interests. It has recently been introduced into schools in California. The competition has proved very popular with 500 schools participating (Fitzclarence *et al.* 1993).
9 In the latest advertising campaign the class that collects the most dockets wins a trip to the set of 'Beverly Hills 90210' in Hollywood.
10 See the concluding chapter of Kenway and Willis, with the Education of Girls Unit of SA (1993) for a discussion of this issue with regard to feminist work in schools.

References

Australian Education Council (1993) *National Code of Practice: Commercial Sponsorship and Promotion in Schools Education* (Melbourne: AEC).

Bigum, C., Fitzclarence, L., Green, B. and Kenway, J. (1993) 'Multimedia and monstrosities: reinventing computers in schools again', *Australian Educational Computing*, 8 (Special Conference Edition): 43–9.

Bigum, C., Fitzclarence, L. and Kenway, J., with Croker, C. and Collier, J. (1993) 'That's edutainment: restructuring universities and the Open Learning Initiative', *Australian Universities Review: Special Issue on Marketing Education in the 1990s*, 36 (2): 21–8.

Brand, S. (1987) *The Media Lab: Inventing the Future at MIT* (Harmondsworth: Penguin).

Calvert, J., with Kuehn, L. (1993) *Pandora's Box: Corporate Power, Free Trade and Canadian Education*, Our schools/our selves monograph series; No. 13 (Toronto: Our Schools/Our Selves Education Foundation).

Collins, C. (ed.) (1993) *Competencies: The Competencies Debate in Australian Education and Training* (Canberra: Australian College of Education).

Collins, M. (1993) 'Global corporate philanthropy – marketing beyond the call of duty', *European Journal of Marketing*, 27 (2): 46–58.

Davidson, K. (1993) 'TAC best-suited to caring for victims', *The Age*, 19 June: 7.
Duncan, B. (1992) 'TV Inc in the classroom', *Education Forum* (Fall): 18–21.
Durie, J. (1992) 'Planning the school of profit', *Higher Education Supplement, The Australian*, 21 October: 18.
Ewen, S. (1976) *Captains of Consciousness* (New York: McGraw-Hill).
Featherstone, M. (1991) *Consumer Culture and Postmodernism* (London: Sage).
Fitzclarence, L. (1993) ' "I Shop Therefore I Am": the origins of a market based culture – a critical postmodern reading of material history as it applies to developments in education', foundation paper for the research project Marketing Education in the Information Age, Deakin University, Geelong.
Fitzclarence, L. and Kenway, J. (1993) 'Social justice in the post-modern age', in B. Lingard, J. Knight and P. Porter (eds) *Schooling Reform in Hard Times* (London: Falmer): 90–106.
Fitzclarence, L., with Bigum, C., Green, B. and Kenway, J. (1993) 'The Rock Eisteddfod: media culture as a de facto National Curriculum', paper presented at the Annual Conference of the Australian Curriculum Studies Association, Brisbane, July.
Giroux, H. (1994) *Disturbing Pleasures: Learning Popular Culture* (New York: Routledge).
Hall, S. (1988) 'Brave New World', *Marxism Today* (October): 24–9.
Hinkson, J. (1991) *Post-modernity, State and Education* (Victoria, Australia: Deakin University Press).
Holmes, S. (no date) 'The emerging corporate culture in schools', unpublished paper, Ormiston College, Brisbane.
Hutnyk, J. (1991) 'What is to be done about Arizona Junkets? The Firm Review, IBM and international profiteering', unpublished paper, University of Western Sydney, Kingswood.
Jameson, F. (1984) 'Post-modernism, or the cultural logic of late capitalism', *New Left Review* (146): 53–93.
Kenway, J. (ed.) (1993a) *Economizing Education: The Post-Fordist Directions* (Geelong: Deakin University Press).
Kenway, J. (ed.) (1993b) *Marketing Education: Some Critical Issues*, Pilot Monograph (Geelong: Deakin University Press).
Kenway, J., with Bigum, C. and Fitzclarence, L. (1993) 'Marketing education in the post-modern age', *Journal of Education Policy*, 8 (2): 105–23.
Kenway, J. and Willis, S., with the Education of Girls Unit of SA (1993) *Telling Tales: Girls and School, Changing Their Ways* (Canberra, Australian Government Publishing Service).
Lantz, B. (1994) 'Shop class sponsored by Black and Decker, chemistry by Dow', *London Free Press*, 21 January: 87.
Leonard, M. (1992) 'The response of the private sector: foundations and entrepreneurs', *Teachers College Record*, 93: 376–81.
Levidow, L. (1990) 'Foreclosing the future', *Science as Culture* (8): 59–79.
Lingard, B. (1993) 'Corporate federalism: the emerging approach to policy making for Australian schools', in R. Lingard, J. Knight and P. Porter (eds) *Schooling Reform in Hard Times* (London: Falmer): 24–35.
Lingard, B., Knight, J. and Porter, P. (eds) (1993) *Schooling Reform in Hard Times* (London: Falmer).
Lobman, T. (1992) 'Public education grant making style: more money, more vision, more demands', *Teachers College Record*, 93 (3): 282–402.
Mahoney, D. (1990) 'The new economics and education', in *Australian College of Education, Evolving Partnerships in Education*, papers presented at the 30th National

Conference of the Australian College of Education Bond University, Queensland, 16–31.

Marginson, S. (1986) 'The free market approach to education: are students human capital?' in R. Gillespie and C. Collins (eds) *Education as An International Commodity, Proceedings of the Fourteenth Annual Conference of the Australian and New Zealand Comparative and International Education Society*, Queensland University, 89–133.

Molnar, A. (1993) *Giving Kids the Business: The Corporate Assault on American Public Education* (Milwaukee: University of Wisconsin).

Probert, B. (1993) 'Restructuring and globalisation: what do they mean?' *Arena Magazine*, April–May: 18–22.

Pusey, M. (1991) *Economic Rationalisation in Canberra: A National Building State Changes Its Mind* (Sydney: Cambridge University Press).

Ranson, S. (1990) 'From 1944–1988: education, citizenship and democracy', in M. Flude and M. Hammer (eds) *The Education Reform Act 1988: Its Origins and Implications* (London: Falmer).

Rosenau, P. (1992) *Post-modernism and the Social Sciences* (New Jersey: Princeton University Press).

Sharp, G. (1985) 'Constitutive abstraction and social practice', *Arena*, 80: 48–82.

Sherman, B. and Judkins, P. (1992) *Glimpses of Heaven, Vision of Hell: Virtual Reality and its Implications* (London: Hodder & Stoughton).

Skeggs, B. (1991) 'Postmodernism: what is all the fuss about?', *British Journal of Sociology of Education*, 12 (2): 225–67.

Wilson, H. (1992) 'Marketing the canon', *Discourse*, 12 (2): 116–26.

Yeatman, A. (1990) *Bureaucrats, Technocrats, Femocrats: Essays on the Contemporary Australian State* (Sydney: Allen & Unwin).

2 Localization/globalization and the midwife state

Strategic dilemmas for state feminism in education?

Jill Blackmore

Deakin University, Victoria, Australia

Source: *Journal of Education Policy*, 14 (1): 33–54, 1999.

Feminism and the logic of globalization

Globalization has provided the justification for the restructuring of the workplace, and of educational work more specifically, in most Western liberal capitalist nation states in the past decade. The general logic of most theories of globalization is that globalization is a threat to national and cultural identity due the totalising impact of information technologies and global markets and the demands of more culturally diverse and shifting populations (Waters 1995; Green 1996). Paradoxically, the typical policy 'response' in most Western liberal nation states to globalization is that of localization (Lawton 1992). The global pattern in educational restructuring has been marked by a shift to self management to produce greater flexibility at the level of the local in order to be 'responsive' to global markets (Taylor *et al.* 1997). More optimistic post-Fordist readings of the labour market and work organization see this as producing flatter, more democratic, organizations in which responsibility is devolved to individuals, thus enabling them to work collaboratively, productively, reflexively and creatively in teams. Such readings are seductive to feminists who have communitarian proclivities. More pessimistic neo-Fordist readings of post-modernist theory confirm feminist materialist accounts of workplace reform. They focus upon the apparent re-assertion of executive prerogative arising from the strong centralizing mechanisms of accountability back to the centre so typical of devolved systems of management, and upon the arising anomie and individualizing nature of life in self managing institutions informed by the principles of market liberalism (Harvey 1989; Hargreaves 1994; Brown and Lauder 1996; Blackmore and Sachs 1997). 'To describe these changes as "cultural" is not just rhetoric; the aim is to produce new cultural values and workers who are "enterprising" or self motivating, or, as Rose has put it, "self steering"' (Fairclough 1992: 7).

From whatever perspective, it is evident that the new global order is marked by 'widespread tensions between increasingly international imported practices and local traditions' (Fairclough 1992: 7), tensions particularly evident in education reform. While state education systems and organizations have devolved responsibility for implementation decisions to smaller localized units of production 'at the chalkface' (e.g. self managing schools, teams or departments) in culturally specific ways (site based management in the USA, self governing schools in New Zealand, self managing schools in Australia, grant maintained schools in the UK), the pattern has also been for governments to retain strong central coordination of policy and funding at the core (Ball 1994; Wylie 1995; Whitty 1996). This core-periphery model of organizational governance, and the tensions it produces, has implications for feminist work in education, both theoretically and strategically.

Theoretically, both post-modernism and feminist post-structuralism have displayed a fetish with the local, exemplified in their interest in Foucault and their emphasis on the differentiating rather than universalizing tendencies of globalization (Ramazanoglu 1993; Hekman 1996). But feminist post-structuralism's rejection of universalizing metanarratives (including that of universal womanhood), and its emphasis on the partiality and 'situatedness' of knowledge, the historically contingent nature of subjectivity and a politics of difference around issues of race, class and gender, as well as sexuality, produces moral and political dilemmas for feminism (Haraway 1988; Fraser and Gordon 1994; Yeatman 1994). Feminist post-structuralism questions whether there is any normative dimension upon which a feminist politics can ground its claims for equity in a liberal state (Young 1990, 1994). Indeed, feminist post-structuralism's concentration on the local, the cultural, the linguistic and the aesthetic, has often been at the expense of attending to the historical and material aspects of globalization and therefore a more *systemic* understanding of the politics of difference, at the very instance that global restructuring has undermined many feminist achievements (Grewal and Kaplan 1994). Kathleen Jones (1995) cautions us that to:

> dispense with the female subject at this point is particularly dangerous... Having money permits one to fantasise escaping corporeality and history. It also enables one to ignore the political-economic system of global inequality that constructs differential opportunities...the political-economic context remains, fantasies of paranoic floating signifiers not withstanding, and is more extraordinarily more fixed and materially more powerful than ever... Systems of law, global economic inequalites, the structured disenfrachisement of most women and most men in the world, the influence of the military-industrial complex...are working to constitute and to fix very specific subjects in very confined and inegalitarian geo-political spaces.
>
> (Jones 1993: 10–11)

Strategically, feminism, as a social movement, is also caught. On the one hand, there is the temptation to call upon universal metanarratives of human rights acceptable to an emerging global political 'community' or networks of global and regional governmental and non-governmental organizations (e.g. UN, UNESCO, European Community) (Bradley and Ramirez 1996). On the other, post-colonial feminists suggest that such metanarratives privilege white middle class Western women's position, 'othering' that which is non-white or non-Western, and thus failing to address the temporal and spatial particularity of women's experience (Mohanty 1990).

To view global/local relations as a binary subverts any capacity to see how the global and local infiltrate each other. To focus only on the local is reductionist, as well as non strategic, as it masks any similarities and links attributable to globalization. Grewal and Kaplan (1994) suggest that the global and the local should be viewed as different aspects of the same phenomenon. You cannot consider one without the other as analyses of the 'micro' always contain some understanding of the larger, the societal, the enveloping 'macro' (Anyon 1994: 125). Indeed, the local exists within larger, often multinational organizations or education systems, through systems of communication networks, themselves manifestations of the often standardizing processes of globalization. The trend towards self management of schools and the new vocationalism, for example, 'disguises the globally dispersed forces that actually drive the production process' which demands new organizational forms and a tighter education-work nexus (Appadurai 1990: 307). The promise of seemingly more democratic, local self management, as espoused in policy texts cross-nationally, masks the overarching framework in which democratic politics and notions of public responsibility are being re-defined in the reduced public sectors of most Western liberal democracies. Similarly, the desire for flexible, multi-skilled workers masks the reality of the attack on the material and professional conditions of teachers' work as governments simultaneously seek greater control, but also more creative responses, to markets in the context of international monetary/market pressures in a deregulated global economy.

Gender is notably absent from mainstream discussions of globalization, either as an organizing principle or a category of analysis. Yet the logic of globalization should raise warning signals for feminists, because globalization is generally associated with the reduction of nation state power and political intervention; the supplantation of politics by the market; an emphasis on the competitive individual rather than community; and the exacerbation of management/worker divides at a time of increased employment insecurity. Feminists in most Western liberal democracies have, in varying degrees, relied upon the welfare state for gender equity reform. To supplant the state with the market is dangerous for women, as the market has never recognized merit or favoured women, and has no obligation to do so. Nor do women tend to fit the model of the self maximizing autonomous individual of competitive social relations central to market theory because, in general, women have responsibilities to others due to their social location in the wider community as 'carers'. And men continue to manage while women remain concentrated on the margins in the paid workforce, despite their increasing presence. Feminist educators and policy makers should therefore consider whether the nation state is being put at risk by globalization, or merely being re-invented to mediate market relations. And if so, how will the state mediate local/global relations and with what repercussions, if any, for the delivery of gender equity?

'State' feminism at risk?

The state is central to matters of gender equity, although women have always had an 'ambiguous relationship' with the state (Franzway *et al.* 1989; Gordon 1990). Since the late nineteenth century, the 'dependence' of women in such Western liberal democracies as Australia, New Zealand, Scandinavia, USA and the UK has increasingly shifted from individual men onto a paternalistic welfare state (Fraser and Gordon 1994; Kovens and Michel 1994). The state has both promoted gender equity through legislation on equal pay parity, child care and employment safety nets, etc. and simultaneously undermined such initiatives through marriage bars, administrative regulations, and discriminatory work and labour market practices. Most feminists no longer view the state as being a monolithic set of structures. The state is conceived to be a range of practices, processes, procedures and structures which work, often in contradiction to each other, but which can provide openings for feminist interventions (Franzway *et al.* 1989). Yet there is still a level of internal coherence to any state's processes of regulation which could be described as patriarchal (Connell 1990).

The second wave of the women's movement has produced a sense of 'global feminism' and policy borrowing between nation states in areas of gender equity policies and equal opportunity. Yet global discourses of human rights, and Western feminist discourses of equal opportunity and affirmative action, articulate differently at the level of the local. To illustrate this point, I make comparison between Australia, Sweden, New Zealand, the USA and England. Historically, these nation states have all had strong feminist movements which have engaged differently with the state. I also explore the implications for the different state feminisms of the general shift from the welfare to the competitive state. Gender reform strategies vary considerably cross-nationally due to the different federal state political structures; industrial relations systems; level and strength of union activism; labour market structures; and cultural differences in emphasis upon different institutions as avenues of social change (e.g. the courts in the USA and the public sector in Australia) (Edwards and Magarey 1995).

The feminist movement in Australia significantly differs from the American, for example, in that there has been a stronger sense of collective action and egalitarianism, a greater focus on schools than on universities, and a pattern of institutionalization of gender equity policies in the public sector, and education in particular (Eisenstein 1992). Australian women's lobby groups began to work in uneasy alliances with male dominated federal and state Labor parties and unions to position feminists within the state bureaucracies (femocrats) after Labor won the federal election in 1972 (Yeatman 1992). Women's Advisers, supported by Equal Opportunity Units, openly worked for gender equity reform in most states, although with uneven success depending upon state politics (Burton 1990; Poiner and Wills 1990; Eisenstein 1992). Australia, during the 1980s, was unique for its combination of strong 'top down' national and state gender equity policies legislated upon nationally and locally, and enacted through Action Plans. These policies both legitimated and provided a language of reform for 'bottom up' feminist grass roots activities in schools (Kenway *et al.* 1997). While there has been significant debate about whether feminists should engage with or work outside, the state, both strategies persisted throughout the 1970s and 1980s. State feminism meant working nationally as well as locally. These approaches arose out of, and were facilitated by, a history of social liberalism originating in the late nineteenth century and the post-war labour settlements between labour and capital which legitimated state intervention in economic and social life, a strong union movement and a centralized wage system which provided a safety for women workers comparable to that of Sweden rather than the localized system of funding education and collective bargaining in Canada and USA (Probert 1995).

Whereas American gender equity policy making has focused upon legislative means and weak intervention in the economy, state feminism in Australia, as in New Zealand and Sweden, has relied heavily on strong state interventions in the economy, and, as Canada, on resourcing EO infrastructure within the bureaucracy for promoting the status of women (Lewis and Astrom 1992). While in each instance, equity discourses have competed against late 1980s global discourses of managerialism and economic orthodoxies of market liberalism about balanced budgets which position equity as a cost, how feminists engage with the state still differs among nations. Canadian feminists view the state as 'containing' feminist activity, and have developed a more activist non-governmental professionalized feminist lobby than Australia. Yet the emphasis in Australia, as Canada, has been on wage justice (unions) and not social justice as in Sweden (Barlow and Robertson 1994; Sawer 1994). While Australia, Canada and the UK have strong radical and socialist feminist traditions which have worked for gender equity through grass roots activities and the unions, Canada's provincial orientation has undermined the emergence of national gender policies typical of Australia or Sweden (Sawer 1994). Swedish feminist political success lay in grounding the welfare state settlement on developing women's economic independence. This meant the integration of social and labour market issues as the basic precondition of welfare state citizenship. Yet in education, because gender was subsumed under the general rubric of social justice, gender specific policies have not been as institutionalized as in Australia (Lewis and Astrom 1992). So while Australia was renowned for its 'state feminism' in terms of government funded services run by women for women similar to those in Sweden, Australia still lags behind Sweden in terms of social policy outcomes, with a lower average wage for women relative to men and lower level of political representation of women than in Sweden (Sawer 1991, 1994).

In the UK, Canada and the USA, where gender equity built on race and class legislation (e.g. Anti Discrimination Act 1975 in England), gender equity policy formation and implementation was more fragmented and localized without the legitimating and resource support of the state (Stromquist 1992; Arnot 1993). Local alliances between feminist teachers, progressive Local Education

Associations, teacher unions and parent organizations, similar to the provincially based activities in Canada, 'took principal responsibility for the delivery of equal opportunities' (Weiner 1995: 75). While many English feminists see interest in the state as being less important, American feminists have either depicted the state as the villain or as gender neutral. Nancy Fraser and Linda Gordon suggest this is because the US state has been relatively less 'welfarist', less protectionist and less economically interventionist state, and, even more importantly, less visible than its European counterparts. This tendency is reinforced by the high level of state decentralization due to the federal system, the mystification accomplished by labelling as 'welfare' only some programs that contribute to a citizen's well being and not others, and the tradition of hostility marking the women's liberation movement in the USA towards the state (Fraser and Gordon 1994: 9). Segal points to the irony that:

> In the countries where there have been longer periods of social-democratic government and stronger trade unions there is far less pay-differential and occupational segregation (both vertical and horizontal) between women and men, and far greater expansion of welfare services... Despite the existence of the largest and most vociferous feminist movement in the world, US women have seen the least *overall* change in the relative disadvantages of their sex compared to other Western democracies.
>
> (1990: 90)

What is dear from the above, is that the nation state continues to be important to gender equity in most instances, but that particular traditions in state feminist practice are more under threat in some states than others, due the move away from a paternalistic (and in the case of Sweden maternalistic), welfare state to a 'midwife' state which mediates global/local markets. Australia's tradition of state feminism has meant there is not the same alternative feminist non-governmental political infrastructure, as say Canada or the USA, through which to mount claims for women if the state withdraws from promoting, even if only symbolically, issues of gender equity.

The midwife state: policy responses to the globalization logic

Paradoxically, policy responses by governments to globalization discourses have tended to be more neo-Fordist than post-Fordist. Premised upon principles of competitive individualism, market liberalism in the context of neo-conservative politics, the effect has been in public sector reform to tighten control over the workplace, rather than democratize, due to the strong bottom up accountability to the centre, and moves to deskill workers and reduce living standards (Brown and Lauder 1997). The convergence of conservative political and liberal market orthodoxies towards 'pure' versions of economic rationalism and public choice theory (compared to earlier, 'soft' versions of human capital theory invoked by Labor governments in Australia), has been facilitated by strong international links between conservative economic think tanks (Hyman 1994). The new economic orthodoxy which tends to be replicated in many nation states is to maximize exports, reduce social spending, curtail state economic regulations, and empower capital to reorganize national economies along transnational trading blocs. There is a strong element of anti-statism, which results in weak domestic policy in the face of globalization. Educational restructuring globally, informed by policy borrowing between nation states, has marked similarities across 'developed' and 'developing' states. The trend is for a shift from welfare to more contractual or competitive states, the privatization of educational costs, workplace restructuring based on more decentralized wage fixing processes, devolution towards self managing organizations, and the corporatization of education as the market penetrates educational organizations, linking them more closely to the economy (Gordon 1991; Yeatman 1992; Codd 1993; Kenway *et al.* 1993; Gewirtz *et al.* 1995; Dale and Robertson 1996; Watkins 1996; Whitty 1996).

Whereas the Keynesian state asserted primacy over the market with its regulatory tendencies, the competitive state tends to mediate the market, intervening only to reduce its excesses (Yeatman 1992; Delhi 1996). The public sector is dismantled or 'corporatized', so that it no longer 'services the welfare state, but instead, services a state which defines its primary objective as one of fostering a competitive economy', thus abandoning the 'rhetoric of social citizenship' which 'underpins the core discourses of the welfare state' (Yeatman 1994: 3–4). The state is thus increasingly withdrawn from its traditional welfare obligations, defining them as merely a domestic problem. With the interpenetration and crystallization of transnational markets and structures, 'the state itself has to act more like a market player, that shapes its policies to promote, control, and maximize returns from market forces in international settings' (Cerny 1990: 230). Indeed 'Governments are acting as the midwives of globalization', as they de-regulate along free market lines (Brodie 1996: 386).

This shapes what Guy Neave (1988) refers to as the shift in the terms of the global debate over education since the 1970s in most Western capitalist democracies. Neave describes it as a shift away from a sense of 'collective social responsibility' and the desire to 'democratize' knowledge, towards a view of education as a 'national enterprise' concerned about output; a highly technical view imbued with notions of managerial rationality. Sally Power and Geoff Whitty (1996: 1) suggest that the 'almost simultaneous emergence of comparable reforms across different continents has led some to suggest that the marketization of education needs to be understood as a global phenomenon'. It is evident in the more instrumental views of education underpinning national trends to 'vocationalize' and 'regulate' the curriculum through national curriculum frameworks, often with highly prescriptive content (Blackmore 1997a; Lingard and Porter 1997). Embedded in new national curricula, Whitty and Power argue, is a hidden curriculum which is reshaping the nature of cultural consumption and the messages imparted to students, that is, the MacDonaldization of curriculum. Market liberal ideologies also re-define education as a private good more than a public good, while educational costs are shifted away from the state and onto the individual and 'self managing educational institutions' through privatization and marketization (Marginson 1997). In Australia, recent national reports argue for 'up-front' full fees for university students combined with pseudo-vouchers, and many policy makers advocate compulsory school fees in a single education market because public/private distinctions are 'dysfunctional'. Furthermore, the internationalization and marketization of tertiary and secondary education means on the one hand, all education sectors seek business sponsorship. The other side of privatization is that schools now demand increased 'voluntary' parental contribution of funds and labour. Ironically, all the above is occurring at the moment when women now constitute a majority of students in education, and indeed when their academic achievements are being lauded Yet it is women who largely constitute the expanding 'voluntary' education labour force. Citizens are converted, through the above processes reconstituting education/state relations, into clients of a competitive 'midwife' state which mediates the education market. Students are 'delivered' as consumers to be sold a customized product. The shift towards the competitive state thus suggests a fundamental change to individual/state relations.

This shift towards a competitive state has implications for 'state feminism'. Most evident in many Western liberal democracies has been the marginalization of key concepts of equality of opportunity and disadvantage, and an emphasis on 'quality', 'effectiveness' and 'the competitive edge' in national educational policy statements (Neave 1988: 277). Values of social justice are now being supplanted by values of individual choice; and democratic notions of a rights based citizenship, a key element to feminist claims on the state, is now being replaced by the economic conceptualization of community as the arbitrary aggregate of rational, self maximizing individual choosers (O'Neill 1996; Peters and Marshall 1996). In Australia, Labor governments maintained an uneasy tension between claims for efficiency, effectiveness and equity during the 1980s. Now the radically conservative governments of recent years are supplanting the more socially egalitarian traditions of gender equity policy of the 1980s, with their focus on group disadvantage and systemic inequality, with a view that equity can be achieved by merely improving any individual's access to a range of market choices. On the premise that we are now on a level playing field, any 'special' treatment is deemed as unfair. In part, this shift has been made possible because the women's movement and multicultural movement during the 1980s have themselves put difference amongst women and cultural diversity on the policy agenda. It was easy for conservative governments to make the move from the growing recognition of the fluidity of the category of woman, 'race' and 'multicultural' as categories of disadvantage to a more individualized notion of diversity. And the notion of diversity conservative governments have promoted, contrary to the concept as it originated in the civil rights movement in the USA in the 1960s, does not rank gender, race and class as first order differences, but merely as equivalent to other individual differences in a range of behaviours, attitudes and skills (Morrison 1992; Bacchi 1997; Blackmore 1998).

At the same time, the globalizing politics of more leftish governments of Blair and Clinton is increasingly evident in the cross-fertilization of ideas, as for example, between the federal Australian Labor Party and Blair in higher education, with Blair copying Australian Labor's funding mechanisms. Previously the left in most Western liberal states was receptive, although to differing degrees, to arguments about group inequality and systemic disadvantage/discrimination, and the social policies of such welfarist states actively encouraged women and children's dependency upon a paternalistic and protectionist state. Now, working within the frame of the midwife state, leftish governments take the worrying position that *all* forms of dependency on the state are bad (Fraser and Gordon 1994). Increasingly, education and training for both official 'left' and 'right' politics is expected to produce an entrepreneurial individual totally independent from the state. This is at the moment that the state is shifting responsibility onto the family for education, health and welfare and self-funding of self managing educational institutions. As many feminist economists suggest, this assumes human capital and neoclassical economic theory's notion of the atomistic individual who emerges like a mushroom fully-grown, with preferences capacities and identity fully developed without parental nurturance or socialization through schooling (Ferber and Nelson 1993; Kuiper and Saps 1995).

So there is a fundamental process of re-privatization and re-gendering of social relations underway which has contradictory effects for gender equity. Structural adjustment policies, so enthusiastically endorsed by international monetary bodies, simultaneously promote access to education and training for women as necessary for economic growth, but demand reduced public expenditure to balance national budgets. Yet the attack on public expenditure undercuts the social wage and capacity of women to exercise choice (Unterhalter 1996: 389). Global market economies demand de-regulation of the public, but at the same time re-regulate the private by 'radically shrinking the realm of political negotiation' of social movements and 'expanding the autonomy of the market and the family' by returning social welfare to the home, 'thereby creating the illusion that they are being returned to some place they naturally belong' (Brodie 1996: 389). The state raises expectations of democratic involvement in local self managing schools, but makes self managing schools increasingly dependent upon voluntary parental labour for funds. Parents, largely women, now 'take up the slack' as the state withdraws from education by acting as surrogate teachers in classrooms and pseudo-administrators on school councils (Dehli 1996; Blackmore 1998). There is a re-commodification underway in that all services (public and private) are relegated to the market, and in so doing are removed from politics, as the market is seen to be value free. These services are thus being reconstituted, but with the family, not the state, as the fundamental building block in society. Thus, state systems of education are constructed as an 'unnecessary interposition between consumers (students and parents) and providers (teachers)' (O'Neill 1996: 406). This is not only a form of economic reconstruction, but, by undermining those very institutions which have historically tempered market relations (e.g. the welfare, state, the unions and education), it is cultural reconstruction. This reconstruction is achieved by corporatizing these very same institutions, and re-organizing them on the basis of market principles of individual choice, demand/supply, and competition (Bryson 1996).

The imposition of public sector reform on education has produced particular tensions between markets and equity, between localized responsiveness and centralized accountability (Gewirtz *et al.* 1995; Wylie 1995). The state has devolved to sub units such as schools decisions to prioritize between a restricted range of options and within budgetary constraints, such prioritizing being well contained within regulatory strategic management, policy and financial management frameworks (e.g. national curriculum). At the same time, strong accountability mechanisms have been imposed to supply feedback to the centre, a process facilitated by new information technologies. The competitive state thus steers increasingly more complex systems from a distance, in many instances by faxing the crises down the line to seemingly more deregulated local units, while simultaneously re-regulating (Cerny 1990; Ball 1994; Watkins 1996). Equally crucial, states seek to simultaneously manage the balance between democratic processes and the reality of increasingly executive style management. This balancing act is achieved, at least rhetorically, by drawing upon discourses which argue that local or devolved systems of educational management are more democratic, more responsive to local need, and more participatory than centralized, bureaucratic systems of governance. Re-regulation for the global economy therefore means that such anti-statist discourses jar against increased state policy mandates, for example, national curriculum, standardized testing. Thus individuals, as citizens, suffer withdrawal of state support; but, as workers, individuals are expected to submit to greater state control to increase national productivity through enterprise agreements and to self surveillance through performance management contracts.

As I have argued elsewhere (Blackmore 1997b), this shift in individual/state relations, in response to the globalization logic, plays out in education in highly gendered ways. Teaching, as a numerically feminized caring occupation located in the public sector, has been particularly susceptible to attacks upon the welfare state and the deregulation of the labour market (Acker 1996; Blackmore 1997b). In Australia, feminist unionists' promotion of affirmative restructuring after 1987 sought to create opportunities to re-define skill, to revalue women's work and to develop a new regulatory framework. Their aim was to facilitate more flexible working arrangements and enable work and social responsibilities to be more readily combined, while still ensuring that women were not confined to poorly paid and dead end jobs (Baldock 1990; Davis and Pratt 1993). But recent research indicates that decentralization of administration and industrial relations (usually accompanied by 'outsourcing' and 'downsizing'), has worked against women. Part time women workers tend not to be covered by collective bargaining or unionized, and, therefore, more susceptible to being 'downsized'. Those in more secure jobs under industrial awards tend to sacrifice personal benefits (recreation leave, superannuation) for family reasons (part time work, flexible hours) under enterprise bargaining agreements (Zetlin and Whitehouse 1996). The move to more individualized contractual employer/employee relations has further exacerbated the gender wage gap in an increasingly casualized education labour market (Blackmore 1997b). The normative principles of industrial regulation under the welfare state, which saw such forms of state regulation as promoting a public good, are now lacking as the midwife state mediates the market (Zetlin and Whitehouse 1996).

Furthermore, feminization, casualization and de-professionalization are highly inter-connected historical processes actively reconstituting the social relations of gender. The competitive individualism, outcomes orientation and surveillance aspects of the strong accountability mechanisms not only reduce the professional autonomy of teachers locally, but the strong policy frameworks of corporate managerialism have led to the reassertion of hierarchy within teaching such that professional judgement is subordinated to management prerogative, both locally and centrally, under performance management contractual arrangements (Blackmore *et al.* 1996). At the same time, there is a de-skilling process occurring within the profession, with, in Victoria, the new position of 'instructor'. Teacher instructors, without teacher qualifications, will serve under fully qualified teachers in the classroom to deliver curriculum, a position which will most likely feminized. Thus the polarization effects of globalization which play out locally with the re-gendering of the authority relations between employer/employee in education as control is re-asserted by re-masculinized central units of policy and finance and the feminization of an increasingly casualized and deprofessionalized teaching workforce (Edwards and Magarey 1995; Westergaard 1995; Bryson 1996). Anne Marie O'Neill's comment about New Zealand has wider application:

> Operational devolution and institutional market responsiveness occur within a context whose parameters are increasingly shaped by decreasing levels of centralized funding and increasing levels of centralized control and surveillance.
>
> (1996: 406)

Devolution driven by market principles also changes the nature of the delivery of social justice at the local level. The New Zealand case is an example of the potentially detrimental impact on women of the combination of devolved education systems and free market economic policies (Court 1993; Gordon 1994a,b). The first to introduce school charters to regulate the relations between the state and self governing schools, the New Zealand government initially devolved considerable authority to boards of trustees, but with a strong equity provision targeting women, Maoris, people of ethnic and other minorities. Schools were expected to include specific equity goals for equal educational and employment opportunity. But political commitment to equity has been superseded by competition between schools, and as elsewhere there has been an increase in gender pay gap within five years and a reduction of women in leadership (Pringle and Timperley 1995). This division of labour is also racially as well as gender biased, with Maoris also under-represented in leadership. Ultimately, a conservative government repealed the equity act and rejected pay equity because it was 'social engineering by the state' (Court 1993). The EEO requirement laid down for charters remained, largely, because they did not demand pay equity, but they did 'enhance' business as women gained flexible hours to do the 'double shift' of family and paid work in return for lower pay (Court 1993). Responsibility for equity policies, when largely devolved to local communities, is often ignored, treated as a luxury or a cost, or viewed instrumentally and not as a human right. Nor is equity as an indicator of success as marketable as good academic results, technologically well resourced educational institutions, or strong entrepreneurial leadership. The market can promote particular norms (e.g. competitive individualism) within schools which, when played out in organizational forms and through curriculum, be neither inclusive or equitable (Gewirtz *et al.* 1995; Power and Whitty 1996).

As a commitment to economic globalization has come to be seen as a national matter of survival since the late 1980s, there has been a rejigging of both the content and nature of policy formation itself which has re-positioned both feminists and educators in the policy production process. First, there has been a closer linking of state education systems to the world market in national policies framed in terms of economic rationalism (albeit with different national versions, for example, Thatcherism, Reaganism, Rogernomics) to improve national productivity and international comparative advantage. This vocationalization and internationalization of education is represented in the dominant readings of global discourses of gender equity encouraging more women and girls to go into science, maths and technology, an emphasis which tends to reinforce high status knowledges of science and maths, and define success narrowly as being largely located in male domains, areas where women are usually not rewarded in the workplace for their educational achievement (Yates 1993; Kenway *et al.* 1997). It has also produced competency and outcome based approaches to curriculum which are seen to disadvantage girls and women pedagogically (Taylor and Henry 1994). Globalization pressures to balance budgets and be more competitive have also led to reduced public expenditure. Thus in Australia, education and training providers have been opened upon to national and international market forces and individual students compete in an increasingly expensive user pays system, which again works against women who tend not to be supported in on-the-job training by employers or the state (Blackmore and Angwin 1997). Leaving equity to the market ignores the evidence that women's educational achievement is not rewarded equally to that of men in the labour market.

At the same time, the nature of policy formation within the competitive state has itself changed, effecting the capacity of feminists to influence state policies. Indeed, the voice of feminist educators have been remarkably absent in the re-formation of Australian education after 1987. In times of greater political and economic volatility, policy is increasingly viewed as a solution to public media generated problems as much as a seeking a solution for social or economic problems (Wallace 1993). One response to the immediacy of managing perceived political crises has been the 'Ministerialization of policy' which has occurred as the power to initiate policy has shifted during the late 1980s largely from bureaucrats to Ministers (Taylor *et al.* 1997; Blackmore 1998). More specifically, gender equity policy has shifted into the hands of state premiers under the Ministerial Committee for Employment, Education, Training and Youth Affairs and out of the hands of public servants, many of them femocrats, as well as feminist academics who had acted as policy advisers. The effect of this is exaggerated by institutional memory loss and de-legitimation of equity discourses. This has occurred first, due to the supplanting of a public service discourse imbued with a notion of service, professional advocacy and the public good, to one in which the bureaucracy serves the government. And second, many femocrats have fled the chilly climate or shifted out of specialist equity policy areas, to be replaced by multiskilled managers without expertise in, or commitment to, gender equity. Not only is possession of knowledge and experience in gender equity (or any other field for that matter) likened to producer capture, but the new managerialism emulating business equates success to doing much more for much less. Third, gender equity policy production is increasingly being outsourced on a contractual basis to consultants who are less likely to speak truth to power due to their reliance upon delivering the goods to continue in business. Finally, loyalty upward to the Minister is deemed more important than any commitment to any constituency, for example, women (Blackmore 1998). The corporatist state, both conservative and social democratic, has, in privatizing the business of state policy making, withdrawn it from open debate and accountability.

Such responses to globalization cannot be separated out from particular ideological readings or contextual differences. Gender equity policies in Australia, as elsewhere, have often operated at the level of the symbolic than actually effecting change. Policy has not been effectively or easily translated into practice, largely due to lack of political will, even under Labor. But a regression has begun under the neo-conservative Federal Coalition, with their dis-investment in gender equity both symbolically, for example, with the abolition of gender neutral language guidelines in government documents, and in reducing the resourcing of gender equity infrastructure established during the 1980s. Nationally, the Office for the Status of Women and the Equal Opportunity and Human Rights Commission have been undermined with 40% funding reductions, the Women's Budget has been abolished, as has the Women's Section of the Bureau of Statistics, and now Affirmative Action policies (as with multiculturalism in 1997) are under review for 1998. What is left of gender equity infrastructure has been devolved to the states in the looser Commonwealth state relations of Liberal policy structures which emphasize state rights. Not only are the structures and processes of state feminism at the federal level being dismantled, but its representational voice is being de-legitimated by suggestions that 'feminists' do not represent the 'true voice of women'.

Even while there is a convergence of neo-conservative and market liberal ideologies which circulate in what are universalizing global discourses, these discourses are articulated locally in highly differential ways within nation states (Hyman 1994; Kenway and Epstein 1996). In the state of Victoria, for example, one finds the radical conservatism of the Kennett government actively exploiting feminist discourses about women as new agents of change and sources of productivity, thus channelling individual women's energy towards market ends by promoting discourses of individual competitiveness and success at a time when there is increased social and gender inequality (Blackmore 1998). At the same time, while the *neo*-conservative Howard federal government and Kennett government deregulate the labour market by seeking to move to individual contractualism and wipe out the safety net, Howard intervenes in conservative moral agendas in actively promoting a narrow view of the family. Equity discourses are being reconstituted around 1950s modernist notions of the nuclear family and homogenist, assimilationist and hegemonic (i.e. sexist and racist) notions of citizenship. Both governments, as conservative governments in the USA, England, Canada, New Zealand and Sweden, continue to dismantle the welfare state, restructure and individualize industrial relations and employment contracts, and shift educational and welfare costs onto the family and individual. So there gender equity policy is being reframed within a more conservative framework at the very moment that the citizen claims of women upon the polity have been de-politicized through increased managerialism and the abandonment of the normative principles of the welfare state premised upon citizenship, publics and public goods.

Thus structural adjustment policies promoted by global financial bodies claiming to address *economic* globalization which circulate globally amongst particular elite communities (politicians, academics, big business) have provided an environment for a political backlash against feminism. But the imperatives implicit in such instrumental and deterministic readings of globalization have been both ideological and economic. Policy 'responses' have not been an inevitable consequence of economic globalization, but reflect particular ideological positions which have been made orthodox through the legitimacy imparted to them by international monetary bodies and other global discourses (Brodie 1996). The logic of globalization, as played out through the restructuring discourses, has thus produced the very effects they assumed to describe at the level of the local through processes of both cultural and economic reconstruction. The issue now is what are the strategic implications of the changing nature and role of a more conservative midwife state for the 'delivery' of gender equity in education?

Implications for gender equity policy of globalization logics

For Australia, where gender equity has been especially reliant upon state feminism, the discursive power of the logic of globalization has raised particular strategic problems.

While globally circulating policies appear to provide common responses to the logic of globalization – workplace restructuring, devolution, a shift from welfare to the competitive state, privatization of educational costs, market liberalism, competitive individualism – these articulate differently in specific contexts (Neave 1988; Gewirtz *et al.* 1995; Peters and Marshall 1996). The dynamics of globalization and localization are occurring simultaneously, but often in contradictory ways, requiring a range of gender equity strategies operating at different levels – at the level of the nation, the state (in federated systems such as Australia, Canada and the USA) and locally, but also at the supra-national level.

At the national level, feminist equity claims have focused upon notions of modern citizenship held in most Western liberal democratic societies. Challenges to the nation state have come from without (e.g. internationalization and globalization, migration and refugee patterns, supra-national bodies of trade and governance and international law). Claims upon the state have also come from within, from previously marginalized groups such as women and indigenous groups (e.g. Maoris in New Zealand, Aboriginal Reconciliation in Australia, Native Indians in USA and First Nation peoples in Canada), now making claims for more inclusive notions of citizenship. The destabilization of the national community, itself an effect of feminist and post-colonial critiques of the white masculine citizen underpinning nationhood, requires us to ask:

> what happens to citizenship claims when the internationalisation or globalization of finance, production and labour markets is working to erode the self determining properties of the nation state . . . as the state is less a unit of governance and more a unit of political management with respect to how its internal subjects and their economic activities articulate with transnational markets and institutions?
>
> (Yeatman 1994: 449)

While the nation state is not a polity necessarily, the corporatization of state policy and the infiltration of the market has oriented the nation state to a new globalized context. Modern citizenship – with all its trappings of a social welfare network and public education infrastructure – has been premised upon a national society which is self determining (Yeatman 1992, 1994). This national-societal approach has produced public policy on gender equity, equal opportunity, equal pay claims and anti discrimination. Now globalization threatens both national geographical boundaries and national sovereignty, with multilateral trade agreements and formation of new regional blocs, many which ignore social equity in their reconstitution (with the exception of the European Community). Furthermore, the orthodoxy that market deregulation is the only response to globalization puts pressure on governments to further deregulate industrial relations systems which have historically been premised upon the national entity of the labour market. Australia, as Sweden, has had a strongly centralized wage system which has protected women workers, and imparted significant power to peak trade union bodies under corporatist state arrangements in the 1980s. The declining popularity of unions coincides with, and indeed is a consequence of a casualized, feminized and polarized labour market, itself a factor of globalization in more service oriented economies (Lash and Urry 1994). The transformation of state/individual relations away from a sense of the collective good is exemplified in the supplanting of highly centralized, public, free education systems premised upon the view that state investment in education is a public good (socially as well as economically) by self managing, increasingly privatized, educational organizations serving a range of education markets in which individual clients exercise choice as a private matter (Marginson 1997). Neither individual or school has a strong sense of obligation to 'the public' in this scenario, or to acting on issues of equity which may be associated with citizenship or group disadvantage other than those which come within an individual rights claim. And what happens to nationally based pay claims, affirmative action or national equity policies premised upon equity as a principle of a democratic nation state, when the basis is not the territorially based and legally oriented jurisdiction of the nation state? Given that social organizations have been culturally and organizationally structured in terms of the national political economy (unions and women's lobby groups etc.), globalization has the capacity to reshape the national polity with:

> a shift to both sub national (logics of devolution and decentralisation) and supranational (transitional institutions of governance) levels where the historically achieved nation-state in most instances remains a critical node of political management mediating between these levels of governance.
>
> (Yeatman 1994: 451)

Tactics

So how can feminists working for gender equity respond to the above conditions both substantively (i.e. how gender is raised as an issue), and strategically (in terms of ways of working with/through/against/upon the state)? Generally, there is a need for both strategic essentialism and strategic pluralism. Spivak's (1993) notion of 'strategic essentialism' requires women to continue to be viewed at particular times and in particular contexts as a class or the universal category of woman in order that local and global patterns of gender inequality are continually foregrounded. It is not an either/or situation. Strategic essentialism does not necessarily lead to conservative politics, nor does recognition of the continuity and ambiguity of each identity render a shared feminist politics across class, race and culture helpless. The agent can be in an ensemble of subject – race, class, gender – positions in which, in one instance, they are dominant, and in others dominated. It is the *articulation* and shifting relations between class, race and gender, local and global, state and individual, which need to be focused upon theoretically and in empirical research, and just the shared common universal experience of womanhood. There is a need therefore to consider the 'situated knowledge' which can inform and be informed by a globalized gender politics. 'Strategic pluralism' means that feminists must work on a range of fronts simultaneously; using a multiplicity of feminist theories and strategies (Taylor 1991); maintaining short term and long term objectives (Cockburn 1992); working at the level of the local but watching for global patterns and articulations (Anyon 1994); and working from the margin and within the mainstream (Eisenstein 1995).

In the short term, at the level of the state and individual local educational institutions in devolved systems, a feminist politics for globalized times would require thinking about how particular contemporary discourses can be reworked in more progressive ways. This may involve tactics which mean working simultaneously with/against managerialist and market value systems, policy frameworks and self managing institutions. It means working from both the top down and the bottom up. It means both co-opting the language of the market, while seeking to shift its meaning. Arnot (1993) argues that the capacity for the women's movement in England to mobilize and argue against New Right notions about the family in the 1980s tempered its conservative effects. As producers and consumers, women can make powerful claims on the market, both individually and collectively. And, as I have argued elsewhere, women principals have indicated a capacity within their own local education markets, to seek to work collectively and individually in a socially responsible way premised upon a strong sense of 'the public' and community (Blackmore 1996).

Others have argued, such as Luke (1997) in the case of universities, that accountability measures, the 'institutional economies' of quality assurance, and the new contractualism can be appropriated for equity ends. This can be achieved by arguing (even if within the parameters of managerialism) for the inclusion of equity objectives, procedures and outcomes in performance management contracts, outsourcing contracts, organizational profiles, institutional charters and outcomes based measures of performance so critical to self governing institutions. While advocating such a tactic, there is a need to recognize that the delegation of responsibility for outcomes to individual managers and the lack transparency of quality assurance and of accountability structures have a tendency to control educational workers through self-management or self surveillance (Luke 1997). Equity can be built into all contractual arrangements between individuals (line managers, executive and at the chalkface) and between individual institutions, as well as between the centre and the periphery, in a form of two way accountability to ensure implementation and outcomes. Top management commitment can be gained on the grounds that equity is more 'productive', which in turn sets up organizational expectations that individuals, particularly those in positions of power, take on responsibility about equity issues in an informed and transparent way (Cope and Kalantzis 1997). And this can be achieved, preferably through consent (professional development/incentives) rather than coercion (performance contracts/withdrawal pay). Consumers (parents and students) can also collectively and individually exert pressure upon organizations to be more inclusive and equitable (Deem *et al.* 1995).

Strategies

These are short term tactics working within parameters not of our own making, yet seeking to address the fastly moving agendas of globalization. A longer term strategy would be to undertake a feminist critique of the underlying assumptions of restructuring in ways which bring together theories of cultural and economic globalization and structural adjustment with concrete local examples in education. Restructuring policies have largely been informed by normative theoretical paradigms derived in a large part from economics, a field which feminists have only recently begun to deconstruct, for example, public choice theory, human capital theory, structural adjustment (Ferber and Nelson 1994; Hyman 1994;

Kuiper and Saps 1995). Feminist economics comes from a range of theoretical perspectives, for example, liberal, Marxist, institutional. But there is agreement that mainstream economists have a particular world view which can be summarized as the atomistic individual making rational choices within a neutral market to maximize their material gain. Theories of rational choice which assume that individuals have the equal capacity, resources and knowledge to make 'rational' choices disregard differential power relations and social relationships of responsibility, and indeed the *social* interdependencies which make *market* relations possible There is need for more empirical research which highlights how the mainstream economic theory fails to adequately explain either global or local features of globalization: persistent income inequality, higher rates of poverty amongst women and children, occupational segregation, discrimination, under-valuing of domestic labour and women's work and the ongoing institutional division of labour along gender lines. If economics actually took into account empirical evidence which indicated that the assumptions underpinning its models did not reflect experience (and particularly women's experience), it may lead to an overturning of such central concepts (Bakker and Miller 1996).

A second long term strategy would be to undertake more cross-national research which takes in a broader range of factors than previous studies. Unterhalter (1996) argues that while there is a growing feminist critique of structural adjustment as a policy response to globalization (e.g. Hyman 1994), they have not considered an alternative discourse which conceptualizes the state as well as the household in the reconfiguration of the public and the private. Such research could offer alternative locally specific policy responses to global metanarratives. As Brodie suggests, 'globalization is a paradigm shift of governing practices' and not some deterministic external inevitable force (Brodie 1996: 386). Yet the standard response by governments has to be less interventionist in the market, that is, weak domestic policy by the state. Yet it could well be argued that stronger domestic economic policies are more necessary on economic grounds in consumption oriented states such as Canada, Sweden and Australia. For these countries, one 'solution' would be to follow the 'high road' of high wage, high skills model, innovation and technology so as to value add on human resources and thus maintain competitive advantage while preserving the standard of living and wages. The high road of strong domestic policy could be expected to benefit women both in terms of their public and private activities (Brodie 1996). But it requires public investment in education and training, not state dis-investment (Marginson 1997).

A third consideration is to undertake more cross-national research to highlight the resonances and variations within specific labour markets, for example, educational labour markets, to understand how educational, economic and social policies – localized labour markets, industrial relations conditions, different forms of school governance and administrative structures – impact on teaching as a 'feminised' profession Such research can better inform local labour policies, but also suggest the types of international and national strategic responses which unions and women's organizations can develop to improve women's work situations. Sandra Acker comments:

> Teacher's salaries are determined locally in the United States but nationally in Great Britain Elementary school principals are mostly male in the United States and Canada but female in Mexico and Israel. Salaries and levels of satisfaction vary widely. Theories that rest in observations about the extent to which teachers lack status, possess autonomy, or experience control also need to be more sensitive to national contexts.
>
> (Acker 1996: 141)

Fourth, analyses in which gender as an organizing principle must also consider other first order differences of race, ethnicity and class. Social polarization arising out of crystallization of centre–periphery arrangements of global, national and organizational labour markets are racialized, classed as well as gendered. While traditional notions of class, always troublesome for women anyway, have been disturbed they are also being solidified (Westergaard 1995). To factor in class also raises issues for feminism about shared citizenship claims, given the polarization between the few individual women who are managerial professionals and who enjoy privileged access to transnational modes of distribution of goods as global citizens compared to class position of the young female instructor with minimal training and a one year contract in a school region.

Feminist claims

Given the reliance upon state feminism in Australia in particular for gender equity reform since the 1970s, it is relevant to consider whether this reliance has impeded the growth of strong independent feminist institutions outside the state. This reliance now suggests future problems as the state withdraws from its progressively interventionist stance. In Australia, there are no obvious alternative institutional frameworks evident as there are, for example, in Canada, to take the state's place as sites of feminist activism (Sawer 1994). How will Australian feminists work for social justice outside the state? What can they learn from feminists in Canada, the UK and USA where there have been weaker state interventions in more decentralized contexts? Another aspect of this problem is to consider where any appeal for equity would best be focused, and how it should be mounted, given that the nation state is less receptive to such appeals. Linda Gordon (1990: 13) talks about:

> the changing legalistic arrangements necessary to facilitate new political organizational frameworks and networks to work at both the supra-national and sub-national levels, and a revitalisation of imagined communities at the level of the local and the global, and not total reliance upon the national.

There is already evidence of new forms of local, national and global activism. Globally, the Beijing Women's Conference in 1996 and the recent condemnation of the UNESCO Women's Committee of Australia's failure to report on equal opportunity signalled the capacity for feminists internationally to put pressure on national governments. Locally, in Victoria, alliances are being formed between women's groups and union, welfare, environmental and multicultural interest groups, for example, in defence of 'the public', and in particular, in defence of public education (e.g. Education Coalition in Victoria and the national movement to Defend Public Education with a former CEO of Victorian state education, a committed feminist, as a key initiator). But as yet, these lack the same infrastructure and legitimising discourses that state feminism had provided in the 1980s.

A further strategic issue is the grounds upon which future claims are to be made against the state, or for that matter supranational or local bodies, in the context of globalized social relations. In substantive terms, the shift from the paternalistic to the midwife state has significantly altered the basis upon which women, individually and collectively, can make claims upon the state in most Western liberal democracies (Orloff 1993). Feminist claims on the welfare state have largely been premised upon needs and rights rather than interests, given that claims on the basis of interest has positioned women as 'connoting selfishness, materialism and essentialism' (Pringle and Watson 1992: 64). Needs discourses centred around the maternalistic and caring state inevitably convey a sense of lack, or of marginality. The effect of this strategy has been that the state offers freedom to men, but protection to women. As Fraser and Gordon (1994) perceive, this produces the mythology of women as dependent rather than emphasizing the interdependence between male autonomy and women's work in maintaining the economic infrastructure.

The rights discourse has largely been operationalized by those seeking equality in the workplace to gain access to power, for example, feminist discourses about women's styles of leadership have been exploited by individual women to gain access to middle management or getting more middle class girls into non traditional male dominated subject areas (Bacchi 1997; Blackmore 1998). But the rights discourse evokes, if not possessive individualism, at least a demarcation of the citizen's realms of freedom from the state. It tends to ignore systemic disadvantage and undermines the sense of the collective interests amongst women. The needs discourse has a whole set of assumptions about the role of the state in meeting certain fundamental needs. The rights discourse of the welfare state has been too easily appropriated by market liberal discourses as exercising client choice within a market state which provides no such guarantee of fundamental needs. The market is treated unproblematically as the mechanism by which to respond both to rights (i.e. individual preference exercised through consumer choice) and needs (education, welfare, health services). This is exemplified in increasingly more individualistic versions of human capital economic theory and public choice theory. The market is also the means by which to manage diversity in a pluralistic society, where diversity is treated as a new source of both consumption (emergence of niche markets), and productivity (managing diversity through flexible specialization to respond to niche markets). One possible strategy for feminists is to explore what social justice policies and claims upon the state might be if based upon interests, a claim which respects difference, rather than needs and rights (Young 1990, 1994).

In conclusion, feminists must work not just with and through, but also on and against the state, by engaging with all levels of political activity locally and globally. These multiple approaches are not to be rejected, but extended, given the volatility of post-modern politics. While national and state gender equity policy units have called upon international conventions as normative models, increasingly, the appeal will be to the global notions of human rights (e.g. United Nations and ILO) and not national legislative norms (Cohen 1996). There is what Mohanty (1990) calls an 'imagined community' of feminism to which women can appeal which can influence governmental policies, nationally and internationally so that, for example, intra-state trade agreements (as in the EU social contract) can include principles of equity. At the same time, while post-colonial feminists sensitize us to how international bodies such as the World Bank and OECD can promote global solutions to local problems which can work to the detriment of women as a group (e.g. reduced public expenditure accompanying balancing national budgets and repaying international debt in the face of financial crisis impacting hardest on women and children, for example, Indonesia 1998), such bodies can be pressured to build in gender and race as part of their analysis of national and global policies as well as their own policy recommendations (e.g. devolution) (Taylor *et al.* 1997). This imagined community would be one which recognizes that there is not some homogenous entity which can be called Western or Third World feminists – but can work through strategic essentialism and strategic pluralism forming alliances and collaborations where there is a shared commitment, though not necessarily a common experience, due to shared interests. Thus the category of woman can be used with a sense of irony, conscious of time and place, recognizing the systemic and structural gender inequality but the politics of difference amongst women.

Acknowledgements

The author is very grateful for the careful and insightful editorial suggestions provided by Sandra Taylor and Suzanne Franzway.

References

Acker, S. (1996) Teachers and gender, in M. Apple (ed.) *Review of Research in Education. 21* (Washington: American Educational Research Association).

Anyon, J. (1994) The retreat of Marxism and socialist feminism: postmodern and post-structuralist theories in education, *Curriculum Inquiry*, 24 (2), 114–34.

Appadurai, A. (1990) Disjuncture and difference in the global cultural economy, in M. Featherstone (ed.) *Global Culture: Nationalism, Globalization and Modernity* (New York: Sage).

Arnot, M. (1993) A crisis in patriarchy? British feminist educational politics and state regulation of gender, in M. Arnot and K. Weiler (eds) *Feminism and Social Justice in Education* (London: Falmer Press).

Arnot, M. and Gordon, T. (1996) Gender, citizenship and marketisation, *Discourse*, 17 (3), 377–88.

Bacchi, C. (1997) *The Politics of Affirmative Action* (London: Sage).

Bakker, I. and Miller, R. (1996) Escape from Fordism: the emergence of alternative forms of state administration and output, in R. Boyer and D. Drache (eds) *State Against Markets: The Limits of Globalization* (New York: Routledge).

Baldock, C. (1990) Award restructuring for women: tool of change? *Feminist Studies*, 12 (Sum), 43–9.

Ball, S. (1994) *Education Reform: A Critical and Post-structuralist Perspective* (Buckingham: Open University Press).

Barlow, M. and Robertson, H. J. (1994) *Class Warfare: The Assault on Canada's Schools* (Toronto: Key Porter Books).

Blackmore, J. (1996) Doing 'emotional labour' in the education market place stories from the field of women in management, *Discourse*, 17 (3), 337–50.

Blackmore, J. (1997a) The gendering of skill in Australian state education 1900–80, in A. H. Halsey, H. Lauder, P. Brown and A. Stuart Wells (eds) *Education, Culture, Economy and Society* (Oxford: Oxford University Press).

Blackmore, J. (1997b) The level playing field? The restructuring and regendering of educational work, *International Review of Education*, 43 (5–6), 1–23.

Blackmore, J. (1998) *Troubling Women: Feminism, Leadership and Educational Change* (Buckingham: Open University Press).

Blackmore, J. and Angwin, J. (1997) Educational outworkers: the impact of educational restructuring upon the work of women educators, *Forum of Education*, 52 (2), 1–23.

Blackmore, J. and Sachs, J. (1997) 'All worked out' – gender, restructuring and the psychic economy of Universities. Paper presented to the Australian Association for Research in Education Annual Conference, Brisbane, December, 1–5.

Blackmore, J., Bigum, C., Hodgens, J. and Laskey, L. (1996) Managed change and self management in schools of the future, *Leading and Managing*, 3 (3), 195–220.

Bradley, K. and Ramirez, F. (1996) World polity and gender parity: women's share of higher education 1965–85, *Sociology of Education and Socialisation*, 11, 63–91.

Brodie, J. (1996) New state forms, new political spaces, in R. Boyer and D. Drache (eds) *State Against Markets: The Limits of Globalization* (New York: Routledge).

Brown, P. and Lauder, H. (1997) Education, globalization and economic development, in A. H. Halsey, H. Lauder, P. Brown and A. Stuart-Wells (eds) *Education, Culture, Economy and Society* (Oxford: Oxford University Press).

Bryson, L. (1996) The proletarianisation of women: gender justice in Australia? *Social Justice*, 16 (3), 87–101.

Burton, C. (1990) *The Promise and the Price: The Struggle for Equal Opportunity in Women's Employment* (Sydney: Allen and Unwin).

Cerny, P. (1990) *The Changing Architecture of Politics: Structure, Agency and the Future of the State* (London: Sage).

Cockburn, C. (1992) Equal opportunities: the short and long agenda, *Industrial Relations Journal*, 213–25.

Codd, J. (1993) Managerialism, market liberalism and the move to self managing schools in New Zealand, in J. Smyth (ed.) *A Socially Critical View of the Self Managing School* (East Sussex: Falmer Press).

Cohen, M. (1996) Democracy and the future of nations: challenges of disadvantaged women and minorities, in R. Boyer and D. Drache (eds) *State Against Markets: The Limits of Globalization* (New York: Routledge).

Connell, R. W. (1990) The state, gender and sexual politics. Theory and appraisal, *Theory and Society*, 19, 507–44.

Cope, B. and Kalantzis, M. (1997) *Productive Diversity* (Annandale: Pluto Press).

Court, M. (1993) 1898–1993: how far have we come in women's employment in education? *New Zealand Annual Review of Education*, 3, 81–126.

Dale, R. and Robertson, S. (1996) 'Resiting the nation, reshaping the state': globalization effects on education policy in New Zealand, in M. Olssen and K. Morris (eds) *Education Policy in the 1990s.*

Davis, E. and Pratt, V. (1993) *Making the Link: Affirmative Action and Industrial Relations* (Canberra: AGPS).

Deem, R., Brehony, K. and Heath, S. (1995) *Active Citizenship and the Governing of Schools* (Buckingham: Open University Press).

Delhi, K. (1996) Between 'market' and 'state'? Engendering education change in the 1990s, *Discourse*, 17 (3), 363–76.

Edwards, M. and Magarey, S. (eds) (1995) *Women in a Restructuring Australia* (Sydney: Allen and Unwin).

Eisenstein, H. (1992) *Gender Shock: Feminismon Two Continents* (Sydney: Allen and Unwin).

Eisenstein, H. (1995) *Inside Agitators: Australian Femocrats and the State* (Sydney: Allen and Unwin).

Fairclough, N. (1992) *Discourse and Social Change* (Cambridge: Polity Press).

Ferber, M. and Nelson, J. (1993) *Beyond Economic Man. Feminist Theory and Economics* (Chicago: Chicago University Press).

Franzway, S., Court, D. and Connell, R. (1989) *Staking a Claim. Feminism, Bureaucracy and the State* (Sydney: Allen and Unwin).

Fraser, N. and Gordon, L. (1994) A genealogy of dependency: tracing a keyword of the US welfare State, *Signs*, 19 (2), 309–36.

Gewirtz, S., Ball, S. and Bowe, R. (1995) *Markets, Choice and Equity in Education* (Buckingham: Open University Press).

Gibson-Graham, J. K. (1996) *The End of Capitalism (as we knew it). A Feminist Critique of Political Economy* (London: Blackwell).

Gordon, L. (1990) The new feminist scholarship on the welfare state, in L. Gordon (ed.) *Women, the State, and Welfare* (Madison: University of Wisconsin Press).

Gordon, L. (1991) The state, devolution and educational reform in New Zealand, *Journal of Education Policy*, 7 (2), 187–203.

Gordon, L. (1994a) Whatever happened to the National Policy for Girls and Women in New Zealand? (University of Canterbury: Unpublished paper).

Gordon, L. (1994b) 'Rich' and 'poor' schools in Aotearoa, *New Zeal and Journal of Educational Studies*, 29 (1–2), 129–36.

Green, A. (1996) Education, globalization and the nation state (University of Sydney: Paper presented to the World Congress of Comparative Education Societies, July 1–6).

Grewal, I. and Kaplan, C. (eds) (1994) *Scattered Hegemonies: Postmodernity and Transnational Feminist Practices* (Indianapolis: University of Minnesota Press).

Haraway, D. (1988) Situated knowledges: the science question in feminism and the privilege of the partial perspective, *Feminist Studies*, 14, 575–96.

Hargreaves, A. (1994) Restructuring restructuring: postmodernity and the prospects of education change, *Journal of Education Policy*, 9 (1), 47–65.

Harvey, D. (1989) *The Postmodern Condition* (Cambridge: Blackwell).

Hekman, S. (1996) *Feminist Interpretations of Michel Foucault* (London: Routledge).

Henry, M. and Taylor, S. (1996) Globalization and national school policy in Australia, in B. Lingard and P. Porter (eds) *A National Approach to Schooling in Australia* (Canberra: Australian College of Education).

Hyman, P. (1994) *Women and Economics: A New Zealand Feminist Perspective* (Wellington: Bridget Williams Books).

Jones, K. (1995) *Compassionate Authority. Democracy and the Representation of Women* (New York: Routledge).

Kenway, J. and Epstein, D. (1996) The marketisation of school education; feminist studies and perspectives, *Discourse*, 17 (3), 301–14.

Kenway, J., Bigum, C. and Fitzclarence, L. (1993) Marketing education in the post-modern age, *Journal of Education Policy*, 8 (2), 105–22.

Kenway, J., Willis, S. with Blackmore, J. and Rennie, L. (1997) *Answering Back: Girls, Boys and Feminism* (Sydney: Allen and Unwin).

Koven, S. and Michel, S. (1994) *Mothers of a New World: Maternalistic Politics and the Origins of Welfare States* (London: Routledge).

Kuiper, E. and Saps, P. (1995) *Out on the Margins: A Feminist Economics* (London: Routledge).

Lash, S. and Urry, J. (1994) *The Economies of Signs and Space* (Oxford: Polity Press).

Lauder, H. (1994) *The Creation of Market Competition for Education in New Zealand* (Wellington: Smithfield Project).

Lawton, S. (1992) Why restructure? An international survey of roots of reform, *Journal of Education Policy*, 7 (2), 139–54.

Lewis, J. and Astrom, G. (1992) Equality, difference and state welfare labor market policies and family policies in Sweden, *Feminist Studies*, 18 (1), 59–87.

Lingard, B. and Porter, P. (eds) (1997) A national approach to schooling in Australia? (Canberra: Australian College of Education).

Luke, C. (1997) Quality assurance and women in higher education, *Higher Education*, 33, 433–51.

Marginson, S. (1997) *Educating Australia: Government, Economy and Citizen since 1960.* (Melbourne: Cambridge University Press).

Middleton, S. (1992) Gender equity and school charters: theoretical and political questions for the 1990, in S. Middleton and A. Jones (eds) *Women in Education in Aoatorea/New Zealand II* (Wellington: Bridget Williams Press).

Mohanty, C. (1990) Cartographies of struggle: Third World Women and the politics of feminism, in Mohanty, C., Risso, A. and Torres, L. (eds) *Third World Women and the Politics of Feminism* (Minneapolis: Indiana University Press).

Morrison, A. (1992) *The New Leaders: Guidelines on Leadership Diversity in America* (San Francisco: Jossey-Bass).

Neave, G. (1988) Education and social policy: demise of an ethic or change of values? *Oxford Review of Education*, 14 (3), 273–82.

O'Neill, A. (1996) Privatizing public policy: privileging market man and individualizing equality through choice within education in Aotearoa/New Zealand, *Discourse*, 17 (3), 403–16.

Orloff, A. S. (1993) Gender and the social rights of citizenship: the comparative analysis of gender relations and welfare states, *American Sociological Review*, 58, 303–28.

Peters, M. and Marshall, J. (1996) *Individualism and Community Education and Social Policy in the Post Modern Condition* (London: The Falmer Press).

Poiner, G. and Wills, S. (1990) *The Gifthorse* (Sydney: Allen and Unwin).

Power, S. and Whitty, G. (1996) Teaching new subjects? The hidden curriculum of marketised education systems (London Institute of Education: Unpublished paper).

Pringle, R. and Watson, S. (1992) 'Women's interests' and the post structuralist state, in M. Barrett and A. Phillips (eds) *Destabilising Theory. Contemporary Feminist Debate.* (Cambridge: Polity Press).

Probert, B. (1995) A restructuring world?, in M. Edwards and S. Magarey (eds) *Women in a Restructuring Australia* (Sydney: Allen and Unwin).

Ramazanoglu, C. (1993) *Up Against Foucault. Explorations of Some Tensions between Foucuault and Feminism* (London: Routledge).

Sawer, M. (1991) Why has the women's movement had more influence on government in Australia than elsewhere?, in F. Castles (ed.) *Australia Compared. People. Policies and Politics* (Sydney: Allen and Unwin).

Sawer, M. (1994) Feminism and the state: theory and practice in Australia and Canada, *Australian-Canadian Studies*, 12 (1), 49–68.

Segal, L. (1990) *Slow Motion: Changing Masculinities, Changing Men* (London: Virago Press).

Spivak, G. (1993) *Outside in the Teaching Machine* (London: Routledge).

Stromquist, N. (1992) Sex equity legislation in education: the state as the promoter of women's rights, *Review of Educational Research*, 63 (4), 379–408.

Taylor, S. (1991) *Equity and the Politics of Change: Education Policy Making in Context.* Paper presented to the Australian Sociological Association conference Perth, Dec. 1–3.

Taylor, S. and Henry, M. (1994) Equity and the new post compulsory education and training policies in Australia: a progressive or regressive agenda? *Journal of Education Policy*, 2, 105–27.

Taylor, S., Henry, M., Lingard, B. and Rizvi, F. (1997) *Educational Policy and the Politics of Change* (Sydney: Allen and Unwin).

Unterhalter, E. (1996) States, households and markets in World Bank discourses 1985–1995, *Discourse*, 17 (3), 389–402.

Walby, S. (1997) *Gender Transformations* (London: Routledge).

Wallace, M. (1993) Discourse of derision: the role of the mass media within the education policy process, *Journal of Education Policy*, 8 (4), 321–37.

Waters, M. (1995) *Globalization* (London: Routledge).

Watkins, P. (1996) Decentralizing education to the point of production: Sloanism, the market and schools of the future, *Discourse*, 17 (1), 85–99.

Weiner, G. (1995) *Feminism and Education* (Buckingham: Open University Press).

Westergaard, J. (1995) *Who Gets What? The Hardening of Social Class in the Late Twentieth Century* (Oxford: Polity Press).

Whitty, G. (1996) Creating quasi-markets in education: a review of recent research on parental choice and school autonomy in three countries, *Review of Research in Education*, 22, 3–48.

Wylie, C. (1995) Contrary currents: the application of public sector reform framework in education, *New Zealand Journal of Educational Studies*, 30 (2), 149–64.

Yates, L. (1993) Feminism and Australian state policy, in N. Arnot and K. Weiler (eds) *Feminism and Social Justice* (London: The Falmer Press).

Yeatman, A. (1992) Women's citizenship claims, labour market policy and globalization, *Australian Journal of Political Science*, 27, 449–61.

Yeatman, A. (1994) *Postmodern Theorisings of the Political* (London: Routledge).
Young, I. (1990) *Justice and the Politics of Difference* (Princeton: Princeton University Press).
Young, I. (1994) Polity and group difference: a critique of the ideal of universal citizenship, in B. Turner and P. Hamilton (eds) *Citizenship: Critical Concepts Vol 2* (London: Routledge).
Zetlin, D. and Whitehouse, G. (1996) Citizenship and industrial regulation: a feminist perspective (Griffith University, Paper presented to the *Culture and Citizenship Conference*, September 30–October 2).

3 The lessons of international education reform

Benjamin Levin

University of Manitoba, Canada

Source: *Journal of Education Policy*, 12 (4): 253–66, 1997.

Introduction

Large-scale education reform is widespread across the 'industrialized' world. Documentation prepared for a recent meeting of ministers of education of OECD countries (OECD 1996) notes that almost every country is undertaking some kind of program of large-scale reform in education.

At the surface level these reform programs seem to embody many common features, and thus appear to be attractive options for other countries considering ways of improving education. Governments do seem inclined to transfer policies across national boundaries (Levin 1998; Rose 1993). However appearances can be deceiving; although reforms in Western countries do have some interesting features, they are far from providing a model that can readily be adopted elsewhere. This article draws on OECD work that spans more than two dozen countries, but focuses primarily on education reforms in three English-speaking countries – England, Canada, and the US (with occasional references to New Zealand), partly because these countries do seem, to a considerable extent, to have drawn from the same well of ideas, and partly because the documentation on their reforms is most readily accessible to an English speaker.

Those coming from systems that have always been centralized and state controlled may benefit from a brief reminder of how differently schools in some other countries have been organized. In Canada, for example, the national government plays almost no role at all in education, which is a responsibility of provincial governments. These in turn have historically delegated much authority to local school districts, which may have anywhere from a few hundred to 100,000 students. Curriculum has been a provincial responsibility, but much of the control over what happens in schools has rested with locally elected boards and the professionals they employ. The US system is in some respects even more decentralized. Although the federal government does play an impotant role in education, much control over curriculum and other policy issues has rested with the country's 15,000 school boards. Neither country has had anything that could be called a national system of education. The courts have played a very important role in shaping education in the US, and increasingly so in recent years in Canada as well.

Most of the references in this paper in regard to Britain refer to England and Wales; Scotland and Northern Ireland are different in important ways. However until the last decade individual schools in Britain had a very great deal of control over their own curriculum and teaching, so that their system, too, could be described as having been highly decentralized.

The changing context for education reform

Before discussing specific reforms, it is important to note that recent education reform is occurring in a very different context than existed for previous eras of major changes in schooling. Every historical period contains competing and contradictory trends, of course, but one could reasonably argue that the current period is a less optimistic one than were the last two large-scale reform processes in education – the massive enlargement of school systems after World War II and the period of liberalization in the 1960s.

These earlier times embodied a strong desire for growth, a sense of optimism and a focus on the positive contribution of schooling to social and economic welfare. In contrast, the current wave of reform is linked to feelings of fear, retrenchment and cynicism. Education change is occurring in the context of large-scale criticism of schools. Government policy documents typically take the view that school systems have failed to deliver what is required, and that the failure is especially lamentable in view of the high level of spending on education. The general tone underlying much reform is negative – an effort to undo alleged damage.

The most common rationale advanced for education reform is economic, particularly in relation to preparation of a workforce and competition with other countries. Education is described as being a key component of countries' ability to maintain or improve their economic welfare. This brief excerpt from an OECD report is an illustration of a line of reasoning that can be found in many, many reports of governments and other organizations in almost every country.

> Only a well-trained and highly adaptable labour force can provide the capacity to adjust to structural change and seize new employment opportunities created by technological progress. Achieving this will in many cases entail a re-examination, perhaps radical, of the economic treatment of human resources and education.
>
> (OECD 1993: 9)

We hear so much of this rhetoric now that it may seem self evident, but 30 or 40 years ago much more was being said about social mobility and individual welfare (Dehli 1995). The current emphasis on the apocalyptic consequences of failure in education were largely absent in that last great period of education reform. Economic rationales are not, to be sure, the only reasons being advanced today for educational reform. Equity goals are still cited, and so is individual social mobility, but the balance has clearly changed in the direction of an economic emphasis.

Another important contextual element is an apparently declining faith in the ability of our major institutions to address important social issues. Although confidence in private organizations, such as business and the media, has also declined sharply (evidence of this is reviewed in Livingstone 1995), schools as public institutions are deeply affected by the increasing cynicism about government and scepticism that governments can in fact address social problems effectively. Unlike the situation 30 years ago, education reformers are often doubtful that schools can or will change appropriately. Such ideas as 'provider capture' – that the system is now organized to serve primarily the needs of those who work in it – or 'resistance to change' – that teachers, administrators and policy-makers are unwilling to change what they have always done – have achieved the status of commonsense truths. Plank and Boyd (1994: 264–5) describe this as 'antipolitics'.

> The two most striking features of American school politics in the past decade have been an obsessive concern with the multiple 'failures' of the educational system and a propensity to embark on a flight from democracy in the search for solutions. The consequence has been the growth of an *antipolitics* of education, in which disagreements about educational policy and practice are increasingly likely to be addressed in conflict over the institutions of educational governance rather than in open debate on the merits of alternative goals and strategies . . . in the hope that new institutions will place braver, wiser, and nobler persons in charge of children's schooling [emphasis in original].

It is also important to note that for the first time large-scale education reform is not generally accompanied by additional money. The funding picture varies around the world, with some jurisdictions making real cuts and others providing modest increases. But governments have largely decoupled reform from funding, and have had some success in convincing people that tackling the problems of education does not require large infusions of new cash. The line about money not solving problems is now heard so often that it has become widely accepted, but that should not blind us to its novelty. It is hard to think of any other major reform in education that was not accompanied by injections of large quantities of money. The attempt to move the gears of education without the grease of financing is producing some very loud noises from the machinery; whether it will be successful is still an open question.

These contextual elements – a negative view of schooling based largely on economic concerns, a distrust in the ability of public institutions to reform themselves, and an unwillingness to spend more on education – have been fundamental in shaping the nature of reform programs in many countries. If preparation of the labour force is key, then reform must include a greater curricular focus on knowledge and skills seen as useful in the workplace. Hence emphasis on science and technology, and on students' behaviour. If institutions cannot reform themselves, then institutional forms must be altered so that real change is possible. Hence the interest in alternative forms of organization for schools, such as the current emphasis on markets and 'privatization' or the focus on decentralization as a way of removing power from bureaucrats and politicians, who are seen as self-interested. If additional funding will not be made available, there must be strong external pressures to push people to change. Hence the interest in choice plans, public examination processes, and reform via legislation and regulation.

It would be wrong, however, to present these views as if they were the only ones in play. In fact there is considerable evidence that the agenda for reform of education is not shared by all, but is being advanced by particular groups based on ideological commitments. The frequent criticism of schools on grounds of poor achievement, capture by a 'progressive' agenda, resistance to change, and excessive cost is not the whole or only story, and evidence to the contrary may be deliberately ignored in the service of a political agenda (Berliner and Biddle 1966; Barlow and Robertson 1994). To take an instance, one former minister of education in a Canadian province had criticized schools because of poor Canadian results in international studies of achievement. When students did very well on a later test he rejected the results on the grounds that the test must have been too easy!

One of the most striking indicators is research by David Livingstone and colleagues. Their set of opinion polls in Ontario (Livingstone *et al.* 1995) has shown that the only group strongly supporting the typical reform agenda (as defined below) is corporate executives. All other groups are more supportive of schools and less interested in large-scale reform. Moreover, at least in Ontario, support for more funding for education has actually risen in recent years. Livingstone (1995) also cites polling data from the US and UK as well as Canada showing that public confidence in schools continues to be higher than those for government or business. Quite a large body of research in Canada and the US shows that parents believe that their local schools are doing a pretty good job (Barlow and Robertson 1994). The limited response to various school choice programs, discussed below, is another indicator that public, and especially parent, dissatisfaction with schools may be less than is claimed by critics.

The next section of the paper describes three common components of education reforms and some of their limitations.

Main common elements of reform programs

The components of reform programs do vary in important ways across countries and, in federal countries such as Canada and the US, between provinces or states. The focus of this discussion, however, is on three proposals which are part of many reform packages: decentralization of authority to schools and the creation of school or parent councils to share in that authority; various forms of choice or other market-like mechanisms; increased achievement testing with publication of results and its corollary, more centralized curriculum.

Local management and school/parent councils

One of the strongest trends in education reform across national boundaries has been the move, referred to here as local management, to shift authority to the level of the local school. The first steps in this direction in the US and Canada involved largely an administrative decentralization (Brown 1990), in which school administrators were given more authority over staffing and budgets. More recently, the emphasis has shifted to a political decentralization which gives an increased role in governing schools to parents, and in some cases to other community members. For example, all Canadian provinces have now passed legislation requiring each school to have some kind of parent or school council, although in most cases the councils have only advisory functions. The large-scale education reform in Kentucky required school-based decision-making councils in each school by 1996, with power to select the principal, affect staffing, and set policy in several areas (Lindle 1995). In Chicago, Local School Councils were created with a large majority of parents and community members, with the power to approve school plans and to hire and fire school principals (Bryk *et al.* 1993).

In England each school has a governing body made up of parents and non-parent community members, especially business people, who can exercise a great deal of power over what the school is and does. Local education authorities continue to exist, but their powers have been sharply curtailed, and almost all funding now flows directly to schools with its use determined by the governing bodies. Changes have also been made in arrangements around teachers' pay to give governing bodies more autonomy in staffing.

New Zealand abolished its education boards as part of its reform program (Peters 1995). Its current legislation requires each school to have a governing body responsible for drafting and fulfilling the school's charter – a statement of what the school will do. The national ministry of education, which used to run the system at a fairly fine level of detail, has been largely disbanded and now serves primarily a monitoring function. The OECD (1989) reports that many other countries are also experimenting with forms of decentralization.

Choice and markets

A second reform proposal (being implemented in many settings) involves the creation of systems that try to mimic the characteristics of economic markets, based on the belief that markets produce high levels of efficiency. In education, market advocates believe that parents can make the best choice of school for their children, while schools will improve if they have to compete for students. This approach is most evident in England, where parents are able to choose the schools their children will attend. Schools are expected to compete for students, since their funding depends largely on enrolments, and are required to make certain kinds of information, including achievement results, available to parents to assist their choice. In the last few years a program of compulsory external inspection of schools has been added, with the inspection reports being given to parents and made available to the public as another source of information on which to base choice of school. New Zealand uses a similar approach, with parents free to choose schools and schools that are popular free to choose students.

Choice has taken a rather different form in the US where it is often bound up with the funding of private or religious schools and with questions of racial integration. American states and districts have experimented with a wide variety of choice plans. Another US variant is 'charter schools'. Charter schools are schools that are developed around a particular focus or purpose. They are separately funded from normal public schools, and may be given exemptions from various regulations governing public schools. Charter school plans do vary considerably from state to state (GAO 1995).

In Canada choice and market plans are relatively undeveloped. Several provinces have indicated that parents and students will have more ability to choose the school they attend, but many Canadian jurisdictions already offer widespread choice even if not under that rubric (Riffel *et al.* 1996). Students in most provinces (at least in urban areas) can already choose between English-language schools, French immersion schools, bilingual schools (English–German, English–Ukrainian, etc.), Roman Catholic schools (publicly funded in provinces with about two-thirds of the Canadian population), private schools (which receive some public funds in most provinces), Aboriginal schools, traditional (basics) schools, and so on.

Testing and accountability

One of the key arguments about the alleged failures of schools concerns poor levels of achievement, which in turn are held to threaten economic prosperity. Accordingly, many jurisdictions have adopted reforms that increase the amount of testing of student achievement and that make the results of this testing more public.

As with other reforms, testing regimes vary across jurisdictions. England and Wales are implementing a series of national tests at four age levels, keyed to the National Curriculum (about which more shortly), but the process has been very difficult. Teachers boycotted the first set of tests in 1993 leading to an inquiry and a major redesign of both the testing program and the curriculum. Meanwhile, reported results on the national GCSE exams written at about age 16 (the results are typically expressed as the percentage of students receiving good scores in five subjects) are a main feature of reporting on school achievement and part of the basis on which parents and students choose schools.

Canada has long had provincial curriculum-based examinations at the end of high school; more extensive examination programs in secondary schools were largely abolished in the 1960s. In the last few years most provinces have extended their exam requirements, including more subjects and grade levels and giving them more weight in students' overall evaluations. Reporting practices vary from reporting only overall provincial scores to reporting school by school results.

The US has quite a different approach to testing. Because curriculum has been so decentralized, school systems and governments have relied on standardized tests that were thought to be valid across most school settings. Moreover, many US systems report the results of standardized tests in very public ways, such as publishing school by school results in newspapers (Cohen 1992). US research, too, tends to rely on standardized general achievement tests for assessing school outcomes, even when noting how problematic such reliance is. The result is that testing is decoupled from curriculum to a much greater extent than in other countries. However there have been recent efforts to reform testing in ways that link it more closely to curriculum and teaching.

One of the results of a greater commitment to testing is that it tends to lead to a more centralized curriculum. If all students need to learn certain knowledge and skills, then it seems logical that these items should form the basis of a common curriculum. Hence England, where curriculum was largely left to the discretion of schools and teachers, has now developed a National Curriculum. New Zealand, too, has now a much more centralized curriculum framework than it did before reform. In Canada, which has had provincial curricula, there are now large projects to integrate curricula across provinces – sometimes regionally and sometimes nationally. The US has too many states and districts to make national curricula feasible, but efforts are underway to develop what are called national standards in various subject areas. The first of these, in mathematics, appears to be having powerful effects although efforts in other subject areas, such as English or history, have been plagued with controversy. US states have also taken a more active role in shaping curriculum requirements. However there is deep distrust in many quarters in the US of any moves towards state control of curriculum, particularly by religious groups, and projects such as outcomes-based education, which involves the specification of particular outcomes for students, have been the subject of enormous political struggle (Boyd *et al.* 1996).

The problems of reform strategies

Contradictions in purpose

A first problem is that the three areas of reform embody contradictory elements. Local management and parent involvement are only sensible if one presumes a genuine interest in the community in the work necessary to create and sustain a vital school. This implies that parents and others are willing to invest substantial amounts of time and energy in their school. Choice, on the other hand, assumes that parents influence quality not by working to improve a particular school, but by choosing the school that they feel will best suit their children. If choice is meaningful there is no reason for parents to invest in the process of governance and improvement, any more than consumers will work hard to improve the product of a particular company as opposed to switching to another company instead. Hirschmann (1970) has referred to these alternatives as exit (for choice) and voice (for involvement aimed at improvement).

Both choice and local management are also potentially inconsistent with the move towards more centralized curricula and assessment. Choice is only meaningful if the things to be chosen differ in some respect. Similarly, local management is only meaningful if there are some real decisions about organizational form and purpose to be made. Both local management and choice are about encouraging diversity in schooling arrangements. Common curriculum and assessment push in exactly the other direction. If all schools are expected to teach the same thing, why bother with local management or with choice? Moreover, institutional theory points to the tendency for all institutions of a certain kind to take on a common form (Powell and Dimaggio 1991). In schools, where assessment practices are held to have a strong influence on the entire nature of the institution, it seems likely that more standardized assessment will lead to schools looking more and more like each other rather than becoming more diversified.

Variability in implementation

Writers on politics such as Edelman (1988) and Stone (1988) are among those who suggest that the purpose of policy is at least as much symbolic as political. If that is so, it should be no surprise to find that policies that look similar on paper end up looking quite different in practice. A considerable literature on implementation has documented these differences in particular countries (McLaughlin 1987; Fullan and Stiegelbauer 1991; Conley and Goldman 1995), but the difference is even greater between countries.

Decentralization and local management provide a good example. Various plans embody important differences between administrative and political decentralization, in the degree to which school councils are advisory vs being given decision making powers, and in the range of issues they can address. OECD research (1995) points to a very wide range in the powers of local school councils across countries; even in systems purporting to be school-based, some schools have control over most decisions, and others control very few. In short, the common terminology around decentralization actually represents an enormous range of practices, some of which appear very little different than the supposedly more centralized approaches they have supplanted.

Choice plans, too, differ greatly not only from one country to another, but within countries or states. Many jurisdictions have begun with an ideological commitment to choice, but choice plans in practice vary widely. Indeed, it is hard to find two that are very much the same, whether one looks across national boundaries (e.g. Britain, New Zealand) or subjurisdictions (e.g. Milwaukee, Minnesota; see Hirsh 1994). Some plans include private schools, while others do not. Some plans allow choice at any point in a child's schooling, while others focus it at certain transition ages. Some plans require schools to achieve equity targets while others do not. Some favour local residents or siblings of current students, while others do not. Some fund transportation costs while others do not. And so on. The combination of these details can result in huge differences in the practical implications of choice. These differences are one reason that one can find people on opposite ends of the political spectrum arguing in favour of choice plans (Nathan 1996).

In all settings, much depends on the details of any choice plan and on the particulars of a given context. Population density is one obvious factor – choice looks very different in rural areas. Schools' and parents' responses to choice are influenced by the economic, ethnic, and class structure of the community, by the entire set of schools within an area, and by the reputation these schools had when the new policy came into play (Lauder *et al.* 1994). In the US, race has been a critical factor in many discussions of choice. In some settings, girls-only schools are popular partly because of parents' religious beliefs. Edwards and Whitty (1995) have argued that in England the entire market/choice system can only be understood within a framework in which rankings are what matter, and most people's objective is to have their children as high on the academic totem pole as possible, regardless of the substantive merits of any given school's program.

Testing, too, takes quite different forms in different settings. As noted, the US relies on standardized achievement tests, while Canada and England have placed more emphasis on tests linked to particular curricula. In England the GCSE exam results are a more and more powerful influence, but these are not all of a piece either, as there are several different providers of GCSE curriculum and exams with different levels within each. Countries will differ also in the grade levels at which testing occurs, the value of the test in terms of the student's overall standing, the number and range of subject areas tested, whether the test is universal or optional, and in other respects that can make an enormous difference to the results and to their uses. Cibulka's study of testing policies in three US states (1991) is highly revealing of the powerful differences created by political and social contexts.

This discussion should not be taken to suggest that variability in policy implementation is something to be feared. Differences in context require differences in policy; to do the same thing in every setting would be foolish. Insofar as some current reforms aim to encourage greater local autonomy, we should expect more variation in practice to result. The proviso to keep in mind is that the greater the local variation, the less meaningful the overall label of a reform or policy becomes. US policy analyst Aaron Wildavsky's famous slogan – If planning is everything, maybe it's nothing (1973) – could equally be true of such widely touted reforms as choice, decentralization, or testing.

Link to outcomes

The third, and most important problem with these reform strategies rests on the weak connection between the strategies and the outcomes they are supposed to influence. In theory the links might be described as follows:

- Local management will lead to better decisions about teaching and learning because people closest to the scene are most likely to understand what practices will be successful; the result will be more effective use of resources, more effective practices, and better outcomes.

- Choice will allow parents to pick the schools that are most suitable for their children. Because schools are funded based on their enrolment, they will have a powerful incentive to improve in order to attract additional students.
- More powerful assessment strategies will motivate students to put more effort into their schooling. They will also provide a means for parents to make judgements about the relative effectiveness of schools and therefore put additional pressure on schools and teachers to improve. Centralized curricula will focus the attention of schools on the knowledge and skills that are most important for students.

All of these assumptions require some leaps of faith, and the evidence on each of them appears mixed at best.

Although it is now conventional wisdom in management generally as well as in education that local actors closest to the scene are most likely to understand what needs to be done, a little thought suggests that the picture is not so simple. Local actors will, of course, have more knowledge of local conditions than will those more distantly situated. They may, however, have less knowledge about larger issues that are just as important in determining an appropriate course of action. Indeed, many of the moves towards local management in schools are hedged with exclusions and prohibitions precisely because we cannot be confident that local judgement will always be the most suitable. We use multi-tier systems of government because local perspectives do need to be balanced against larger-scale views; checks and balances are necessary. It may be that in education local concerns have been unduly subjugated to those of central bodies, or that central bodies have not been sufficiently sensitive and diligent in carrying out their work. This does not mean, however, that only local actors are important. Indeed, the entire move towards local management is the result of actions taken by central bodies rather than because of any mass demand from parents or others in local communities (Barlow and Robertson 1994; Dehli 1995).

Some have advanced a less charitable view. They argue that moves to create local management have been less the result of a desire to empower parents than of a desire to reduce the role of others who have resisted the demands of central government, such as school districts in Canada and the US, and local education authorities in Britain. Local management (and, in England, grant-maintained schools, which are directly funded by the national government) can be seen as ways of increasing the authority of central governments by greatly weakening or removing from the scene another set of political actors with the resources and organization to resist, something few local school councils are likely to have.

A considerable body of evidence also suggests that changes in governance arrangements are only weakly related to teaching and learning, and hence to outcomes of schooling. David Cohen (1992) provides an excellent review of this issue. He identifies four important elements that limit the impact of governance on practice: the degree to which government and policy-making structures are decentralized; other factors that shape instructional practice, such as materials, assessment practices, and teacher education; the limited impact of instructional guidance on school practice; and the impact of the larger culture and values.

> If American politics and education run true to form, reformers... will introduce many different schemes to make education more consistent, but they will be less able to produce consistency among those schemes, to greatly reduce the clutter of previous programs and policies, or to fundamentally change teaching.
>
> (Cohen 1992: 41)

In regard to local management and parent councils themselves, the evidence suggests that they are not as effective as proponents thought. It appears that relatively few parents are actively involved, that involvement may drop off after the first few years, that councils are often dominated by school administrators, and so on (Deem 1994; Coe *et al.* 1995; Furtwengler *et al.* 1995; Levacic 1995). In England and Wales, although budget authority officially belongs to school governors, program and financial decisions are being made predominantly by heads (principals) (Maychell 1994; Thomas and Martin 1996). In the Canadian province of Quebec, a decade after legislation required local school councils, two researchers concluded that the effort 'to grant more authority to the local school can only be described as a failure' (Henchey and Burgess 1987: 56). Wylie (1995) concluded that local management in New Zealand has not had very much impact on teaching and learning, though it does affect education politics. The research indicates that effective parent involvement is not simply a matter of structures, but also involves issues of training, mandate and composition. Moreover, the preference of most parents is not for involvement through school governing bodies, but for involvement in their own children's learning (Epstein 1995). From their comprehensive review of the research on school-based management (SBM), Leithwood and Menzies (1996: 23) conclude: 'There is an awesome gap between the rhetoric and the reality of SBM's contribution to student growth, especially in light of the widespread advocacy of SBM'.

The enormous debate over the value of choice and market mechanisms is evidence that a positive view of their impact on schools is far from unanimous. While advocates suggest that markets will cause improvements, critics worry that markets could also lead to high social costs, especially more provision for the most able at the expense of the least (Ball 1993). As Lindblom (1980: 94) puts it, 'market systems achieve high rates of change and innovation, together with frequent great injury to other firms, the environment, and to their own customers.' Others believe that the nature of schools is such that they will not change dramatically as a result of market mechanisms (Levin and Riffel 1997).

Early evidence on the consequences of choice and market-like systems also suggests that these vehicles have many unanticipated consequences (Hirsh 1994). In New Zealand, Lauder *et al.* (1994) found substantial evidence that schools were becoming more segregated by social class. In the US it appears in most cases that relatively few parents exercise choice to move their children from the local school (Ascher 1995). In Minnesota, participation in inter-district choice grew over seven years from tiny numbers initially to about 5% of enrolment in 1994–95 (Nathan 1996). Reviewing US research, Maddaus (1990: 289) concluded that 'many parents have a more holistic view of "good schools" than appears to be held by policy makers. This view encompasses moral, social, emotional, and cognitive dimensions of education'. Surprisingly, Goldring (1997) found that schools of choice in several countries do not have higher levels of parental involvement, which may be related to the voice/exit issue defined earlier.

The most extensive research on impacts of choice has been done in Britain. Although a thorough review of the research is beyond the scope of this paper (see Levin 1995c; Glatter *et al.* 1997), but some interesting findings are appearing relating to the responses of families and of schools.

Parental choice of school is a complicated matter influenced by many factors, only one of which is perceived academic achievement in the school. Other important variables include the atmosphere of the school, the wishes of the student, the location of schools, and the choices of friends (Adler 1993; West *et al.* 1995). Choosing a school is not a simple matter in most families.

Schools, on the other hand, are not necessarily seeing the advent of choice and markets as requiring them to improve or change what they do. Much effort has focused on marketing devices and improved facilities rather than substantive changes in teaching and learning, with the exception of information technology. As West and Hopkins (1995) put it, schools may be more interested in selling what they already make than in making what they could readily sell. Similar conclusions have been suggested by several other research teams as well (Fitz *et al.* 1993; Gewirtz *et al.* 1995; Bagley *et al.* 1996).

Using student assessment as a reform strategy implies a top-down and rather coercive model of change – that we can punish or shame people into doing better. This strategy seems inconsistent both with the best available knowledge about school improvement (Fullan and Stiegelbauer 1991) and with current thinking about the changing workplace. It seems contradictory that we talk of the workplace as being increasingly about cooperation, teamwork and autonomy, but adopt a strategy with very different values in our efforts to improve the way schools prepare students for that workplace.

A belief in the efficacy of testing also implies that knowledge is available as to how to improve achievement – that if we can identify problems in achievement, we can fix them. Whether this is so is an open question; the effective schools literature does not demonstrate that levels of achievement can be regularly improved and maintained (Reynolds 1996; West and Hopkins 1995). If schools could readily produce better achievement results, it is hard to believe that they would not already be doing so.

In regard to the impact of stricter and more public assessment measures, evidence is limited. Bishop (1994) suggests that provincial examinations in Canada are associated with higher achievement as well as with a variety of other positive measures. However an OECD report (1996, chapter 6: 15) notes that the countries with the highest apparent national achievement are not particularly focused on more assessment and have in fact given professional educators more autonomy in teaching and assessment than is the case in the English-speaking countries. Kallen (1996) also notes that the emphasis on testing is particular to a few countries. Cibulka (1991: 198) suggests that in Illinois an attempt to use performance reporting as a tool for citizen action did not work. 'To generate a system which provides meaningful performance information to parents at a classroom level and yet links that information to national standards – for parents' use as well as accountability to a broader public – may prove to be a political and technical nightmare.'

What is striking about all three reform strategies, whatever the evidence on their effects, is how little attention goes to the heart of education – learning and teaching (Levin 1995a). To be sure, there are comments about such matters as higher standards and the development of critical thinking skills. Some efforts are being made in these areas, especially in the US. But the kinds of strategies that might really change the educational basis of schooling – in particular placing students and their learning at the centre of the educational process (Levin 1995b) – have not been at the centre of government-sponsored reforms. Partly this may be because they are so difficult to put into practice. We know how to pass laws changing governance but we don't know much yet about how to change instructional practices. Partly it may be because such changes are less visible than testing and governance changes, and so lack immediate political appeal. Whatever the reason, it is hard to believe that programs of reform will lead to better outcomes, in any sense, if they do not centre around what students do.

Conclusion

This paper should not be read as being simply a critique of the strategies of decentralization, choice, and assessment. Each strategy could, depending on its application, have useful outcomes. Decentralization could allow local communities, and especially non-educators, to play a more important role in directing their schools and in meeting local needs provided that communities did have real scope to direct their schools and to provide the training and support to allow lay people to participate effectively. Choice could push parents and students to think more about the kind of school that would be of greatest benefit, and it could push schools to think more about the needs of those they serve. Measures to avoid school choice becoming a means of social segregation would be especially important. So would policies that encouraged real diversity in school programs, not only in appearances. Assessment can be a means of giving everyone involved with education more meaningful information about how well students are doing, as long as multiple measures are in place and parents and others are given assistance in understanding the nature and limits of any particular assessment measure. The key is to move beyond ideological commitments to particular strategies in order to look at what the real impacts of policies are and how these can be shaped in desirable ways.

Two other points can be made in conclusion. First, it is important to focus attention on those things that are likely to make the greatest difference. That means, in schools, looking at ways of improving and increasing students' learning (Levin 1995a,b). There can be – there is – much debate about just how to achieve this goal. But a strategy that from the outset appears largely unrelated to learning is not one on which we should concentrate our limited resources and energies. The improvement of learning is likely to require changes in many aspects of schooling – not only in curriculum and instruction, but also in school organization and governance – but the latter changes must follow from some clear sense of the former rather than hoping that the reverse will take place, that improved learning will somehow flow from changes in governance. Reform programs need to pay as much attention to what students do as to what governing bodies and testing agencies do.

Second, and most important, we need to be very, very cautious about what Halpin and Troyna (1995) have called 'policy borrowing'. Especially for countries with very different organizational, political, social, and educational traditions, copying the reforms of other countries, while superficially attractive, is highly likely to prove ineffective. Surely we need to learn from each other, and to that end much more international exchange of ideas and research would be very useful. Currently research plays a very modest role in shaping education policy (Guthrie 1996). There are, however, no easy short cuts in the matter of education reform. As each country is different, so will each country have to find its own way, with help from others but finally having to choose what makes sense in a unique setting.

References

Adler, M. (1993) Parental choice and the enhancement of children's interests, in P. Munn (ed.) *Parents and Schools* (London: Routledge), 47–64.

Ascher, C. (1995) Retravelling the choice road, *Harvard Educational Review*, 64 (2), 209–21.

Bagley, C., Woods, P. and Glatter, R. (1996) Scanning the market, *Educational Management and Administration*, 24 (2), 125–38.

Ball, S. (1993) Parents, schools and markets: the repositioning of youth in United Kingdom education, *Youth*, 3 (3), 68–79.

Barlow, M. and Robertson, H.-J. (1994) *Class Warfare* (Toronto: Key Porter).

Berliner, D. and Biddle, B. (1995) *The Manufactured Crisis: Myth, Fraud and the Attack on America's Public Schools* (New York: Addison Wesley).

Bishop, J. (1994) Impact of curriculum-based examinations on learning in Canadian secondary schools. Working paper 94-30, Center for Advanced Human Resource Studies, Cornell University.

Boyd, W. L., Lugg, C. and Zahorchak, G. (1996) Social traditionalists, religious conservatives, and the politics of outcome-based education: Pennsylvania and beyond, *Education and Urban Society*, 28 (3), 347–65.

Brown, D. (1990) *Decentralization and School-based Management* (London: Falmer).

Bryk, A., Easton, J., Kerbow, D., Rollow, S. and Sebring, P. (1993) *A View from the Elementary Schools: The State of Reform in Chicago* (Chicago: Consortium on Chicago School Research).

Cibulka, J. (1991) Educational accountability reforms: performance information and political power, in S. Fuhrman and B. Malen (eds) *The Politics of Curriculum and Testing* (Philadelphia: Falmer Press), 181–201.

Coe, P., Kannapel, P., Aagaard, L. and Moore, B. (1995) Non-linear evolution of school-based decision-making in Kentucky. Paper presented to the American Educational Research Association, San Francisco, April.

Cohen, D. (1992) Policy and practice the relations between governance and instruction, in G. Grant (ed.) *Review of Research in Education*, 18 (Washington: AERA), 3–49.

Conley, D. and Goldman, P. (1995) Reactions from the field to state restructuring legislation, *Educational Administration Quarterly*, 31 (4), 512–38.

Deem, R. (1994) The school, the parent, the banker and the local politician: what can we learn from the English experience of involving lay people in the site-based management of schools? Paper presented to the American Educational Research Association, New Orleans, April.

Dehli, K. (1995) Travelling tales: thinking comparatively about education reform and parental choice in postmodern times. Paper presented to the American Educational Research Association, San Francisco, April.

Edelman, M. (1988) *Constructing the Political Spectacle* (Chicago: University of Chicago Press).

Edwards, T. and Whitty, G. (1995) Marketing quality: traditional and modern versions of educational excellence. Paper presented to the American Educational Research Association, San Francisco, April.

Epstein, J. (1995) School/family/community partnerships: caring for the children we share, *Phi Delta Kappan*, 76 (9), 701–12.

Fitz, J., Halpin, D. and Power, S. (1993) *Grant Maintained Schools: Education in the Market Place* (London: Kogan Page).

Fullan, M. and Stiegelbauer, S. (1991) *The New Meaning of Educational Change* (New York: Teachers College Press/OISE Press).

Furtwengler, C., Furtwengler, W., Holcomb, E. and Hurst, D. (1995) An assessement of shared decision-making and school site councils. Paper presented to the American Educational Research Association, San Francisco, April.

GAO (United States General Accounting Office) (1995) *Charter Schools: New Model of Public Schools Provides Opportunities and Challenges* (Washington: GAO). Document GAO/HEHS-95-42.

Gewirtz, S., Ball, S. and Bowe, R. (1995) *Markets, Choice and Equity in Education* (Buckingham: Open University Press).

Glatter, R., Woods, P. and Bagley, C. (eds) (1997) *Choice and Diversity in Schooling: Perspectives and Prospects* (London: Routledge).

Goldring, E. (1997) Parental involvement and school choice: Israel and the United States, in R. Glatter, P. Woods and C. Bagley (eds) *Choice and Diversity in Schooling: Perspectives and Prospects* (London: Routledge), 86–101.

Guthrie, J. (1996) Evolving political economies and the implications for educational evaluation, in *Evaluating and Reforming Education Systems* (Paris: OECD), 61–83.

Halpin, D. and Troyna, B. (1995) The politics of policy borrowing, *Comparative Education*, 31 (3), 303–10.

Henchey, N. and Burgess, D. (1987) *Between Past and Future: Quebec Education in Transition* (Calgary: Detselig Press).

Hirsch, D. (1994) *A Matter of Choice* (Paris: OECD).

Hirschman, A. (1970) *Exit, Voice, and Loyalty* (Cambridge: Harvard University Press).

Kallen, D. (1996) New educational paradigms and new evaluation policies, in *Evaluating and Reforming Education Systems* (Paris: OECD), 7–23.

Lauder, H., Hughes, D., Waslander, S., Thrupp, M., McGlinn, J., Newton, S. and Dupuis, A. (1994) *The Creation of Market Competition for Education in New Zealand.* Report to the Ministry of Education, March.

Leithwood, K. and Menzies, T. (1996) Forms and effects of school-based management: a review. Paper presented to the Canadian Society for the Study of Education, St. Catharines, ON, June.

Levacic, R. (1995) *Local Management of Schools: Analysis and Practice* (Buckingham: Open University Press).

Levin, B. (1995a) Changing basic delivery systems, in B. Levin, W. Fowler and H. Walberg (eds) *Organizational Influences on Educational Productivity* (Greenwich: JAI Press), 195–213.

Levin, B. (1995b) Improving educational productivity through a focus on learners, *Studies in Educational Administration*, 60, 15–21.

Levin, B. (1995c) Will school choice make a difference? *Educators' Notebook*, 7 (1), 1–4.

Levin, B. (1998) An epidemic of education policy: (What) can we learn from each other? *Comparative Education*, 34 (2), 131–41.

Levin, B. and Riffel, J. (1997) School system responses to external change: implications for parental choice of schools, in R. Glatter, P. Woods and C. Bagley (eds) *Choice and Diversity in Schooling: Perspectives and Prospects* (London: Routledge), 44–58.

Lindblom, C. (1980) *The Policy-making Process*, 2nd edn (Englewood Cliffs: Prentice-Hall).

Lindle, J. (1995) School reform in Kentucky, in B. Levin, W. Folwer and H. Walberg (eds) *Organizational Influences on Educational Productivity* (Greenwich: JAI Press).

Livingstone, D. (1995) Popular beliefs about Canada's schools, in R. Ghosh and D. Ray (eds) *Social Change and Education in Canada*, 3rd edn (Toronto: Harcourt Brace), 16–44.

Livingstone, D., Hart, D. and Davie, L. (1995) *Public Attitudes Towards Education in Ontario: 1994* (Toronto: OISE Press).

McLaughlin, M. (1987) Learning from experience: lessons from policy implementation, *Educational Evaluation and Policy Analysis*, 9 (2), 171–8.

Maddaus, J. (1990) Parental choice of school: what parents think and do, in C. Cadzen (ed.) *Review of Research in Education 16* (Washington: AERA), 267–95.

Maychell, K. (1994) *Counting the Cost: The Impact of LMS on Schools' Patterns of Spending* (Slough: NFER).

Mulgan, G. (1994) *Politics in an Antipolitical Age* (Cambridge: Polity Press).

Nathan, J. (1996) 'Do we hear the people sing?': evidence regarding school choice programs. Paper presented to the American Educational Research Association, New York.

OECD (1989) *Decentralization and School Improvement* (Paris: OECD).

OECD (1993) *Education at a Glance* (Paris: CERI/OECD).

OECD (1995) *Decision-making in 14 OECD Education Systems* (Paris: OECD).

OECD (1996) Meeting of the Education Committee at Ministerial Level: Lifelong Learning for All. Report of the Secretariat (Paris: OECD).

Peters, M. (1995) Educational reform and the politics of the curriculum in New Zealand, in D. Carter and M. O'Neil (eds) *International Perspectives on Educational Reform and Policy Implementation* (London: Falmer), 52–68.

Plank, D. and Boyd, W. L. (1994) Antipolitics, education, and institutional choice: the flight from democracy, *American Educational Research Journal*, 31 (2), 263–81.

Powell, P. and Dimaggio, P. (1991) *The New Institutionalism in Organizational Analysis* (Chicago: University of Chicago Press).

Reynolds, D. (1996) Turning around the ineffective schools: some evidence and some speculations, in J. Gray, D. Reynolds, C. Fitz-Gibbon and D. Jesson (eds) *Merging Traditions: The Future of Research on School Effectiveness and School Improvement* (London: Cassell)

Riffel, J., Levin, B. and Young, J. (1996) Diversity in Canadian education, *Journal of Education Policy*, 11 (1), 113–23.

Rose, R. (1993) *Lesson Drawing in Public Policy* (Chatham: Chatham House).

Stone, D. (1988) *Policy Paradox and Political Reason* (Glenview: Scott, Foresman).

Thomas, H. and Martin, J. (1996) *Managing Resources for School Improvement* (London: Routledge).

West, A., David, M., Hailes, J. and Ribbens, J. (1995) Parents and the process of choosing secondary schools: implications for schools, *Educational Management and Administration*, 23 (1), 28–38.

West, M. and Hopkins, D. (1995) Reconceptualising school effectiveness and school improvement. Paper presented to the British Educational Research Association/ European Conference on Educational Research, Bath, September.

Wildavsky, A. (1973) If planning is everything, maybe it's nothing, *Policy Sciences*, 4 (2), 127–53.

Wylie, C. (1995) School site management: some lessons from New Zealand. Paper presented to the American Educational Research Association, San Francisco, April.

4 Specifying globalization effects on national policy

A focus on the mechanisms

Roger Dale

University of Auckland, New Zealand

Source: *Journal of Education Policy*, 14 (1): 1–17, 1999.

Introduction

There has been and continues to be an enormous amount of discussion about the nature and meaning of globalization. The recent experience of the global origins and consequences of the crash of East Asian stock markets and economies has reduced the ranks of doubters about the existence of at least some economic forces that are beyond the control of even the most powerful nation state; and it is significant that one of the most 'globalist' interpretations of the current world economy comes from an author who subsequently became Secretary for Trade in the Clinton administration (Reich 1992).

However, accepting that globalization 'exists', at least to the extent of curtailing states' capacities and policy making discretion (which was never as untrammelled for any state as is often implied, and was distinctly limited for most), is only the start of the problem. 'Globalization' is not, as sometimes appears to be implied, the answer to any questions about the nature and orientation of national policies, but it does require one to consider anew how those policies are formed, shaped and directed. The key problem then becomes understanding the nature of globalization in ways that enable one to trace more precisely how, and with what consequences, it affects national policies. If 'global' factors affect national policies, what is the nature and extent of their influence?

In addressing these questions, this paper shall argue that globalization does constitute a new and distinct form of relationship between nation states and the world economy, but that it takes many different forms. While globalization has certainly not made nation states either irrelevant or obsolete it has affected both the content and form of at least some of the policy making procedures and outcomes of all states – which is one of its defining characteristics. However, states have not been rendered impotent in the face of an overwhelming challenge, much less replaced by it; rather, while they have all retained their formal territorial sovereignty more or less intact, they have all, to a greater or lesser degree, lost some of their capacity to make national policy independently. Globalization, then, does create broadly similar patterns of challenge for states that shape their possible responses in similar ways. Absolutely central to arguments about the effect of globalization on public services like education is that those effects are largely indirect; that is to say, they are mediated through the effect of globalization on the discretion and direction of nation states. As Habermas (1996: 292) puts it, 'While the world economy operates largely uncoupled from any political frame, national governments are restricted to fostering the modernization of their national economies. As a consequence, they have to adapt national welfare systems to what is called the capacity for international competition.'

However, while globalization does represent a new set of rules, there is no reason to expect all countries to interpret those rules in identical ways, or to expect them all to play to the rules in identical ways. Indeed, it could be argued that the curtailment of individual states' policy discretion is no more likely to bring about greater convergence between their policies than the formal freedom they previously enjoyed. As will be made clear below, that freedom was often exercised through mechanisms as similar as any so far induced by globalization. It is not then so much the diversity of policy responses to globalization that is discussed here, as the effects of the different mechanisms through which those effects are delivered. This paper also suggests that the variety of mechanisms through which globalization affects national policy is itself a diversifying factor; globalization cannot be reduced to the identical imposition of the same policy on all countries.

However, while it is widely acknowledged that globalization does affect national policies in a range of areas, precisely how is rarely questioned, let alone analysed. There is increasing recognition that national differences remain despite the spread of globalization, and accompanying doubts about tendencies towards convergence. Paradoxically, however, globalization itself, and certainly the ways it affects national policy, remains homogenized. One is, in fact, faced with a classic 'black box' analysis, where input is clearly related to output, but where the means by which the transformation is brought about are not apparent (or, by implication, important).

The main argument in this paper will be that the mechanisms through which globalization affects national policy are crucially important in defining the nature of that effect. Those mechanisms are not merely neutral conduits, but modify the nature of the effect they convey. Thus, at one level the argument is that the 'delivery mechanisms' themselves have an independent influence on the message, on how globalization affects national policy, and that this is a significant source of diversity within and across the effects of globalization. It must, of course, also be noted, though this paper shall not go into this in any depth, that the nature and impact of globalization effects varies enormously across different countries, according to their position in the world and regional economies.

This paper will also suggest that the mechanisms through which globalization operate are themselves qualitatively different from traditional mechanisms of external policy influence; this argument also strengthens the conception of globalization as a distinct phenomenon. In particular, it shall be suggested that the main dimensions along which globalization mechanisms differ from 'traditional' mechanisms are that their locus of viability is external, that their scope embraces policy goals as well as policy processes, that they are externally initiated, that they draw on a wider range of forms of power, and that they cannot be directly sourced to other individual nations. Specifically, this paper shall point to variations in the mechanisms through which globalization affects education policy and argue that though these effects are largely 'indirect', the mechanisms not only produce different types of responses from the states affected but they also independently shape and channel the form and strength of the effects of globalization.

The next section briefly sets out what the author understands by globalization and suggests, in broad terms, how it might effect education policy. The second part of the paper outlines and discusses some of the precise mechanisms through which global dynamics affect national education policies, The paper will conclude with an attempt to draw conclusions about the explanatory value of this approach to understanding education policy.

Globalization

There is no space here to go into an extended analysis of the nature of globalization, or even to produce a digest of the massive literature that it has spawned. (Extended discussions of the nature of globalization and its consequences for education can be found in two complementary essays; see Dale 1998, 2000.) The purpose of this section is to set out, very briefly, what seem to be the major features of globalization as they effect the issues at hand. The absolutely basic features of globalization for this paper are that it has economic, political and cultural strands, though it is the political that is being emphasized here; that 'global' to a large extent masks the fact that three major regional economic groupings have separate, as well as collective, effects; that the impact of globalization can occur at different levels of national societies, such as the regime, sectoral (e.g. the education system) and organizational (e.g. schools, or educational bureaucracies) levels; and that the effects of globalization are mediated, in both directions and in complex ways, by existing national patterns and structures, summarized here as the societal effect and the cultural effect.

Globalization is not a homogeneous process, nor are its effects homogeneous. As well as operating through different strands, it is associated with three quite distinct forms of regionalization (in Europe, Asia and America) which themselves generate and mediate different policies and mechanisms (for an analysis of the relationship between regionalization and education policy, see Dale and Robertson (1997a)).

Globalization emerged from the particular set of circumstances that attended the decline of the post-war economic and political settlement, that centred on the set of international financial agreements and institutions known collectively as the Bretton Woods agreement. This settlement was also premissed on American hegemony and a world divided into two major blocs. The conditions that gave rise to those arrangements no longer hold. The Cold War is over, American hegemony, certainly economically, is eroded and the financial agreements proved incapable of responding to new global financial forces. These factors have together eroded both individual states' capacities to control their own affairs and their mutual arrangements for the collective management of their common interests.

Turning to the political aspect of globalization, as Cerny (1997: 253) puts it:

> Globalization as a political phenomenon basically means that the shaping of the playing field of politics is increasingly determined not within insulated units, i.e. relatively autonomous and hierarchically organized structures called states; rather, it derives from a complex congeries of multilevel games played on multilayered institutional playing fields, above and across, as well as within, state boundaries.

Very simply, states' reactions to these changing circumstances can be argued to have taken two broad forms; individually they have taken on what Cerny (1997: 263 ff.) calls a 'competition state' form, and collectively they have become more concerned with setting up a framework of international organizations through which they seek to establish what Rosenau refers to as 'governance without government' (Rosenau 1992). Most prominent among the organizations that are involved in attempting to install governance without government are the IMF, the OECD, G-7, the World Bank and other similar, often regional organizations, through such very different institutional forms as, for example, the European Union, North American Free Trade Area and the Asia Development Bank. However, while all these organizations have different, albeit often overlapping, missions, approaches and capacities, they are all driven by a broad set of ideological preferences that have developed as the 'orthodox' response to the problems posed to rich countries by changing global economic circumstances. (And it should be noted that the existence of this common ideology demonstrates clearly that though those countries may have individually ceded some of their national political capacity to international organizations, they have done so voluntarily, in order to maintain their own privileged positions in the world economy; indeed, Cerny argues that this has become a significant driver of the globalization process.)

That common ideology has been given some different labels, but the most succinct summary of its key features is provided by John Williamson under the title of the 'Washington Consensus' (Williamson 1993). He isolates 10 features of the consensus, which it will be useful to bear in mind in the second half of this paper. These are fiscal discipline, public expenditure priorities, tax reform, financial liberalization, exchange rates, trade liberalization, foreign direct investment, privatization, deregulation and property rights. Together, these constitute the preferred ideological filters that inform the directions in which national policy decisions are to be shaped.

States' individual responses to changing global realities centre on making themselves more competitive. This has a number of specific consequences, not least for education policy; indeed, as suggested above, it could be argued that the clearest effects of globalization on education policy come from the consequences of states' reorganization of their priorities to make them more competitive, for instance in attracting Trans National Corporations to locate in their territory. The key characteristic of the competition state is that it prioritizes the economic dimensions of its activities above all others. However, this does not mean that the effects of globalization are confined to the 'regime' level of nation states. It is clear that different sectors of national societies are more likely to be influenced by changing global dynamics than others and in different ways. It is also dear that some global effects are very direct and narrowly focused on particular organizational practices; the clearest examples of these are the work practices introduced by TNCs, which can entail major, but isolated, shifts in traditional practices.

It is also essential to recognize the continuing significance of national societal and cultural effects whose prominence and importance are hardly diminished by globalization. Globalization may change the parameters and direction of state policies in similar ways but it does not inevitably override or remove existing national peculiarities (or different sectoral peculiarities within national societies). This is evident from a number of studies. For instance, Maurice *et al.*'s (1984) concept of the societal effect shows dearly the existence of nationally specific collections of organically related policies (such as legal, financial, education and training policies) that comprise structures to which innovations must accommodate. For a further elaboration of the societal approach to education see Dale (1991). Another powerful nationally mediating factor is the 'cultural effect'. This is based on the work of Hofstede (1994). Hofstede compared the values of similar people in 64 different national subsidiaries of IBM and discovered that they varied considerably in ways relevant to their performance of the same set of duties across the four major dimensions of Power Distance, Uncertainty Avoidance, Masculinity and Individualism. This provides a further demonstration of how external policies are likely to be differently interpreted and differently acted on in different countries, even at the organizational level, where their impact is most direct.

The remainder of this paper will concentrate on the mechanisms through which the effects of globalization are delivered. It will tackle this by setting out a typology of mechanisms of external influences on policy.

Dimensions of variability between external effects on national education policies

This section of the paper shall (a) compare mechanisms of externally influenced policy change that have been used before and during the phase of globalization and (b) discuss the nature and outcomes for national education policy making of a wide range of policy transfer mechanisms. It will consider five mechanisms of external effect on education policy that could be seen to be associated, though not exclusively, with globalization, as parts of a 'globalization effect'. These are labelled 'harmonization', 'dissemination', 'standardization', 'installing inter-dependence' and 'imposition'. These are compared with two 'traditional' or 'orthodox' mechanisms of external effect on national education policies, 'policy borrowing' and 'policy learning' (note that the author is not suggesting that these two 'traditional' mechanisms have been eliminated or somehow outlawed in a global era; they might be expected to persist, though in forms crucially shaped by globalization).

The purpose of presenting these mechanisms of policy transfer is not so much to assess the validity or success of the approaches, as to test the idea that globalization represents a distinct phenomenon that also operates and achieves its effects through distinct mechanisms. What shall be shown in this section then is that (a) it is possible to distinguish globalization effects from more traditional effects on education policy, such as 'policy borrowing' and 'policy learning' and (b) mechanisms of globalization effects are themselves diverse rather than homogeneous.

A simplified digest and comparison of the eight mechanisms is set out in Figure 4.1. The nature and consequences of the differences between the approaches are elaborated below. It will be useful to start by giving some explanation and elaboration of the dimensions on which they are compared.

The first dimension of variability, the degree to which the reforms were voluntarily accepted by the recipient nation, is included because of the common assumption that externally influenced reforms are necessarily 'forced on', or at least unwillingly accepted by, the recipient nation. That seems often to be the case with more 'conspiracy' inclined accounts of the consequences of globalization. However, as the discussion above of the nature of 'governance without government' suggests, imposition of policy is not the only way that globalization can affect education policy.

The second dimension focuses on how explicit the process is; again, this is used to highlight the apparent assumption that many reforms are introduced 'behind the back' of the recipient nation. However, on the one hand, much of the external influence may be quite explicit, as in the case of 'policy borrowing', and on the other, we should note that the external effect can be implicit without being suspicious; unconscious imitation is not unknown in many spheres of life!

The third dimension, the scope of the externally influenced reform, is extremely important. While traditionally externally influenced reforms might have been expected to be piecemeal and restricted in their scope, one cannot assume either that 'borrowing' or 'learning' are necessarily limited in scope or that the other types of effect are necessarily broad in scope. The key issue here is whether the effects are restricted to policy *programmes* and *organization* or whether they can also involve policy *goals*. Traditionally, only the former were taken to be susceptible to external influence, with goals and values remaining strictly 'internally' determined. Peter Hall's work on policy learning does provide a partial and very significant exception to this and will be discussed further below (see Hall 1989).

The fourth dimension concerns the 'locus of viability' of the mechanism. The viability of any policy is usually assumed to be judged at a national level and according to existing national norms and expectations. The argument for political globalization suggests that that may no longer necessarily be the case, while the argument about the variability of forms of globalization also suggests that more than a simple shift from a 'national' to a 'global' locus of viability may be involved.

CHARACTERISTICS OF EFFECT MECHANISMS	MECHANISMS OF EXTERNAL EFFECTS							
	BORROWING	LEARNING		HARMON-ISATION	DISSEMIN-ATION	STANDARD-ISATION	INSTALLING INTERDEPEN-DENCE	IMPOSITION
		'NORMAL'	'PARADIGMATIC'					
NATURE OF RELATIONSHIP	VOLUNTARY	VOLUNTARY	FORMALLY VOLUNTARY	FORMALLY VOLUNTARY	FORMALLY VOLUNTARY	FORMALLY VOLUNTARY	VOLUNTARY	COMPULSORY
EXPLICITNESS OF PROCESS	EXPLICIT	VARIES	VARIES	EXPLICIT	EXPLICIT	QUITE IMPLICIT	EXPLICIT	EXPLICIT
SCOPE	PARTICULAR POLICY PROCESS	RECOGNISED PARAMETERS/ POLICY PROCESS	POLICY PROCESS AND POLICY GOALS	MULTIPLE POLICIES	MULTIPLE POLICIES	MULTIPLE POLICIES	POLICY GOALS	PARTICULAR POLICY GOALS
LOCUS OF VIABILITY	NATIONAL	NATIONAL	EXTERNAL	REGIONAL ORGANIS-ATION	EXTERNAL/ NATIONAL	INTERNAT-IONAL FORA	COMMON HERITAGE OF HUMANKIND	INTERNAT-IONAL ORGANIS-ATION
PROCESS	BORROWING/ IMITATION	'LEARNING'	'TEACHING'	COLLECTIVE AGREEMENT	PERSUASION/ AGENDA SETTING	CONDITION OF MEMBERSHIP	PERSUASION	LEVERAGE
PARTIES INVOLVED	BILATERAL	BILATERAL/ INTERNAT-IONAL	INTERNAT-IONAL	MULTI-NATIONAL	INTERNAT-IONAL	MULTI-NATIONAL	GLOBAL - 'BOTTOM UP'	MULT-INATIONAL
SOURCE OF INITIATION	RECIPIENT	NATIONAL 'POLICY COMMUNITY'	INTERNAT-IONAL MODEL	COLLECTIVELY BY MEMBERS	SUPRA-NATIONAL BODY	'INTERNAT-IONAL COMMUNITY'	NGOs ('GLOBAL CIVIL SOCIETY')	SUPRA-NATIONAL BODY
DIMENSION OF POWER	CONSCIOUS DECISION	CONSCIOUS DECISION	AGENDA SETTING/ RULES OF GAME	CONSCIOUS DECISION	AGENDA SETTING	RULES OF GAME	AGENDA SETTING	ALL THREE DIMENSIONS
NATURE OF EFFECT ON EDUCATION	DIRECT (ON SECTOR OR ORGANISATION)	VARIES	VARIES	IMPLIED - REGIME AND SECTOR	DIRECT - SECTOR	DIRECT - REGIME - SECTOR RELATION	INDIRECT - REGIME DIRECT - ORG.	INDIRECT - REGIME
EXAMPLE FROM EDUCATION	SCOTVEC IN NEW ZEALAND	HUMAN CAPITAL THEORY IN 1960S	INCREASING USER CHARGES FOR EDUCATION	MAASTRICHT TREATY	OECD/CERI ACTIVITY (SEE PAPADOPOULOS, 1992)	UNESCO SCIENCE POLICY UN DECLAR-ATION ON HUMAN RIGHTS	'GREEN' CURRICULUM MATERIALS	WORLD BANK EDUCATION LOANS

Figure 4.1 A typology of mechanisms of external effects on national policies.

The fifth dimension concerns the process by which the external influence is introduced. This, too, might be expected to alter somewhat the (at least implicitly) relatively cooperative and collaborative processes that accompanied the traditional forms. However, it is important to recognize the difference between policy borrowing and policy learning as *processes* or *media* of introducing or implanting external influences on education systems and the way they are being employed here, as *models of mechanisms* for the introduction of external effects. As such, their importance exceeds the processes they embody, though it should also be noted that those processes may be employed by any of the other mechanisms listed in Figure 4.1.

A further clear difference between the 'traditional' models and those associated with globalization is the range of partners to the transaction. Both 'borrowing' and 'learning' assume a relatively narrow range of partners to the relationship. These would normally be expected to be restricted to other nation states or some kind of 'policy community'. While the size and specificity of this community may vary according to whether the attempted transfer is occurring at regime, sectoral or organizational level, it might be expected to be limited by existing commonalities of interest (as implied in the term 'policy community'). At the very least it assumes some kind of mutual recognition of relevant parties, but *prima facie* something more distant and anonymous is involved in a 'global' relationship.

The sixth dimension concerns the central issue of the source of initiation of the reform; here again, it is implicit in the borrowing and learning models that it is the recipient (a more neutral and less emotive term than either beneficiary or victim!), rather than the external party, who would initiate the reform. This assumption too, is challenged by the possibility of externally initiated reforms. This may be an appropriate juncture at which to raise the issue of the difference between globalization and 'imperialism' or 'colonialism', since it is quite plausible to suggest that the difference between globalization and imperialism/colonialism is that what once happened only to third world or colonized countries is now happening to the most powerful states, previously the initiators rather than the recipients of external pressures on their national policies. In a nutshell, the difference is that globalization is not the result of the imposition of a policy by one country on another, possibly backed up by the threat of bilateral military action, but a much more supranationally constructed effect. The result may be little different as far as the recipient countries are concerned – indeed, as suggested above, the point of constructing the supra national organizations was not to weaken or dissipate the power of the already powerful states, but to strengthen their ability to respond collectively to forces that none of them could control individually any longer – but the nature of the process is significantly changed.

The seventh dimension is called 'dimension of power' after Steven Lukes' theoretical development of the forms of power (Lukes 1974). Put simply, Lukes argues that power may be exercised in three distinct ways, that vary in their visibility and explicitness. The first dimension involves the relatively 'naked' use of superior power and/or is exercised through dearly defined decision making fora.

The second dimension centres around the politics of non-decision making and highlights the importance of the ability to exercise power through such means as agenda setting. The final dimension of power concerns the ability to control the 'rules of the game', the processes through which power is defined and exercised. These forms of power are successively less overt and correspondingly more difficult to counter. The increasing use of less direct means of power is a further manifestation of the changing nature of the relationship between states. Power over third world states is now much less likely to be bilaterally applied and much more likely to be achieved through a supranationally organized rearrangement of the rules of the game.

The final dimension concerns how the effect on education of the externally introduced change is mediated. Such effects are typically assumed to be direct; policy transfers are assumed to affect the appropriate policy area. However, if we confine ourselves to external effects that announce themselves as being concerned with education we will miss many of the most significant effects of extra national influences on national education systems. As argued previously, the more we confine ourselves to the level of education politics – that is, to policies and practices that are clearly of direct and immediate relevance to education policy or practice – the greater the risk that we will neglect the level at which the agenda for education politics is set, that of the politics of education (see Dale 1994). This becomes even more important when the ambit of possible external influences is extended geographically. This variable acknowledges the possibility of indirect, or implied, effects, as well as those that declare themselves explicitly. It is also important to note that the nature of the effect has to be registered at the appropriate level; it cannot be assumed that for an external factor to have an effect on an education system it has to be directed towards the education sector or even to educational organizations. Of course, these are extremely important; however, it is crucial not to neglect the consequences of changes at the regime level on education policy and practice.

A comparison of policy transfer mechanisms

The central focus of this paper is on claims about the distinctiveness of globalization as an influence shaping national education policies. The alternative view is implied by Halpin and Troyna (1995) who refer to 'policy borrowing' as 'a trend that has accelerated as the move towards a "global village" becomes an increasing reality' (304), while explanations that fall under the broad heading of 'policy learning' have been increasingly invoked to explain the apparent similarity of policy shifts carried out almost simultaneously in different countries (see Bennett and Howlett 1992). The comparison is made tighter and its potential validity enhanced if it is recognized that all the features of what is referred to above as the societal effect and the cultural effect modify, filter, channel, interpret and select from all the modes of external effect that will be discussed. That is to say, in none of the cases to be discussed is the external effect assumed to be either so compatible with existing practices, or to be so overwhelmingly imposed, that the societal effects etc. are rendered nugatory.

This latter proposition is perhaps hardest to sustain in the case of the first policy transfer mechanism to be discussed, borrowing. Here it sometimes seems to be assumed that some considerable level of relevant compatibility exists between the 'borrowing' and 'lending' partners. The representation of what transpires as 'borrowing' certainly sustains the compatibility assumption; we don't usually 'borrow something we don't know we have a use, even a need, for, or indeed, that we won't return! And of course, borrowing implies a 'lender'. The notion of borrowing is, however, misleading. Bennett (1997) lists several terms that more accurately describe the nature of the relationship – imitation, emulation, copying. The literature on education policy borrowing reflects some of the uncertainties raised by Bennett. In particular, it tends to find evidence of 'borrowing' as such rather lacking. As Whitty *et al.* (1993) put it, describing Whitty and Edwards' work on the extent of policy borrowing between Britain and the US, in the City Technology College and Magnet school initiatives, 'policy makers in both countries were working with similar frames of reference and producing parallel policy initiatives, rather than directly "borrowing" policies from one another' (166). The policy borrowing literature is also somewhat sceptical about its success as a strategy (though there is some questioning of the exact nature of the strategic aims of 'policy borrowing'). McLean (1995: 14), for instance, argues that it simplifies the policy process, puts it out of the reach of potential opponents and is used to enable politicians to justify pre-determined reform intentions. Halpin and Troyna (1995) also emphasize the use of policy borrowing as a form of political legitimation and as driven by political expediency. However, there do exist cases of direct policy borrowing. Peddie (1991) cites several examples of policies directly borrowed by New Zealand from Britain (including the direct adoption of school designs that retained their south facing aspect!). More recently, several countries have expressed considerable interest in the German apprenticeship system, while Kappert (1997) describes New Zealand's attempts to introduce elements of both the English and Scottish systems of qualification and accreditation

The point here, however, is not to evaluate policy borrowing as a strategy, but to compare it with globalization as a mechanism of introducing external influences to national education systems. As a mechanism of policy transfer, the key features of policy borrowing in terms of the variables outlined above are that it is carried out *voluntarily* and *explicitly*, and that its *locus of viability is national.* It involves *particular policies* that one country seeks to *imitate, emulate or copy, bilaterally*, from another. It is the *product of conscious decision making*, and it *is initiated by the recipient.* The nature of its effects on education could be expected to be *direct* and they would tend to be restricted to the sectoral or organizational level, that is to the level of education politics.

The issue of policy learning is somewhat more complex and more instructive. For one thing, it takes a wide variety of forms. In a very useful review of the policy learning literature Bennett and Howlett (1992: 289) conclude that 'the all-embracing term "policy learning"... can be seen to actually embrace three highly complex processes: learning about organizations, learning about programs and learning about policies'. Such a broad compass means that some form of policy learning is likely to be present in any mechanism of policy transfer. This broad compass enables one to specify more closely what it is that distinguishes globalization mechanisms from traditional mechanisms. The 'compatibility' of 'policy learning' with both traditional and globalized mechanisms makes examining how it might fit into the different contexts a very effective way of comparing the two sets of mechanisms. The best way to illustrate how this might be done is through the example of the pre-eminent work of comparative policy learning, Peter Hall's edited collection of writings on the diffusion of Keynesian ideas across different countries (Hall 1989). This enables one to compare the place of policy learning in traditional and global mechanisms across five key dimensions; such a comparison enables one to reach one of the main goals of this paper, that of specifying factors that distinguish and differentiate traditional and global mechanisms.

The first variable to be considered is the locus of viability. In his concluding chapter (see especially pp. 370–1 and figure 14.1), Hall argues that the main factors affecting the reception of Keynesian ideas were their economic viability (their perceived ability to resolve the economic problems at hand); their political viability (their fit with existing goals and interests of the dominant party and the associations the ideas acquired in the political arena); and in particular, their 'administrative viability', 'the degree to which the new ideas fit the long-standing administrative biases of the relevant decision makers and the existing capacity of the state to implement them' (Hall 1989: 371). The emphasis here is entirely on the individual nation state as the locus of viability. The central point about globalization is the diminution of the nation state as the ultimate locus of viability over a range of policies. Thus, globalization assumes that the viability test of policy is carried out at a supranational level. Rather than having to demonstrate their compatibility with existing national state structures and practices, policies have to demonstrate their compatibility with supranational expectations. In certain policy areas, then, the adjustment is in the opposite direction to that required of Keynesian polices in the 1930s and 1940s – although, of course, the process involved may still be one that could be described as learning. In terms of the variables outlined above one can see that policy learning in the traditional mode was largely voluntary; the purpose of Hall's book is to show why some countries decided to adopt Keynesianism and others did not, which clearly assumes a high level of voluntarism. As this paper shall show, globalization mechanisms tend not to make this assumption.

The second important variable here is the dimension of power through which the desired end was to be achieved. The Keynesian case clearly rests on conscious decision making; there appear to have been significant elements of 'real' choice for the countries discussed, though the presence of Keynesian policy in some countries clearly had some effect on the broader international agenda. The means by which policy learning has been involved in accommodating globalization mechanisms of policy transfer may be rather more implicit and arms length, to be achieved through agenda setting or the rules of the game.

In the case of the source of initiation of policy change, all the countries that adopted Keynesian policies, or decided not to, essentially initiated the change themselves, rather than having it formally brought to them by a 'lender' state or a supranational body (though this is not to say that the fact that other countries were, or were not, adopting the same set of ideas was irrelevant to their decision). By contrast, it is a dominant characteristic of the globalization mechanisms that they are initiated outside the recipient country (albeit that the organization initiating the transfer or influence may well have been set up by the country and encouraged to initiate such policies). It might be noted here that while the 'borrower-lender' metaphor may not be wholly apt, it is possible and useful to distinguish the different status of 'policy learning' and 'policy teaching'. Some of the mechanisms to be discussed below display a clear and sometimes explicit teaching orientation.

The most significant differences come in the scope of the policy learning and the nature of the parties involved. As Bennett and Howlett (1992) point out, all the policy learning work they consider 'extends only to programs and . . . to instruments . . . and not to the adoption of new policy goals' (287). The exception to this is Peter Hall's work. Hall does recognize the possibility of policy learning extending to policy goals as well as policy instruments – and the circumstances in which he sees this as likely to occur are of considerable importance to the argument being advanced here. As Bennett and Howlett summarize his position, for Hall, 'normal politics' or policy-making is associated with learning about instruments, while 'learning about policy goals occurs only in special circumstances associated with shifts in "policy paradigms" or changes in the dominant set of policy ideas which shape discourse in the policy-making process' (Bennett and Howlett 1992). The author's argument about globalization is that it induces precisely this kind of paradigm shift in national policy making assumptions. Essentially, globalization removes some matters from the control of individual states and this requires paradigm shifts in the ways that they respond through policy. One consequence of this is the achievement of a new state 'settlement', which has been described as 'the competitive-contractual state settlement' (see Dale and Robertson 1997b); this shift essentially makes international competitiveness the dominant criterion of state policy making and contractualism the dominant source of administrative bias and structural capacities.

This development, though indirect, is an extremely important consequence of globalization. A more direct and more immediately relevant consequence is the development of *supranational* responses to common problems for states in a globalized context. This represents the final major dimension of difference between globalization and 'traditional' mechanisms of policy influence. As pointed out above, what distinguishes globalization from imperialism and colonialism is that it is supranational; it is not initiated by a single country, or carried out by nations on nations, but by supranational organizations, albeit dominated by the same group of nations that were previously involved separately in bilateral mechanisms.

So, the different forms they take, especially the variations on 'governance without government', are what underlie the globalization inflected mechanisms of policy transfer and influence that will be discussed next. Before doing that this paper will very briefly summarize the implications of the comparisons of the place of policy learning in traditional and globalization mechanisms. The distinctiveness of globalization mechanisms lies in their extra-national locus of viability, their use of less 'direct' forms of power, the fact that they are externally rather than internally initiated and that their scope, as a result of the paradigm shift brought about by globalization, extends to policy goals as well as to policy processes.

The first of these mechanisms of policy transfer to be discussed is what has been called 'harmonization'. This draws largely on the model of the European Union. That development itself could be seen as a form of paradigm shift. As Brigitte Unger argues, in an article that examines the convergence effect of the EU, the installation of major policy change such as the EU requires the kind of stimulus represented by globalization to induce change in states where 'the more policy content, procedure or intended outcome affect the core of (political) institutions and the cultural values that underlie them, the stronger the resistance to change will be' (Unger 1997: 107). The EU example also requires one to focus on the different regional forms of globalization, although it is important to recognize that the harmonization mechanism is largely restricted to Europe. Grieco (1997) has suggested three dimensions for the comparison of what he refers to as the 'process of institutionalization' of economic relations between countries (and of course, the EU extends beyond economic relations). These are the 'locus of internationalization', the 'legal-organizational basis of association among partners': 'the scope of activity', the number of issues covered by regional arrangements: and the 'level of institutional authority', which refers to the amount of pooled responsibility for joint activities by national governments (Grieco 1997: 165). As Grieco emphasizes, on all these dimensions, the Asia region is relatively underdeveloped compared to America and especially Europe. For the purposes of this paper this serves to emphasize the heterogeneity of the mechanisms produced by globalization.

However, the focus here is on European integration, officially referred to as 'harmonization'. The point is that the process involved requires all member nations to cede and pool some of their national policy making capacity to the regional organization. The harmonization mechanism operates through a process of collective agreement, which may be its most important defining variable. The limit case of harmonization (or of almost any form of globalization) is monetary union or the EMU (European Monetary Union). Unger (1997: 106) refers to this:

> 'Maastricht-style convergence' as deliberate(ly) impos(ing) a set of convergence criteria on countries wanting to join the currency club . . . (where)

> convergence is not the result of imitation of technology or of market forces, but the result of political norms and collective enforcement.

It is at present unclear whether monetary union will ever be achieved or whether it will set a pattern for harmonization. Unger implies that it will not. However, as Mann (1996: 303–4) argues,

> Europe remains fundamentally an economic planning agency . . . The EC has not moved into class or other group relations, such as the regulation of labour relations, public order, religion, or the welfare state, though where welfare and the labour market meet in national education policy, it is active.

Unger (1997: 122) suggests, on the basis of a comparison of 14 policy fields, that,

> financial market liberalization, multinational firms' threats of relocation, the spread of political ideologies, and EU-harmonization laws are the main factors affecting national economic policies in (Europe). Of these, state competition for the location of firms seems to be more important for convergence than has the enforcement of EU-harmonization laws. And imitation of political ideology seems more important than market forces.

This is a very interesting list, especially in the way that it ranks the more 'imposed' and the more 'cooperative' mechanisms for change.

The next mechanism of policy transfer, dissemination, differs from harmonization mainly in the process, initiation and dimension of power dimensions. The best example here is found in the work of supranational organizations like the OECD. The OECD works predominantly through an agenda setting strategy. Most of its major documents seek to indicate to member nations likely future directions in a wide variety of policy fields. It should also be noted that the OECD's work is influential at all three major levels distinguished above, regime, sector and organization. Unusually, education has been a sector of particular interest, and the sectoral and organizational scope of the OECD approach to education has been clearly set out in a history of the organizastion's involvement in education by a member of its education secretariat (see Papadopoulos 1994). Papadopoulos (1994: 13) points out that the organization's influence on national policies:

> must be sought in terms of a 'catalytic role', through a process (whose) starting point is the identification of major new policy issues which emerge on the educational horizon, and which might call for priority attention in the countries. These are issues which are somewhat ahead of actual country developments and thinking . . . These issues are then put together within a structured framework, leading to a number of questions which arise for policy-making. Arriving at a convincing statement of such issues and questions, of how and why they arise, and of their implications, is already half the work done.

And he concludes the book by stating that:

> The educational agenda for the nineties is . . . both fresh and exciting . . . It remains to be seen whether the Member countries can rise to the challenge. Certainly, the experience of the last 30 years . . . places the OECD in a unique position to continue its task of assisting them to do so.
>
> (Papadopoulos 1994: 195)

A key example of this mechanism would be OECD's attempts to develop international indicators of and for education systems (see CERI 1992) that go well beyond its stated function of meeting the growing demand for more and better information about the quality of education. It has dear implications for the goals as well as the processes of policy, something that is also clearly implicit in the process described by Papadopoulos. There is in both these examples an element of 'anticipatory policy convergence', or self denying policy ordinance around an internationally approved agenda.

The idea of 'standardization' draws heavily on the work of the 'global institutionalists' (see, for example, Meyer *et al.* 1992, 1997). Their fundamental argument is that,

> many features of the contemporary nation state derive from worldwide models constructed and propagated through global cultural and associational processes . . . Worldwide models (which) have become especially important . . . as cultural and organizational development of world society has intensified at an unprecedented rate) define and legitimate agendas for local action, shaping the structures and policies of nation-states and other national and local actors in virtually all domains of rationalized social life . . . the institutionalization of world models helps explain many puzzling features of contemporary societies, such as structural isomorphism in the face of enormous differences.
>
> (Meyer *et al.* 1997: 144–5)

It is fortunate, for the purposes of this paper, that the work of Meyer *et al.* has concentrated especially on the spread of a particular institutional form of education, which they take as a key example of the spread of the Western cultural project (this issue is discussed at greater length in Dale 1998). The extent of educational isomorphism is exemplified through a study of school curricula, which Meyer *et al.* (e.g. 1994) argue have shown signs of becoming common across the world. This argument and its implications are not quite as startling as may appear at first blush. Their focus is 'curriculum categories', rather than 'what is taught'. Indeed, they willingly concede that what is taught may well vary across countries. The processes they describe occur chiefly through the work of international organizations, especially those that are 'open' in their membership, such as those associated with the United Nations. Essentially, these organizations operate to bring about congruent policy changes by making, or assuming, adherence to particular broad policy principles a requisite of membership of the particular sector of the international community they represent. As Meyer *et al.* (1997: 158) put it,

> Entry into the system occurs, essentially, via application forms (to the United Nations and other world bodies) on which the applicant must demonstrate appropriately formulated assertions about sovereignty and control over population and territory, along with appropriate aims and purposes.

This may not only bring benefits, especially for smaller and poorer countries, but it almost seems to be suggested by the global institutionalists that they are not regarded as real states if they do not or have not such defining characteristics of modernity.

However, the processes through which global isomorphism comes about are not clear. Two representatives of the approach put forward two means of 'promoting attention to international norms' – that are useful with less and more developed countries respectively – 'pressure', through the imposition of costs for violation, and 'the use of the norms as "resources" that reinforce the purposes actors are already aligned around' (Strang and Chang 1993: 244). This seems somewhat *ad hoc*, however, and not as useful for the purposes of this paper as Lukes' typology, to which it can clearly be subsumed. The Strang and Chang article is, though, useful, in that it indicates that international organizations (in this case the ILO) can both apply 'progressive' norms and that they can be effective in 'bringing into line' advanced as well as developing countries. Another example that sheds some light on the process (though not explicitly) is provided in Finnemore's (1993) account of how UNESCO spread the idea of national science policy. She refers explicitly to this process as the 'teaching of norms' by international organizations. Specifically, she argues that:

> UNESCO 'taught' states the value and utility of 'science policy organization' and that this was 'a reflection of a new norm (that held that coordination and direction of science are necessary tasks of the modern state and that a science policy bureaucracy having certain well-specified characteristics was the appropriate means to fulfill those tasks) elaborated within the international community'.
>
> (Finnemore 1993: 466)

The success of this prescriptive policy is evident from the fact that it was successful in the Congo, which at the time had only nine scientists in R&D jobs, while in Sudan, 'UNESCO officials had trouble finding enough qualified scientists to draft a proposal for the new science policy body, let alone staff it once it was created' (Finnemore 1993: 591). Standardization, then, clearly has some of the crucial features of globalization effects – it extends to policy goals, it has an external locus of viability, and is externally initiated by a supranational body; however, it employs a rather smaller and less assertive range of dimensions of power.

The next type of mechanism is called 'Installing Interdependence'. Its starting point is the notion of the 'common heritage of humankind' (Sousa Santos 1995: 264–5). The defining feature of this mechanism is that it is driven essentially by a concern for *issues* (such as environmental, human rights and peace) that extend beyond the scope of any nation state, rather than by a concern with international or even multinational policies and processes. Thus, it differs along several dimensions from most of the other mechanisms discussed. Its scope is very much centred on policy goals, indeed on the purpose of national policy. It is initiated by what might be referred to very loosely as 'global civil society' (though the amorphousness of this concept might be reduced through the development of the idea of a 'world polity', based around the work of Non-Governmental Organizations (see Boli and Thomas 1997)). It operates from the 'bottom up' and can pursue its ends only through persuasion. One other crucial feature of this mechanism is that it has no effective locus of viability (as is empirically evident from the 'non-results' of the many world environmental summits etc.). Consequently, one might expect that its effects on education will be relatively direct and focused on sectoral, or more likely, organizational, levels, where the agenda setting possibilities of the mechanism might be most effective.

The final mechanism to be considered, 'imposition', is the one that is probably the first to come to most people's minds when they think of globalization. Despite the attention paid here to the variation in mechanisms of globalization, Unger's comments quoted above about the superior effectiveness of MNCs' threats over EU-harmonization alert to the continuing central importance of imposition. Because the mechanism of imposition has been so widely canvassed it is probably not necessary to describe it in even the sketchy amount of detail that has been used with the other, less familiar, mechanisms. The broad parameters and exemplars of imposition, such as structural adjustment and TNC leverage have been very fully documented in the literature on globalization. However, since a central aim of this paper is to indicate the diversity of globalization mechanisms, it is useful to point to the two dimensions on which imposition differs most significantly from the other mechanisms: it is the only mechanism able to compel recipient countries to take on particular policies and it is the only one that does not need to rely on some form of learning, persuasion or cooperation to bring about its desired changes.

Conclusion

This paper has attempted to open up the black box of mechanisms through which globalization affects national policies. In doing so, it has sought to demonstrate the qualitative differences implied by the term globalization and to extend the understanding of its diversifying consequences. In developing and elaborating the typology, it indicated five key dimensions on which the mechanisms associated with globalization differed significantly from those typical of 'traditional' mechanisms of policy transfer. These were the scope of the mechanisms (whether they included policy goals as well as policy processes), the locus of viability, the mode of power employed through the mechanism, the initiating source of the policy change and the nature of the parties to the exchange. Overall, this demonstrated the necessity of breaking down the gross concept of globalization along a range of dimensions if its nature and consequences are to be adequately understood and acted upon. Specifically in the field of education it has been argued that the effects of globalization are largely indirect, the result of the stances adopted by nation-states in response to globalization, rather than a direct effect of globalization. Two possible exceptions were considered. The 'global institutionalist' view that world-wide models of political institutions are leading to convergence of the categories states use to organize and define their business was seen as correct in a formal sense, but lacking in any effective and demonstrable outcomes on individual states, beyond a kind of lip service compliance. The possibility that the 'common heritage of humankind' may come increasingly to have a direct effect, unmediated by states, on education at the organizational level is suggested.

Notes

This article is one of three linked papers on globalization that are intended to be mutually complementary (see also, Dale 1998, 2000). The whole project has benefited enormously from a continuing conversation with Susan Robertson on this issue and I would like to acknowledge the extent of her contribution to it.

References

Bennett, C. J. (1997) Understanding ripple effects: The cross-national adoption of policy instruments for bureaucratic accountability, *Governance*, 10(3), 213–33.

Bennett, C. J. and Howlett, M. (1992) The lessons of learning: Reconciling theories of policy learning and policy change, *Policy Sciences*, 25, 275–94.

Boli, J. and Thomas, G. M. (1997) World culture in the World polity: A century of international non-governmental organizations, *American Sociological Review*, 62, 171–90.

Centre For Educational Research and Innovation (1992) *The OECD International Education Indicators: A Framework for Analysis* (Paris: OECD).

Cerny, P. (1997) Paradoxes of the competition state: The dynamics of political globalization, *Government and Opposition*, 32(2), 251–74.

Dale, R. (1991) International Comparisons or a 'Societal Approach' for New Zealand?, Paper presented to New Zealand Planning Council Seminar on Education Models from Overseas, Wellington.

Dale, R. (1998) Comparative education through globalisation, in J. Schriewer (ed.) *Discourse Formation in Comparative Education* (Berlin: Peter Lang).

Dale, R. (2000) Globalization and education: Demonstrating 'Common world educational culture' or locating a 'Globally structured educational agenda'? *Educational Theory*, 50(4), 427–80.

Dale, R. and Robertson, S. (1997a) Resiting the nation, reshaping the state, in M. Olssen and K. Morris-Matthews (eds) *Education Policy in New Zealand* (Palmerston North: Dunmore), 209–27.

Dale, R. and Robertson, S. (1997b) The contours and consequences of the competitive/contractualist state settlement. Unpublished Paper, University of Auckland School of Education.

Finnemore, M. (1993) International organizations as teachers of norms: the United Nations Educational, Scientific, and Cultural Organization and science policy, *International Organization*, 47(4), 565–97.
Grieco, J. (1997) Systematic sources of variation in regional institutionalization in Western Europe, East Asia and the Americas, in E. O. Mansfield and H. V. Milner (eds) *The Political Economy of Regionalism* (New York: Columbia University Press), 164–85.
Habermas, J. (1996) The European nation-state – its achievements and its limits. On the past and future of sovereignty and citizenship, in G. Balakrishnan (ed.) *Mapping the Nation* (London: Verso), 281–94.
Hall, P. A. (ed.) (1989) *The Political Power of Economic Ideas: Keynesianism across Nations* (Princeton, NJ: Princeton University Press).
Halpin, D. and Troyna, B. (1995) The politics of education policy borrowing, *Comparative Education*, 31(3), 303–10.
Hofstede, G. (1994) Management scientists are human, *Management Science*, 40(1), 4–13.
Kappert, P. (1997) Educational Utopia? The New Zealand Standards Approach Considered in the Light of the German Experience in Vocational Training, Unpublished PhD thesis, Victoria University of Wellington.
Lukes, S. (1974) *Power: A Radical View* (London: Macmillan).
McLean, M. (1995) *Educational Traditions Compared* (London: David Fulton).
Mann, M. (1996) Nation-states in Europe and other continents: Diversifying, developing, not dying, in G. Balakrishnan (ed.) *Mapping the Nation* (London: Verso), 295–316.
Maurice, M., Sellier, F. and Silvestre, J.-P. (1984) *Social Foundations of Industrial Power* (Cambridge: MIT Press).
Meyer, J. W., Kamens, D. and Benavot, A. (1992) *School Knowledge for the Masses: World Models and National Primary Curricular Categories in the Twentieth Century* (London: Falmer).
Meyer, J. W., Boli, J., Thomas, G. M. and Ramirez, F. (1997) World society and the nation-state, *American Journal of Sociology*, 103(1), 144–81.
Papadopoulos, G. A. (1994) *Education 1960–90: The OECD Perspective* (Paris: OECD).
Peddie, R. (1991) Comparative studies in education: lessons for New Zealand?, Paper presented to New Zealand Planning Council Seminar, Education Models form Overseas Wellington.
Reich, R. (1992) *The Work of Nations* (New York: Vintage).
Rosenau, J. (ed.) (1992) *Governance Without Government: Order and Change in World Politics* (Cambridge: Cambridge University Press).
Sousa Santos, B. (1995) *Towards a New Common Sense: Law, Science and Politics in the Paradigmatic Transition* (London: Routledge).
Strang, D. and Chang, P. M. Y. (1993) The International Labor Organization and the welfare state institutional effects on national welfare spending, 1960–80, *International Organization*, 47(2), 235–62.
Unger, B. (1997) Limits of convergence and globalization, in S. D. Gupta (ed.) *The Political Economy of Globalization* (Boston, MA: Kluwer), 99–127.
Whitty, G., Edwards, T. and Gewirtz, S. (1993) *Specialisation and Choice in Urban Education* (London: Routledge).
Williamson, J. (1993) Democracy and the 'Washington Consensus', *World Development*, 21(8), 1329–36.

5 Educational change and new cleavages between head teachers, teachers and parents

Global and local perspectives on the French case

Agnès van Zanten

CNRS Centre National de la Recherche Scientifique (National Center for Scientific Research), Paris

Source: *Journal of Education Policy*, 17 (3): 289–304, 2002.

Introduction

The purpose of this article is twofold. At a first, theoretically informed, empirical level, it presents an analysis of the effects of educational changes over the last 20 years on the relationship between head teachers, teachers and parents, that is on the micro-politics of schools (Ball 1987). At a second, more epistemological level, it hopes to highlight the importance of combining a global, national and local perspective. The concept of 'educational change' rather than 'educational reform' has been chosen to emphasize the fact that, although many of these transformations were brought about by political decisions, they also stem from more general social and cultural shifts which have created receptive audiences for new policies (Kenway *et al.* 1993). Five kinds of transformations – decentralization, marketization, accountability, managerialism and professionalization – will be examined in terms of their impact on definitions of the social and professional identities of different educational agents and on the redistribution of power among them inside and outside schools. This will be done through a classical approach in comparative studies: the case study of national and local practices in relation to global patterns. Ties within the different scales will be analysed to provide a more comprehensive empirical and theoretical understanding of educational processes (Popkewitz 2000a).

The first section of the paper will briefly examine the main shifts in policy and practice that these transformations were designed to effect from the perspective of policy-makers as well as how they have been disseminated through transnational discourses. However, it will also show how the global success of these transformations is due to educational changes that have created new contexts of receptivenes. The second section will analyse the interaction between these global discourses and transformations of French educational models and realities at the level of the nation-state. The emphasis will be on French national policy-makers' discursive resistance and ultimately pragmatic accommodation and reinterpretation of global trends. The third section will show how deliberate reform projects, on the one hand, and changes brought about by the unplanned convergence of the actions of individual agents on the other interact at the local level. By considering two contrasting sites located in the Parisian periphery, this section will show the degree to which local reinterpretation of policy can vary depending on local social class configurations.

Global models and global processes

Although world models have long been in operation as shapers of states and societies, they have become much more important in the last decades because of the intensification of cultural and organizational developments and of international exchange (Meyer *et al.* 1997). As concerns the educational domain, it is easy to show that decentralization, accountability, marketization, managerialism and professionalization have become key concepts in the reform discourses of policy-makers in many countries around the world. These concepts have a normative function. They constitute a small but solid set of policy models, that are ideal representations of the ends of schooling and of the means of attaining those ends, which can be reinterpreted to a certain extent and combined in different ways, but which are expected to produce similar or convergent effects in educational settings around the world (Ball 1998). Although the goals that are officially put forward when advocating these policy-making concepts concern an increase in the global efficiency and effectiveness of educational systems and individual schools, the discourse around these concepts is also permeated with diverse representations of the social identities and power relations between different educational agents. Behind the official text, there are in fact diffuse ideological discourses on parentocracy, the nature of professional work, the management of men and women and the relationship between the public sector and the State (Brown 1990; Ball 1994; Goodson 2001a).

Key concepts and their implications

Decentralization offers perhaps the mildest version of contrived change. The administrative, political and pedagogical rationales that are put forward tend either to present it as a transformation that is needed if local diversity is to be taken into account or as a consensual move towards enlarged participation and grass-root democracy. However, this applies more to decisions to strengthen regional and local authorities in countries with traditions of centralized education than to countries with a long tradition of decentralization where the redistribution of responsibilities between schools and local authorities has mostly been justified in terms of effectiveness (McLean and Lauglo 1985). Nonetheless, in both cases, it is clear that decentralization may be used to impose new modes of educational management, based on a remote steering of the system that increases State legitimacy while considerably reinforcing local agents' vulnerability to internal and external criticism (Weiler 1990). It may introduce changes not only in the locus but also in the strength of control (Broadfoot 1985). Power relations may be altered as certain groups, such as teachers, lose part of the influence they had at the national level through the action of unions and become more exposed to individualized and more immediate pressures from the administration, head teachers or parents at the local level.

Decentralization and accountability have been promoted together in several countries from the 1970s on. Stemming from the same global critique of the inefficiency and ineffectiveness of centralized and bureaucratic systems of control, they can be seen as the two faces of the same policy coin. In fact, increased monitoring and evaluation counterbalance local autonomy. The rationale for accountability may vary according to national traditions. In centralized countries, accountability has meant a change of State control from process to product evaluation with little reference to 'clients' except at a very abstract level. In decentralized countries, more emphasis has been put on concrete ways of making product evaluation more accessible to parents at the local level (Broadfoot 1996; Poulson 1996). In both cases, however, there is a clear move toward external surveillance and regulation of educational professionals that tends to alter their roles and their relationships with each other and with parents. Head teachers and teachers are no longer conceived as colleagues, but as occupying distinct positions, the first very much oriented toward external demands and the second toward internal tasks (Ball 1994). The relation of both groups to parents are seen as potentially conflicting.

In the model of the market, a neat and potentially antagonistic division is created between parents and educational professionals. Parents are supposed to create new dynamics in the educational system by constraining educational professionals to respond to their expressed desires in order to avoid the potential negative consequences of parents opting out of specific schools. At the same time, external competition between providers in educational markets is mainly conceived as the task of head teachers, while teachers are supposed to deal with internal tasks at the classroom level. Furthermore, head teachers are supposed to reorganize their schools in order to make them more attractive to potential consumers. As a result, new cleavages and new arenas for potential conflict are created between head teachers and teachers (Gewirtz *et al.* 1995). It is thus not as members of a consensual educational community, but as individuals having potentially diverging interests that parents and professionals are expected to act in order to improve the quality of educational provision.

On the contrary, the management model that is promoted in many countries is intended to reduce potential for conflict among school professionals by transforming close coercive mechanisms into new forms of self-control. As in other public organizations, the legitimacy of bureaucratic hierarchies is dismissed in favour of the personal vision and the capacity to mobilize individuals and to organize group work by an educational leader (Boltanski and Chiapello 1999).

Teachers are also valued for capacities other than those traditionally deployed in the classroom such as their loyalty to the organization and their aptitude to engage in collective projects and in external partnerships. Nevertheless, it is easy to see that divisions and potential for conflict not only remain, but also may increase when this model is applied. In fact, bureaucratic or collegial relationships give way to manipulative strategies from head teachers whose training, recruitment and professional responsibilities are becoming extremely different from those of teachers and who must play a crucial mediating role between teachers, parents and local and national administrations (van Zanten 1999; Gewirtz 2002).

In contrast to discourses of accountability, marketization or managerialism, discourses of professionalization that circulate internationally seem to cross ideological positions: professionalization is related to autonomy in liberal discourses and to empowerment in progressive ones (Popkewitz 2000b). It is perhaps possible to see in this contradiction a global process of 'deprofessionalization' and 'reprofessionalization' (Seddon 2000). Positive discourses on the professionality of teachers can be seen as either sincere or hypocritical attempts to rehabilitate teachers' work in face of reforms that have tended to emphasize distrust and criticism from parents, head teachers and local and national educational authorities. These discourses have come from educational decision-makers but also from educational researchers in many countries who have insisted on teachers' capacity to act as 'reflective practitioners' or to develop collegial responsibility (Schön 1983; Talbert and McLauglin 1996). However, some discourses on teachers' professionalization are in fact ways of introducing managerial modes of control in subtle ways. This, for instance, is the case of discourses focused on co-operation which, when they come from the administration, are perceived by teachers as forms of 'contrived collegiality' (Hargreaves 1992). It is important to note that although the relationship between school professionals is not the same in each case, in both the distance between them and parents is reinforced.

Dissemination and hybridization

How are these policies diffused? This implies taking into account the role of multinational corporations, international agencies and think tanks as active agents of a new kind of 'cultural imperialism' that applies not only to Third World countries but to others as well. These groups in fact constitute important sites of construction, dissemination and legitimation of transnational discourses. Their power has increased because of economic globalization and the symbolic retreat of the state from the scene of education in many countries. However, these groups should not be conceived as coherent bodies promoting perfectly convergent points of view. Although the existence of a common core classic liberal ideology based explicitly or implicitly on rational choice theory, which has colonized policy-making around the world, can be easily demonstrated (Archer and Tritter 2000), a more detailed analysis shows that other ideologies coexist and interact in complex ways with liberalism. This is the case for instance with the European Union's discourse on education and training, which emphasizes three main themes – competition, quality and citizenship – and tries to weave them into a common 'modernist but social welfare conscious' fabric (Novoa 2000).

It is also important to go beyond the rhetoric of public declarations and government documents. The common global discourse that plays a crucial role in the legitimation of policy can in fact mask extremely divergent conceptions of the same idea at the national level. Likewise, the capacity for international agencies to enforce policy decisions directly should not be overestimated. Even in Third World countries placed in a highly dependent position, it has been shown that resistance to outside influences, as well as subtler processes of adaptation and progressive transformation of external models are at work (Anderson-Levitt and Alimasi 2001). Among countries occupying a leading position, the 'lending' and 'borrowing' of policy can be a much more complex process, implying a *bricolage* of ideas, strategies and tools where the role of individual carriers, such as consultants, experts or researchers, as well as that of fortuitous meetings, can be essential and where legitimation needs will orient the degree of visibility and the ideological 'turn' given to external models (Brown and Lauder 1996; Phillips and Lauder 2001). It is fact the notion of 'hybridization' that provides the best conceptualization of the way in which global models interact with different national realities (Popkewitz 2000a; van Zanten and Ball 2000).

To understand hybridization, it is necessary to go beyond political discourse to examine the various factors that have created a receptive ground for its dissemination. Although to provide a comprehensive perspective many factors should be considered, not only in the sphere of schooling but also in those of family relations, culture and work, here I will attend to those educational changes that have had direct effects on the views and practices of administrators teachers and parents. In many rich countries, important educational reforms were implemented after the Second World War. These reforms focused on increasing the number of pupils completing secondary schooling and improving the educational chances of specifically targeted 'educationally disadvantaged' groups. These changes lend themselves to criticism for the increase in bureaucratic control, complexity and inefficiency. Moreover, as it became apparent that these efforts at educational reforms were not producing the expecting results, still harsher criticisms were levelled against reformers and administrators on grounds of ineffectiveness and inequity. These attacks led these groups to become much more cautious, in many cases cynical, about the power of schooling to equalize the life chances of children from different social and ethnic backgrounds and opened the way to the individualization of educational discourse and to liberal-oriented reforms (Farrell 1999; Gillborn and Youdell 2000).

At the same time, the massive influx of lower-class pupils into secondary academic schooling had also produced enormous pedagogical and social control problems for teachers, especially in mixed-ability and socially mixed classrooms and schools. This created feelings of disorientation, discouragement and disengagement, and made teachers both more receptive to discourses on professionalization and more vulnerable to external forms of management and control (Bernstein 1967) while leading many of them to withdraw their 'hearts and minds' from teaching and schools (Goodson 2001b). This situation also generated uncertainties and backlash reactions among parents. Did middle-class families ever really support the 'comprehensive ideal'? (Pring and Walford 1997). Many of them saw the comprehensive schools as a way of making up for scarcity of place in selective grammar schools, *lycées* or *gymnasiums* and used them as a way of transforming other assets into cultural ones at a period of economic expansion (Butler and Savage 1995). However, with the arrival of economic recession and massive numbers of working-class and ethnic minority children in comprehensive systems, these parents became much less confident in the schools' capacity to provide their children with a good education. They started to develop 'closure' strategies based on the unofficial reconstruction of segregated school careers through ability and social tracking or setting inside schools and reinforced them through unofficial choice which was later legitimized by market reforms.

Globalization, national models and national contexts

In order to understand the interaction between global processes and national processes it is necessary to examine national educational models and realities in more detail. Some researchers argue that the national level has lost a great deal of its importance because globalization and neoliberalism have created 'hollow States' (Peters 1993). The position adopted here is different. It is true that the influence of world models tends to produce a gap between official national rhetoric and the real hybridization of global and local processes. This 'decoupling' is in fact endemic both because world culture contains many variants of dominant models leading to conflicting principles and because in all countries, and especially in centralized ones such as France, there are important differences between formal models and observable practices. However, this does not necessarily mean a weakening of state control as nation-states are reaffirmed in their 'modernizing' and integrative functions (Meyer *et al.* 1997). Fragmentation can in fact lead to a restructuring of decision-making processes: the central State lays down essential principles and leaves the burden of connecting them to social environments to local agents at the periphery who are forced to reconstruct their identities, forge new alliances and invent new organizational and pedagogical responses to crucial problems (van Zanten 2001). What we observe here is, thus, a radical transformation of the educational arena implying changes in composition and power relations between various groups of actors (Popkewitz 2000b).

National models, resistance and change

Compared to other national educational systems, the French system has relied, since the end of the 19th century, on a very consensual and powerful ideological model: a philosophical, political and pedagogical construction that has contributed to the formation, maintenance and continuous legitimation of specific policies, structures and practices. At the centre of it, is the Enlightenment idea of knowledge as a supreme liberating force from natural and social chains, as well as the more recent 19th-century ideology of merit as a way of breaking up traditional hierarchies based on wealth and tradition. There is also a strong moral component as the school is supposed to promote universal values against specific religious and local lay beliefs and to constitute, in that sense, a distinct public sphere (van Zanten 1997a). Because of its insistence on universal rationalism and national cohesion, this ideology was highly consistent with the administrative centralized form that had been gradually developing for several centuries under very different political regimes and which was considerably strengthened and extended by the development of a national system of education. In fact, centralization itself became part of an ideological construction: the 'centre' stood for rationality, progress and equality whereas 'local forces' stood for irrationality, conservatism and favouritism of different kinds (Grémion 1968).

The centralized form has given way to a specific policy cycle. As analysed by Archer (1979), this cycle is characterized by short periods of intense but opaque negotiation at the centre while the policy is formed – and frequently distorted by multiple compromises between different parties – and long periods of latency while the policy is being implemented but also altered or discreetly shelved by local-level bureaucracies and teachers. Considered from this perspective, the French model appears based on an alliance between the State and teachers, represented by powerful teacher unions who are not only considered partners in all national negotiations concerning educational reforms, but who also influence policy through public manifestations and strikes. As in Portugal, this compromise between an 'educational State' and a 'Republic of teachers' has had the effect, until recently, of excluding parents from the decision-making process although representatives of parents' associations are formally part of most official educational bodies and commissions (Barroso 2000). It has also contributed to protecting teachers from head teachers' authority as their recruitment, careers and the essential components of teacher evaluation are controlled by the central administration.

This gives, however, a distorted picture of the functioning of the system, even at the height of central planning in the 1960s. It does not take into account the interactions between centre and periphery in policy formation and the considerable leeway enjoyed by educational officials who implement very general principles and norms at the local level. Furthermore, it is necessary to take into account recent changes in the policy-making process at both national and local levels, changes that have been so rapid and diffuse that they invite us to revise our whole vision of the system. On the one hand, at the national level, since the 1970s, there has been a proliferation of 'councils' and 'commissions' bringing together Ministry officials, representatives of teacher unions and teacher disciplinary associations, representatives of professional or economic sectors and researchers with more and more appeals being made to 'experts', mostly from the university. Although many of these groups and individuals are merely 'consulted' and not directly involved in the decision-making process, they do exert some influence on both content and form of reforms. On the other hand, decentralization has considerably increased the influence of local political bodies – regions, departments and municipalities – especially in the area of educational provision. It has also considerably developed the need for local dialogue between these political bodies and local educational authorities – that is, in France, the *Rectorats* and the *Inspections Académiques* – and between these authorities and the central political and administrative ones.

Although the traditional model of strong direct moral and organizational control by the centre is presently undergoing profound changes, that model is still used for the purposes of rejecting internal influences. Nevertheless, apparent political consensus on many of its components hides the fact that in the 1980s, through different political 'forums', a new neo-liberal 'referential' penetrated that model (Jobert and Théret 1994). As concerns education, and the five main global concepts presented in the first section of this paper, this position translates into a political and administrative discourse that rejects marketization, but integrates in various degrees the principles of decentralization, accountability, managerialism and professionalization under the banner of 'the modernizing of public services'. School choice and school autonomy concerning pupil and teacher recruitment are officially rejected but schools are expected to use the limited financial and pedagogical autonomy conferred through decentralization measures to work more efficiently and adapt to their local environment. Managerial-style rhetoric is promoted as concerns the internal co-ordination of work inside schools by head teachers and its external control by local educational authorities. The importance of external accountability is underlined and this has translated into the development of individual evaluations of pupils at different stages of their school career as well as evaluations of individual schools and policies. At the same time, the need for new teaching professionals, possessing new pedagogic and organizational skills to allow them to work in this new modern environment, is also emphasized with support from the teacher unions and with the newly created *Instituts Universitaires de Formation des Maîtres.* This discourse is not only that of the central State. Local political bodies also espouse it insisting on the key terms of 'projects', 'professional training of teachers and educational managers' and 'evaluation' (van Zanten 1997b).

From national models to national realities

In looking at the impact of globalization, it is nevertheless essential to distinguish educational rhetoric from educational realities or, more precisely, to analyse the intricate relationship between the two. This is particularly necessary in countries such as France, where there is both a widespread faith in the power of political discourse to act as a moral regulating force and a widespread tolerance of the inevitable gaps between general discursive ideals and local realities. For instance, if one looks not at discourse on school choice but at actual policies and practices, the educational system seems far more 'liberal' than its official image. In fact, despite strong positions against giving more power to individual parents, choice has been officially, although discreetly, promoted though a policy called *désectorisation*, which gives parents the possibility to express three or five different preferences for secondary schools (van Zanten 1996). This policy was first applied experimentally in five departments and then extended to many others through local initiatives, without any form of direct control from national authorities. At the same time, various studies show a growing gap between official discourses and practices in this area at the local level. Not only has the use of the private sector substantially increased in the last 20 years with almost one family out of two using it for one of their children at one point of their school career (Langouët and Léger 2000), but 'school switching' inside the public sector has also developed. Although the percentage of pupils that are not schooled in their catchment school is nationally only 10%, this covers a wide range of situations across the country with percentages nearing 25% having been documented in our own research on urban areas around Paris (Broccolichi and van Zanten 2000). Clearly, as will be shown in more detail below, this 'switching' has profound implications for the activities of parents, teachers and head teachers, and for the transformation of power relations at the local level.

An almost opposite example of the gap between official discourse and local realities is that of accountability through external evaluation. On the one hand, in the last 15 years prominent researchers and decision-makers have emphasized the importance of developing a 'culture of evaluation' in schools (Thélot 1993). From 1987 to 1997, the Department of Evaluation came to occupy such a central place at the Ministry of Education that the latest Ministry has considerably curtailed its responsibilities. This has not prevented the development of multiple types of evaluation, however, conducted at the local level by the local educational authorities or political bodies (Demailly *et al.* 1998). On the other hand, analysis of the actual uses of evaluation show that it serves more as a rhetorical device to generate feelings of inadequacy among school professionals, with the expectation that this will lead to changes in their actual practice, than as a corrective mechanism implying outside interventions and sanctions from the administration. Moreover, local political bodies, especially municipalities, tend to use evaluations of their investment in schools as a device to legitimize and popularize their action with their electors (van Zanten 1997b; Dutercq 2000). Furthermore, for local educational actors, both head teachers and teachers, the growth of evaluation appears both as an extension of bureaucratic modes of control through norms and procedures by the national State (Broadfoot 1996) and as a new mode of 'politicized' control by local political bodies.

The development of limited autonomy for schools through decentralization has also been accompanied by administrative rhetoric presenting head teachers, at least in secondary schools, as 'new managers' of the educational system with corresponding changes in their training – almost non-existent before – allowing for the introduction of courses on the management of financial and human resources. Although popular among a sizeable minority, these discourses and practices have not been embraced by the majority of head teachers who feel that their autonomy is not only very limited by law but also by the recent increase in State and local control and by parents' new attitudes towards schooling. It is important however to distinguish between the external and the internal activity of head teachers, especially of those working in large urban secondary schools. Many of them have integrated new managerial skills in the local promotion of their school and in financial and administrative negotiations with local political authorities and bodies. Very few, however, are willing to apply managerial techniques in dealing with their school personnel. This is so not only because their capacity to act is strongly limited by the pedagogical and administrative autonomy of teachers, but also because they see their career as based on frequent horizontal moves from one school to another (van Zanten 1999). Young teachers, trained in the *Instituts Universitaires de Formation de Maitres* created in 1989, have also been exposed somewhat to managerial discourses and techniques. Many of them have in fact come to equate professionalization with new organizational techniques such as group work or new communication skills. They tend to see the possession of these skills as an important component of their identity as opposed to that of 'old' teachers who are viewed as either 'traditionalists', using old-fashioned methods, or as 'ideologists', promoting unrealistic aims. Moreover, from this new managerial and professional perspective, they have also tended to develop a critical discourse on head teachers.

Perhaps the greatest observable transformation that has come about through policy enactment is due to decentralization. If this is so, it is because in centralized countries such as France, decentralization is not just a specific policy orientation but a much more general restructuring of State/civil society distinctions, one that encompasses highly diverse reforms and social movements (Popkewitz 2000b). Decentralization in fact in the last 20 years in France has developed well beyond legislation, especially in the areas of educational provision and financing, because it corresponds to structural and political changes in the role of the State, regions and localities and this at not only the national but also the international level. It has progressed rapidly and frequently invisibly and in a disorderly way because of the lack of organized local communities and strong local administrations. Neo-liberal tendencies as expressed by the increase of parental choices have developed at the same time as inequalities in provision and financing resulting from differences in local political bodies' capacity and will to invest in education. The problematic of 'local governance' has thus become a crucial one in France today (Le Galès 1998) but very little progress has been made toward such governance in the area of education.

Local reinterpretations and configurations

At this stage, it is nevertheless important to point out that the interaction between global, national and local processes does not affect all localities in the same way. Many researchers have pointed out that because of their specific position, both as regards accumulation of resources and integration into exchange networks, metropolitan areas are more likely to be affected by globalization processes (Sassen 1997). At the same time, because of their importance, both numerical and symbolic, at the national level, these metropolitan areas – especially, in France, Paris and its suburbs – are seen as sites where national policies are formed, experimented with and transformed. Education policy has in fact become essentially, urban policy (Grace 1991; van Zanten 1991). However, metropolitan sites differ greatly in terms of their social class and, in many cases, ethnic configurations. We have studied two different areas, both located in the Parisian conurbation, that represent two different types of emblematic sites and two different types of local recontextualizations of national and global trends (Taylor 2000).[1] The first is a lower-class *commune*, administrated by a communist mayor, which exhibits all the problems associated with urban 'deprivation': social and ethnic segregation in social housing areas, school failure, juvenile delinquency and adult unemployment. The second is a predominantly middle- and upper-middle-class *commune*, which enjoys concentrated economic, urban, social and school resources and thus represents urban affluence: that is, the apparent accessibility of material and symbolic goods, that has for centuries attracted so many internal and foreign migrants to Western cities.

Dynamics of withdrawal, adaptation and conflict in 'disqualified' areas

Decentralization and accountability take very specific forms in poor, 'disqualified' areas. On the one hand, given the weight of educational and social problems, local educational administrators and inspectors tend, much more than in other areas, to delegate unofficially to the schools themselves the work of finding 'solutions'. Deviance from official norms in terms of internal organization, curriculum or disciplinary sanctions is tolerated, if not encouraged. At the same time, decentralization has also meant the development of various specific policies of positive discrimination such as the creation of educational priority areas. However, because financial support has been limited and fluctuating and because pedagogical support for developing and evaluating projects aimed at improving pupils' results has been wanting, these policies have not been successful and have even aggravated the situation in some cases. In fact, educational professionals tend to view them as an increase in 'procedural' control (new directives to follow and forms to fill out) while developing many projects that are either geared rather toward the less 'problematic' faction of the school population or that tend to reproduce the current situation. Nor can schools expect much help from municipalities that are torn between two competing directions of action. On the one hand, there are the pressing needs of the new underclass in terms of employment, schooling and social integration. On the other hand, there are the pressing demands of the stable factions of the working class and of the middle class in terms of residential and school quality and cultural development and the fear that these groups may not only leave the schools but the city itself, thereby reinforcing processes of urban impoverishment and segregation (Bacqué and Fol 1997).

In fact, in 'disqualified' areas, such as the one studied, there is considerable tension between members of the less stable factions of the working class and immigrant groups on the one side, and members from the more stable factions of the working class and from the lower-middle classes on the other side.

Public schools are central sites for the display of this tension because they constitute one of the only public spaces where these groups are formally forced to interact and because they play a crucial role in social reproduction and social mobility. In the majority of cases, parents from the first group adopt a position of retreat while, in a minority of cases, they react with anger towards teachers and other parents. Parents of the second group develop strategies of 'colonization' of the public school which imply both participating in school councils to increase their 'voice' and constructing 'good learning environments' for their children through pressure on head teachers and teachers to recreate academic tracks. A small but significant percentage of these parents also develop avoidance strategies in reaction to these 'demonized' schools (Reay and Lucey 2003). Playing 'exit' rather than 'voice' (Hirschman 1971), they try to get their children into more prestigious public and private schools, mostly located in Paris. There are risks, however, involved in this strategy as in those contexts, parents and children are in competition with other more 'skilled' parents and 'brighter' children from the upper factions of the Parisian middle class. In fact, these parents enter the unofficial educational metropolitan market with the wrong currency and are very far from the ideal model of a well-informed, rational and resourceful consumer (Gewirtz *et al.* 1995; Broccolichi and van Zanten 2000).

Such parental attitudes exert a powerful influence on schools. Teachers see their work with pupils as being made more difficult by all the parents they perceive as 'invisible' or 'unpredictable', but also by the small group of parents who are trying to protect their children's interests. Head teachers' activity is much more reactive to the pressure of this last category of parents. In order to limit parental 'flight' from these disqualified schools, two main strategies are developed: strong emphasis on security and discipline and creation of the 'good' classes that these parents ask for. Neither strategy has much effect on school flight, but they do have significant effects on the internal functioning and climate of schools (Duru-Bellat and Mingat 1997; Thrupp 1999). Head teachers also have conflicting relations with the 'invisible' and 'unpredictable' parents whom they see only in problematic situations such as disciplinary exclusions and pedagogical reorientations for pupils with learning difficulties. These contextual factors lead school professionals to blame parents, much more than the competitive strategies of Parisian and private schools or the lack of support from local educational and political authorities, for their daily problems.

Furthermore, this social configuration creates a variety of tensions among teachers and between teachers and head teachers. It is in these kind of schools that conflicts between 'old' and 'new' teachers are more likely to arise, both because there are important ideological cleavages between the professional ethics of the two groups and because solidarity appears as an essential dimension for professional success. Old and stable teachers are much more oriented toward a 'humanitarian' ethic that gives meaning to their activity in 'disqualified' school contexts, even when pupils do not make any significant achievement progress (Becker 1952). Most young and mobile teachers just develop 'survival strategies' (Woods 1977), some of them based on the use of managerial techniques, to cope with situations that they hope are transitory; theirs is a much less ideologically informed professional ethic. Moreover, in this type of school, there are numerous disagreements and disputes between teachers and the significant, growing number of non-teaching personnel such as educational and career counsellors, school supervisors, school nurses and social workers (Kherroubi and van Zanten 2001). In addition, in these schools, teachers and non-teaching personnel have higher expectations concerning the pedagogic and educational role of the head teacher who should, they believe, be able to ensure that national norms are adapted to the local situation. Given the enormous responsibility that this represents, head teachers are much more likely to seek compensation in activities outside schools than to play a leading role within them. Again, different categories of school personnel tend to blame each other, using the vocabulary of professionalism or managerialism, without any clear sense of political responsibilities.

Dynamics of appeal, selection and professional distance in attractive areas

The situation of the middle-class *commune* administrated by a right-wing coalition is quite different. The municipality we studied has profited from decentralization laws to develop an exceptionally explicit policy of attracting middle-class and upper-middle-class families through residential projects elaborated in relation with property developers. It has also invested high sums of money in the development of day nurseries, cultural activities and sports facilities for children and youth as a central dimension of its urban strategy. Primary schools, which depend on the municipalities for financial aid, except for teachers' salaries, have not been neglected. Services of various kinds such as child-minding facilities before and after school hours, after-school and Wednesday clubs, as well as different kinds of sport and cultural activities are provided free of charge. Most of the schools have been enlarged and embellished and have good computer and music facilities at their disposal. The major problem remains, however, of some of the public junior secondary schools over which the powers of the municipalities are very limited being much less attractive than the primary schools. This is to a great extent compensated for by the good reputation of the three private secondary schools – all of them Catholic – and of the public *lycée*. For a long time, local educational authorities were very tolerant of the municipality's practices, which included, some years ago, changing the outline of one catchment area to allow the inhabitants of a new residential area to send their children to the primary school with the best reputation. In recent years, they have, however, become more aware of the increase in school and urban segregation both inside the *commune*, which does include one social housing area, and even more, in the larger surrounding area which includes much more socially-mixed *communes*.

Parental attitudes here are very different from those in disqualified areas. Most parents are very ambitious for their children's educational and occupational future and have deliberately chosen their place of residence because of the supposed quality of the local schools (Robson and Butler 2001). Children are encouraged from a very young age, to increase their 'cultural capital' through various extracurricular activities and placed in the best classes within schools. Nevertheless, these ambitions are frequently limited by other factors having to do with the children's safety and happiness (Coldron and Boulton 1991). In a sprawling urban space, some parents hesitate to send young children to far-away schools and have them use public transportation daily. Others fear that some school environments may be too competitive for children who are not very good pupils or 'immature'. Still others dislike taking their children away from local friends and neighbourhood activities. Parental ambition is even more limited by lack of slots and selective procedures in private schools and lack of diversity and choice in public schools. Although the apparent richness and closeness of the local school market heightens parents' aspirations, there is in fact fierce competition for places in schools that require either good grades and economic capital (private schools) or good grades and social capital in order to bypass official restrictions on choice (public schools). Thus, a considerable proportion of parents leave their children in local secondary schools of average reputation, at least until the end of *college.* Because of this, many of them are also very active in schools combining individual pressure on teachers and collective pressure on head teachers and the administration through extremely dynamic parents' associations, two of which are independent from national federations, quite exceptional in France.

Schools respond to these parental pressures differently according to their position in the reputation scale. As in 'disqualified' areas, schools located at the bottom of the hierarchy established by parents have to prove that they are able to provide high-quality teaching at least in the 'good' classes if they want to retain middle-class children. This is true, however, to a certain extent, of all public schools because parents of the best pupils in the public system can always threaten teachers and schools principals with pulling their children out and moving to the nearby private schools. In order to maintain their standing, the best public schools are thus led to imitate the private schools' selection practices, internal tracking and evaluation standards. This is done with tacit agreement from local educational authorities who justify their deviation from official norms as being the only way for public schools to defend their position against the unfair competition from private schools. There is thus unofficial acknowledgement of the existence of a public–private market but this has not had any serious impact on the development of new modes of regulation at the local level.

Moreover, the internal response of public schools is far from being totally coherent. Teachers in the 'best' schools, those with high qualifications and seniority, consider themselves almost as members of a liberal profession and are very reluctant to pursue collective projects and become accountable to external groups. Local educational authorities, head teachers and parents' associations have in fact very little power to change their ways and make them more responsive to their demands. In the other schools, the situation is more like that of the schools in 'disqualified' areas – although less critical – with little co-ordination among school professionals. The situation is quite the opposite in private schools. In these schools, the head teacher has complete freedom to recruit teachers and other school personnel according to specific criteria. These teachers are generally much less likely to express a strong professional point of view, not only because, as opposed to teachers working in the public sector, they can be dismissed, but because they have lower qualifications than public school teachers. They are more willing to do pastoral work and co-operate with parents who are also asked to participate in school activities. Coherence is further increased by continuous reminders of school values and norms closely related to Catholic ideals.

Conclusion

The purpose of this paper has been to argue for the necessity of taking into account the complex interweaving of transnational, national and local trends and movements that have altered the pace and the conditions for educational change when examining policy formation and policy enactment today (Goodson 2001a). Globalization is a powerful process but does not entail the disappearance of national state policies. States cannot avoid global pressures to change in specific directions, but they can twist and transform them to fit national purposes and opportunities. Moreover, globalization does not affect all areas within each country to the same degree and in the same way. Local processes are also very important. Global and national pressures and incentives for change have no chance of altering the working of educational systems if they are not fitted to local discourses and locally accepted ways of doing things at schools. However, because local realities can be very different according to social geographies and institutional configurations, policy terms such as marketization, management or accountability may take different and sometimes very contrasting meanings. In turn, local recontextualizations of policies, in variable ways according to the emblematic character of each location, will alter national and global policies.

France provides an interesting case of this complex interweaving for at least three reasons. The first is its position on the international scene. Having been for a long period a world leader in the cultural and educational spheres, it has now come to play a minor role as regards the global liberal trends promoted by the USA and the UK. This has given way to an interesting process of dealing with world influences, namely the claim for 'exceptional' status. The second reason is the fact that – as opposed to less articulated national positions on the role of schools – France developed a very strong and consensual educational model in the 19th century that has only started to be questioned in the last 20 years. This model, which is, in many respects, at odds with the dominant models circulating internationally, is still used with some success to promote the image of a rational, responsible state, still capable of holding external influences at bay. So, in a sense, France might seem as a counter-model for the study of the impact of globalization. However, the French case also provides a good perspective for the study of the interaction between transnational, national and local levels of educational policy making and change for a third reason. As I have tried to argue here, the two previous processes have resulted in extensive, profound delegation of the problem of resolving crucial educational dilemmas at the local level without any serious political effort to create new modes of regulation.

This makes France an interesting case for the study of the effects of global influences on the increasing 'decoupling', 'fragmentation' and 'localization' of centralized national systems that have undergone a 'decentralization' process far beyond official legislation. It also allows for important insights on the way these processes contribute to excessive responsibilities being thrown on local actors who, in the absence of clear political directions, tend to develop individualistic defensive or offensive attitudes and practices and tension-ridden, conflicting interactions. Cleavages between parents of different factions of the working and the middle classes, and between parents and educational professionals, are reinforced by the operation of unofficial markets and their impact on school and urban segregation. Cleavages between head teachers and teachers are likewise strengthened by managerial and accountability pressures that have important effects in contexts where internal problems of teaching and social control make it difficult to reach national standards, but also in those where public schools are subject to competitive pressures from the private sector. Cleavages between teachers and between teachers and other educational actors are also reinforced by reductionist interpretations of professsionalization, which serve mainly to protect teachers from external pressures without allowing them to improve their practice and develop a collective ethic of work.

Note

1 For this analysis, we rely on two different local studies. The results of the first one, conducted between 1993 and 2000 through various research programmes, have been brought together recently in a book (van Zanten 2001). Those of the second, still in process, will be published in a research report due in April 2002.

References

Anderson-Levitt, K. M. and Alimasi, N. I. (2001) Are pedagogical ideals embraced or imposed? The case of reading instruction in the Republic of Guinea, in M. Sutton and B. A. Levinson (eds), *Policy as Practice* (Norwood, NJ: Ablex).

Archer, M. S. (1979) *Social Origins of Educational Systems* (London: Sage).

Archer, M. S. and Tritter, J. Q. (2000) *Rational Choice Theory. Resisting Colonization* (London: Routledge).

Ball, S. J. (1987) *The Micro-Politics of the School* (London: Methuen).

Ball, S. J. (1994) *Education Reform. A Critical and Post-Structural Approach* (Buckingham: Open University Press).

Ball, S. J. (1998) Big Policies/Small World: an introduction to international perspectives in education policy, *Comparative Education*, 34 (2), 119–30.

Ball, S. J. and van Zanten, A. (1998) Logiques de marché et éthiques contextualisées dans les systèmes scolaires français et britannique, *Education et sociétés*, 1, 47–71.

Barroso, J. (2000) Autonomie et modes de régulation locale dans le système éducatif, *Revue française de pédagogie*, 130, 57–71.

Becker, H. S. (1952) The career of the Chicago public school teacher, *American Journal of Sociology*, 57, 470–7.

Bernstein, B. (1967) Open schools – open society? *New Society*, 14, 351–3.

Boltanski, L. and Chiapello, E. (1999) *Le nouvel esprit du capitalisme* (Paris: Gallimard).

Broadfoot, P. (1985) Toward conformity: educational control and the growth of corporate management in England and France, in J. Lauglo and M. McLean (eds), *The Control of Education* (London: Neinemann).

Broadfoot, P. (1996) *Education, Assessment and Society* (Buckingham: Open University Press).

Broccolichi, S. and van Zanten, A. (2000) School competition and pupil flight in the urban periphery, *Journal of Education Policy*, 15 (1), 51–60.

Brown, P. (1990) The 'third wave': education and the ideology of parentocracy, *British Journal of Sociology of Education*, 11 (1), 65–85.

Brown, P. and Lauder, H. (1996) Education, globalisation and economic development, *Journal of Education Policy*, 11, 1–24.

Butler, T. and Savage, M. (eds) (1995) *Social Change and the Middle Class* (London: University College London Press).

Coldron, J. and Boulton, P. (1991) 'Happiness' as a criterion of parents' choice of school, *Journal of Education Policy*, 6 (2), 169–78.

Demailly, L., Deubel, P., Gadrey, N. and Verdiere, J. (1998) *Evaluer les Établissements Scolaires. Enjeux, Expériences, Débats* (Paris: L'Harmattan).

Duru-Bellat, M. and Mingat, A. (1997) La constitution de classes de niveau par les collèges: les effets pervers d'une pratique á visée égalisatrice, *Revue française de sociologie*, 38, 759–90.

Dutercq, Y. (2000) *Politiques Éducatives et Évaluation. Querelles de Territoires* (Paris: Presses universitaires de France).

Farrell, J. P. (1999) Changing conceptions of equality of education. Forty years of comparative evidence, in R. F. Arnove and C. A. Torres (eds), *Comparative Education. The Dialectic of the Global and the Local* (London: Rowan and Littlefield).

Gewirtz, S., Ball, S. J. and Bowe, R. (1995) *Markets, Choice and Equity in Education* (Buckingham: Open University Press).

Goodson, I. F. (2001a) The personality of change. Paper presented at the Conference on Social Geographies of Educational Change: Context, Networks and Generalizability, Barcelona, Spain, 10–12 March.

Goodson, I. F. (2001b) Social histories of educational change theory, *Journal of Educational Change*, 2 (1), 45–63.

Grémion, P. (1976) *Le Pouvoir Périphérique. Bureaucrates et Notables dans le Système Politique Français* (Paris: Seuil).

Hargreaves, A. (1992) Cultures of teaching: a focus for change, in A. Hargreaves and M. Fullan (eds), *Understanding Teacher Development* (New York: Teachers College Press).

Hirschman, A. (1971) *Exit, Voice and Loyalty: Responses to Decline in Firms, Organizations and States* (Cambridge, MA: Harvard University Press).

Jobert, B. and Théret, B. (1994) France: la consécration républicaine du néolibéralisme, in B. Jobert (ed.), *Le tournant néolibéral en Europe* (Paris: L'Harmattan).

Kenway, J., Bigum, C. and Fitzclarence, L. (1993) Marketing education in the postmodern age, *Journal of Educational Policy*, 8, 105–22.

Kherroubi, M. and van Zanten, A. (2002) La coordination du travail dans les établissements d'enseignement: collégialité, division des rôles et encadrement éducatif, *Éducation et Sociétés*, 6, 65–91.

Langouët, G. and Léger, A. (2000) Public and private schooling in France: an investigation into family choice, *Journal of Education Policy*, 15 (1), 41–9.

Lauder, H. and Brown, P. (2001) Educational policy importation: transplant or transubstantiation? Paper presented at the Conference on Social Geographies of Educational Change: Context, Networks and Generalizability, Barcelona, Spain, 10–12 March.

Le Galès, P. (1998) Régulation, gouvernance et territoire, in J. Commaille and B. Jobert (eds), *Les Métamorphoses de la Régulation Politique* (Paris: LGDJ).

McLean, M. and Lauglo, J. (1985) Rationales for decentralization and a perspective from organization theory, in J. Lauglo and M. McLean (eds), *The Control of Education* (London: Neinemann).

Novoa, A. (2000) The restructuring of the European educational space. Changing relationships among states, citizens and educational communities, in T. S. Popkewitz (ed.), *Educational Knowledge. Changing Relationships between the State, Civil Society, and the Educational Community* (Albany, NY: State University of New York Press).

Peters, B. G. (1993) Managing the hollow state, in K. Eliassen and J. Kooman (eds), *Managing Public Organizations* (London: Sage Publications).

Popkewitz, T. S. (2000a) Globalization/regionalization, knowledge, and the educational practices, in T. S. Popkewitz (ed.), *Educational Knowledge. Changing Relationships between the State, Civil Society, and the Educational Community* (Albany, NY: State University of New York Press).

Popkewitz, T. S. (2000b) Rethinking decentralization and the state/civil society distinctions, in T. S. Popkewitz (ed.), *Educational Knowledge. Changing Relationships between the State, Civil Society, and the Educational Community* (Albany, NY: State University of New York Press).

Poulson, L. (1996) Accountability: a key word in the discourse of educational reform, *Journal of Education Policy*, 11 (5), 579–92.

Pring, R. and Walford, G. (ed.) (1997) *Affirming the Comprehensive Ideal* (London: The Falmer Press).

Reay, D. and Lucey, H. (2003) The limits of 'choice'; children and inner city schooling, *Sociology*, 37 (1), 121–42.

Robson, G. and Butler, T. (2001) Coming to terms with London: middle-class communities in a global city, *International Journal of Urban and Regional Research*, 25 (1), 70–86.

Sassen, S. (1991) *The Global City: New York, London, Tokyo* (Princeton, NJ: Princeton University Press).

Schön, D. A. (1983) *The Reflective Practitioner. How Professionals Think in Action* (New York: Jossey-Bass).

Seddon, T. (2000) Education: deprofessionalized or reregulated, reorganised and reauthorised?, in S. Ball (ed.), *Education: Major Themes* (London: Routledge).

Talbert, J. E. and McLauglin, M. W. (1996) Teacher professionalism in local school contexts, in I. Goodson and A. Hargreaves (eds), *Teachers' Professional Lives* (London: Falmer Press).

Taylor, C. (2000) Hierarchies and 'local' markets: the geography of the 'lived' market place in secondary school provision, *Journal of Education Policy*, 16 (1), 197–214.

Thélot, C. (1993) *L'Évaluation du Système Éducatif* (Paris: Nathan).

Thrupp, M. (1999) *Schools Making a Difference: Let's be Realistic!* (Buckingham: Open University Press).

Weiler, H. (1990) Decentralisation in educational governance: an exercise in contradiction, in M. Granheim, M. Kogan and U. Lundgren (eds), *Evaluation as Policymaking. Introducing Evaluation into a National Decentralised Educational System* (London: Jessica Kingsley Publishers).

Woods, P. (1977) Teaching for survival, in P. Woods and M. Hammersley (eds), *School Experience. Explorations in the Sociology of Education* (London: Croom Helm).

van Zanten, A. (1996) Market trends in the French school system: overt policy, hidden strategies, actual changes, *Oxford Studies in Comparative Education*, 6 (1), 63–75.

van Zanten, A. (1997a) Schooling immigrants in France in the 1990s: success or failure of the Republican model of integration? *Anthropology and Education Quarterly*, 28 (3), 351–74. Reprinted in S. J. Ball (ed.) (2000) *The Sociology of Education. Major Themes* (London: Routledge).

van Zanten, A. (1997b) L'action éducative à l'échelon municipal: rapport aux valeurs, orientations et outils, in F. Cardi and A. Chambon (eds), *Les Métamorphoses de la Formation. Alternance, Partenariat, Développement local* (Paris: L'Harmattan).

van Zanten, A. (1999) Les chefs d'établissement et la justice du système d'enseignement, in D. Meuret (ed.), *La Justice du Système Éducatif* (Bruxelles: De Boeck).

van Zanten, A. (2001) *L'école de la périphérie. Scolarité et ségrégation en banlieue* (Paris: Presses universitaires de France).

van Zanten, A. and Ball, S. J. (2000) Comparer pour comprendre: globalisation, réinterprétations nationales et recontextualisations locales, *Revue de l'Institut de Sociologie*, 1 (4), 113–31.

6 In search of structure[1]

Theory and practice in the management of education

David Hartley

University of Dundee, Scotland

Source: *Journal of Education Policy*, 13 (1): 153–62, 1998.

Introduction

The management of education seems to be pulled in different directions, enmeshed in different discourses, revealing different influences. These influences are intellectual, cultural and economic. The concern here is mainly with the intellectual and the cultural, less so the economic. Dissonance is rife: neither among theorists nor within the culture is there much degree of consensus. Take the theorists: their theories are a mix of approaches derived from functionalism, social construction, chaos theory and postmodernist theory. On the one hand, there are those who point to fundamental incompatibilities among them, arguing that neither singly nor collectively can they serve as the basis for practice. On the other hand, there are others who, in their search for structure, suggest that a theoretical reconciliation is indeed possible – and necessary in order to inform management practice.

But the management of education is not only informed by theory within academe; rather, it is also set within the broader culture. Contemporary culture is referred to as postmodernism – fragmented, fickle and relativistic. In part, it is a consequence of a contemporary capitalism which continuously advertises change, choice and consumption. Furthermore, it is the metaphor of the market which increasingly structures policy and practice in education, privileging the consumer over the producer, requiring more to be done with less, in the interests of competition and efficiency. Having considered these issues, I then discuss some of the ways in which managers may use these cultural and intellectual changes in order to effect policy. That is to say, we may soon begin to see evidence of managers and policy makers incorporating aspects of both post-modernist theory and of the culture of postmodernism so that they can be seen to flow with the contemporary intellectual and cultural stream. But, I argue, this will be little more than a makeover, an attempt to retain the certainties of modernity whilst appropriating selectively the cultural and intellectual vernacular of the times.

Management theory: a modernist makeover?

Modernist organization theory has its intellectual roots in Bentham's (1791) proposals for a Panopticon. This marked a shift in the technology of compliance: away from physical coercion towards self-control. It was an architectural design best suited to prisons, factories and schools. Although it was never built it provided a blueprint for a new management, and Bentham's *Chrestomathia*, published in 1816, sets out clearly five 'Principles of School Management', some of which would sit easily with those of officialdom today. Bentham's insights were applied to factories in the 19th century, and are well documented (Pollard 1965; Shenhav 1995). Further refinements came with F. W. Taylor's *Principles of Scientific Management* (1947[1911]), and with Henry Ford's subsequent insight that technology itself could structure control. Beyond that, in the late 1920s, industrial psychologists were said to have revealed that the worker's social needs should be recognized, and that if this were to be done then productivity would increase. Thereafter, organization theory adopted a more systemic perspective, calling for an interrelationship between an organization and its environment, arguing that knowledge has universal properties, and that theory can be tested empirically, using the scientific method which the physical sciences have developed.

Since 1970, this model has not gone unchallenged. It was first questioned in the 1970s by the phenomenologists and the symbolic interactionists. They regarded it as being overly deterministic, emphasizing passivity not agency. Organizations were not reified structures which were independent of the actions of actors; rather they were social constructions which had the mere appearance of being objective givens. They were always in process, never fixed (Greenfield 1975). What systems theorists referred to as 'structure' was nothing but a constellation of definitions of the organizational situation held to by its members at a given time. In this way, structure and agency are brought together, the former explained by the latter, the 'objectification of the subjective' (Berger and Luckmann 1967). Greenfield's concern was to understand social reality within an organization – a cultural hermeneutics. He had no truck with a unitary theory of organizations, nor did he regard educational administration as a social science, for there can be no truth; only truths for the moment, contingent and provisional.

Systems theorists were initially not easily moved by Greenfield (Hills 1980). There were, for example, attempts to incorporate 'culture' within the epistemic frame of systems theory. That is to say, Greenfield's cultural hermeneutics of the organization appeared to be similar to earlier organizational climate studies (Halpin and Croft 1963), but despite their semantic similarity, the two were rooted in different paradigms. The ideal-typical organizational climate study tended to be ahistorical, quantitative, empiricist and firmly rooted within the discipline of psychology. Organization culture studies rested on a social constructionist sociology which generated contextually grounded first-order meanings which were coded as qualitative second-order constructs (Denison 1996: 625). Whilst it seems that the shift from 'climate' to 'culture' did indeed occur, nevertheless some adherents to a positivist methodology proceeded to 'co-opt' culture as a 'variable' within that methodology (White and Jacques 1995: 46). In sum, systems theorists claimed that the common-sense theories of actors could never serve as a general theory of organizations. They reduced Greenfield's approach to little more than a methodology for understanding the definitions of, and cultural processes within, organizations.

But systems theory had yet to face the postmodernist critique. This undermined the fixity of meaning, deconstructing texts, disrupting all that purported to be certain. Meanings could never be final. There was said to be nothing but a constant deferral of meaning, an infinite regression in search of a certainty which never comes. It followed, therefore, that the very notion of being organized did not sit well with an intellectual approach which was set on disruption and disorganization. The central objection of the postmodernists turned on the issue of representation: against the systems theorists they claimed that no universal theory was possible; and against the phenomenologists and social constructionists they asserted that no second-order constructions or representatives could hold. In other words, neither the grand narratives of the systems theorists nor the meta-narratives of the social constructionists were admissible. Jeffcutt summarizes the position: 'Postmodernism articulates a postmodern condition of undecidability and perpetual redefinition' (Jeffcutt 1994: 239).

This postmodernist critique has provoked denials and uncertainty, if not pessimism, and the move towards a reconciliation has begun. There is perhaps a parallel to be drawn here between the search for a stable and coherent self-identity within the cultural flux of postmodernism and the quest for a coherent explanation of organizational reality within academe. Evers and Lakomski offer a diplomatic solution: 'the various research traditions, even if incommensurable, are equally legitimate and not necessarily in conflict' (Evers and Lakomski 1991: 222). Like Jeffcutt, they agree that both the systems theorists, on the one hand, and the phenomenologists and social constructionists, on the other, assume 'that there is something there to be represented' (p. 383), and that post-modernist theory makes a contrary assumption. But, they say, both are flawed: the systems theorists assume a universalism, context-free; and the logical problem for the postmodernists lies in the following contradiction: 'it does seem odd to propose an epistemology in order to defend the claim that epistemology is impossible' (p. 391). Influenced by this analysis, Aspin and Chapman (1994) go so far as to refer to a 'new science' of educational policy administration and management' (p. 26), calling for a pragmatic approach:

> There is never a time when we can haul our theoretic craft up into some kind of intellectual dry dock, investigate it all over and decide to do a complete overhaul or to build a fresh boat from scratch: we have to be flexible, adaptable and inventive in the repair and reconstruction of our theory, criticizing, making do and mending as we go along.
>
> (Aspin and Chapman 1994: 184)

This search for structure and for a reconciliation with modernism can go even further. In the offing is a new metaphor which may enable it, one based on the notion of chaos. Arguing that 'the control model is now largely discredited', Dobuzinskis nevertheless equivocates: 'it is not quite dead yet.' What is required, he argues, is an explanatory metaphor which can encompass the disparate discourses of public choice theory, critical theory and postmodernist theory (Dobuzinskis 1992: 361–2). The metaphor which Dobuzinskis has in mind is that of chaos. What is chaos? Scientists are said to distinguish among three states: first, stable equilibrium, whereby elements are usually in a state of what open systems theory calls a dynamic equilibrium, or homeostatic balance; second, bounded instability (or chaos), which seems both orderly and disorderly, with much seeming unpredictability, but which nevertheless reveals basic patterns; and third, explosive instability, where no order or pattern prevails (Glass 1995: 101).

Chaos theory appears to have some appeal, with affinities to the culture of postmodernism, to postmodernist theory and even to neo-liberal economics. That is to say, first: chaos theory has a superficial semantic affinity with a culture marked by disorder, second, whereas postmodernists stress the indeterminacy of knowledge so chaos theory suggests a superficial indeterminacy of events; and, third, Dobuzinskis (1992: 364) sees chaos theory as possibly analogous to 'Austrian economics'. Even Prigogine and Stengers, whose seminal *Order out of Chaos* sets out the case for a chaos theory of natural phenomena, make an important allusion to its cultural and political expression:

> We know now that societies are immensely complex systems involving a potentially enormous number of bifurcations exemplified by the variety of cultures that have evolved in the relatively short span of human history. We know that such systems are highly sensitive to fluctuations. This leads to hope and a threat: hope, since even small fluctuations may grow and change the overall structure. As a result, individual activity is not doomed to insignificance. On the other hand, this is also a threat, since in our universe the security of stable, permanent rules seems gone forever.
>
> (Prigogine and Stengers 1985: 312–15)

The concept of self-organization is important because it is occasioned only when there is a disruption to the stability of the system. For that to occur, the system must be open, not closed. Systemic closure leads to entrophy. The management implications of this approach would lead us to discard bureaucracy and to replace it by a structure which admits *some* disequilibrium, contingency and connectivity.

So far I have dealt briefly with three considerations of functionalist management theory: from symbolic interactionists; from postmodernists; and from chaos theorists. In particular, the pessimism occasioned by the postmodernists has prompted a defensive reaction, and there are attempts to bring order to the paradigmatic disputes. I have suggested that, far from portending a paradigmatic shift in management theory, these emergent theoretical developments (i.e. postmodernist theory and chaos theory) may come to be appropriated in order to refine modernist management theory, to take it forward. Before elaborating on this possibility, however, I refer now to a further context which frames policy making and management in education, namely that of contemporary culture: postmodernism.

Contemporary culture: the search for certainty

The Protestant ethic which was said to have underpinned the growth of industrial capitalism is in relative decline. On the ascendancy is the 'ethic' of consumerism, at least for those fortunate enough to be able to 'buy into' it. The full (male) employment envisaged by the architects of the postwar welfare state is no longer regarded as an achievable goal in late capitalist societies (Aronowitz and Fazio 1994). Part-time employment (whose other side is part-time unemployment) is increasingly a feature of most advanced economies. A further feature is the consumption of cultural products. As consumers gradually acquire the material goods which they need, business has come to produce and market cultural goods in order to sustain demand and to generate new markets. Capitalism also generates uncertainty. It requires constant product innovation and change. Advertisers continually lure customers to acquire a new image, at a price; and they do so by subliminal appeals to the irrational. Few advertisements inform us about the technicalities of a product; rather they associate it with the emotions. And there is no obvious pressure to conform to consumerism. If we can afford it then we choose it. Confronted constantly by having to choose, we must reflect, sometimes facilitated by therapists. In the search for the self, constant reflection is required: 'A world that lives by complexity and difference cannot escape uncertainty, and it demands from individuals the capacity to change form (the literal meaning)' (Melucci 1996: 2). This, argues Melucci (1996: 84), 'has led to the wholesale therapeutization of everyday life, so that it now seems more imperative to heal life than to live it.'

These cultural goods symbolize the self. They serve to generate identities. They make a public statement about the projected inner selves of those who disport them. And they are fleeting. Equally emphemeral are contractual relationships, be they marital or employment. Not only is there an ephemerality about this culture of postmodernism, but there is forever a sense of urgency and immediacy: a dipping into and out of a book, a switching of television channels, last-minute holidays. The moral code fractures; relativism is the 'order' of the day. There is uncertainty: 'The constitutive dimensions of the self – time and space, health and sickness, sex and age, birth and death, reproduction and love – are no longer a datum but a problem' (Melucci 1996: 2). There seems to be a superficial affinity between, on the one hand, the fragmentation of life and the loss of meaning within the culture of postmodernism, and, on the other, the undermining of certainty within academe by postmodernist theorists. I go on now to consider how these intellectual and cultural trends may affect how education may come to be governed and managed.

The management of education: postmodern means for modernist ends

What consequences may these intellectual and cultural changes have for policy makers and managers in education? First, policy makers can simply ignore the roots and expressions of uncertainty, and assert old ways; second, they may draw selectively upon the culture of postmodernism in order to manage the consent of professionals and other participants in education; third, some of the ideas of postmodernist theory may come to be appropriated within modernist discourses, assuming a compatibility which does not hold; and fourth, the metaphor of chaos may also be worked into an essentially modernist discourse. These are now discussed in turn.

The return of the iron cage of bureaucracy

One reaction both to cultural instability and to the destabilization of modernist management codes by postmodernists is to try to ignore them, and to continue blindly to observe the time-served codes and concepts of modernity. The modernist conceptual framework is thereby strengthened, producing a strait-jacket of standards and procedures under the guise of 'quality-management' and efficiency gains. At every level of education – especially in England – very elaborate schemes of standardization are being constructed, apparently with the purpose of producing an articulated structure spanning all levels. The English National Curriculum is a clear example of the nation-state seeking to rein in the multicultural and fragmentary cultural trends which consumer capitalism has set in train.

Take a further example. The current debate in British higher education about 'graduateness' has generated a contradictory logic which speaks on the one hand of systematization, comparability, explicitness and formalization; but, on the other hand, makes assertions that the very curriculum and pedagogy of higher education will remain immune from standardization. If this continues, then comparability and formalization will serve to produce uniformity of syllabi, as is now in the offing for a national curriculum for university-based teacher education in England (OFSTED/TTA 1996). This national curricular 'framework', defined by government – not by the teaching profession or by academics – contains an elaborate bureaucratic arrangement of areas, which are: the central assessed area, namely 'Teaching Competence of Students and of NQTs'; its major contributory area, namely the 'Quality of Training and Assessment of Students'; and other contributory areas, namely the 'Selection of Quality of Student Intake', the 'Quality of Staffing and Learning Resources' and the 'Management of Quality Assurance'. Each area has its component cells, 16 in total, with its own set of criteria, giving over 120 criteria in all. Each of the 16 individual cells will 'normally' be graded on a four-point scale: 'very good' (1); 'good' (2); 'adequate' (3) and 'poor quality' (4).

The force of these bureaucratizing tendencies is not to be under-estimated. The political room for manoeuvre is limited. Whilst the modernist conceptual frameworks do not logically fit the emergent cultural, intellectual and political forms, nevertheless very concerted attempts to make them fit are being made. This is not to say that all of officialdom's attempts at generating a rhetoric of legitimization have been abandoned. The forms of control are not only those of the bureaucratic directive; rather, as I shall suggest below, elements of the culture of postmodernism, of the postmodernist epistemological critique and of chaos theory may all be incorporated within modern management discourse. This would be no postmodern management; it would be a remodernized management.

Therapeutic illusions

Elements of the culture of postmodernism are already being appropriated into a new managerial discourse. That is to say, managers within a self-centred and consumerist culture may seek to ground their rhetoric so that is resonates with what is called the 'hermeneutics of the self' (Rose 1989: 247). But whilst this process purports to free us – to lead us to self-awareness, authenticity and fulfilment – it does no such thing. It only appears to free us, for with our freedom we choose to become complicit in, or to have a sense of ownership of, the political, economic and social structures of our time:

> Their significance is less the fact that they extend domination than in their functioning, at the same time, as practices that promote the obligation to be free. We are obliged to fulfil our political role as active citizens, ardent consumers, enthusiastic employees, and loving parents as if we were seeking to realize our own desires.
>
> (Rose 1989: 258)

Take some examples. Consider the common usage of the term 'reflective practitioner' and other forms of self-audit. Reflexivity is now a cultural practice, be it at the level of the self, or in the many 'audits' which are conducted at all institutional levels within education. Add to these the notion of 'ownership' (usually expressed as a sense of ownership; and usually only of tactics, not strategy), then the infusion of consumerist notions into modernist management takes on further salience.

The incorporation of postmodernist theory

In the management of education, the postmodernist critique appears to have generated two responses. First, there is a clear denial or avoidance of postmodernist theory, and the advocacy of best-practice advice derived from observing good managers. For example, Boje *et al.* (1996: 61) have analysed the attempts by the 'orthodox administrative science subcommunity' in *Administrative Science Quarterly* to resist critical postmodernism. Second, others have attempted a pragmatic adaptation or incorporation of some aspects of postmodernist theory, as expressed in the work of Gergen (1992) and of Fullan (1993). Gergen, in a pragmatic interpretation of postmodernism, agrees that the modernist discourse has lost its 'lived validity' (Gergen 1992: 212), and he seems at one with Cooper when he states, 'The view of knowledge-making as a transcendent pursuit, removed from the trivial enthrallments of daily life, pristinely rational, and transparently virtuous, becomes so much puffery' (Gergen 1992: 215). But, he argues, let there be some disruption of conventional thinking in an organization; let 'alien realities' (p. 223) be admitted, for if they are not then the organization may become overly isolated from its environment, and may thereby atrophy. In sum, let there be dissensus and renewal. Now Fullan: in his 'Eight basic lessons of the new paradigm of change' he makes similar calls for 'connection with the wider environment' and for non-experts as well as experts to be instrumental in effecting change (Fullan 1993: 21–41).

Both Gergen and Fullan see merit in breaching the limits of the organization by admitting the insights of strangers from the outside or of non-managerial voices from within. But this could lead either to their co-option or to their neutralization. And management may seek safe and agreeable 'dissenters', perhaps giving them functional (but separate) autonomy, an organization within an organization, seen but sidelined. Like appeals to chaos theory, this kind of managed dissent, which seems to accord with the disruptions and deconstructions of postmodernist theory, could also serve as a conservative rhetoric. In other words, 'deconstruction' could be appropriated in much the same way as 'empowerment' has been (Ellsworth 1989).

Gergen's pragmatic approach appears to be at one with postmodernist theory. It also resonates, apparently, with critical postmodernism (Giroux and McLaren 1994) and critical realist theory (Reed 1997). Giroux and McLaren, for example, advocate the following: admit the deconstructions and disruptions advocated by postmodernists, and allow once-marginalized 'voices' to be heard and to contest the hitherto privileged meanings which count as organizational wisdom. So, from Giroux's perspective, deconstruction becomes a political means to an emancipatory end, one which could put paid to the privileges of, for example, adult, middle-class, white, able-bodied, male and Christian majorities. Reed emphasizes that individual constructions of reality are set within existing social structures, and are thereby to be seen in relation to them, rather than being wholly autonomous of them. Whilst there are indeed definitions of the situation, the situation itself must be explained. Based on different motives, therefore, both Gergen and Giroux take issue with the relativism and nihilism implicit in deconstruction. But the political questions in the management of education remain: Who are the alien realists? How do they enter the arena? What shall be the rules of the dialogue? How will conflicts be resolved?

Managed 'chaos'

The application of chaos theory in educational administration and management has been very limited. To apply chaos theory to the social world is to commit a category error (Hunter and Benson 1997: 89): social phenomena do not appear to structure themselves in a universally patterned manner, unlike natural phenomena, from which chaos theory is derived. Indeed chaos theory, far from being critical, is said by Maxcy (1995: 55) to be both modernist and conservative, not post-modernist, for beneath the flows and fluctuations on the surface there exists a deep structure of patterned regularities. Moreover, the 'chaos' within the culture of postmodernism may indeed be functional for capitalism. Like Melucci (1996), Berman points up the dilemmas of postmodernism: between a desire for stability and a desire for new knowledge and experience; between a search for our roots and our tendency to uproot everything; between our individualism and our search for national, ethnic and class identities; between our need for a moral standpoint and a desire to go to the limit (Berman 1983: 35). But he is doubtful that much of this is news, and indeed the very title of his book, *All That is Solid Melts into Air*, is based on an extract from the *Communist Manifesto*, by Marx (quoted in McLellan 1977: 224; emphasis added):

> Constant revolutionizing of production, uninterrupted disturbance of all social relations, everlasting uncertainty and agitation distinguish the bourgeois epoch from all earlier times. All fixed, fast-frozen relationships, with their train of ancient and venerable prejudices and opinions, are swept away, all new-formed ones become antiquated before they can ossify. All that is solid melts into air, all that is holy is profaned, and man is at last compelled to face with sober senses his real conditions of life, and his relations with his kind.

What Berman is suggesting is that we should not expect culture to be other than it is, given the logic of capitalism:

> The one specter that really haunts the modern ruling class, and that really endangers the world it has created in its image, is the one thing that traditional elites (and, for that matter, traditional masses) have always yearned for: prolonged solid stability. In this world, stability can only mean entropy, slow death.... To say that our society is falling apart is only to say that it is alive and well.
>
> (Berman 1983: 95; emphasis added)

Chaos theory has yet to suffuse official management discourse in education. But there may be opportunities for market-driven theorists to concede that the market does indeed throw up unpredicted instabilities as consumers choose different and unforeseen courses of action. And they might go on to argue that these instabilities are nevertheless compatible with market forces: after all, the workings of markets will 'find their own level', so to say, and this 'level' will be tantamount to the deep structure which is to be found beneath its surface 'irregularities'. In this way, the discourse of chaos theory might be incorporated into the legitimatory rhetoric of policy makers and managers in education.

Conclusion

I have argued that in the wake of the post-positivist critique of management theory in education, three broad trends of thinking are emerging. The first is an atheoretical, politically driven management discourse defined by central government, particularly in England. It is a barely disguised return to the iron cage of bureaucracy, and it has efficiency as its goal. There is another trend which sees the incorporation of postmodernist culture within management discourse. That is to say, notions such as 'ownership', 'choice' and 'diversity' begin to enter this discourse in an attempt to get people to 'buy into' its bureaucratic agenda. This is the soft sell. And this 'ownership' can even be cast in nationalist terms: our nation's education system. (The recent White Paper in Scotland *Raising the Standard* [Scottish Office Education and Industry Department 1997] is a clear example.) The third and fourth trends constitute an emerging discourse which draws on intellectual ideas now being debated within academe, such as postmodernist theory and chaos theory, both of which, given their appearance of disruption and indeterminacy, seem to be at one with the instabilities of postmodernist culture and with the fluctuations of the market.

Already there are signs of these trends beginning to intersect. In respect of the first trend, its bureaucratic discourse may soon reach the limits of its legitimacy to manage consent. Its hard edge will need to be softened. Indeed management rhetoric is already suffused with references to consumerism (the second trend). The speculation being made here is that aspects of postmodernist theory, and perhaps chaos theory, will also be incorporated within management discourse. For example, the constructs of postmodernist theory may become operationalized, thereby rendered pragmatic, as Gergen and Fullan have already hinted at. Their ideas may represent the beginning of what Coates (1995) calls a 'postmodern means to a modernist end'. And they portend what White and Jacques (1995: 47) see as a time when academics may be speaking about, for example, 'operationalizing the postmodern construct', 'testing the reliability and construct validity of deconstructive data analysis' or 'postmodern change practices for efficiency, productivity and world-class competitiveness'. By then, the modernist makeover would be complete.

Note

1 The phrase 'in search of structure' draws on Hamilton (1977).

References

Aronowitz, S. and Fazio, W., 1994, *The Jobless Future: Sci-tech and the Dogma of Work* (Minneapolis: University of Minnesota Press).

Aspin, D. and Chapman, J., 1994, *Quality Schooling: A Pragmatic Approach to Some Current Problems, Topics and Issues* (London: Cassell).

Berger, P. and Luckmann, T., 1967, *The Social Construction of Reality* (Harmondsworth: Penguin).

Berman, M., 1983, *All That is Solid Melts into Air* (London: Verso).

Boje, D. M., Fitzgibbons, D. E. and Steingard, D. S., 1996, Storytelling at *Administrative Science Quarterly*: warding off the postmodern barbarians, in D. M. Boje, R. P. Gephart Jr. and T. J. Thatchenkery (eds), *Postmodern Management and Organization Theory* (Thousands Oaks: Sage).

Coates, G., 1995, Is this the end? Organising identity as a post-modern means to a modernist end. *Sociological Review*, 43 (4), 828–55.

Cooper, R., 1987, Information, communication and organisation: a post-structural revision. *Journal of Mind and Behaviour*, 8 (3), 395–416.

Denison, D. R., 1996, What is the difference between organizational culture and organizational climate? A native's point of view on a decade of paradigm wars. *Academy of Management Review*, 21 (3), 619–54.

Dobuzinskis, L., 1992, Modernist and postmodernist metaphors of the policy process: control and stability vs chaos and reflexive understanding. *Policy Sciences*, 25, 355–80.

Ellsworth, E., 1989, Why doesn't this feel empowering? Working through the repressive myths of critical pedagogy. *Harvard Educational Review*, 50 (3), 297–324.

Evers, C. W. and Lakomski, G., 1991, *Knowing Educational Administration* (Oxford: Pergamon).

Fullan, M., 1993, *Change Forces: Probing the Depths of Educational Reform* (London: Falmer Press).

Gergen, K., 1992, Organization theory in the postmodern era, in M. Reed and M. Hughes (eds), *Rethinking Organization: New Directions in Organization Theory and Analysis* (London: Sage).

Giroux, H. and McLaren, P., 1994, Multiculturalism and the postmodern critique: toward a pedagogy of resistance and transformation, in H. Giroux and P. McLaren (eds), *Between Borders: Pedagogy and the Politics of Cultural Studies* (London: Routledge).

Glass, N., 1995, Chaos non-linear systems and day-to-day management. *European Management Journal*, 14 (1), 98–106.

Greenfield, T. B., 1975, Theory about organization: a new perspective and its implications for schools, in M. Hughes (ed.), *Administering Education: International Challenge* (London: Athlone Press).

Halpin, A. W. and Croft, D. B., 1963, *The Organizational Climate of Schools* (Chicago: Midwest Center of the University of Chicago).

Hamilton, D., 1977, *In Search of Structure: Essays from a Scottish Open-plan Primary School* (London: Hodder & Stoughton for the Scottish Council for Research in Education).

Hills, J., 1980, A critique of Greenfield's 'New Perspective'. *Educational Administrative Science Quarterly*, 6 (1), 20–44.

Hunter, W. J. and Benson, G. D., 1997, Arrows in time: the misapplication of chaos theory to education. *Journal of Curriculum Studies*, 29 (1), 87–100.

Jeffcutt, P., 1994, The interpretation of organization: a contemporary analysis and critique. *Journal of Management Studies*, 31 (2), 225–50.

McLellan, D. (ed.), 1977, *Karl Marx: Selected Writings* (Oxford: Oxford University Press).

Maxcy, S. J., 1995, *Democracy, Chaos and the New School Order* (Thousand Oaks: Corwin Press).

Melucci, A., 1996, *The Playing Self: Person and Meaning in the Planetary Society* (Cambridge: Cambridge University Press).

Office for Standards in Education/Teacher Training Agency, 1996, *Assessment of Quality and Standards in Initial Teacher Training* 1996/97 (London: Ofsted).

Pollard, S., 1965, *The Genesis of Modern Management* (London: Arnold).
Prigogine, I. and Stengers, I., 1985, *Order out of Chaos: Man's New Dialogue with Nature* (London: Flamingo).
Reed, M. I., 1997, In praise of duality and dualism: rethinking agency and structure in organizational analysis. *Organization Studies*, 18 (1), 21–42.
Rose, N., 1989, *Governing the Soul: The Shaping of the Private Self* (London: Routledge).
Scottish Office Education and Industry Department, 1997, *Raising the Standard* (Edinburgh: HMSO).
Shenhav, Y., 1995, From chaos to systems: the engineering foundations of organization theory, 1879–1932. *Administrative Science Quarterly*, 40, 557–85.
Taylor, F. W., 1947, *The Principles of Scientific Management* (London: Harper & Brothers).
White, R. F. and Jacques, R., 1995, Operationalizing the postmodernity construct for efficient organizational change management. *Journal of Organizational Change Management*, 8 (2), 45–71.

7 Subjected to review

Engendering quality and power in higher education

Louise Morley

University of Sussex, Brighton, UK

Source: *Journal of Education Policy*, 16 (5): 465–78, 2001.

The micropolitics of quality

Subject Review is a quality assurance procedure for teaching and learning in UK higher education. The Quality Assurance Agency oversees this exercise. However, the assessors are recruited from the academic community. There are six aspects audited: learning resources; curriculum development and organization; teaching, learning and assessment; quality management and enhancement; student progress and achievement; and student support. There is an Aspect Group meeting for each area in which assessors interrogate staff. Often, staff are required to produce further documentary evidence, at short notice, as a consequence of concerns raised by assessors in Aspect Group meetings. Each aspect is scored out of four. The highest score for an institution is 24. There are three sources of data: observation of teaching sessions; interviews with students, staff and employers; and scrutiny of documentation. The latter is housed in a baseroom. This contains volumes of information about courses, quality assurance procedures, organizational policies, samples of student work, minutes of meetings, information to students, etc. For some, Subject Review is viewed as a valuable opportunity for organizational development and reflection. While others experience it as a highly corrosive form of performance and regulation.

Hence, it could be argued that quality assurance, as a regime of power, has both creative and oppressive potential in the academy today. However, the micro-level of experience can often be where the effects of power are felt (Morley 1999). I wish to argue that the quality assurance movement in higher education is having profound effects on the micropolitics of the academy. Quality has its own micropolitics and also exposes organizational micropolitics. Coalitions, inclusions, exclusions, networks, negative interpersonal relations and subterranean influences become particularly noticeable when organizations are under pressure.

I interviewed 20 women academics and managers in social science departments and faculties in 6 different institutions. All have been Subject Reviewed within the last 18 months. I was keen to gather some qualitative data relating to women's experiences of Subject Review. I was also interested in gendered interpretations of the process. The gendered division of labour and the themes of inclusion/exclusion and visibility/invisibility recurred throughout my data. One informant commented on the surface and subterranean distribution of responsibility:

> What was very noticeable was that not a senior male colleague was in sight during the extensive preparations for Subject Review. Most of the work was done by women on lecturer grade, administrators, librarians.... The morning the assessors arrived, the women were almost literally shooed off and a tier of senior men in suits came on the scene to represent the organisation. (Lecturer)

There seems to be a key issue of embodiment here, with message systems about who is seen to be in control, rather than who does the work. It would appear that women are often the organizational Morelocks – the creatures who live underground and service the 'Upper World' people (Wells 1971). Smith theorized the social division of labour as far back as 1987. She highlighted how women's invisible labour promotes men's authority. Davies (1996) also wrote about women's 'adjunct' roles whereby male professionals are kept aloof and elite by armies of women who deal with all the clutter. It would appear that women's labour is being appropriated in the extensive preparations for Subject Review, and that this is often unrecognized and unacknowledged.

The war effort

Subject Review can be experienced as a battle, a war, and a mobilization against a common threat. This can encourage a particular form of masculinity that is oppressive to those men and women who do not subscribe to macho combative interactions. One of my informants commented, that, when certain male colleagues were involved, the entire process seemed like a virility test!

> They found the stress exhilarating.... Also, the male assessors only really seemed to value what other men were saying.... In the Aspect Group meetings, they interrupted women, told them that time was running out every time that they attempted to speak. (Personnel Officer)

Collegiality and the strengthening of professional relations as a consequence of the enhanced contact preparing for Subject Review was highlighted by several of my informants. Some theorists have deconstructed collegiality and exposed it as a gendered form of social relations, whereby men are seen as more equal colleagues than women (Bensimon 1995; Deem and Ozga 2000). However, some of my informants used the term collegiality to describe support from certain other women that was noticed as a consequence of working through the night to produce evidence for assessors for the next morning.

> It was like a kind of war effort! The assessors were all so obnoxious and authoritarian that we all formed a united front. . . . I now have much stronger bonds with some of my women colleagues. (Senior Lecturer)

It is interesting to note that the emphasis was on the positive relationship building, rather than on the unhealthy working practices and long hours culture demanded by the methodology. This observation also suggests that women's emotional labour, that is, offering support to colleagues under stress, is being appropriated in the service of quality assurance. However, a sense of collegiality can be a potent antidote to the feelings of isolation and separation many professional women experience.

A further reading could be that 'soft' management skills are being deployed to manipulate colleagues into working long hours. I question whether collegiality is a form of capillary power, with colleagues reinforcing dominant cultures and corporate goals. Furthermore, 'war effort' and collegiality can also reinforce hegemonies, by assuming shared values, goals and lifestyles. Nixon *et al.* (1998: 283) suggest that collegiality 'is one of those words . . . that often masks complex power relations and the manipulative practices to which these can give rise.' It would be erroneous to represent women academics in terms of victim narratives and to ignore hierarchies and power relations among women. One of my lesbian informants noted:

> During the run up to Subject Review, many of the 'straight' women at work gained a lot of points by going on about how they hadn't seen their husbands and children all week as they had been working such long hours. . . . As a lesbian, I was not entitled to speak about the effect of overwork on my relationship . . . because it isn't a real relationship, is it? (Lecturer)

It would appear, from this observation, that work-related sacrifices are perceived as greater if made within a heterosexual relationship.

(E)qual opportunities?

Women's exclusion from positions of authority in the academy has been well documented. Overall women hold 35% of lecturer posts, but account for only 10% of professors. Latest figures from the Higher Education Statistics Agency (HESA) show that the average female academic will earn four to five years' less salary than an average male colleague for the same number of years worked and that 42% of women academics have full-time permanent positions compared to 59% of men. Women are 33% more likely than men to be employed on fixed-term contracts and 550% less likely to be professors (*Guardian* 1999).

Some of my informants felt that Subject Review offered them the opportunity to gain authority and to influence their organizations, particularly in relation to equity issues, student services and staff development. They also commented on the opportunities for women's enhanced visibility and career opportunities as a consequence of their centrality in Subject Review.

> The women in our organization always come out really well in Subject Reviews . . . their organisation skills are noticeable and also it provides an opportunity to parade all the student services that are usually invisibly carried out by women. (Quality Assurance Officer)

However, the visibility could also be about making women more governmentable and knowable. Subject Review can enable women to enter the managerial elite in organizations, and sometimes help fulfil ideological and career aspirations concerned with influence and change agency. For feminists, the move into quality management can often be accompanied by the imperative to moderate radical ideals and compromise values (Deem and Ozga 2000). Two informants stressed how women who had 'performed' well in Subject Review frequently went on to more senior management posts elsewhere within a year. Another informant noted how processes such as Subject Review:

> take women out of their invisible corners and place them nearer to the centre of power in their organisations . . . they get to see 'the bigger picture' in higher education and suddenly become known, noticed and valued by their Deans. (Assistant Registrar)

This raises questions about whether Subject Review creates career opportunities for women, or pushes them into a career pathway strongly associated with organizational housekeeping. In much of professional life there is a thin line between opportunity and exploitation. In relation to Subject Review, some women move away from the status of research activity and into the world that ties them to organizational development, new managerialism, presenteeism and responsibilization. In a two-tiered higher education system, it would be interesting to track where these women go to further their careers. Women are already disproportionately concentrated in areas and institutions with the lowest levels of research funding (Lafferty and Fleming 2000).

Women, in general, apply for fewer research grants than men (The Wellcome Trust 1997). A recent survey carried out by the National Centre for Social Research discovered that women academics are less likely than men to be eligible to apply for research funding as a consequence of being on fixed-term contracts, or being in more junior posts (NCSR 2000). Gender discrimination in the academy means that women do not always meet the eligibility criteria. This produces a vicious circle – women are too busy teaching or administrating, too junior, too precariously employed to gain major research grants. They are then ineligible to apply for senior posts, as they have no major research grants. In addition to these structural barriers, there are attitudinal barriers. In Sweden, Wenneras and Wold (1997) found that eligibility criteria were gendered and that women needed to be two and a half times more productive in terms of publications than their male counterparts to get the same rating for scientific competence.

Some of the most elite research organizations also have the worst record on gender equity. For example, Cambridge did not allow women graduates full status until 1947. Today, only 6% of Cambridge professors are women (compared to a national average of 10%). Even at lecturer level, women only make up 15% compared with 20% nationally (Cole 1999). The 'student experience' is also highly gendered in these institutions, with more male students awarded first class honours degrees (Leman and Mann 1999).

The two accounting systems in the UK (research and teaching and learning) are gendered and are contributing to polarized employment regimes. There is a danger that women will eventually be squeezed out of high status research work. This has serious implications for the ideological base of the knowledge that is produced and disseminated, and for women's career development. The exclusion of many women from research opportunities might account for why so many get sucked into quality assurance procedures for teaching and learning. For them, this provides a welcome opportunity to be included and valued.

The unhealthy organization

Economic rationalism and the reassessment of the economic benefits of educational spending has created considerable pressure to produce and perform. The quality discourse in the UK is not being applied to employment conditions. Academics are expected to mine their resources to be increasingly creative, supportive and managerial. Fast capitalism is requiring more of people and creating an unhealthy imbalance between work and life (Knight and Trowler 2000). The demand for more marketable educational products, or the vocational drift, is redefining academics as service providers and consumers of resources. They have to be the disembodied facilitators of others, with no needs, or fallabilities. The industrialization of higher education means that the product, the production plant and its workers must exhibit zero defect properties. The continuous improvement discourse is reminiscent of the cultural pressures on women in general to strive for perfection. It also echoes another major regulatory force, that is, that of original sin. Women enter the academy as flawed and imperfect academics and they have to struggle to redeem themselves.

While quality assurance can create discursive space for professionals to reflect and refine practice, taxonomies of effectiveness are predetermined and non-negotiable. Funding is based on performance indicators which are often experienced as reductive and over-simplistic. There is an obsession with classifications and boundaries – disciplinary, administrative boundaries to regulate the chaos of massification. Feminists have long argued that disciplinary boundaries are social constructions, invariably representing the interests of the dominant group. Subject Review currently audits by 42 academic disciplines. Interdisciplinary provision, such as Women's Studies, has to be inserted into the old classifications. Henkel (2000) argues that boundaries between the state, the market and the academy have also been reconceptualized. Employers increasingly demand information about the content of qualifications. Hence subject benchmarking is now well underway. This process, orchestrated by the Quality Assurance Agency, identifies key components of qualifications. This could be paving the way for a national curriculum for higher education in Britain.

The world of impression management, judgements and penalties is creating new professional subjectivities, new modes of description and new organizational identities. Complex organizations are granularized, that is, reduced to a myriad of parts and reconstituted to represent a 'pure' whole, containing certain knowledge about processes and practices (Guile 2001). Impression management or the process of making tacit practices explicit requires an element of performativity and textual representation that is temporally and emotionally demanding and potentially demoralizing (Jeffrey and Woods 1996). Prescribing what must be recorded and how, is itself a system of power and governmentability. Sennett (1998) suggests that there is a mathematics of fear. In the high risk, low trust culture, academics and managers have to decode, calculate and identify and avert risk and reconstruct themselves textually in what is sometimes seen as creative retrospective archiving. While quality assurance purports to challenge routinization and time-serving complacency, it can also produce these dispositions. For example, performing within prescribed categories can be another form of routinization at work. The suspension of critical knowledge can be a form of occupational stress for academics. While one of the justifications for quality assurance is to protect standards and prevent the 'dumbing down' of higher education, one of my informants felt that Subject Review itself represented a major form of 'dumbing down'.

> I feel that Subject Review is anti-intellectual, as it allows no space for critical engagement...we are just told what to do and we have to dumb down and present ourselves as certain and closed as complexity, ambiguity and contestation get low scores.... If you are judged against your own aims and objectives, it is better not to be too ambitious! (Head of Department)

The audit culture can appear to promote discursive space for reflection on practice, but when it is so highly performative, this can produce a 'counterfeit reflection' (Clegg 1999: 177). The reflection is prescribed and circumscribed by external agents. The reflection can be seen as another example of capillary power, with academics policing themselves and others in the service of quality assurance. This can result in an alienation that leads to disaffection. De Groot (1997: 134) characterized academic work in the 1990s in terms of three themes: 'alienation, anxiety and accountability'. By alienation she means:

> the growing sense of separation between work and personal identity experienced by many academics and to the experience of loss of control or even influence over many aspects of teaching, learning and research.
>
> (De Groot 1997: 134)

Ball (1999: 11) argues that alienation is a result of 'inauthentic practices and relationships'. Caught between the state, employers, the market, industry, student/consumers and the wider economic concepts of globalization, employability and international competitiveness, universities and academics in Britain are struggling with a hybrid identity that can be demoralizing and confusing.

There is a distorted belief that increasing workload leads to enhanced efficiency. More quality procedures are seen to equate with increased quality of services. There is a psychic economy involved in quality assurance. Occupational stress is one of the major challenges to the education profession (AUT 1997). There seems to be some correlation between high stress levels and high levels of regulation. Interestingly, this appears to be being globalized as well. For example, Lafferty and Fleming (2000) reported that, in the Australian Workplace Industrial Relations Survey, 35% of educational professionals reported high work intensification and stress, compared to 28% for all workplaces. All my informants commented on the intensification of labour demanded by Subject Review. The long hours culture *per se* did not cause resentment, it was the fact that long hours were required for performance within an alien discourse.

Without wishing to offer correlation/causation explanations, the over-regulation of public service professionals, compounded with low pay and decreasing security of tenure, might offer some explanatory power for the current recruitment and retention crisis in many sectors. Henkel (2000) reports how by 1997 more than one in ten lecturing staff in universities were on fixed-term contracts. She notes a tension between the traditional notion of intrinsic motivation among scholars dedicated to intellectual inquiry and the newer belief that quality can be enhanced by the creation of insecurity among academics. It appears that academics are being asked to demonstrate increasing commitment to their organizations, while the same commitment to them is not exhibited in terms of contracts and conditions of employment.

In their Australian study, Currie *et al.* (2000) discovered that what academics most valued and enjoyed doing was research. However:

> Most of academics' time, though, is not devoted to tasks associated with research or teaching.
>
> (Currie *et al.* 2000: 270)

Some of my informants commented that many of the men in their organizations protected their research time by refusing to be involved with any part of Subject Review.

> Many of our male professors were actually out of the country the week of Subject Review.... Then when they returned, they wanted to know why we had only got 23 instead of 24! (Lecturer)

There are questions about who takes the credit and who takes the blame. Low involvement, investment and visibility, but these senior men retained the right to call more junior women to account. There is also a contradictory consciousness at work here. While many critical thinkers in the academy are sceptical and intellectually opposed to the reductivism involved in Subject Review, they also seem to internalize the values attached to the scores.

Naming and shaming: the affective implications

Subject Review is a form of assessment and it has long been argued that there is a powerful affective impact of assessment in so far as it influences confidence, self-esteem and identity (Broadfoot 1998). Assessment also translates dominant discourses into broad social understandings and specific practices (Bernstein 1996). Quality, in the public services, invariably relates to performance, standards and output, rather than to inputs such as academic employment conditions.

New organizational regimes demand considerable temporal investment and emotional labour. Quality procedures require the activation and exploitation of a range of feelings such as guilt, loyalty, desire, greed, anxiety, shame and responsibilization, in the service of effectiveness and point-scoring (Ozga and Walker 1999). These feelings are easily activated and manipulated in today's fear-laden academic culture. Top-down bureaucratic requirements seem to be serving disciplinary functions, as one senior lecturer indicated:

> Managers used the threat of a low score in Subject Review to force us to attend endless meetings, which always felt tense and punitive. We were pushed to produce countless documents (many of which weren't even used for Subject Review).... We were told that a low score would mean fewer students and the possibility of redundancies... nasty bullying work practices ruled the day. (Senior Lecturer)

The language that many of my informants used was evocative of narratives of violence against women. Terms such as 'abusive', 'violation', 'bullying' were frequently invoked to describe the sense of invasion. The Quality Assurance Agency uses the terms 'light touch' and 'heavy touch', also implying an invasion of body space to a greater or lesser degree. Maybe academics need a 'Just Say No' campaign to reinstate boundaries!

The violence is encoded in the 'visitation' (note the religious undertones!), and also in the scoring. The quality machinery is labelling organizations and individuals by association. The labelling reaches interior spaces as well as public league tables. There are profound ontological issues at stake in the scoring of organizations. The culture of scrutiny implies deficiency and incompetence. It impacts on interpersonal relationships, self-esteem and organizational cultures. Quality audits represent a type of organizational trauma. Ostensibly, the scoring purports to offer value-added information. However, a low score is a badge of degradation. Within a performance culture to gain a low score is to be addressed and labelled injuriously.

Naming is a significant aspect in the constitution of identity. Butler (1997: 2) observed that: 'to be called a name is one of the first forms of injury that one learns.'

The labelling of universities iterates and inscribes the discourses in a complex chain of signification. Audit and the ensuing certification and grading means that private in-house matters are now in the public domain. The results of audit provide a reified reading, which becomes a truth. There is a strong relationship between identity and reputation. For universities at the bottom of the league tables, identity is a form of negative equity. The damage to reputation becomes an attack on the competence of every organizational member. For those at the top, there is an artificial halo effect, which invites the projection of a range of positive attributes on to their services. These identities have cash value in the market place, as they purport to speak directly to newly empowered student consumers.

Reconstructing students as consumers

The student voice is not that of the empowered citizen or social change agent, but that of the discerning consumer. Students' experiences are now more firmly located within the framework of customer care and consumer entitlements such as course handbooks, student charters and opinion surveys. The use of the definite article 'the' in relation to 'student experience' also homogenizes a diverse body. A further question is whether students can fully evaluate the quality of education they are receiving. Like surgery and legal advice, it is difficult for purchasers to evaluate at the point of delivery. Evaluation is often more related to the quality of service by which it is provided (Scott 1999). So, what is important now are features such as turnaround time for marking essays, access to tutors, transparent assessment procedures, etc. Meadmore (1998) argues that what is being taught or researched has become less important than it should be done 'excellently'. However, in a demand-led economy in which the customer is always right, it becomes more difficult to set boundaries of time and space. Several of my informants noted that it was becoming increasingly dangerous to try and set aside time for writing and research, as the dominant culture now is to be permanently accessible to students for fear of grievance procedures and negative student evaluations.

It is pertinent to ask what students have gained from quality assurance, and if processes like Subject Review have added any value to 'the student experience'. One of my informants felt that superficially services might seem to have improved. However, they were based on market exchange relations, rather than humanitarian commitment.

> As student recruitment, retention and completion are performance indicators, I think that, increasingly, student welfare is linked to keeping students on track for their economic value to the organisation. (Lecturer)

It is questionable whether students' interests are promoted in Subject Review.

In the market culture, are all student services manipulative? Students too, are being incorporated into the managerialist project. They are constantly asked to evaluate courses, to take time off work to sit on committees, meet Subject Reviewers and mentor new students. They have to live with the tension of quality audits and are often expected to represent their institutions as the authentic student voice. The emphasis on outcomes-based education is reducing their academic experiences to trades-based notions of competencies.

However, one informant felt that Subject Review had provided the opportunity to get better facilities for students with disabilities and for international students. This corresponds with Luke's observations (1997) that quality audits can bring marginalized groups of students under the spotlight. Yet again, quality is experienced as manipulative and oppressive by some, and as a creative and transformative space by others.

In terms of pedagogical practices, feminist discourses of empowerment are precariously positioned in the closed culture of predictable learning outcomes and teacher prescribed aims and objectives. Henkel (2000: 100) discovered that the closure enforced by Subject Review was disempowering students:

> Concepts of quality that elevated clarity of exposition, comprehensive handout material, contained and predictable learning formats above other values were encouraging passivity and dependence in students.

On the one hand, feminist pedagogy's concerns with student empowerment are being rearticulated in discourses of what constitutes quality teaching and learning. For example, groupwork, interactive approaches, rather than transmission, are heavily promoted as examples of 'good practice'. On the other hand, the emphasis on predictable learning outcomes represents a form of premature closure and teacher direction that contradicts the principles of negotiation, participation and the decentring of authority. Furthermore, the endless production of documentation for students, evaluation procedures and student consultations could also be perceived as another form of domination, with students' voices and time constantly colonized for the purposes of continuous improvement.

Quality as a greedy institution

The cost of quality assurance is difficult to estimate. The official figure is 0.1% of the Higher Education Funding Council's teaching budget dedicated to Subject Review (Yorke 1999). David Triesman, the former Secretary of the Association of University Teachers, recently reported that the costs of the inspections alone came to 300 million pounds, or the equivalent to 8,500 lecturing posts. So far, only six courses have found to be failing and four of those were franchised (2001). This figure excludes the costs incurred by institutions and the substantial opportunity costs of staff allocated to extensive preparations. When the whole organization, faculty or department is the unit of analysis, vast amounts of time are used ensuring ownership and information flow. Newton (2000) describes quality audits as 'feeding the beast', with ritualistic practices by academics seeking to meet accountability requirements.

Approximately 10,000 people – most of them academics – have been involved in inspecting universities and higher education colleges over the past seven years. More than 2,000 individual institutions have undergone Subject Review. Academics in the Economics Department at Warwick estimated that Subject Review cost their department between £150,000 to £200,000 in staff time alone (*Guardian* 30/1/2001). In his response, John Randall, the former chief executive of the Quality Assurance Agency, argued that academic time should be spent on monitoring standards and ensuring fitness for purpose anyway, not just for the purposes of Subject Review (*Guardian* 6/2/2001). However, my informants commented both on the material costs and the opportunity costs, with questions about the compatibility of the two accounting systems:

> I lost nine months research time, as a consequence of all the documentation that I had to produce for Subject Review. I had to re-negotiate a deadline for a book that would have done my career more good! (Senior Lecturer)

This raises important questions about collective and individual good, with the above woman academic sacrificing her own career interests for the good of the organization. Henkel (2000: 217) also noted a newly emerging division of labour:

> staff, previously valued for their contribution to institutional and departmental reputations, could find themselves valued instead for shouldering teaching loads that would enable others to bring in research resources and make reputations.

Henkel does not attempt to gender this division of labour. I wish to argue that Subject Review, and the accompanying preoccupation with teaching and learning, requires significant amounts of self-sacrifice which is profoundly gendered. This is evocative of Handy's (1993) notion of the psychological contract between employees and their organization. This self-sacrifice is often resented when irrationalities and profligacy are observed:

> Money is very tight in our organisation. We can never afford to go to conferences, buy in visiting speakers etc. However, vast amounts of money were suddenly found for our Subject Review... extra secretarial hours, new equipment, fancy documentation for the reviewers. (Lecturer)

Foyerization and impression management is very noticeable. It is feeding the power of the assessors. At a national workshop I attended on preparation for Subject Review, we were briefed by an assessor for the natural sciences about what to provide for assessors in the baseroom. She told us to provide fresh, not instant coffee, fresh fruit, mineral water, flowers, natural light, lists of good restaurants in the area, etc. As I mentioned earlier, quality assurance is producing new systems of power in the academy, with organizations being held hostage to the caprices, obsessions and agendas of assessors.

While the evidence for the cost of Subject Review is fairly uneven, so too is the evidence of the benefits. In a policy context of best value and evidence-based research, what value do the QAA Subject Review and Research Assessment Exercise add? How reliable are they as tests? In Subject Review, there is a correlation/causation link between teaching and learning, with an assumption that good learning follows excellent teaching. The organization is seen as the central site for intervention, with socio-economic considerations carefully edited out of the equation. This raises questions about the central premise and the methodology of Subject Review.

The end of the peer show

Subject Review purports to be more collegial as it is executed by peers. Equally, in the tradition of academic endeavour, externality is seen to represent objectivity (Reay 2000). With peer review there is both a blurring and marking out of boundaries. One of my informants was very cynical about the concept of 'peerness':

> To call these ghastly, low-calibre people peers was over-generous! . . . They had fewer publications between them than any one of us had in our department. . . . They had appalling interpersonal skills and spent the week revelling in the power they had acquired as very mediocre academics. (Head of Department)

This raises questions about shared values in the so-called academic community. The London School of Economics voted 70 to 2 to reform, transform or terminate the QAA. One of their many concerns also related to the quality and prior agendas of the assessors:

> Our colleagues have been perturbed by the nature of review teams, and great variations in their calibre – in their preparation and professionalism; academic competence and reputation; dispositions towards both the departments visited and towards the LSE; and their intentions to impose their own pedagogical agenda.
>
> (Draft resolution to LSE Academic Board, 14 March 2001)

This is open to multiple readings. Is this resistance to the domination of the QAA, or the refusal of an elite organization to make itself accountable to a wider constituency? Either way, it raises questions about the nature of peerness, and whether it actually exists in stratified higher education systems.

Excellent studies have been produced on the impact of policy changes on the academic profession (e.g. Henkel 2000). However, gender is only mentioned *en passant* as a constituent of identity. Social structures and diversity relating to race, class, sexuality and disability do not enter into the debate on 'peerness'. The pervasive clichés of 'best/good practice' and 'excellence' imply discursive orthodoxy, normalization techniques and common goals. One of my informants commented on how bruised she had felt by a colleague's observation of her teaching in preparation for Subject Review:

> I was told that my teaching was too emotional and that I was forcing gender issues down my students' throats.... It took me ages to see that as my observer's problem, rather than mine. (Lecturer)

The scoring of Subject Review is supposed to be based on how organizations meet their own aims and objectives. They are not to be judged against national or local benchmarks. The market culture has created considerable competition among organizations. Yet, peers are expected to enter organizations altruistically and with no prior agendas, expectations or prejudices. Whose interests do assessors represent – the evaluative state, the academic 'community', their own, sometimes fractured identities? The peer issue poses questions about whether feminists should be assessors. Can feminists claim to be value free? This reflects the age-old debate about change from within or without. By accepting to act as assessors are academics colluding in an oppressive technology, or protecting their colleagues from a worse fate? One of my informants noted that in her opinion, it could not get much worse!

> I have been inspected by OFSTED and the QAA now...they always say that the QAA peer review is more collegial...I don't agree. At least with OFSTED, there is some accountability and rights of appeal. There is some notion of professionalism.... Whereas our Subject Reviewers were amateurish and seemed to be totally unaccountable in the way that they behaved. (Senior Lecturer)

The lack of accountability and the limited opportunity to reply suggest that Subject Review is currently a one-way gaze, reminiscent of pornographic objectification.

The whole truth

The methodology of Subject Review is open to feminist and postmodernist critique, as there are elements of positivism with audits claiming to be able to unearth a 'truth' about the complexities of organizational life, simply by consulting the 'right' documents and asking the 'right' people. The readings become 'truths', encoded in league tables and reified for several years. This is in direct opposition to postmodern and feminist research paradigms which suggest multiple readings, situated interpretations and discontinuities. The crisis of representation and the plurality of texts are not considered in Subject Review. The imperative to represent one's organization textually imposes a modernist rationality and a set of certainties that cannot exist in complex organizations. For example, organizations are regularly required to provide audit trails documenting how issues/student concerns etc. move through the committee cycle to a satisfactory resolution.

These imply a linear rationality which completely overlooks micropolitics, creative non-implementation, and the politics of non-decision-making (Lukes 1974).

Elsewhere, the methodology has also been criticized for being too 'soft' and open to distortion. Economists at Warwick felt that:

> The method is not scientific. We supplied the hypothesis, the evidence and the witnesses. We chose the students and employers, the samples of student work, and the internal documentation to be seen by the panel.
>
> (*Guardian* 30/1/2001)

Whatever the ideological hue, there are widespread beliefs that the methodology of Subject Review is characterized by *ad hocery*, instability and unreliability.

Conclusion

The academy has always been an unfriendly and fairly dangerous place for women. There are differing views about whether Subject Review is an ally or enemy to women's interests. The quality assurance movement is a system of coercion and domination. Women academics' precarious and predominantly junior positions in the academy make them more vulnerable to bullying, manipulation and compliance. Quality assurance is producing docile bodies as the consequences of resistance are too high. There is a powerful rhetoric of inevitability, or a TINA effect ('there is no alternative'), and a ludic engagement with quality assurance (Morley 2001). Walkerdine (1989) argued long ago that femininity is performance. I argue that quality assurance too is performance. Women's gender socialization makes them particularly well-schooled players. This can produce both losses and gains. In some cases, women report identity enhancement and increased career opportunities, along a management track. In other cases, women express a sense of loss and deviation from research-based, high-status academic careers. Subject Review is contradictorily perceived as developmental, stressful, wasteful and simultaneously instrumental in career progression and career demise.

The impact of quality assurance on the affective domain, professional identities and creativity is under-theorized in relation to gender in the academy. Narratives of declining standards and quality procedures activate and exploit a range of feelings in the service of effectiveness and point scoring. School-based education in Britain is currently facing a crisis in recruitment and retention of teachers. The effect of OFSTED inspections on the self-esteem of teachers is beginning to be carefully documented. Hargreaves (1994) notes how the increased expectancy of service arouses intense feelings of guilt and shame in schoolteachers. In the academy, the process of naming and shaming speaks directly to women academics' outsider status and reinforces narratives of deficit and lack.

It could also be argued that the two major accounting systems in the UK reproduce the gendered division of labour in the academy, with women playing a central role in the domestic labour of quality assurance of teaching and learning. There is a psychic economy involved in Subject Review which is part of a gendered care chain. Women are being responsibilized in the service of quality assurance, with emotionally literate women recruited to ease the path of managerialism. This raises questions about whether the goals of feminist educators have been superseded or co-opted into the quality machinery.

The wastage of material and human resources in the service of Subject Review is a political scandal. Data gathering invariably entails extra work for women. The preparation of baserooms, documentation and audit trails are consuming women's time in a way that does not necessarily serve their long-term professional interests. Quality assurance is actively constructing, rather than measuring the academy and this has implications for women in terms of what is valued, rewarded or suppressed in the academy.

References

AUT (1997) *Combating Stress at Work* (London: AUT).

Ball, S. (1999) Performativities and Fabrications in the Education Economy: Towards the Performative Society? Paper presented at the AARE, Melbourne.

Bensimon, E. (1995) TQM in the academy: a rebellious reading, *Harvard Educational Review*, 4, 593–611.

Bernstein, B. (1996) *Pedagogy, Symbolic Control and Identity* (London: Taylor & Francis).

Broadfoot, P. (1998) Quality standards and control in higher education: what price life-long learning? *International Studies in Sociology of Education*, 8 (2), 155–80.

Butler, J. (1997) *Excitable Speech: A politics of the Performative* (London: Routledge).

Clegg, S. (1999) Professional education, reflective practice and feminism, *International Journal of Inclusive Education*, 3 (2), 167–79.

Cole, P. (1999) To what extent is the culture of a university department supportive of equal opportunities for women? *International Studies in Sociology of Education*, 8 (3), 271–97.

Currie, J., Harris, P. and Thiele, B. (2000) Sacrifices in greedy universities: are they gendered? *Gender and Education*, 12 (3), 269–91.

Davies, C. (1996). The sociology of professions and the profession of gender, *Sociology*, 30, 661–78.

Deem, R. and Oaga, J. (2000) Transforming post-compulsory education? Femocrats at work in the academy, *Women's Studies International Forum*, 23 (2), 153–66.

De Groot, J. (1997) After the ivory tower: gender, commodification and the 'academic', *Feminist Review*, 55 (Spring), 130–42.

Guardian (1999) Class acts, *Guardian Higher Education*, 9 March, i.

Guardian (2001) Trial by ordeal, 30 January, 12.

Guardian (2001) Belief system, 6 February, 15.

Guile, E. D. (2001) MA Seminar at the Institute of Education, 13 March.

Handy, C. (1993) *Understanding Organizations*, 4th edn (Harmondsworth: Penguin).

Hargreaves, A. (1994) *Changing Teachers, Changing Times: Teachers Work and Culture in the Postmodern Age* (London: Cassell).

Henkel, M. (2000) *Academic Identities and Policy Changes in Higher Education* (London: JKP).

Jeffrey, B. and Woods, P. (1996) Feeling deprofessionalized: the social construction of emotions during an Ofsted inspection, *Cambridge Journal of Education*, 26 (3), 325–43.

Knight, P. and Trowler, P. (2000) Editorial, *Quality in Higher Education*, 6 (2), 109–14.

Lafferty, G. and Fleming, J. (2000) The restructuring of academic work in Australia: power, management and gender, *British Journal of Sociology of Education*, 21 (2), 257–67.

Leman, P. and Mann, C. (1999) Gender differences in students' performances in examinations: the Cambridge University project, in P. Fogelberg, J. Hearn, L. Husu and Mankkinen (ed.) *Hard Work in the Academy: Research and Interventions on Gender Inequalities in Higher Education* (Helsinki: Helsinki University Press), 83–92.

London School of Economics (2001) Draft resolution to LSE Academic Board, 14 March.

Luke, C. (1997) Quality assurance and women in higher education, *Higher Education*, 33, 433–51.

Lukes, S. (1974) *Power: A Radical View* (London: Macmillan).

Meadmore, D. (1998) Changing the culture: the governance of the Australian pre-millennial university, *International Studies in Sociology of Education*, 8, 27–45.

Morley, L. (1999) *Organising Feminisms: The Micropolitics of the Academy* (London: Macmillan).

Morley, L. (2001) Comedy of manners: quality and power in higher education, in P. Trowler (ed.) *Higher Education Policy and Institutional Change* (Buckingham: SRHE/Open University Press).

NCSR (National Centre for Social Research) (2000) *'Who Applies for Research Funding?'* (London: National Centre for Social Research).

Newton, J. (2000) Feeding the beast or improving quality? Academics' perceptions of quality assurance and quality monitoring, *Quality in Higher Education*, 6 (2), 153–63.

Nixon, J., Beattie, M. and Walker, M. (1998) What does it mean to be an academic? A colloquium, *Teaching in Higher Education*, 3 (3), 277–98.

Ozga, J. and Walker, L. (1999) In the company of men, in S. Whitehead and R. Moodley (eds) *Transforming Managers* (London: UCL Press), 107–19.

Reay, D. (2000) 'Dim dross': marginalised women both inside and outside the academy, *Women's Studies International Forum*, 23 (1), 13–22.

Scott, S. (1999) The academic as service provider: is the customer 'always right'? *Journal of Higher Education Policy and Management*, 21 (2), 193–202.

Sennett, R. (1998) *The Corrosion of Character: The Personal Consequences of Work in the New Capitalism* (New York: Norton).

Shaw, J. (1995) *Education, Gender and Anxiety* (London: Taylor & Francis).

Smith, D. (1987) *The Everyday World as Problematic: A Feminist Sociology* (Milton Keynes: Open University Press).

Triesman, D. (2001) Keynote address to the AUT Annual Women's Conference, London, 8 March.

Walkerdine, V. (1989) Femininity as performance, *Oxford Review of Education*, 15 (3), 267–79.

Wellcome trust (1997) *Women and Peer Review: An Audit of the Wellcome Trust's Decision-making on Grants* (London: The Wellcome Trust).

Wells, H. G. (1971) *The Time Machine* (London: Heinemann).

Wenneros, C. and Wold, A. (1997) Nepotism and sexism in peer review, *Nature*, 387, 341–3.

Yorke, M. (1999) *Leaving Early: Undergraduate Non-completion in Higher Education* (London: The Falmer Press).

8 'Bodies are dangerous'

Using feminist genealogy as policy studies methodology

Wanda Pillow

University of Illinois, Urbana-Champaign

Source: *Journal of Education Policy*, 18 (2): 145–59, 2003.

Introduction

'Yes, but is what you're doing policy analysis?' was the question put to me after a presentation on my use of 'embodied analysis' on a panel with other educational policy colleagues at AERA. I think I stumbled over the question a bit, likely providing a response that was not satisfactory to the questioner, but this query has hung with me as I continue to think about, and others want to, determine where my work fits. If I do bodies, do I really do policy?

This question arises not only because as a qualitative researcher connections to policy analysis seem tenuous in a field dependent upon rational numbers, but also because of the theoretical and methodological lens I work through – namely race-feminisms[1] and post-structuralisms, including specifically uses of Foucault's genealogy. A genealogical analysis necessarily focuses upon bodes and tracing the discursive reproductions of bodies. Perhaps the question above was posed because attention to bodies, particularly in education, seems taboo, too personal or playful; certainly not real policy work and unrelated to viable policy recommendations. Is there a place in the field of policy studies, an arena dependent upon rational data even in the midst of 'messiness', for the theories of race-feminism and post-structuralism, the use of genealogies and discussions of bodies? After all, as a school administrator instructed me during my research on teen pregnancy, 'bodies are dangerous'.

Yet, at the same time and likely precisely because 'bodies are dangerous' policies are all about bodies – controlling, regulating, shaping and (re)producing bodies. Bodies, nevertheless, remain uncontrollable in many ways, receptive to and disruptive of power. What would it mean then to pay attention to the body, literally and figuratively, in policy analysis? While attention to the body as a methodological site from which to theorize, analyse and practice is not new (Diprose 1994; Grosz 1995; Pillow 1997b; Williams and Bendelow 1998), attention to bodies in educational policy research remains largely absent. The previous two decades have, however, produced a plethora of new works and theories critiquing and developing reconceptualizations of power, the state and the policy process. MacKinnon's (1989) ground-breaking work on the state and feminist theory, increased influences of the writings of Foucault, and the proliferation of critical policy research (Troyna 1994) have all contributed to the beginnings of a rethinking of patriarchy, power and control in the arena of policy studies. This effort has included, but is not limited to, a multidisciplinary research focus upon the state's role in the reproduction of male dominance and racialized inequities (Connell 1987; Gordon 1990; Solinger 1992; Parker 1998); reconceptualizations of power and the power of the state (Ball 1990; Scheurich 1994); reconsideration of agency, resistance and of the policy text (Ball 1994; Haney 1996; Pillow 1997a); and critiques of traditional forms of policy development and analysis (Marshall *et al.* 1989; Carlson 1993; Kelley and Maynard-Moody 1993; Scheurich 1994; Marshall 1997; Pillow 1997a,b; Parker 1998).

This work has been necessitated in part by the recognition that institutionalized policies often have many shortcomings and may even serve to debilitate the exact condition they wish to advocate (Elmore 1983; McLaughlin 1990, 1991). Yet, despite this influx of critique and critical discussion, the arena of policy studies remains dependent upon a technical-rational assessment framework to predict, influence and explain the policy process from development to implementation and outcome, even while those involved in the policy process find it to be highly politicized and even irrational. Since its inception, educational politics and policy has largely centred around the questions of who gets what or the informal and formal mechanisms by which individuals or groups influence the decision-making process as well as resulting policy outcomes[2] (Stout *et al.* 1994; Stone 1998) and the arena of educational policy studies has been criticized for relying upon positivistic methods assuming a political neutrality, ignoring larger sociological, cultural influences and inadequately studying the interactions of gender, race, class and sexuality (Ladner 1987; Ladson-Billings and Tate 1995; Mac an Ghaill 1996; Marshall 1997). Only recently has policy studies reliance upon such rational, scientific models of explanation been put under suspicion (Ball 1990; Griffith 1992; Carlson 1993; Scheurich 1994; Hargreaves 1996). These works turn the lens of analysis upon policy studies itself, tracing the limits of its ideology and methods.

This paper continues this line of critical questioning by exploring the possibilities for the methodological work of race-feminist poststructuralism in policy studies[3] through a methodology I term *feminist genealogy* (Pillow 1997a). Feminist genealogy builds from the work of Foucault read through and with race-feminisms and focuses specific attention upon the discursively structured raced, gendered and sexed body. Feminist genealogy *embodies* policy analysis, forefronting and refiguring conceptualizations of bodies, power and knowledge in policy studies. Specifically, I consider the uses of feminist genealogy in developing and analysing policy for certain types of bodies – in this case teen pregnant female bodies.[4]

A feminist genealogy as methodology can provide several avenues of analysis within educational policy analysis. It can, for example, be used to reinterpret power, truth, ontology and subjectivity (Ferguson 1991; Mahon 1992; McCoy and Pillow 1995). In this paper, I focus specifically upon genealogy as a form of historical, discursive critique, which 'recognizes that the things, values and events of our present experience have been constituted historically, discursively, and practically' (Mahon 1992: 14). Further, genealogy as critique 'reveals the contingency, even arbitrariness, of what appears natural and necessary and thereby it serves to open possibilities' (Mahon 1992: 14). Feminist genealogy locates the work of genealogy as critique within the body, a methodology that *embodies* policy analysis.

Why bodies?

Before considering just what feminist genealogy is and what use it is as an educational policy studies methodology, I first want to make a case for bodies. As will be detailed later in this paper, Foucault's discussion of genealogy is focused upon the body and, thus, feminist genealogy cannot be separated from an understanding of the importance of the body in social organization, theorizing, power and practice. Here I provide a narrative of how I came to turn, and return, to bodies in my research. These turns occurred because of the many paradoxes I observed in development, implementation and analysis of teen pregnancy policy in schools – often an utter disconnect between policy and the lives of teen mothers – and, my need to attempt to understand how such policies seemed rational.

For two years I was a researcher and itinerant teacher in a school-based teen pregnancy programme. This programme, implemented in nine states, requires the teen mother to return to school two weeks after the birth of her child or have welfare support suspended. The programme, operating under an ideology of 'tough love' and an assumption that the visibility of teen pregnancy can make it spread like a virus,[5] does not advocate the provision of school-based or assisted child care for teen mothers and, indeed, in most schools stuck with a strict rule of 'No Children Allowed'.[6] Thus, during my research, I found myself struck by the irony of sitting in a 7:35 am class for teen mothers listening to lessons on appropriate parenting (including bonding and breast feeding as well as best practice tips on speaking, playing and reading to your baby) while the young women and myself were all separated from our infants and children.

How/why did it make sense to those who developed and oversaw implementation of this programme to develop such policies and guidelines? How is it that the educational policies and programmes I observed were so far removed from the lived experiences of teen mothers? It would be easy here to say the discrepancy between the policy and the needs of new mothers and their children is due to the fact that the majority of policy players, state-level decision makers, are male – and I would agree this demographic does impact the development of gendered and raced policies. However, I believe this story and analysis is more complicated than a tale of 'bad patriarchical' policy-makers. While it is true the majority of decision makers who first developed and approved of the teen pregnancy programme I analysed were male, there were females involved in all steps of development and implementation, and many of these males and females were parents themselves, and, thus, it would seem, knowledgeable about the demands of parenting. Furthermore, all of the teachers in the school-based programmes I observed were female. Yet, the majority of teachers ignored the physicality of the pregnant teen body, even when faced daily with the needs of this body (Pillow 1997b).

I needed to find a way to both address and readdress the issues and paradoxes evident in teen pregnancy educational policy. When I began collecting data – conducting observations and interviews with teen mothers – I assumed I would write a story with the girls about teenage pregnancy. A story that would highlight the girls voices and their constructions of their lives as young women, mothers and students. However, I began to feel the gaps in such a story, gaps which continued to place the focus of attention and responsibility on the teen mother herself without questioning larger social constructions of teen pregnancy as a social, education and policy problem. At the same time, I was struck by both the silences and proliferation of discourses surrounding teen pregnancy. The teen pregnant girl as a subject is both silenced and over produced in discourses (political, social, moral) of teen pregnancy. Further discourse surrounding teen pregnancy is in the US highly differentiated by race and class, thus marking which girls and teen mothers are the problem in the problem of teen pregnancy.

I wanted to shift the gaze of inquiry from the girls themselves to the discourses shaping and defining teen pregnancy, without losing the context of the girls lived experiences. My attempts to question the relationships between macro- and micro-level policy development and implementation led me over and over gain, radically, back to the body. Reading Trinh's (1989) mobile subjectivities with Ferguson's (1991) ironic interventions, through Spivak's (1993) notion of working within and against, Butler's (1993) bodies that matter, Quinby's (1994) 'pissed criticism', Lesko's (1995) 'leaky needs' and Singer's (1993) conceptualization of erotic welfare, I find myself drawn to the possibilities of an interruptive excessiveness of bodies and theory.

At first, my readings and connections between feminist and post-structural constructions of the body and policy were timid. The messy physicality of a talk of bodies felt somehow taboo, forbidden and out of place in rational policy discourse. *Body* is a promiscuous term. However, in attempting to understand policy in the context of specific lives, I repeatedly returned to a notion of embodiment. This move to the body is not merely a romanticized celebration of the body (a goddess worshiping of the body), but as Grosz (1995: 2) states 'more an enjoyment of the unsettling effects that rethinking bodies implies for those knowledges that have devoted so much conscious and unconscious effort to sweeping away all traces of the specificity, the corporeality, of their own processes of production and representation'.

Bodies represent and are represented. Whether rendered invisible, portrayed romantically, described with statistics, fear, repulsion or pity, policies are about and for bodies. Our body is inescapable and cannot be lost in a chain of reference. Bodies are always already cultural artifacts (Foucault 1974/1990). Silverman (1988: 146) writes: 'Even if we could manage to strip away the discursive veil that separates the subjects from his or her "actual" body, that body would itself bear no unmistakable stamp of culture'. Culture, power, inscribes both on and in the body. Bodies are sites and centres of struggles between different power formations. Bodies bear the marks of these struggles and are also marked differently – processes and constructs of gender, race and class impact which bodies are marked and how they are marked. As Fay (1987: 146) points out that 'oppression leaves its traces not just in people's minds, but in their muscles and skeletons as well'. Bodies then also bear the weight of discursive representations. Women's bodies have been especially marked. On the one hand, motherhood is as Wilton (1990: 182) states a 'political status through which a woman achieves a place in the socio-political order'. On the other hand, Wilton (1990: 182) continues it is '*precisely* because of their ability to mother that women's bodies (and their political and social selves) have been so rigidly controlled within all patriarchal political systems'. States intervene in the child-bearing of women when at any time they feel a threat – morally, culturally or economically. Threats may occur through hegemonic alarm over who should give birth – for example, should unmarried women be supported on public welfare – or who is perceived to be giving birth, as captured by the fear of a 'browning of America' in the 1990s.[7] The threat of what and who is constructed as irresponsible childbearing means that some women are subjected to direct state control, surveillance and intervention of their sexual practices. As Thomas (1998: 439) notes, past and current framings of the problem of unwed motherhood and resulting policy responses cannot be understood nor separated from the 'history of racism, sterilization abuse and the devaluation of African American motherhood' in the US. Further to these discourses, practices and resulting social science literature have reproduced long-standing stereotypes pathologizing the sexuality, morals and mothering of African American, American Indian and most recently Latina's in the US.

Teen pregnancy encapsulates the above fears, stereotypes and threats and is repeatedly targeted as a national policy problem. The body is inescapable (although both proliferated and silenced) in teen pregnancy research and policy (Pillow 1997a,b). The teen pregnant body is a site of state regulation and control not only of the teen mother, but also a site for the regulation and reassertion of societal norms, morals and values on issues such as female sexuality, single-parenting, welfare, birth control and abortion. Teen pregnancy as an educational policy issue specifically challenges norms, morals and values around adolescent sexuality, female sexuality and sex education. The teen pregnant body has also proven to be a body that cannot be simply contained or fixed; it is excessive and leaky, not easily predicted or programmed for under traditional policy studies.

Feminist genealogy and bodies

If I begin from a position that 'bodies matter', how can I carefully pay attention to bodies in policy analysis. Foucault's reformulation of Nietzsche's genealogy is particularly useful for such a project. Foucault's use of genealogy reconceptualizes history, power, subjects and political discourse. The form of critical inquiry Foucault calls genealogy provides a forum for decentring what we think we know and for tracing how we come to know it. Such knowing according to Foucault is always embedded within power relations. Power operates as a productive, positive force not only as a repressive force and the discourses and practices of power are present not only in legitimate or institutionalized centres of power, but in the micro-levels of experience. This is biopower – power that operates upon the body.

Genealogy pays implicit attention to details, thus unmasking and questioning what seems innate or natural; it exposes the power of the norm. Genealogy as a form of analysis interrupts simple reversal strategies of displacement. As Ferguson (1991: 3) states, 'genealogical reversals do not restabilize cause/effect relations in the opposite direction so much as they unsettle any effort to conceptualize singular or linear relations between events and practices'. A genealogy, thus, brings notions of subjects, agency and bodies into genealogy as inquiry'. In this way, genealogy provides a means to situate and understand the discourses of power and practice that influence the naming, defining and living of teenage pregnancy. This process interrupts traditional notions of subjectivity, takes into account the 'politics of the gaze' and focuses attention on not only the politics of what gets said about girls who are pregnant but how what is said about girls who are pregnant defines what we say.

Foucault's (1984: 83) discussion of genealogy is as a methodology that is 'grey, meticulous, and patiently documentary. It operates on a field of entangled and confused parchments, on documents that have been scratched over and recopied many times'. Foucault (1984: 83) also describes genealogy as an analysis of descent, 'situated within the articulation of the body and history. Its task is to expose a body totally imprinted by history and the processes of history's destruction of the body'. This historical tracing of descent (and also emergence) is not about a search for origins, but rather genealogy accounts for the 'disparate details, events and accidents found at any beginning' (Mahon 1992: 110). Further, historical work traces and locates conditions not only in macro-level structures but in micro-level practices, within bodies.

Genealogy as methodology is not counter to Foucault's discussion of archaeology, which Scheurich (1994) adapted into a new policy studies methodology in his article in this journal. While an archaeological analysis focuses upon an 'analysis of unconscious rules of formation' (Mahon 1992: 104) evident in discourses (see Scheurich 1994), genealogy, reveals 'the historical conditions of existence' and is concerned with 'technologies of power embodied in social practices' (Mahon 1992: 104). A genealogical analysis may engage in 'an archaeological analysis of discursive rules' while focused upon as Foucault states 'how those discursive events have determined in a certain way what constitutes our present and constitutes ourselves – either our knowledge, our practices, our type of rationality, our relationship to ourselves or to others' (Mahon 1992: 105). Similarly, my use and reformulation of Foucault's genealogy builds from Scheurich's work on archaeology as discursive policy studies methodology.

Thus, specifically, genealogy as policy studies methodology offers not only an analysis and critique of the policy problem at issue, but also an on-going analysis and critique of the arena of policy studies itself. Genealogy specifically challenges policy studies to rethink itself, and its subjects, across four axis: power, truth, rationality and subjectivity. Foucault's reformulation of power under genealogy disrupts understandings of power as one-way relationships and locates power in bodies. Further, genealogical analysis is suspicious of truth claims based upon assumed rationality and disputes understandings of subjects as singular, easily identifiable, linear subjects. Genealogy works to interrupt the common trend of commentary supporting 'tidy generalities' while ignoring 'messy realities' in policy studies (Ball 1990: 9).

Feminist genealogy builds from Foucault's work by focusing analysis upon historically and culturally situated decision-making, with particular attention to how gender, race and class shape in this case the policy process. Feminist genealogy pays explicit attention to 'messy realities' and questions that which seems the most natural, the most hegemonic, thus providing an ongoing critique and questioning of discourses (re)inscribing power, body, knowledge relationships. Influenced by Foucault's use and description of genealogy, this work turns repeatedly to the body and theories of the body to interrupt normative practices, unmask liberatory discourses, displace binaries and resist hierarchical arguments. However, a feminist genealogy is also immersed in the work of race-feminist theorists leading to a commitment to conduct analysis in such a way that the 'agency' of teen parents, while troubled, is not silenced. Thus, the analysis utilized in feminist genealogy is not simply resistant, but is meticulous in its search for the discursive strategies of power as they are camouflaged in the assumptive discourses and practices of policy theory, implementation and evaluation. A feminist genealogy further explores how these discourses are articulated, regulated, incorporated and resisted in programme discourses, classrooms, architecture, bodies and discourses of the self.

Turner (1984) describes four tasks of society related to the body that are useful to rethinking an embodiment of policy analysis through feminist genealogy: reproduction, regulation, restraint and representation. Feminist genealogical analysis of these four tasks of embodiment, four ways in essence that a society seeks to control and organize itself collectively, offers possibilities to interrupt the modernist problematics inherent in policy studies. Turner's typology forefronts the role policy plays in not only regulating and restraining bodies but also its role in representing and reproducing certain bodies – revealing how policy produces what Foucault (1979: 194) terms 'domains of objects and rituals of truth'. Through consideration of these tasks of embodiment educators, researchers and policy analysts are confronted with what is embodied within the 'problem' of teen pregnancy. Thus, a feminist genealogy begins to ask, not only how teen pregnancy is a problem, but rather how is the teen pregnant body represented, reproduced, regulated and restrained – and to what effects?

A feminist genealogical exposure of what is embodied but not said in teen pregnancy policy

Policies are value statements, rules to guide actions, interactions and construct bodies. Genealogy focuses upon the conditions that make the practices of policies 'acceptable at a given moment' (Mahon 1992: 129). According to Foucault, discourses and practices intertwine, supporting and reconstructing each other in a web of power/knowledge relations. Feminist genealogy provides a methodology through which to identify and trace these discursive practices and their effects.

In respect to analysis of teen pregnancy as an educational policy issue, I have utilized feminist genealogy to trace historical and present-day discourses impacting how the teen mother is defined and who she is defined as and how these discourses in turn impact and delimit the development and implementation of educational policy for the teen mother.[8] I utilize the meticulousness of feminist genealogy to locate ruptures and disjunctures in shifting definitions of the problem of teen pregnancy within economic, political, racial and moral climates. This tracing links and makes obvious that in the US who we think the teen mother is, who she is depicted as, is integrally linked with what type of education we think this teen mother needs and deserves (Pillow 2002).

In this way, feminist genealogy does not begin with an assumption or acceptance that how the problem of teen pregnancy has been defined is real or true. Rather feminist genealogy questions what is invested in such truths. This is not to deny that there are not lived ramifications of being a young mother. Building from recent social historical works which detail the gendered and raced ideological framework of the US welfare state and provide insight into the processes by which unwed motherhood in the US has been socially constructed (Abramovitz 1988; Gordon 1990; Solinger 1992; Kunzel 1993; Thomas 1998), feminist genealogy links the problem of early parenting to the status of unwed motherhood and also begins to link differences in treatment options available to the unwed mother to the race of the un-wed mother.[9] Consider, for example, the myriad of ways teen pregnancy has been constructed as a problem. Is teen pregnancy a problem of too early child-bearing or a problem of unwed motherhood? A problem of national decline of family values or of (certain) female sexual immorality? Compounding these questions are further questions of who teen pregnancy is a problem for – the teen mother, her child, society – and when is teen pregnancy a problem – only when the teen mother is unmarried, only when the teen mother is school-aged, or only when the teen mother is deemed irresponsible by measures of age, race and income?

Feminist genealogy also helps me trace and forefront what is silenced in teen pregnancy research and policy – specifically how gender, race and sexuality impact the defining of the problem of teen pregnancy. Rarely is teen pregnancy discussed as a gender, race and sexed issue, as in fact, MacIntyre and Cunningham-Burley (1993: 63) cite one of their favourite conclusions of teen pregnancy research: '*probably* one of the most immediate causes of adolescent birth is intercourse itself'. Feminist genealogy works at several levels to disrupt such claims and silences. Around the construct of gender, for example, a feminist genealogy of teen pregnancy not only names and questions the impact of the polemical dualism of male and female, but also attempts to trace how we define what we think we know about teen pregnancy through that dualism. A feminist genealogical analysis in this sense would seek to interrupt and disrupt the circularity of assumptions about the authentic experiences of teen pregnancy by examining assumptions about gender roles, race and sexuality.

In a society that assumes heterosexuality, assumes childbearing as part of a women's life and assumes male power, dominance and sideline participation in responsibility for these actions, teen pregnancy programmes are developed with little or no attention given to both the normative and proliferative affects of gender on teen pregnancy. By ignoring and, thus, silencing issues of gender, race and female sexuality related to teen pregnancy, school-based programmes for teen mothers have remained entrenched in normative assumptions and moralistic ideology.

Understanding how these silences are perpetuated and reproduced while at the same time women's sexuality is being constantly marketed and proliferated is crucial to developing effective school-based programmes for teen mothers. Feminist genealogy through its close analysis of the embodied effects of discourses offers a lens through which to analyse the embodiment of teen pregnancy through and in the girls who are teen mothers. What does embodiment mean for understanding teen pregnancy as a policy issue? What would we come to know if we moved beyond a traditional policy studies approach of teen pregnancy to an embodied analysis? How might policies be developed and implemented if policy-makers were faced with the *leaky* needs of the female pregnant body – the body that swells, changes, stretches, grows, lactates, cramps, leaks, bleeds? What would happen if the pleasures of the body were put on the table? How would the problem of teen pregnancy be defined if young women were part of the discussion? How might schools interpret their mission to provide education to teen mothers if they considered how paradoxes of gender, race and female sexuality affect young women's self-esteem, sexuality, educational outlook and economic opportunity? The affects of pregnancy pre- and post-partum are felt and experienced by the teen mother – they are embodied. How should schools respond to these changing embodied needs? To date, such questions are not considered in policy debates surrounding teen pregnancy (except as such issues are raised to point to the inappropriateness of the female pregnant body in schools), and many of the above questions could easily be situated as irrelevant under existing teen pregnancy research. Yet, through a feminist genealogy such questions are brought to the forefront. With these questions, I am not only discussing the actual embodied fluctuations and needs of the pregnant teen body but importantly how society interprets, names, judges and prescribes for these needs. Embodiment does not ignore the complex relationships between women, mothering and the state. Nor is embodiment neutral – it includes the constituted politics of gender, race and class.

The above examples point repeatedly to the need to confront and question the construction of teen pregnancy as a social and educational policy problem. While space limits explicating the above examples, I want to further articulate how feminist genealogy yielding an embodied analysis can aid in interruptive critique. Specifically, I see four ways an embodied policy analysis, through feminist genealogy, can inform and interrupt policy studies.

(1) *Bodies interrupt and decentre the study of power relations* – they both incorporate ideas and generate them. As Foucault's works point out, bodies are objects of power and as well as sites of resistance to power. Teen pregnant bodies are figuratively and literally regulated, produced,

> monitored and measured – for the good of the young woman, the unborn child and society. Yet, the pregnant bodies I observed were not the passive bodies written up in research briefs. When I began paying attention to the bodies of teen mothers, I began to identify how educational policies and programmes attempt to regulate, restrain and remake the teen pregnant/parenting body (Pillow 1997b). Additionally, I also began to see how young women learned to use their bodies as sites from which to resist power and assert themselves.

For instance, many adults are uncomfortable with the obvious physicality of the teen pregnant body. Teen pregnancy interrupts the lines between adult/child, teacher/student, asexual/sexual that education is dependent upon. I repeatedly observed young pregnant women use the discomfort their bodies caused in others to get what they wanted – out of class, out of an assignment, a form signed.[10] Teen pregnancy policies are intently focused on controlling the teen pregnant body. Thus, observing the body and observing from the body reveals how young women negotiate the myriad of conflicting demands, desires and accountability placed upon them as young women, pregnant women, often poor women and un-wed mothers. This view from the body interrupts a simplistic, rational, linear telling of these stories and does not discount the agency of the pregnant teen.

> (2) Bodies place us within partial subject positions that are interruptive of modernist practices. Haraway (1988: 585) describes the view from the body as 'always a complex, contradictory, structuring, and structured body, versus the view from above, from nowhere, from simplicity'. Policy studies has traditionally taken the 'view from above or from nowhere', the seemingly objective and neutral position, vs acknowledging its own embodied, subjective position in the policy process. This practice allows policy analysts, developers and implementors to situate teen pregnancy as a given problem – there is no need to discuss the problem of teen pregnancy because it is known to be a problem. Indeed, there is a proliferative amount of information that policy studies assumes to be correct and known about teen pregnancy.
>
> (Pillow 1997a)

Additionally, in this way, the pregnant teen girl as policy subject is known and situated as an 'Other' – she is the problem, different and separate from 'our' lives. Thus, the policy process ignores that the teen pregnant body is both a constructed and constructing body. The teen pregnant body is a 'located' body – defined and constructed as much by societal norms and needs as by the pregnant female herself. Likewise, as discussed within the problematic of 'norms', locating the unacceptable and marginalized teen pregnant body works to also locate and regulate the acceptable public female body. Yet, policy studies' masking of this process ignores how deeply embodiment is indeed an integral part of defining the problem of teen pregnancy.

For example, I was unprepared initially in my research, based upon what I had read about teen mothers, to find a number of similarities between the pregnant teens and my own life as a 'single' mother. I found that the lived experiences of the teen mothers' and the issues they raised with me – juggling childcare, mothering, relationships, work, school, healthcare – and our joys and frustrations in each of these areas, were the same issues I discussed with my girlfriends. I could not ignore these shared intimacies and realities and, thus, used them as sites of analysis. What would happen if myself, or my girlfriends, or educators and policy analysts were put under the same scrutiny and regulation as teen mothers? What if it were our sexual and love lives, our mothering, our relationships, our dietary and health habits, our fiscal responsibility, our familial relationships, our career choices and moral fortitude which were continually monitored and judged? Who could withstand this type of scrutiny? Would any of us be 'good' mothers?

This scenario points again to questioning the construction of teen pregnancy as a problem. If, as recent research suggests, the long-term negative effects of being a teen mother are negligible and, furthermore, that the negative impact of single-parenting in the US is much more closely linked with access to healthcare, economic opportunity and childcare (Furstenberg *et al.* 1987; Upchurch and McCarthy 1990; Nathanson 1991; Geronimus and Korenman 1992; Weinstein 1998), then how might we rethink the problem of teen pregnancy as not just about teen mothering, but about continued gender and racialized inequities evident in US society? In other words, if it was acknowledged that teen parenting cannot be separated from the role and status of mothering in the US (and varying depictions historically by race and class), what kinds of policies and programmes might be pursued?

(3) *Bodies are interruptive of modernity's reliance upon a unified mode of thought – rational pre-defined and continuous over time.* Bodies exploit rather than conceal and, in this way, bodies are necessary to an interruptive embodied analysis. As Quinby (1994: xxiii) notes, bodies are 'pivotal for countering universal truth claims, for questioning totalizing myths of origin'. What is the origin of the problem of the pregnant teen body? The pregnant body, post-partum body and mothering body are bodies in flux with shifting needs and desires. How does policy attempt to account for the fact that sexuality, intimacy, pregnancy and mothering/parenting are processes – not distinct events easily defined or programmed for? When is the young woman a social or educational problem – when she 'first' becomes sexually active? or only if she becomes pregnant? only if she is poor? or perhaps only if she is attending school? Which body are we referring to and programming for in schoolbased teen pregnancy programmes – all young women, the 'at-risk' teen, the already pregnant teen, or the teen mother? And whose needs are we locating – the young woman's or society's? The teen pregnant female body bears the marks of societal paradoxes concerning female sexuality, race, socio-economic class and single mothering.

An embodied analysis challenges the policy analyst to ask such questions and raise such complexities broadening the scope of discussion surrounding teen pregnancy.

(4) *An embodied analysis proliferates the asking of what has not been questioned, a telling of what has been unspoken and unspeakable, creating spaces for multiple subjectivities, theories and practices to operate.* An embodied analysis of teen pregnancy necessitates critical discussion of how the intersections of gender, race, sexuality and class impact how teen pregnancy is defined as a problem and how this process affects policy interventions. Such an analysis exposes the silences and discrepancies in teen pregnancy research and practice. For example, while the problem of teen pregnancy is obviously linked with the 'problem' of female sexual activity, research on female sexuality remains mired in scientific studies perpetuating gendered constructions. Correspondingly, there is little critical, feminist research on female teen sexuality and even less is known about teen mothers' sexuality (Fine 1988, Tolman 1994, Burdell 1996). Also, the historical social construction of the 'problem' of teen pregnancy in the US has corresponded more to who is getting pregnant, when, and how (e.g. un-wed mothers and a pathology of pregnancy and mothering by race) than to actual teen birth-rate increases or decreases (Solinger 1992, Lawson and Rhode 1993, Luker 1996). Thus, many issues impacting teen pregnancy – female sexuality, un-wed mothering, gender roles, racism – have remained unspoken in policy studies, while at the same time these constructs – unwed mothering, gender, race – are utilized to identify and name the problems of unwed parenting and teen pregnancy, which in turn identify the subjects of policy discourse and practice.

Yet, I have also argued that while the adults around them find these issues of race, gender, sexuality unspeakable (except to define or frame the problems of teen pregnancy), teen mothers themselves are quite aware of the impact of these issues on their lives (Pillow 1997b). They bear the weight of society's paradoxical relationship to their roles as gendered, raced and classed student, woman, mother. When given the opportunity to be heard beyond the 'rites of redemption' promoted by many teen pregnancy programmes,[11] teen mothers can and do speak out about their needs and desires and voice the complexities of their positions. Policy studies, however, has avoided speaking to and with the teen pregnant girl – the un-fit policy subject.

Beginning and ending with bodies

A feminist genealogy of teen pregnancy as an educational policy issue provides an embodied analysis that demonstrates policy theory's inability to deal with specific kinds of bodies, in this case teen, unmarried, pregnant bodies. An embodied analysis – one that is contextual and takes explicitly into account the lived experiences of the teen pregnant body – takes pleasure in working to disrupt simplistic accounts and make evident non-sensical practices – while at the same time offering a critique of the field of policy studies itself. Forefronting the body interrupts the Cartesian dualism between mind and body and at the same time works from the 'irrationality' of the body as a site of information. Talk of the body toward an embodiment of policy analysis interjects the *messiness* of the talk of bodies into the policy process.

This turn to the body and talk of bodies is aimed not at tidying up policy theory, but rather at focusing attention on how bodies implode and interrupt the supposed neutrality of policy studies, forefronts policies role in regulating bodies and exposes the lived experiences of subjects of policy. The use of the body as a tool to interrupt a policy process which is about controlling bodies, like teen pregnancy policy, performs a double move to both expose the category of body, here specifically pregnant teen girls bodies and give the category of the body another meaning.

McNay (1994: 27) points out that once the 'fundamental notion of "enlightenment" is undermined – this is to say the idea that scientific and rational thought progressively acquires a greater proximity to the truth, thereby attaining a greater humanity – then a whole series of social practices can be viewed in a new light'. Here, I propose that feminist genealogy is not the way but one more way to engage in interruptive analyses and practices, to bring to bear the weight of what, as Britzman (1995: 154) states 'hegemonic discourses of normalcy cannot bear to know'. Feminist genealogy yields an embodied analysis that brings feminist, queer and post-structural theories into policy studies. In this way, feminist genealogy's can perform an 'impertinent performance: an interest in thinking against the thought of one's conceptual foundations' (Britzman 1995: 155) and serve as methodology that can engage in an 'historical analysis of the limits that are imposed on us and experiment with the possibility of [what my be] beyond them' (Foucault 1977/1984: 50).

Further, an embodiment exposed through feminist genealogy alters what is meant by policy studies. It opens spaces for questioning the construction of the policy process – now policy studies becomes in essence the subject of analysis – and challenges analytic methodological practices. Embodied analysis provides a way to speak up and speak back to the paradoxes in existing policies and expose the ineffectiveness of reliance upon assumptive, seemingly natural, rational policies. Embodied analysis is attention getting – in the same way a pregnant teen body is attention getting. It works to neither hide nor capture the teen pregnant body but to keep what has been invisible and unsaid out front while taking what has been proliferated and re-telling the tale – in my case, from the bodies of young mothers.

Notes

1 I use the term 'race-feminisms' to forefront that I understand, use and practice feminisms that are not only inclusive of but are changed by analyses of race, racialization and racism and contact with race theory. The term race-feminisms also works to situate

analyses of race on equal foundation with analyses of gender, not subsumed *under* feminism. My use of the term feminist genealogy in this paper should be understood and read as working out of race-feminisms.

2 For example, as Stone (1998: 8) explicates the '*model of reasoning*' for policy studies is 'rational decision making' resulting in a series of 'well-defined steps' that is very familiar to policy researchers:

   1 identify objectives;
   2 identify alternative course of action for achieving objectives;
   3 predict the possible consequences of each alternative;
   4 evaluate the possible consequence of each alternative; and
   5 select the alternative that maximizes the attainment of objectives.

   The fact that these steps are so commonly understood and accepted without question is part of the problem I am discussing in this essay. Stone's (1998: 9) further depiction of the '*model of society*' as 'the market model' and the '*model of policy making*' as 'a production model, where policy is assumed created in a fairly orderly sequence of stages almost as if on an assembly line' are also integral to my critique of such understandings of the policy process.

3 In this essay, policy studies is used as a broad term, encompassing the range of work in policy studies, policy analyses and politics of education focused upon one or more of these areas.

4 This discussion is intricately informed and influenced by my experiences researching educational policy affecting teen mothers, my confrontation with the limits of traditional policy theory and analysis and my attempts to name and forefront the inconsistencies and paradoxes evident in US teen pregnancy social and education policies and practices. See Pillow for book length discussion of these issues.

5 Repeatedly, I hear from teachers, administrators and school personnel that teen pregnancy can 'spread like a virus'. Although research on school-based programmes and teen pregnancy frequency data does not support these claims such a conceptualization of teen pregnancy calls for and reinforces measures of containment and control.

6 This rule was a rational action based upon the belief that the presence of teen mothers with their children in school settings would create an environment that reinforced teen pregnancy – in effect act as a causal agent. I have written elsewhere on how the visibility and invisibility of teen pregnancy programmes, the students and their children differs by a schools location and socio-economic status. In brief, I found that in lower income schools teen pregnancy programmes were more visible and integrated into the school while in higher income schools teen pregnancy programmes were non-existent or operating on the margins of the school. However, the type of education provided in these schools is also highly differentiated, with low-income, mainly US 'minority' schools offering only basic education curriculum, while middle-income and 'white' schools offer college preparatory curriculum even to teen mothers (see Pillow 1997b).

7 *Time* magazine ran a feature cover story in 1990 depicting a 'browning of America'. As Lesko (1990: 121) observes of the *Time* article:

   > Girls of different colours, shapes, ages with babies in their arms or on their laps stare out from the pages of *Time*.... Young women with extended bellies or small children both represent and are the problem of sexual irresponsibility and failure to delay motherhood.

   The *Time* story visualizes a white, middle-class fear that given present trends in lower birthrates to white middle-class mothers and higher birthrates to Black mothers, US society would move from *white* to *brown* to *black*.

8 Title IX, enacted in the US in 1974, specifically addresses the right of pregnant teens to remain in school and, furthermore, states that any decision to attend a separate

programme must be voluntary. Additionally, the separate programme must be comparable to programming offered non-pregnant students. Although Title IX prohibits schools from not serving teen girls who are pregnant, there is little consensus on how to serve pregnant girls, and little case law, so as Stamm (1998: 1216) states 'it is unclear whether existing programmes satisfy the regulations'.

9 I specifically apply analyses of the racialized discourses impacting unwed, low-income mothers and resulting social welfare policies to an analysis of these discourses on teen mothers in Pillow.

10 In prior presentations of this work, I have been challenged to think about whether the resistance I speak of here is useful to the young women – are they resisting in ways that are to their benefit? For me, this question assumes that the adults around the pregnant teen have her best interests in mind, something I found I cannot assume. In shadowing pregnant teens, I found that they have to speak up and speak out for themselves and their child an inordinate amount of time – with a myriad of social workers, counsellors, teachers, school administrators, medical personnel, family members, boyfriend(s). And, as in this example, I observed that young women would 'use' their bodies, to at times do the talking for them.

11 Such 'rites of redemption' include the expectation that teen mothers will come to recognize and vocalize their 'mistakes', how they are paying for their mistakes now, and what they will do to be a good mother and good citizen. Being able to speak about their behaviour redemptively is seen as a sign of progress and maturity. Some programmes as part of their 'treatment' include a requirement that teen mothers speak (give testimony) in public about the dangers of a teen pregnancy (see Lesko 1990).

References

Abramovitz, M. (1988) *Regulating the Lives of Women: social welfare policy from colonial times to the present* (Boston, MA: Harvard University Press).

Ball, S. J. (1990) *Politics and Policy Making in Education/Explorations in Policy Sociology* (London: Routledge).

Ball, S. J. (1994) *Education Reform: a critical and post-structural approach* (Buckingham: Open University Press).

Britzman, D. (1995) Is there a queer pedagogy? Or, stop reading straight, *Educational Theory*, 45(2), 151–65.

Burdell, P. A. (1996) Teen mothers in high school: tracking their curriculum, in M. Apple (ed.), *Review of Research in Education, 21* (Washington, DC: AERA Publishers), 163–207.

Butler, J. (1993) *Bodies That Matter On The Discursive Limits of 'Sex'* (New York: Routledge).

Carlson, D. (1993) The politics of educational policy: urban school reform in unsettling times, *Educational Policy*, 7, 149–65.

Connell, R. W. (1987) *Gender and Power* (Cambridge, UK: Polity Press).

Diprose, R. (1994) *The Bodies of Women: ethics, embodiment and sexual difference* (London and New York: Routledge).

Elmore, R. F. (1983) Complexity and control: what legislators and administrators can do about implementing public policy, in L. S. Shulman and G. Sykes (eds), *Handbook of Teaching and Policy* (New York: Longman), 342–69.

Fay, B. (1987) *Critical Social Science* (Ithaca, NY: Cornell University Press).

Ferguson, K. E. (1991) Interpretation and genealogy in feminism, *SIGNS*, 16(21), 322–39.

Fine, M. (1988) Sexuality, schooling and adolescent females: the missing discourse of desire, *Harvard Educational Review*, 58(1), 29–53.

Foucault, M. (1974/1990) *The History of Sexuality/An Introduction/Volume I* (New York: Vintage Books) (original work published 1976).

Foucault, M. (1977/1984), P. Rabinow (ed.), *The Foucault Reader* (New York: Pantheon Books).

Foucault, M. (1979) *History of Sexuality*, Vol. 1 (New York: Pantheon Books).

Furstenberg, F. Jr, Brooks-Gunn, J. and Morgan, S. P. (1987) *Adolescent Mothers in Later Life* (Cambridge: Cambridge University Press).

Geronimus, A. T. and Korenman, S. (1992) The socioeconomic consequences of teen childbearing reconsidered, *Quarterly Journal of Economics*, 107, 1182–98.

Gordon, L. (ed.) (1990) *Women, the State, and Welfare* (Madison, WI: The University of Wisconsin Press).

Griffith, A. I. (1992) Educational policy as text and action, *Educational Policy*, 6, 415–28.

Grosz, E. (1995) *Space, Time Perversion* (New York: Routledge).

Haney, L. (1996) Homeboys, babies, men in suits: the state and the reproduction of male dominance, *American Sociological Review*, 61, 759–78.

Haraway, D. (1988) Situated knowledges: the science question in feminism and the privilege of the partial perspective, *Feminist Studies*, 14(3), 575–99.

Hargreaves, A. (1996) Transforming knowledge: blurring the boundaries between research, policy, and practice, *Educational Evaluation and Policy Analysis*, 18(2), 105–22.

Kelly, M. and Maynard-Moody, S. (1993) Policy analysis in the post-positivist era: engaging stakeholders in evaluating the economic development districts program, *Public Administration Review*, 53(2), 135–42.

Kunzel, R. (1993) *Fallen Women, Problem Girls: unmarried mothers and the professionalization of social work, 1890–1945* (New Haven, CT: Yale University Press).

Ladner, J. (1987) Black teenage pregnancy: a challenge for educators, *Journal of Negro Education*, 56(1), 53–63.

Ladson-Billings, G. and Tate, W. F. IV (1995) Toward a critical race theory of education, *Teachers College Record*, 97, 47–63.

Lawson, A. and Rhode, D. L. (eds) (1993) *The Politics of Pregnancy/Adolescent Sexuality and Public Policy* (New Haven, CT: Yale University Press).

Lesko, N. (1990) Curriculum differentiation as social redemption: the case of school-aged mothers, in R. Page and L. Valli (eds), *Curriculum Differentiation/Interpretive Studies in US Secondary Schools* (Albany, NY: State University of New York Press), 113–36.

Lesko, N. (1995) The 'leaky needs' of school-aged mothers: an examination of US programs and policies, *Curriculum Inquiry*, 25(2), 177–205.

Luker, K. (1996) *Dubious Conceptions/The Politics of Teenage Pregnancy* (Cambridge, MA: Harvard University Press).

Mac an Ghaill, M. (1996) Towards a reconceptualised sex/sexuality education policy: theory and cultural change, *Journal of Education Policy*, 11(3), 289–302.

McCoy, K. and Pillow, W. (1995) *Genealogical Inquiry. The 1995 Volume, Qualitative Research* (Athens, GA: UGA).

MacIntyre, S. and Cunnigham-Burley, S. (1993) Teenage pregnancy as a social problem: a perspective from the United Kingdom, in A. Lawson and D. L. Rhode (eds), *The Politics of Pregnancy/Adolescent Sexuality and Public Policy* (New Haven, CT: Yale University Press), 59–73.

MacKinnon, C. A. (1989) *Toward a Feminist Theory of the State* (Cambridge, MA: Harvard University Press).

McLaughlin, M. W. (1990) The rand change agent study revisited: macro perspectives and micro realities, *Educational Researcher*, 19, 11–16.

McLaughlin, M. W. (1991) Learning from experience: lessons from policy implementation, in A. R. Odden (ed.), *Education Policy Implementation* (Albany, NY: SUNY), 184–92.

McNay, L. (1994) *Foucault: a critical introduction* (Cambridge: Polity Press).

Mahon, M. (1992) *Foucault's Nietzschean Genealogy/Truth, Power, and the Subject* (Albany, NY: SUNY Press).

Marshall, C. (ed.) (1997) *Feminist Critical Policy Analysis I: a primary and secondary schooling perspective* (London: Falmer Press).

Marshall, C., Mitchell, D. and Wirt, F. (1989) *Culture and Educational Policy in the American States* (New York: The Falmer Press).

Nathanson, C. A. (1991) *Dangerous Passage/The social control of sexuality in women's adolescence* (Philadelphia, PA: Temple University Press).

Parker, L. C. (1998) From Brown to Ayers-Fordice: the changing shape of racial desegregation in higher education, *Journal of Education Policy*, 13, 699–715.

Pillow, W. (1997a) Decentering silences/troubling irony: a feminist postmodern approach to policy analysis, in C. Marshall (ed.), *Feminist Critical Policy Analysis I: a primary and secondary schooling perspective* (London: Falmer Press), 134–52.

Pillow, W. (1997b) Exposed methodology: the body as a deconstructive practice, *International Journal of Qualitative Studies in Education*, 10(3), 349–63.

Pillow, W. (2002) *Unfit Subjects: educational policy and the teen mother, 1972–2002* (New York: Routledge).

Quinby, L. (1994) *Anti-apocalypse: exercises in genealogical criticism* (Minneapolis and London: University of Minnesota Press).

Rich, A. (1986) *Of Woman Born* (New York: Norton).

Scheurich, J. J. (1994) Policy archaeology: a new policy studies methodology, *Journal of Educational Policy*, 9(4), 297–316.

Silverman, K. (1988) *The Acoustic Mirror* (Bloomington, IN: Indiana University Press).

Singer, L. (1993) *Erotic Welfare: sexual theory and politics in the age of epidemic* (New York: Routledge).

Solinger, R. (1992) *Wake up Little Susie: single pregnancy and race before Roe v. Wade* (New York: Routledge).

Spivak, G. C. (1993) *Outside in the Teaching Machine* (New York: Routledge).

Stamm, M. J. (1998) A skeleton in the closet: single-sex schools for pregnant girls, *Columbia Law Review*, 1203–37.

Stone, D. A. (1998) *Policy Paradox: political reason* (Boston, MA: Scott, Foresman & Co.).

Stout, R. T., Tallerico, M. and Scribner, K. P. (1994) Values: the 'what' of the politics of Education, in J. D. Scribner and D. H. Layton (eds), *The Study of Educational Politics: the 1994 commemorative yearbook of the politics of education association (1969–1994)* (Washington, DC: Falmer Press), 5–20.

Thomas, S. (1998) Race, gender, and welfare reform/the antinatalist response, *Journal of Black Studies*, 28(4), 419–46.

Tolman, D. L. (1994) Doing desire/adolescent girls' struggles for/with sexuality, *Gender & Society*, 8, 324–42.

Trinh, M.-H. T. (1989) *Women Native Other* (Bloomington, IN: Indiana University Press).

Troyna, B. (1994) Critical social research and educational policy, *British Journal of Educational Studies*, 42(2), 70–84.

Turner, B. S. (1984) *The Body and Society: explorations in social theory* (New York: Basil Black well).

Upchurch, D. M. and McCarthy, J. L. (1990) The timing of a first birth and high school completion, *American Sociological Review*, 55, 224–34.

Weinstein, M. (1998) The teenage pregnancy 'problem': welfare reform and the personal responsibility and work opportunity reconciliation act of 1996, *Berkeley Women's Law Journal*, 13, 117–52.

Williams, S. and Bendelow, G. (1998) *The Lived Body/Sociological Themes, Embodied Issues* (New York: Routledge).

Wilton, T. (1990) *Lesbian Studies: setting an agenda* (London: Routledge).

9 Critical policy sociology

Historiography, archaeology and genealogy as methods of policy analysis

Trevor Gale

Monash University, Victoria, Australia

Source: *Journal of Education Policy*, 16 (5): 379–93, 2001.

Introduction

Cognizant of Stephen Ball's remonstrance that 'much of what passes for theoretically informed research lacks any sense of critical distance or reflexivity about its own production and procedures and its claims to knowledge about the social' (1997: 269), this paper seeks to outline three research methods with the potential to more explicitly inform social policy analyses. They are represented here as policy historiography, policy archaeology and policy genealogy. This is preceded by an account of the distinguishing features of policy sociology, particularly its sociological antecedents and its deference to historical methods, and the research questions that such alliances generate. A case is made for the importance of a *critical* policy sociology set apart from other policy work and favourably disposed to the critique of oppressive social practices. Following Dale's (1989) distinction, these matters constitute the *topic* of the paper's discussions whereas research into issues of Australian higher education entry policy (Gale 1999b) provide its *resource.* Although not heavily theorized here, a subtext to this biography of critical policy sociologists and ways of engaging in and representing their analyses, is the notion of 'temporary policy settlements' (see Gale 1999a).

Policy sociology and methodology: some reflections

It would seem that one of the more critical features of policy analysis in recent times has been its reflexivity and self-appraisal; that is, its willingness to ponder matters related to its own research activity. In 1990, for example, Ball noted that 'the field of policy analysis is dominated by commentary and critique rather than by research' (1990: 9). Yet, becoming 'too abstract' was itself a reaction by policy analysts to much atheoretical and apparently objective accounts of policy, particularly that emanating from the empiricism of 'policy science' but also from managerialist and technocratic perspectives of the policy process (Ozga 1990). Given this to-ing and fro-ing between theory and data, it is hardly surprising that methodological issues should more recently occupy the writings of critical policy researchers, particularly since, compared with earlier qualitative inquiry, their research has appeared 'unsophisticated' and 'somewhat naive' (Maguire and Ball 1994: 281).

This paper, then, forms a response to recent self-criticism (see, for example, Ball 1994b, 1997; Halpin and Troyna 1994; Maguire and Ball 1994) by critical policy analysts that 'little attention has been given to research methodology' (Taylor 1997: 23) and particularly that 'most [policy] analysts leave the interpretational relationships between data and analysis heavily implicit' (Ball 1994b: 107). In an edited collection by David Halpin and Barry Troyna, written to address these shortcomings, Ball (1994b) identifies Gewirtz and Ozga's confession concerning the 'heavily implicit' methodological assumptions in their writings, drawing attention to the importance of explicating policy research issues. The relevant passage discloses that 'constraints on space and the fact that the work is still in progress (not to mention the difficulty of the task) inhibit us from offering here an exposition of the developing relationship between the informing theoretical perspective, its associated propositions, and the empirical data' (Gewirtz and Ozga 1990: 41). In responding to such criticism, this paper constitutes a deliberate attempt to create space away from the constraints of a work-in-progress to specifically address these issues of policy methodology.

Policy sociology critique

In particular, the paper seeks to contribute to the field known variously as 'critical policy analysis' (Prunty 1985; Henry 1993; Marshall 1997; Taylor 1997), 'critical policy scholarship' (Grace 1998) and 'policy sociology' (Payne *et al.* 1981; Ozga 1987; McPherson and Raab 1988; Ball 1990; Bowe *et al.* 1992; Maguire and Ball 1994). Definitions of the latter are often attributed to Jenny Ozga (1987: 144) who characterizes policy sociology as 'rooted in the social science tradition, historically informed and drawing on qualitative and illuminative techniques'; as I read them, characteristics with parallels to Van Manen's (1990: 27–9) (analytic) distinctions between research methodology, method and techniques.

For some (Raab 1994; Troyna 1994a,b) Ozga's definition lacks a degree of integrity, particularly in relation to the explicit claim in this approach to be an exercise in sociology. Troyna's (1994a: 71) critique, for example, is that policy sociology appears to differ little 'from other social and political science analyses of policy' that 'takes policy analysis to be a multi-disciplinary field that cuts across existing specializations to employ whatever theoretical or methodological approach is most relevant to the issue or problem under investigation' (Codd 1988: 235). Troyna (1994a: 72) regards interdisciplinary and cross-disciplinary work as 'no bad thing', although he is concerned that emphasising the sociological character of policy sociology could inhibit such 'trespassing' (Apple 1996), while Henry (1993) is critical of the 'theoretical eclecticism' evident in this form of research, embodied in Ball's (1993, 1994a) 'toolbox' approach to policy analysis. As Troyna and Henry see it, the main problem is the absence of 'a particular strategic edge' (Troyna 1994a. 82) to policy sociology, not just its lack of a 'clearly distinctive approach' (Raab 1994: 23). For these critical researchers, rectifying such absence necessarily requires a closer and more explicit relationship between policy sociology and critical social science which would potentially highten policy analysts' interests in feminist and antiracist issues (Troyna 1994a) and matters of social justice and equity more generally (Henry 1993).

This concern with being critical, and particularly with developing a critical disposition for 'overt political struggle against oppressive social structures' (Harvey 1990: 20), seems a more cogent argument than questioning policy sociology's disciplinary credentials. As Apple (1996: 125, emphasis in original) notes in his recent review, 'what actually *counts* as the sociology of education is a construction... [Its boundaries] are often the results of complex "policing" actions by those who have the power to enforce them and to declare what is or is not the subject of "legitimate" sociological inquiry'. Indeed, concern about whether policy sociology is or is not sociological in orientation and whether it can be multi-disciplinary *and* legitimately sociological seems reminiscent of Mills' observation regarding history: 'the weary debate over whether or not historical study is or should be considered a social science is neither important nor interesting' (1959: 143). Moreover, Mills' (1959: 22–4) *Sociological Imagination* provides some history to relations between sociology and other social science disciplines, which appears consistent with a more recent 'picture of the state of sociology of education that is broad and that cuts across disciplinary boundaries' (Apple 1996: 125).

Critical policy sociology – like critical policy analysis and critical policy scholarship – is perhaps a better description of what is intended here. Put simply, sociology is interested in the workings of the social world and, in particular, in the relations between 'personal troubles' and 'public issues' (Mills 1959: 8). Clearly, these are not interests foreign to policy analysts and their analyses; indeed, how personal troubles are dealt with as public issues and how public issues are expressed in personal troubles, contribute to defining the work of policy studies. Further, critical sociology imagines a particular relationship between the specific and the general of social life in a way that has social researchers thinking simultaneously about these things (Apple 1996). For Apple (1996: 141):

> it is exactly this issue of simultaneity, of thinking neo and post together, of actively enabling the tensions within and among them to help form our research, that will solidify previous understandings, avoid the loss of collective memory of the gains that have been made, and generate new insights and new actions.

Again, critical policy sociologists have been willing to embrace such simultaneity, even though at times their work has been represented otherwise. (See Gale 1994a for an account of opposing caricatures of critical policy analysis.) Roger Dale, for example, while clearly advocating the retention of broad analyses of social formations in policy work, does not simply argue the merits of grand narratives. As he puts it:

> Severing implementation from formulation of policy involves not only a distortion but a serious misunderstanding of the role of the State in education policy. It is a misunderstanding connected to the view that the State involvement in education implies ownership, control and operation of education systems, with a functional division of labour between formulation and implementation of policy.
>
> (Dale 1992: 393)

In short, the critical in policy sociology is worth pursuing, far more than dubious debates over what is sociological about its orientation, and provides the potential to redress concerns over its theoretical eclecticism and its politics without delimiting contributions from the social sciences more broadly.

Illuminative research technique

Policy analysts, and other social researchers, often jump from these theoretical and political matters to those of data collection (and analysis); for those who are policy sociologists, the methodological leap is to 'qualitative and illuminative techniques' (Ozga 1987). Here I want to continue this progression, although only momentarily; first, because space prevents a fuller account and also because I want to move more quickly to Ozga's second characterization of policy sociology, particularly given that research techniques within this approach have already received somewhat more attention (see, for example, Ball 1994b; Maguire and Ball 1994; Ozga and Gewirtz 1994; Wallace *et al.* 1994). Briefly, then, ethnographic and 'life history' methods, such as participant and non-participant observations but more commonly semi-structured interviews, tend to generate the primary sources of data in this research genre, producing textual representations of policy discourses – themselves the subject of interpretation (Rizvi and Kemmis 1987: 12–19) – for interpreting policy and/or its processes of production. As Raab (1994: 23–4) explains:

> In each case . . . knowledge of the former [process and product] is to be gained empirically and not on the basis of inference from the latter [motive and action] or by deduction from grand theory. Hence the importance of going beyond the pronouncements of 'policy makers' and actually talking to them, for meanings and 'assumptive worlds' are essential parts of the policy process and require to be understood if action itself is to be understood.

Written documentary evidence often provides a supplement to such data production. But not as evident in policy sociology, at least to date, is the collection and analysis of more quantitative statistical data. Again, space does not allow for a fuller account of these matters but what is intended here is what Brown *et al.* (1997)

refer to as 'a new *political arithmetic* [of the social world] as a form of "social accountability"' (p. 37, emphasis in original) and 'as part of a *committed* policy scholarship' (p. 38, emphasis added). That is, quantitative data can also prove illuminating, particularly when it is subjected to the methodological assumptions of critical social science. To dismiss such data as the stuff of positivism is to curtail 'our ability to raise and answer critical questions about the large-scale effects' (Apple 1996: 127) of policy.

Historically informed method

However, it is Ozga's second characterization of policy sociology, as historically informed, that I want to foreground in this paper, although, as already demonstrated (critical) social science traditions and qualitative and (quantitative) illuminative techniques are not far from the paper's interests and discussions. A regard for history is not unusual in sociology and is similarly emphasized in critical policy studies. Indeed, 'all sociology worthy of the name is "historical sociology." It is, in Paul Sweezy's excellent phrase, an attempt to write "the present as history"' (Mills 1959: 146). Ball (1990: 1), for example, describes his early policy analysis 'both as an exercise in contemporary history and as a contribution to what Ozga (1987) calls "policy sociology"'. Yet, deferring to an historical research method – what I understand by Ozga's (1987) depiction of policy sociology as 'historically informed' – does not always bring clarity to policy research. History, as Petersen (1992) observes, is itself crowded with definitions. It is almost too simple, then, to 'hold fast to the original Greek verb: *Historeo* (1) I find out by inquiry, (2) I narrate what I have found out. Inquiry and narration – that is my craft' (Hancock 1954, in Petersen 1992: 2). To employ a common expression, such definition raises more questions than it answers, questions that I want to dwell on here in order to explore ways of doing critical policy sociology.

Given the uncertainties embedded in Hancock's craft, one initial question for historically informed policy sociologists is *what am I looking to find/produce?* In their search for policy related data, too many analysts treat this simply as an empirical question. For them:

> the meaning of policy is taken for granted and theoretical and epistemological dry rot is built into the analytical structures they construct . . . much rests on the meaning or possible meanings that we give to policy; it affects 'how' we research and how we interpret what we find.
>
> (Ball 1994a: 15)

More recent theoretical accounts of what to look for have tended to emphasize policy as text and discourse (see, for example, Ball 1994a; Taylor 1997; Gale 1999a). This in itself raises epistemological and ontological questions about the activity of research: that is, is data on policy 'out there' to be found or do researchers produce it? It would seem reasonable to assume, for example, that policy analysts who define policy in terms of text, discourse and ideology will necessarily 'find' different things in their research from others who have regard for one or more of Hogwood and Gunn's (1984: 13–19) nine popular definitions. But reworking policy in this way, on the basis that 'the established conceptual tools [of policy analysis] seem blunt and irrelevant' (Ball 1990: 8), is more than simply a theoretical exercise: for 'the master's tools will never dismantle the master's house' (Lorde 1984: 112). What to look for, then, is also related to a researcher's political disposition. As argued above, critical policy sociology is informed 'by the conviction that "things," especially policy discourse, must be pulled apart' (Troyna 1994a: 71) to determine whose interests they serve. Troyna (1994a: 72–3) identifies two questions central to these critical determinations: 'what is really going on?' – the presumption here is that there is something to be uncovered – and 'how come?' Hence, research questions that ask what influences the production of (Australian higher education entry) policy – the research from which illustrations below are derived – necessarily arrive at empirical answers informed by theoretical and political considerations of what policy is and who benefits from it.

Second, *where and how will I find/produce it?* In many ways this is a difficult question to separate from the first. What the policy analyst is looking for, what is regarded as 'the policy' and/or as 'policy making', necessarily frames where and how data about policy will be found/produced. In the quotation above, for example, Raab (1994) emphasizes the search in policy sociology for meanings and assumptions, and suggests that one of the best places to find/produce these is in/through the words and reasonings of communities or networks of policy actors. Hence, asking about these in interview, although not necessarily the only research technique available, becomes a logical form of data collection/production. More broadly, Maguire and Ball (1994: 278–81), in their overview of recent research in policy sociology, provide a contextual account of how 'where to look' is related to 'what to look for'. In their review, they identify three broad orientations: 'elite studies' (otherwise known as 'situated studies of policy formation'), 'trajectory studies' and 'implementation studies'. Clearly, such orientations reveal more than the (productive) locations of data. For example, disclosed in these characterizations of policy research is a surprising unacknowledged dichotomy between policy formulation and policy implementation; surprising, given Ball's earlier work (Bowe *et al.* 1992) on theorizing contexts of policy making. (See Gale 1999a for a critique of the separations between these policy contexts.) Again, illustrated here is that ways of conceiving of policy – as divided into formulations and implementations or as part of the one endeavour – produce different forms of data.

Third, *how is what is found/produced (to be) represented?* It is tempting to think about representing or 'publishing' data after the work of finding/producing it has been completed. However, the realities of (policy) analysis are very different from the divisions of doing (reading) and writing research implied in such thinking. That is, at the heart of issues of representation is an *a priori* question that asks, what lenses do I use to look (read) with? In this respect, policy analysts can appear very similar to policy makers who seek to construct policy problems in ways that match the answers they already have available (Beilharz 1987; Gale 1994b).[1] I do not mean to 'slip back' into positivism here – as researchers, we must be careful not to simply fill predetermined theoretical buckets with policy data – but I do want to signal that analysts do not enter policy fields with 'blank slates'. As argued above, 'critical theories offer lenses for looking' (Marshall 1997: 11).

There are several 'lenses' that could fit this criterion and many of them potentially overlap, increasing their various hues. In particular (critical) ethnographies (see Hammersley 1994) and (critical) case studies (see Deem and Brehony 1994) – the latter described by some as quasi-historical research (Bartlett 1987) – seem to dominate policy sociology. Without discounting these, in the sections that follow I outline three alternative and overlapping historical lenses with which to 'read' and 'write' policy research: specifically, *policy historiography*, *policy archaeology* and *policy genealogy*. In effect, all are policy historiographies or different ways of storying policy, although 'in the tradition of what may be called *critical erudition*' (Petersen 1992: 3, emphasis in original) they come under the influence of a similar 'radical revisionist' (Kincheloe 1991) historiography.

I should confess here, if it is not already evident, to some fluidity in how I use the term *historiography*: as both a general term that encompasses a range of historical discourses and as a more specific term that refers to one particular collection of these. My defence for such ambiguity, short of also confessing to not knowing what else to name them, is that the social sciences have the same regard for terms such as *methodology*: meaning, the range of ideas and activities (methods, techniques, procedures and so on) that come under the broad banner of social research *and*, more specifically, 'the theory behind the method' (Van Manen 1990: 27). My confessions also extend to not being fully attentive to Foucault's renditions of archaeology and genealogy, even though these have influenced the methods of policy analysis I imagine here. But then Foucault himself provides such licence:

> If one or two of these 'gadgets' of approach or method that I've tried to employ . . . can be of service to you, then I shall be delighted. If you find the need to transform my tools or use others then show me what they are, because it may be of benefit to me.
>
> (Foucault 1980: 65)

Without claiming absolute distinctions between their interests, the following sections couple policy historiography with the substantive issues of policy at particular hegemonic moments, policy archaeology with conditions that regulate policy formations and policy genealogy with social actors' engagement with policy. In claiming that these have things to say about the representation of policy sociology, I am not concerned so much with their schematic structures, how their narratives are ordered and arranged, but with the subject of these narratives, what is included in these 'stories' about policy (and what is not).

Policy historiography

Historical accounts of education come in all shapes and sizes (see Connell 1987) but they commonly share an interest 'to trace the processes of educational change and to expose the possible relationships between the socio-educational present and the socio-educational past' (Kincheloe 1991: 234); although, histories of the present and their comparison with the past sometimes remain implicit.[2] Mills (1959: 22) similarly describes tendencies in sociology:

> It is at once historical and systematic – historical, because it deals with and uses the materials of the past; systematic, because it does so in order to discern 'the stages' of the course of history and the regularities of social life.

Drawing on this heritage, policy historiography asks three broad questions: (1) what were the 'public issues' and 'private troubles' within a particular policy domain during some previous period and how were they addressed?; (2) what are they now?; and (3) what is the nature of the change from the first to the second? Critical policy historiography adds to these a further two: (4) what are the complexities in these coherent accounts of policy?; and (5) what do these reveal about who is advantaged and who is disadvantaged by these arrangements?

It is perhaps best to illustrate these research questions by referring to a specific example of policy historiography: an analysis of Australian higher education entry policy, March 1987 to March 1996 (Gale 1999b). In this critical historiography of policy, data analysed were predominantly documentary and included primary sources (such as government policy texts, departmental records and reports, commissioned research, media releases, and minutes of meetings) and secondary sources (such as relevant academic literature and newspaper articles). In analysing such policy records I was interested to do several things, including to detail:

- 'a systematic account of selected past events; initially through their analytical separation from present events and from those that do not contribute to an understanding of "entry" but also through their subsequent "division" into distinctive historical epochs' (Gale 1999b: 70); and
- 'a critical examination of the data that is concerned not just with an episode in the history of ideas but also, and more crucially, with critical sociological questions about who benefits from particular university entrance arrangements' (Gale 1999b: 70).

With regard to the first of these intentions, I was concerned not to represent these historical periods and their policies as necessarily self-evident and consensual, and the transition from one to another as a consequence of 'progress'. This in mind and informed by the work of Hall (1984), Offe (1984) and others, I conceived of temporary policy settlements: 'a moving discursive frame' (Ball 1994a: 23) that at a particular historical and geographical moment defines the specifics of policy production. I also understood these hegemonic settlements to *contain* crises or other settlements 'in waiting' and, hence, I characterized them as asymmetrical, temporary and contextual (see Gale 1999a).

Theorizing policy in this way, I represented university entry policy in the first three-quarters of the twentieth century as dominated by a 'qualified-entry' settlement, followed by a period (beginning in the 1970s and extending into the 1990s) of more explicit policy crisis, and then, subsequently, by a 'diversified-entry' arrangement. Specifically, the qualified entry period foregrounded issues of merit and school-to-university pathways, which were settled to the extent that most, if not all, students who submitted for university entrance examination and were successful, gained entry; albeit with some adjustment around the edges in the latter years, given faculty prerequisites and quotas. The evolving period of (explicit) crisis was primarily expressed as 'unmet demand': dramatically more students undertaking and successfully completing senior secondary schooling, and, hence, qualifying for university entrance, than universities could/would accommodate. During this period, there was also greater recognition given to the under-representation in university student populations of particular social groups. 'Resolution' of these issues and the resettling of Australian higher education entry policy came in the form of a 'diversified-entry' policy settlement that focused on increased, targeted, open and displaced access arrangements. In brief, these measures widened existing pathways to university and, in addition, created new ones. Moreover, pathways leading out of senior secondary schooling were established to destinations other than university. The school-to-university route, it appeared, now had some viable alternatives.[3]

But my intention was also to highlight whose interests these arrangements served. Drawing on Turner's (1971) two ideal–typical normative patterns of upward mobility, I suggested that in settling the crisis of qualified-entry around a new diversified-entry arrangement, the organizing logic of entry policy had shifted, at least in its rhetoric, from 'elite sponsorship' (selection by association) to 'fair contest' (selection via competition). Yet, what became evident was that even though more students were gaining access to Australian universities (as undergraduates) under diversified-entry arrangements (from 99,820 entrants in 1983 to 152,113 in 1993), including increases in the representation of Australia's indigenous populations (from 0.5% in 1987 to 1.0% in 1993), university entry was not as fair as it might have seemed. For example, the proportion of university students from low socio-economic backgrounds did not increase under this new policy regime and some institutions even recorded a decrease. Moreover, targeted groups in general tended to congregate in lower status courses and institutions; for example, in 1991 two-thirds of indigenous students were enrolled in arts and education and in five predominantly regional institutions. Neither did the pathway between school and university seem as wide for all students: 'in 1989 more than 70% of those graduating from independent secondary schools entered higher education. The rate for government schools was a little less than 40%' (Williams *et al.* 1993: 99).

If these figures raised questions about the fairness of the competition – that there are 'powerful mechanisms of privilege and exclusion [ensuring that universal access] does not function in a universal way' (Connell 1994: 145) – so did the introduction of open access arrangements, in the form of Open Learning Australia (OLA), question the demise of elite sponsorship. Not only were OLA students predominantly urban, able-bodied, employed in middle-class occupations, with senior secondary qualifications and some prior studies at a tertiary level (Atkinson *et al.* 1995), the 'openness' of the system was being actively utilized by elite schools and universities to ensure the progression of particular kinds of students from school to university. That is, through OLA mechanisms or 'high achiever' programmes organized by (mostly traditional) universities, university subjects were offered in (mostly private) schools to assist (mostly elite) students in gaining advanced standing following their entry into university courses.

In short, my critical historiography sought to analyse the role of Australian higher education entry policy in 'the perpetuation of hegemonizing influences within those historically specific moments and those particular cultural configurations' (Kincheloe 1991: 237) that I called 'qualified entry' and 'diversified entry'. I concluded that, like racism, privileging the dominant in university entry arrangements 'is virus-like, constantly mutating into new forms in the changed social structures and cultural configurations of different historical moments' (Kincheloe 1991: 238).

Policy archaeology

A second level of analysis of Australian higher education entry policy was engaged and represented through the lens of policy archaeology. James Scheurich (1994) has written an instructive account on this historical method and its relevance to policy analysis, much of which has appeal to critical policy sociologists. In his explanation, policy archaeology spans four broad arenas that could be expressed in terms of the following research questions: (1) what are the conditions that make the emergence of a particular policy agenda possible?; (2) what are the rules or regularities that determine what is (and is not) a policy problem?; (3) how do these rules and regularities shape policy choices?; and (4) how is policy analysis similarly regulated? Without engaging in a full discussion of these arenas, there is, I think, some overlap with my own account: parts, although not all, of (1) and (2) seem possible within policy historiography; the reflection and self-critique by policy analysts, discussed above, are echoed in (4); while (3) speaks of what I discuss below as policy genealogy.

Here I want to focus on those parts of Scheurich's (1994) characterization that seem implied in a policy archaeology that 'tries to establish the rules of [policy] formation' (Foucault 1972: 207). I suspect that I take this to mean a little less than Scheurich – that is, I restrict policy archaeology to the analysis of constitutive rules and position 'the conditions of their realization' (Foucault 1972: 207) as the interest of policy genealogy – and perhaps I mean a little more than Scheurich, including the licensing of policy makers and their relations as part of the process of policy formation. In this account, critical policy archaeology asks: (1) why are some items on the policy agenda (and not others)?; (2) why are some policy actors involved in the production of policy (and not others)? and (3) what are the conditions that regulate the patterns of interaction of those involved? Representing Australian higher education entry policy in this way, I drew on the documentary records listed above but also on 27 semi-structured, in-depth interviews with policy actors located at various levels of the Australian state: politicians and political advisors (PPA), bureaucrats and policy advisors (BPA), independent authorities (IA) and academics and university administrators (AUA).[4]

The research produced a number of strategies in the legitimation of policy agendas: the prescription, incorporation, leverage, currency, mediation, and dislocation associated with dominant policy discourse and their utilization in the determination of higher education entry policy. Embedded in this analysis was also a sense of 'chronology' of agendas and events, important for understanding the strategies employed to advance some agendas over others. A similar excavation delivered a number of licensing strategies: the authorities, changes, conditions, spaces and places legitimated by the state[5] in the production of higher education entry policy. While these strategies were largely presented as discrete, the research was also cognizant of interaction among them. For example, the strategy of licensing some actors and groups of actors, so that 'only certain voices are heard at any point in time' (Ball 1994a: 16), was not just concerned with controlling who will 'speak' policy but also with what agendas are heard. Similarly, determining the 'who' of policy production (as object) necessarily influenced aspects of their interaction.

Again, some illustration is valuable here to better explain this policy archaeology work. For example, excavations of the processes involved in the production of diversified-entry policy identified the agenda-setting strategy of incorporation, employed by policy actors to make competing agendas subservient. The strategy operated on two levels; by raising a specific discourse to a more general level and by appealing to some discourse pervading broader contexts. The following interview extract provides an example of the latter in which a policy actor, a federal bureaucrat, relates the discourse that, at the time, repositioned education as the handmaiden of the economy:

> this human capital stuff is fairly hard to untangle but what I think was being said was that the OECD [Organization for Economic Cooperation and Development] countries – the major western industrial democracies – were going to become more sophisticated producers of goods and services and that that would need to be driven by a more highly educated workforce than had been the case hitherto, where we nourished some fairly traditional professions and left it largely at that.
>
> (BPA2)

A further and related way of framing these matters of university entry involved the exclusion of some discourses and their speakers from policy agendas. This strategy of dislocation sought to represent some discourses as irrelevant. In this vein, notice how the politician in the following extract portrays the efforts of the Queensland National Party as 'too little, too late':

> Ahern [the National Party Premier of Queensland from 1988 to 1989] – who did have a genuine interest in education – when he became Premier he made a last despairing effort, but it was too late. In the budget immediately prior to the '89 election, which meant it came out in September, he made a big play for education but, of course, it was too late. They'd had 32 years prior to that and they hadn't done it [commit State funds to secure additional university places]. He was genuine. I don't think he was doing it just for political gain. He was a guy who had a university education himself and had an interest, but it was too late.
>
> (PPA1)

Other strategies included authoritative claims by policy actors to jurisdiction in policy production matters. In a context where Australian universities are entities created by State legislation, there were interesting interactions with federal government bureaucrats who made various claims to their overarching importance. Their claim was often grounded in a:

> rail gauge logic. If you want trains to run from one State to another, they are more efficient if they're on a standard gauge. Well, if you want people to be able to move as skilled labour across the country, it's more efficient if the educational infrastructure is common.
>
> (BPA1)

A final example illustrates how formal and informal contexts of policy production were also strategically used to achieve certain ends and how they could be restricted to specific policy actors. It also provides an example of the relations between policy actors who are differently licensed to participate in the policy production process. As one federal bureaucrat commented with regard to one agenda setting event:

> The agreement was [reached as a result of] political pressure from [the Queensland Premier]. Now, I wasn't party to that discussion personally. I only know the way in which it was vented, but there was just a lot of heat put on to do with the need to provide for certain marginal seats in Queensland. This is not atypical government activity, nor is it necessarily wrong.
>
> (BPA1)

I should explain, before I move on, some apparent differences that arise in these illustrations between how policy archaeology in this account deals with policy actors and how Scheurich and Foucault deal with them. Scheurich (1994: 314), for example, recognizes his 'debt to critical theory' and its influence in his rendition of policy archaeology, although without giving 'centre stage to the conscious actions of social agents' as in other critical work. Perhaps here he interacts too closely with Foucault (see Scheurich 1994: 297), for archaeology in Foucault's hands is purposely devoid of conscious subjects. In the policy archaeology outlined above, however, I have not been interested in a subjective analysis of policy actors but in their objectification. That is, what is important to uncover is not so much who speaks but what is spoken, what positions it is spoken from, and how this is mediated by the speaking positions of others; an architecture of policy positions. Moreover, this is not dissimilar to the interests of critical theorists who have long been sceptical of 'great man' theories of policy production. In this sense, an interest in policy actors is not an interest in authorship but in vocality. To avoid an archaeology of policy actors is to see only that policy problems are constructions without fully understanding the conditions of their construction.

Policy genealogy

A third lens with which to analyse policy could be termed policy genealogy, which has at heart an interest in the particulars of temporary policy settlements – the 'modalities of power' (Davidson 1986: 224) – an appropriate foil to policy archaeology's interest in policy settlement parameters. Indeed, it is genealogy that enables insight into policy 'realizations' that are defined by (archaeological) rules of their formation (Foucault 1972: 207). This should not be taken to mean the discovery of simple continuities between past and present, and parameters and particulars, for 'genealogy seeks out discontinuities where others found continuous development' (Dreyfus and Rabinow 1986). Policy genealogy, then, is not convinced by analyses of policy production explained by 'bounded rationality' (Simon 1960) or 'incrementalism' achieved through 'partisan mutual adjustment' (Lindblom 1959). Certainly, it asks (1) how policies change over time, but it also seeks to determine (2) how the rationality and consensus of policy production might be problematized and (3) how temporary alliances are formed and reformed around conflicting interests in the policy production process. Intentionally, 'what emerges out of this is something one might call a genealogy, or rather a multiplicity of genealogical researches, a painstaking rediscovery of struggles together with the rude memory of their conflicts' (Foucault 1994: 22).

The explorations below of diversified-entry policy in Australian higher education are more sporadic in their representations than those above and are offered in the form of descriptive and analytical vignettes, informed by interviews with policy actors described above. There is not the same impetus in policy genealogy to present a sequential account that weaves itself through an analysis of strategies of negotiation. In part, this is because the broad narratives of higher education entry have already been advanced through its historiography and archaeology, but it also reflects genealogy's different emphases. That is, the delineation here of negotiation strategies is focused on a particular dimension of the Australian higher education entry settlement and on the encapsulation of these strategies in 'local' specific knowledges.

The research disclosed six strategies in the negotiation of settlement particulars developed from the data: strategies of trading; bargaining; arguing; stalling; manoeuvring and lobbying. While their separations imply a certain discreteness, they are more cogently understood as interrelated. For instance, a certain amount of stalling can be exercised in the process of bargaining, lobbying can involve a degree of trading and argument, while a strategic manoeuvre might involve several strategies of negotiation. Each of these strategies is illustrated in turn.

Trading: negotiating the exchange of interests

> [one policy maker] would come to the Reference Committee and she would listen to them and then she would say, 'No, I don't like that, I won't do that'... [but] she's a very good operator, because at the same time, when she is strong and makes her position, she'll tend to give a bit of ground somewhere else. So, she doesn't alienate people, or there's a minimum of that.
>
> (IA7)

Bargaining: negotiating the moderation of interests

> we went out publicly and got the school leaver targets back because the [Federal] Government was getting hit over the head with the huge retention increases to Year 12 – social pressure from parents and kids – and the universities themselves had argued with the Government that they needed to expand the sector in order to accommodate the Year 12 increases. So we thought at least on that we could hold them, so we included these school leaver targets. Then they came back to [us to] say by using them we were denying mature age access.
>
> (BPA1)

Arguing: negotiating the persuasion of interests

> We had a lot of big fights about important things... I tried very hard to talk them into one form of scaling – I tried really hard – and if you read Maxwell's argument (the first appendix) you can see why I couldn't and anyone who wants to get rid of one form of scaling, has to answer Maxwell's argument. And that's why it's there as the first appendix [in the policy document].
>
> (AUA6)

Stalling: delaying the negotiation of interests

> one of the sources of greatest frustration for me and for this Board all through the early 80s was the fact that we could never ever get any dialogue with the Federal government. It was a stone wall... I went to Canberra on a number of occasions and interviewed numbers of different people. ... They'd always be interviewed off the record, particularly if they were senior public servants. Never on the record. ... We believed that Queensland was

> being given a raw deal in terms of allocation of places and funds and all the rest of it.
>
> (IA7)

Manoeuvring: negotiating the circumvention of interests

> one group who'll be pushing it is the Commonwealth, again because it'll get them off this policy hook about shifting load. If they can say, 'Well, anyone can apply anywhere and go anywhere easily and there are no formal barriers to that', then that gets them a bit off that policy hook that they really need to put political pressure on Victoria to get rid of places. So they'll be supporting it. But the other bunch that are supporting it – this is what makes me really cross – is the bloody Directors of Admission Centres because they can become a national empire, you know.
>
> (BPA4)

Lobbying: negotiating the coalition of interests

> imbibe all this macro stuff about the economic environment and we construct rationales that are influential in those terms. Now, a lot of it's unresearched and untested, but there's no doubt that we argue for certain things in terms of what we describe as perceived economic advantage. And then you also try to create a coalition of interests with what you know to be the Minister's personal interests... [S]ome ministers are better than others at principles and policy broadly and some are much more framed by personal experiences and understandings.
>
> (BPA4)

Conclusions

Reflecting on the use of these methods of doing critical policy sociology, there seem a number of observations worth making. First, if we were to organize these methods in a triangular relationship – and I am as yet unsure about the wisdom of doing so – interests in 'policy' seem to gravitate towards policy historiography whereas interests in 'policy production' (understood broadly as both formulation and implementation, see Gale 1994a) tend towards policy genealogy. Moreover, interests in both policy and policy production seem accommodated within policy archaeology. Similarly, in the utilization of data – and I should stress that this is a specific observation of my own research into the production of Australian higher education entry policy – doing policy historiography seemed to rely more on documentary and statistical data whereas policy genealogy required the data produced through semi-structured interview. Again, policy archaeology drew fairly evenly on both of these data.

A second set of observations concern *what*, *how*, and *why* questions of policy (Kenway 1990; Taylor *et al.* 1997; Gale 1999a) and, although not absolute, their relations between the respective interests of policy historiography, policy genealogy and policy archaeology. Similarly, and within the context of my research discussed above, policy historiography seems disposed to providing an overall account of temporary policy settlements whereas policy archaeology enables a detailing of the parameters of these settlements and policy genealogy its particulars. But I should caution that I do not mean to signal completion, having found the perfect combination of policy methods to unravel all policy matters. They are merely what I found useful and plausible in my questioning of and theorizing influences in the production of higher education entry policy in Australia. I could imagine other methods; policy narratology, for example, with its interests in text, story, and fabula (see Bal 1997), could be another worth pursuing to discern how narratives (both policy and policy analysis) are ordered and arranged. These, of course, are early thoughts and will need further exploration as will the policy methods outlined above.

Notes

1 Such comparisons cast doubt over the value of 'analysis of' and 'analysis for' (Gordon *et al.* 1977; Kenway 1990: 5–6) distinctions in policy work or Hammersley's (1994) more general three ideal–typical models of the research–practice relationship in policy analysis.
2 In archaeology and genealogy the emphases are somewhat different. Both foreground a history of the present or a contemporary history, although in archaeology a history of the past appears absent whereas in genealogy there is recognition of continuities and discontinuities between past and present.
3 I suspect there is now a new crisis in higher education entry that reads something like: 'Australia cannot afford to maintain universities at current (academic, numeric and financial) levels. Besides which, a university education is more of a personal benefit than a public one and, therefore, individuals should contribute (in part and/or in full) to its cost.' Settling this crisis seems to revolve around principles inspired by the market that, to some degree, have displaced or at least backgrounded issues of merit and have reworked matters of social justice.
4 When referencing the comments of interviewees, the acronyms PPA, BPA, IA and AUA are used throughout to protect individuals' anonymity while also giving the reader a sense of the 'vocalities' of interviewees with respect to entry policy in Australian higher education.
5 Throughout this paper, a distinction is made between: 'State' (first letter capitalized), which refers to one territory in a federation of territories that constitute a nation, as in 'the State of Queensland'; and 'state' (without capitalization), which refers to a nation's collective political governance, as in 'the Australian state'.

References

Agger, B. (1998) *Critical Social Theories: An Introduction* (Colorado: Westview Press).
Apple, M. (1996) Power, meaning and identity: critical sociology of education in the United States, *British Journal of Sociology of Education*, 17 (2), 125–44.
Atkinson, E., Conboy, I., Dodds, A., McInnis, C. and Atkinson, J. (1995) *Evaluation of the Open Learning Initiative: Interim report, March 1995* (Melbourne, Australia: Centre for the Study of Higher Education).

Bal, M. (1997) *Narratology: Introduction to the Theory of Narrative*, 2nd edn (Toronto, Canada: University of Toronto Press).

Ball, S. (1990) *Politics and Policy Making in Education: Explorations in Policy Sociology* (London, UK: Routledge).

Ball, S. (1993) What is policy? Texts, trajectories and toolboxes, *Discourse*, 13 (2), 10–17.

Ball, S. (1994a) *Education Reform: A Critical and Post-Structural Approach* (Buckingham, UK: Open University Press).

Ball, S. (1994b) Researching inside the state: issues in the interpretation of elite interviews, in D. Halpin and B. Troyna (eds) *Researching Education Policy: Ethical and Methodological Issues* (London, UK: Falmer Press), 107–20.

Ball, S. (1997) Policy sociology and critical social research: a personal review of recent education policy and policy research, *British Educational Research Journal*, 23 (3), 257–74.

Bartlett, L. (1987) Issues in the construction of an historical narrative, *Curriculum Perspectives*, 7 (1): 1–6.

Beilharz, P. (1987) Reading politics: social theory and social policy, *Australian and New Zealand Journal of Sociology*, 23 (3), 388–406.

Bowe, R., Ball, S. and Gold, A. (1992) *Reforming Education and Changing Schools: Case Studies in Policy Sociology* (London, UK: Routledge).

Brown, P., Halsey, A., Lauder, H. and Stuart Wells, A. (1997) The transformation of education and society: an introduction, in A. Halsey, H. Lauder, P. Brown and A. Stuart Wells (eds) *Education: Culture, Economy, and Society* (Oxford, UK: Oxford University Press), 1–44.

Codd, J. (1988) The construction and deconstruction of educational policy documents, *Journal of Education Policy*, 3 (3), 235–47.

Connell, R. (1994) Poverty and education, *Harvard Educational Review*, 64 (2), 125–49.

Connell, W. (1987) Research and writing in the history of education, in J. Keeves (ed.) *Australian Education: Review of Recent Research* (Sydney, Australia: Allen & Unwin).

Cox, R. (1980) Social forces, states and world orders' millennium, *Millennium: Journal of International Studies*, 10 (2), 126–55.

Dale, R. (1989) *The State and Education Policy* (Milton Keyenes: Open University Press).

Dale, R. (1992) Recovering from a Pyrrhic Victory? Quality, relevance and impact in the sociology of education, in M. Arnot and L. Barton (eds) *Voicing Concerns* (Wallingford, Triangle).

Davidson, A. I. (1986) Archaeology, genealogy, ethics, in D.C. Hoy (ed.) *Foucault: A Critical Reader* (Oxford: Basil Blackwell), 221–33.

Deem, R. and Brehony, K. (1994) Why didn't you use a survey so you could generalize your findings? Methodological issues in a multiple site case study of school governing bodies after the 1988 Education Reform Act, in D. Halpin & B. Troyna (eds) *Researching Education Policy: Ethical and Methodological Issues* (London, UK: Falmer Press), 154–69.

Dreyfus, H. and Rabinow, P. (1986) *Michel Foucault: Beyond Structuralism and Hermeneutics* (Brighton, UK: Harvester Press).

Fairclough, N. (1992) *Discourse and Social Change* (Cambridge, UK: Polity Press).

Foucault, M. (1972) *The Archaeology of Knowledge* (London, UK: Tavistock).

Foucault, M. (1994) Two lectures, in M. Kelly (ed.) *Critique and Power: Recasting the Foucault/Habermas Debate* (Cambridge, MA: MIT Press), 17–46.

Gale, T. (1994a) Beyond caricature: exploring theories of educational policy production and implementation, *Australian Educational Researcher*, 21 (2), 1–12.

Gale, T. (1994b) Story-telling and policy making: the construction of university entrance problems in Australia, *Journal of Education Policy*, 9 (3), 227–32.

Gale, T. (1999a) Policy trajectories: treading the discursive path of policy analysis, *Discourse*, 20 (3), 393–407.

Gale, T. (1999b) Fair contest or elite sponsorship? Entry settlements in Australian higher education, *Higher Education Policy*, 12 (1), 69–91.

Gewirtz, S. and Ozga, J. (1990) Partnership, pluralism and education policy: a reassessment, *Journal of Education Policy*, 5 (1), 35–46.

Gordon, I., Lewis, J. and Young, K. (1977) Perspectives on policy analysis, *Public Administration Bulletin*, 25, 26–35.

Grace, G. (1998) Critical policy scholarship: reflections on the integrity of knowledge and research, in G. Shacklock and J. Smyth (eds) *Being Reflexive in Critical Educational and Social Research* (London: Falmer Press), 202–17.

Hall, S. (1984) The rise of the representative/interventionist state 1880s–1920s, in G. McLennan, D. Held and S. Hall (eds) *State and Society in Contemporary Britain: A Critical Introduction* (Cambridge, UK: Polity Press), 7–49.

Halpin, D. and Troyna, B. (eds) (1994) *Researching Education Policy: Ethical and Methodological Issues* (London, UK: Falmer Press).

Hammersley, M. (1994) Ethnography, policy making and practice in education, in D. Halpin and B. Troyna (eds) *Researching Education Policy: Ethical and Methodological Issues* (London, UK: Falmer Press), 139–53.

Harvey, L. (1990) *Critical Social Research* (London, UK: Allen & Unwin).

Henry, M. (1993) What is policy? A response to Stephen Ball, *Discourse*, 14 (1), 102–5.

Hogwood, B. and Gunn, L. (1984) *Policy Analysis for the Real World* (Oxford: Oxford University Press).

Kenway, J. (1990) *Gender and Education Policy: A Call for New Directions* (Geelong: Deakin University Press).

Kincheloe, J. (1991) Educational historiographical meta-analysis: rethinking methodology in the 1990s, *Qualitative Studies in Education*, 4 (3), 231–45.

Lenzo, K. (1995) Validity and self-reflexivity meet post-structuralism: scientific ethos and the transgressive self, *Educational Researcher*, 52 (1), 17–23.

Lindblom, C. (1959) The science of muddling through, *Public Administration Review*, 19, 79–88.

Lorde, A. (1984) *Sister Outsider* (New York, USA: Crossing Press).

McPherson, A. and Raab, C. (1988) *Governing Education: A Sociology of Policy* (Edinburgh, UK: Edinburgh University Press).

Maguire, M. and Ball, S. (1994) Researching politics and the politics of research: recent qualitative studies in the UK, *Qualitative Studies in Education*, 7 (3), 269–85.

Marshall, C. (1997) Dismantling and reconstructing policy analysis, in C. Marshall (ed.) *Feminist Critical Policy Analysis I: A Perspective from Primary and Secondary Schooling* (London, UK: Falmer Press), 1–39.

Michel Foucault (1980) Truth and power, in Colin Gordon (ed.) *Power/Knowledge, Selected Interviews and Other Writing* (New York: Pantheon).

Mills, C. W. (1959) *The Sociological Imagination* (Oxford, UK: Oxford University Press).

Offe, C. (1984) *Contradictions of the Welfare State* (Cambridge, MA: MIT Press).

Ozga, J. (1987) Studying educational policy through the lives of policy makers: an attempt to close the macro-micro gap, in S. Walker and L. Barton (eds) *Changing Policies, Changing Teachers* (Milton Keynes, UK: Open University Press), 138–50.

Ozga, J. (1990) Policy research and policy theory: a comment on Fitz and Halpin, *Journal of Education Policy*, 5 (4), 359–62.

Ozga, J. and Gewirtz, S. (1994) Sex, lies and audiotape: interviewing the education policy elite, in D. Halpin and B. Troyna (eds) *Researching Education Policy: Ethical and Methodological Issues* (London, UK: Falmer Press), 121–35.

Payne, G., Dingwall, R., Payne, J. and Carter, M. (1981) *Sociology and Social Research* (London: Routledge & Kegan Paul).

Petersen, R. (1992) *History of Education Research: What it is and How to do it* (Sydney, Australia: William Michael Press).

Prunty, J. (1985) Signposts for a critical educational policy analysis, *Australian Journal of Education*, 29 (2), 133–40.

Raab, C. (1994) Where we are now: reflections on the sociology of education policy, in D. Halpin and B. Troyna (eds) *Researching Education Policy: Ethical and Methodological Issues* (London, UK: Falmer Press), 17–30.

Rizvi, F. and Kemmis, S. (1987) *Dilemmas of Reform* (Geelong: Deakin University Press).

Scheurich, J. (1994) Policy archaeology: a new policy studies methodology, *Journal of Education Policy*, 9 (4), 297–316.

Shacklock, G. and Smyth, J. (eds) (1998) *Being Reflexive in Critical Educational and Social Research* (London, UK: Falmer Press).

Simon, H. (1960) *The New Science of Management Decision* (Englewood Cliffs, NJ: Prentice Hall).

Taylor, S. (1997) Critical policy analysis: exploring contexts, texts and consequences, *Discourse*, 18 (1), 23–35.

Taylor, S., Rizvi, F., Lingard, B. and Henry, M. (1997) *Educational Policy and the Politics of Change* (London, UK: Routledge).

Tripp, D. (1998) Critical incidents in action inquiry, in G. Shacklock and J. Smyth (eds) *Being Reflexive in Critical Educational and Social Research* (London, UK: Falmer Press), 36–49.

Troyna, B. (1994a) Critical social research and education policy, *British Journal of Educational Studies*, 42 (1), 70–84.

Troyna, B. (1994b) Reforms, research and being reflexive about being reflexive, in D. Halpin and B. Troyna (eds) *Researching Education Policy: Ethical and Methodological Issues* (London, UK: Falmer Press), 1–14.

Turner, R. (1971) Sponsored and contest mobility and the school system, in E. Hopper (ed.) *Readings in the Theory of Educational Systems* (London, UK: Hutchinson), 71–90.

Van Manen, M. (1990) *Researching Lived Experience: Human Science for an Action Sensitive Pedagogy* (New York: University of New York Press).

Wallace, G., Rudduck, J. and Harris, S. (1994) Students' secondary school careers: research in a climate of 'moving perspectives', in D. Halpin and B. Troyna (eds) *Researching Education Policy: Ethical and Methodological Issues* (London, UK: Falmer Press), 170–83.

Williams, T., Long, M., Carpenter, P. and Hayden, M. (1993) *Entering Higher Education in the* 1980s (Canberra, Australia: AGPS).

10 The construction and deconstruction of educational policy documents

John A. Codd

Massey University, Palmerston North, New Zealand

Source: *Journal of Education Policy*, 3 (3): 235–47, 1988.

Introduction

For a long time, the field of policy analysis has been fraught with argument over its purposes and methods. What began as a 'policy orientation' within social science (Lasswell 1951) was later elevated by some proponents to the level of 'a new supra discipline' (Dror 1971: ix). A widely accepted view, however, takes policy analysis to be a multidisciplinary field that cuts across existing specializations to employ whatever theoretical or methodological approach is most relevant to the issue or problem under investigation. According to Ham and Hill:

> the purpose of policy analysis is to draw on ideas from a range of disciplines in order to interpret the causes and consequences of government action, in particular by focusing on the processes of policy formulation.
>
> (Ham and Hill 1984: 11)

Policy here is taken to be any course of action (or inaction) relating to the selection of goals, the definition of values or the allocation of resources. Fundamentally, policy is about the exercise of political power and the language that is used to legitimate that process. Policy analysis is a form of enquiry which provides either the informational base upon which policy is constructed, or the critical examination of existing policies. The former has been called analysis *for* policy, whereas the latter has been called analysis *of* policy (Gordon *et al.* 1977: 27).

Analysis *for* policy can take two different forms: (*a*) *policy advocacy* which has the purpose of making specific policy recommendations; and (*b*) *information for policy* in which the researcher's task is to provide policy-makers with information and data to assist them in the revision or formulation of actual policies.

Analysis *of* policy can also take two different forms: (*a*) *analysis of policy determination and effects*, which examines 'the inputs and transformational processes operating upon the construction of public policy' (Gordon *et al.* 1977: 28) and also the effects of such policies on various groups; and (*b*) *analysis of policy content*, which examines the values, assumptions and ideologies underpinning the policy process.

The central focus of the following discussion is on the analysis of policy content, more specifically, the analysis of the content of policy documents. It is argued that such documents should be regarded as texts which are capable of being decoded in different ways depending upon the contexts in which they are read. It is suggested, moreover, that policy analysts can use some of the methods and theories of textual analysis that have been developed and refined within the field of literary criticism to examine the language content of policy documents. The discussion begins by challenging the dominant account of how official documents function within the policy formation process and questions the theory of language that it presupposes. An alternative approach, derived from a materialist theory of discourse, is then outlined. It is suggested that such an approach to the analysis of policy documents could be construed as a form of textual deconstruction in which ideological effects can be critically examined.

The state and educational policy

The orthodox liberal view of education and society emphasizes the role that schooling plays in promoting social mobility. Within this view, the state has a neutral function to protect the interests of all members of society by a system of universally accepted rules and regulations. Accordingly, the state will promote policies which are in 'the public interest' and whether or not individuals take advantage of those policies is assumed to be a matter that is largely their own responsibility. In this view, the overriding purpose of state policies is to provide an equitable means for the distribution of social goods (such as education) among competing groups on the basis of their needs or deserts. This is a view which, in New Zealand, we have seen exemplified in the writings of Renwick (1986). In recent years, however, this conception of the state has been criticized increasingly from a neo-Marxist point of view (Shuker 1987) in which it is argued that the capitalist Welfare State basically serves the interests of dominant groups within society. Within this critical tradition, Claus Offe's (1984) analysis of the welfare state provides some insights into the purposes, effects and necessary contradictions of many current and proposed government policies.

Offe argues, contrary to the claims of state-derivationist and structural-Marxist theories, that Welfare State policies do not necessarily or automatically serve the interests of the capitalist class. In his view, 'what the state protects and sanctions is a set of institutions and social relationships necessary for the domination of the capitalist class' (Offe 1984: 120) but it nevertheless seeks to implement and guarantee the collective interests of all members of society. In other words, the state works in the interests of the capitalist mode of production rather than exclusively in the interests of one class. In particular, it works to support the process of capital accumulation by providing a context in which the continued expansion of capital is accepted as legitimate. Moreover, the political power of the state depends, indirectly, on the private accumulation of capital which, through taxation, provides the state with its resources. The exercise of this power is legitimated through the democratic processes of election and representation. However, according to Offe, the state's role in the process of capital accumulation, while necessary to advanced forms of capitalism, produces a number of fundamental contradictions at the policy level. These contradictions frequently lead to the failure of policies in areas such as education but they often remain unrecognized because of the language in which such policies are couched. Thus, policies are produced in response to the failure of other policies leading to what Offe refers to as crises of crisis management. Examples within education can be identified in policies relating to assessment and credentialism, transition education and decentralization of curriculum control.

Offe's theory goes a long way towards explaining why the state has a particular interest in promoting public discussions of educational policy such as that which has been recently evidenced in New Zealand by *The Curriculum Review* (1987). Such discussion has become an accepted part of what is called 'the democratic process' through which people come to believe that the policies of the state are the result of 'public consent' rather than necessary forms of social control and crisis management. In other words, if people believe that political decisions are the result of public discussion, and if they have the right to contribute to that discussion, then they are most likely to accept rather than resist existing power relationships.

Because the state has a particular interest in promoting public discussion of educational policy, its agencies produce various policy documents which can be said to constitute the official discourse of the state (Codd 1985). Thus, policies produced by and for the state are obvious instances in which language serves a political purpose, constructing particular meanings and signs that work to mask social conflict and foster commitment to the notion of a universal public interest. In this way, policy documents produce real social effects through the production and maintenance of consent. These effects, however, remain unrecognized by traditional forms of policy analysis which are derived from an idealist view of language and enshrined within technical-empiricist view of policy-making.

The technical-empiricist approach to policy-making

Policy documents are generally interpreted as expressions of political purpose, that is as statements of the courses of action that policy-makers and administrators intend to follow. Within this view, the analysis of a policy document becomes a quest for the authorial intentions presumed to lie behind the text. It is a form of analysis which is frequently part of an instrumentalist approach to the whole policy-making process.

Discrete functions are assigned to the policy researcher (who is a disinterested provider of information), the policymaker (who produces the policy) and the policy recipient (who interprets or implements the policy). The document itself is regarded as a vehicle of communication between these agents within the process.

The traditional view of policy-making is a technical-empiricist one in which the researcher or social scientist is expected to produce a body of knowledge encompassing various factual explanations and causal connections which policy-makers may then draw upon in the formulation of policy proposals and the writing of policy documents. The policy researcher produces the general laws and theories relating to the structures which govern educational processes, while the policy-maker must then decide the 'best means' of achieving certain predetermined goals. Thus, policy analysis is relegated to a totally instrumental function, succinctly described by Fay in the following terms:

> A policy science is supposed to be a device for organizing political thought in a rational way, merely a method for clarifying empirical relationships among alternative actions and for sorting out their likely consequences, and a procedure for making 'correct' decisions; as such, it is supposed to be employable by anyone, regardless of his political views, for any end whatsoever, and its results are supposed to be impartial in the sense of not being dependent upon the particular evaluations of the policy scientist for their truth.
>
> (Fay 1975: 57)

Expressed simply, the technical-empiricist view of policy formation treats educational provision as a set of means to given ends. These ends are expressions of educational aims and belong within the domain of values. How we might go about achieving them is a question for research and belongs within the domain of facts. Thus it is assumed that there are alternative means available to given ends and that the proper role for research is in evaluating the effectiveness and efficiency of alternative means for attaining the chosen ends. It is assumed that research (with its objective methods of data collection and theory validation) provides scientific knowledge about the means available and their relative effectiveness under different circumstances.

Within a technical-empiricist approach to educational policy-making, policy statements or documents relate educational intentions, in the form of values and goals, to factual information resulting from research. These statements must then be interpreted by those who would either discuss or implement the policy. This can be represented diagrammatically as in Figure 10.1.

Because policy documents are construed as *expressions* of particular information, ideas and intentions, the task of analysis becomes one of establishing the *correct* interpretation of the text. When there is controversy surrounding the meaning of a document, it is assumed that some readers have misunderstood what was meant. One of the tasks of the policy analyst within this approach therefore, is to clear up such confusions and establish an authoritative interpretation. However, in the next two sections it is argued that such a task is founded upon mistaken

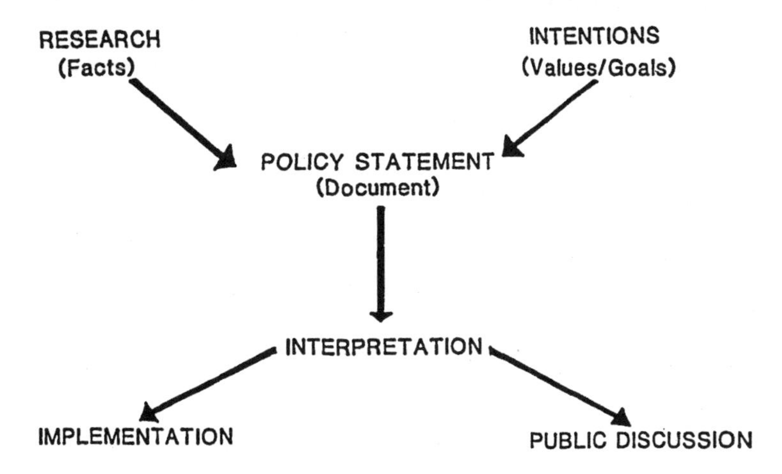

Figure 10.1 Technical-empiricist model of policy analysis.

idealist assumptions about both the nature of intentions and the nature of language itself. It is subsequently argued that these assumptions are widely held because they belong within a liberal humanist ideology which is largely successful in masking fundamental contradictions behind the rhetoric of many state policies.

The intentional fallacy

To assume that policy documents express intentions is to subscribe to a version of what in literary criticism has come to be known as the *intentional fallacy* (Wimsatt and Beardsley 1954). In essence, this particular version of the fallacy holds that the meaning of a literary text corresponds to what the author *intended*, that is the text is taken as being *evidence* of what the author intended to express. As Lyas (1973) points out, the fallacy can be shown to derive from an idealist confusion about the relevant sense of 'intention'. First, it is a mistake to think of intentions as private mental events (arguments which show this to be a mistake can be found in Wittgenstein's *Philosophical Investigations*, 1953). Second, intentions are not the same as 'statements of intention' (people can be mistaken about their own intentions). Third, we must distinguish between an intention in the sense of a prior plan or design and an action that is done *intentionally.* In short, it is the adverbial sense of intention, rather than the nominal sense, that is relevant to the interpretation of texts. The crucial point, however, is that nothing can be said about an author's intentions apart from various features of the text itself and the context in which it is interpreted. As Fay points out:

> Intentional explanations . . . make sense of a person's actions by fitting them into a purposeful pattern which reveals how the act was warranted, given the actor, his social and physical situation and his beliefs and wants. An intention

> is no more 'behind' the action than the meaning of the word is 'behind' the letters of which it is composed, and it is no more an 'invisible mental cause' of an act than is a melody the invisible cause of the pattern of notes that we hear at a concert.
>
> (Fay 1975: 73–4)

The place of intentional explanations in literary interpretation was first challenged by a group of literary critics in the 1940s and 1950s who have come to be associated with what is called the 'New Criticism' (Simonson 1971). These critics insisted upon what they called 'the autonomy of the text' which implied that the meaning of a text could not extend beyond the literary object itself. Some structuralists went even further, insisting upon a complete negation of the concept of authorship within literary analysis. Roland Barthes, for instance, has argued that:

> a text is not a line of words releasing a single 'theological' meaning (the 'message' of the Author-God) but a multi-dimensional space in which a variety of writings, none of them original, blend and clash.
>
> (Barthes 1977: 146)

Barthes goes even further when he adds that:

> a text's unity lies not in its origin but in its destination. . . . the birth of the reader must be at the cost of the death of the Author.
>
> (Barthes 1977: 148)

Another influential literary critic, Northrop Frye (1957) has also totally rejected the invocation of the author as any guarantee that a text can have a single meaning. What this means, essentially, is that for any text a plurality of readers must necessarily produce a plurality of readings.

Now, it should be recognized that there has been considerable debate about the nature of intentional explanations in literary criticism, and their significance for the validity of interpretation (Hirsch 1967). Nevertheless, there are important implications here for policy analysis, given that many policy documents do not even have single identifiable authors and are inevitably addressed to a plurality of readers. Instead of searching for authorial intentions, perhaps the proper task of policy analysis is to examine the differing effects that documents have in the production of meaning by readers. This would involve a form of discourse analysis developed within a materialistic theory of language. Before examining the implications of such an approach, however, it is necessary to consider the linguistic assumptions behind the traditional technical-empiricist approach to policy-making.

Linguistic idealism

Attempts to analyse policy documents by explicating the ideas within them and clarifying their intended meanings, presuppose a theory of language which may be called idealist because of the posited relationships between words, thoughts and things. These relationships were illustrated diagrammatically by Ogden and Richards (1923: 11) in what has come to be called 'the semiotic triangle' (see Figure 10.2).

Ogden and Richards argued that language bears an indirect relationship to the real world, one which is imputed because it is mediated by thought. The relationship between language and thought is direct and causal. Moreover:

> When we speak, the symbolism we employ is caused partly by the reference we are making and partly by social and psychological factors – the purpose for which we are making the reference, the proposed effect of our symbols on other persons and our own attitude. When we hear what is said, the symbols both cause us to perform an act of reference and to assume an attitude which will, according to circumstances, be more or less similar to the act and the attitude of the speaker.
>
> (Ogden and Richards 1923: 10–11)

Given these relationships, conceptual truth becomes a matter of the correctness of language in expressing what is thought and the adequacy of the language in producing a concurrence of thought in a suitable interpreter. Thus, within this

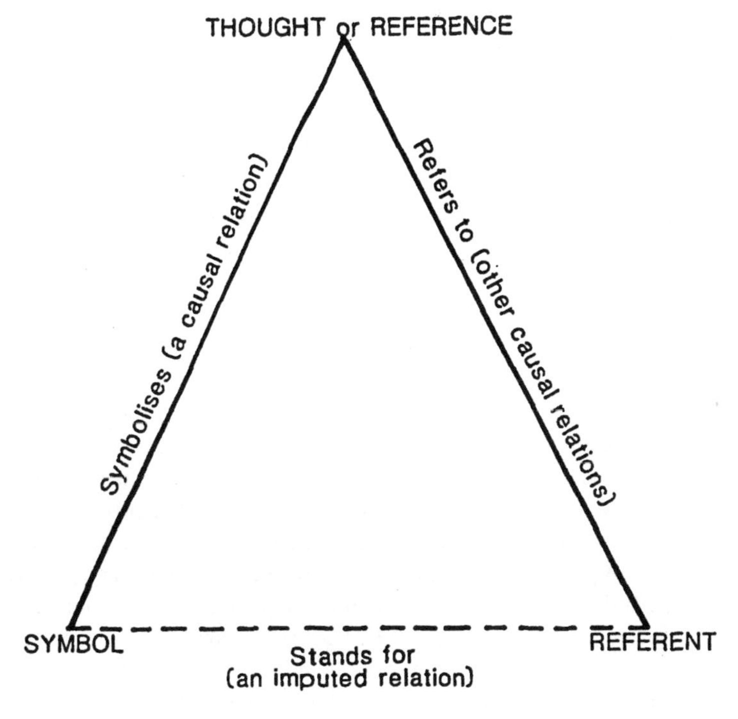

Figure 10.2 The semiotic triangle.

theory of language, symbolic truth (coherence) is distinguished from referential truth (correspondence). Ogden and Richards define symbolic (or conceptual) truth as follows:

> A true symbol = one which correctly records an adequate reference. It is usually a set of words in the form of a proposition or sentence. It correctly records an adequate reference when it will cause a similar reference to occur in a suitable interpreter. It is false when it records an inadequate reference.
>
> (Ogden and Richards 1923: 102)

This means that a proposition can be empirically false and yet also be a correct expression of what the speaker thought. Conceptual clarity is not dependent on empirical truth and Ogden and Richards make the point that:

> It is often of great importance to distinguish between false and incorrect propositions. An incorrect symbol is one which in a given universe of discourse causes in a suitable interpreter a reference different from that symbolized in the speaker.
>
> (Ogden and Richards 1923: 102)

This is the conception of language implicit in the work of policy analysts who seek to clarify the meaning of policy documents. The main point of their work is to make language transparent through correct use in order to produce commensurability of meaning amongst different readers of the text. Essentially, this kind of policy analysis takes language to be a transparent vehicle for the expression of experience. It is a view of language in which:

> Our concepts and our knowledge are held to be the product of experience (*empiricism*), and this experience is preceded and interpreted by the mind, reason or thought, the property of a transcendent human nature whose essence is the attribute of each individual (*idealism*).
>
> (Belsey 1980: 7)

What this empiricist-idealist view of language is unable to take into account, however, is that language itself is a sphere of social practice and is necessarily structured by the material conditions in which that practice takes place. This requires an alternative conception of language which recognizes that words, whether in speech-acts or texts, do more than simply name things or ideas that already exist. It requires a conception of how the use of language can produce real social effects, and how it can be political, not only by referring to political events, but by itself becoming the instrument and object of power. In particular, if it is to inform the analysis of policies produced by and for the state, it requires a conception of how language produces ideological effects by suppressing the contradictions of people's experience in the interests of preserving the existing social formation. Such a materialist conception of langauge has emerged within theories of discourse which can be traced back to the pioneering work of the French linguist, Ferdinand de Saussure.

Theories of discourse

Saussure's work has had a major influence on the structuralist tradition which adheres to the view that language precedes experience at some levels, making the world intelligible by differentiating between concepts. While this is not the place for a detailed account of structuralist theories of language, it shall suffice to say that this tradition has totally rejected the idea that language symbolizes the reality of an individual's experience and *expresses* that reality in a discourse which enables other individuals to recognize it as true.

Saussure challenged the notion that words express pre-existent ideas and the assumption that language can be reduced to a naming process. He argued that language is not simply a static set of signs through which individual agents transmit messages to each other about an externally constituted world of 'things'. Rather, language is a set of social practices which makes it possible for people to construct a meaningful world of individuals and things. In his pioneering work, Saussure distinguished between *langue* (the normative rules or conventions of language) and *parole* (the actual utterances made by speakers in concrete situations).

In opposition to idealist theories of language, Saussure argued that the linguistic sign unites, not a thing and a name, but a concept and a sound image. This is not a causal relationship, but rather, as Saussure pointed out:

> The two elements are intimately united, and each recalls the other. Whether we try to find the meaning of the Latin word 'arbor' or the word that Latin uses to designate the concept 'tree', it is clear that only the associations sanctioned by that language appear to us to conform to reality, and we disregard whatever others might be imagined.
>
> (Saussure 1974: 66–7)

Saussure argued that language is a product of social forces. It is *both* an arbitrary system of signs *and* a domain of socially constituted practices. Like any other social institution it will change over time but always within social and temporal limits. Such limits, or structures, both enable and at the same time check the amount of choice that is available to a community of language users.

> Language is checked not only by the weight of the collectivity but also by time. These two are inseparable. At every moment solidarity with the past checks freedom of choice. We say *man* and *dog* because our predecessors said *man* and *dog*. This does not prevent the existence in the total phenomenon of a bond between the two antithetical forces – arbitrary convention by virtue of which choice is free and time which causes choice to be fixed. Because the sign is arbitrary, it follows no law other than that of tradition, and because it is based on tradition, it is arbitrary.
>
> (Saussure 1974: 74)

Saussure's work was to prepare the way for a materialist theory of language in which the term *discourse* has come to be used to embody both the formal system of signs *and* the social practices which govern their use. In this sense, *discourse* refers not only to the meaning of language but also to the real effects of language-use, to the materiality of language. A discourse is a domain of language-use and therefore a domain of lived experience. It can be ideological in the Althusserian sense because it can become an unconscious, taken-for-granted 'system of representations' (Althusser 1969: 231–6). This form of ideology is *inscribed in* discourse rather than symbolized by it, in other words, it is not synonymous with a set of doctrines or a system of beliefs which individuals may choose to accept or reject. As Catherine Belsey points out:

> A discourse involves certain shared assumptions which appear in the formulations that characterize it. The discourse of common sense is quite distinct, for instance, from the discourse of modern physics, and some of the formulations of the one may be expected to conflict with the formulations of the other. Ideology is *inscribed in* discourse in the sense that it is literally written or spoken *in it*; it is not a separate element which exists independently in some free-floating realm of 'ideas' and is subsequently embodied in words, but a way of thinking, speaking, experiencing.
>
> (Belsey 1980: 5)

Because people participate in a range of discourses (political, scientific, religious) there are manifold ways in which they can signify and represent the conditions of their lived experience. But this does not separate discourse from subjective experience. Rather, discourse itself is constitutive of subjective experience and is also a material force within the construction of subjectivity (Macdonell 1986).

The point has been made earlier that theories of discourse are centrally concerned with the relationship between language and ideology. In this sense, ideology includes all the ways in which meaning (signification) serves to sustain relations of domination (Thompson 1984). To explain this further, it is necessary to invoke the notion of discursive power. Only within a materialist view of language is it possible to show how discourse can mediate the exercise of power, for it must go beyond the meaning of what is said to the act of saying it. As Bourdieu has stated:

> Language is not only an instrument of communication or even of knowledge, but also an instrument of power. One seeks not only to be understood but also to be believed, obeyed, respected, distinguished.
>
> (Bourdieu 1977: 648)

To understand how language can be an instrument of power it is necessary to extend the concept of power itself. At one level, power can be readily understood as coercive force or restraint. What is much more difficult to comprehend is the idea of power being exercise through consent, through what Gramsci called 'ideological hegemony'. To recognize power in terms of sovereignty or exploitation is less problematic than to recognize the forms of power which penetrate consciousness itself. These latter forms of power are normatively exercised within structures of distorted communication and false constructions of social reality. As institutionalized forms of domination they constitute pervasive expressions of power without normally being recognized as such by those who are affected. These are the micro-technologies of power that have been studied with such acute concentration in the work of Michel Foucault.

While rejecting the orthodox Marxist distinction between knowledge and ideology, Foucault has advanced the view that all knowledge is a product of power relations. Within this view, he has developed a non-economic analysis of power and power relations (Smart 1983). Rather than being a possession or commodity, power is exercised through dispositions, techniques, examinations and discourses. Foucault argues that:

> In a society such as ours, but basically in any society, there are manifold relations of power which permeate, characterize and constitute the social body, and these relations of power cannot themselves be established, consolidated nor implemented without the production, accumulation, circulation and functioning of a discourse. There can be no possible exercise of power without a certain economy of discourses of truth which operates through and on the basis of this association.
>
> (Foucault 1980: 93)

The power that is exercised through discourse is a form of power which permeates the deepest recesses of civil society and provides the material conditions in which individuals are produced both as subjects and as objects. It is this form of power which is exercised through the discourses of the law, of medicine, psychology and education.

In most modern societies, the education system is controlled by the state, but it works to maintain relations of power throughout the society as a whole. For this reason, the official discourse of the state relating to educational policies (e.g. core curriculum, transition education, systems of assessment or school management) are obvious instances in which discourse becomes the instrument and object of power. But discourses operate at a number of levels within educational institutions. Teachers, for example, have their own craft discourse relating to pedagogical practice. This discourse will impose limits upon what is possible in areas of classroom organization control and discipline, or the assessment of learning. More importantly, however, the whole schooling process is an apparatus for the distribution, appropriation and stratification of discourses. Foucault writes about schooling in the following way:

> But we know very well that, in its distribution, in what it permits and what it prevents, it follows the lines laid down by social differences, conflicts and

> struggles. Every educational system is a political means of maintaining or modifying the appropriation of discourses, with the knowledge and power they bring with them.
>
> (Foucault 1972: 46)

In addition to these discourses embodied in school curricula, there are many theoretical discourses *about* educational phenomena which have been instrumental in the exercise of power and have had far-reaching effects upon the institution of schooling. The discourse of psychometrics, for instance, is an obvious case in point (Rose 1979; Gould 1981). During a period of 50 years, the language of mental measurement has penetrated the craft discourse of teachers and shaped their practices. A critical analysis of such discourse seeks to expose the connections between psychometric theories and administrative practices, revealing the effects of using this form of technical language to legitimate the exercise of power.

Deconstructing policy documents: the case of 'The Curriculum Review'

The deconstruction of official discourse, in the form of documents, reports and policy statements, treats such texts as cultural and ideological artifacts to be interpreted in terms of their implicit patterns of signification, underlying symbolic structures and contextual determinants of meaning (Burton and Carlen 1979). Policy documents in this kind of analysis do not have a single authoritative meaning. They are not blueprints for political action, expressing a set of unequivocal intentions. They are ideological texts that have been constructed within a particular historical and political context. The task of deconstruction begins with the explicit recognition of that context.

In New Zealand during the 1980s much of the public discussion about education has focused on policies concerning the official, or 'core' school curriculum. In March 1984, a major controversy arose when the politically conservative Minister of Education at that time released a policy document (*A Review of the Core Curriculum for Schools*) allowing a period of only eight weeks for public comment and formal submissions. Among other proposals, the policy contained a list of 'basic' subjects which schools would be compelled to teach for stipulated minimum periods of time. Teachers' organizations, academic commentators and spokespeople on the political 'left' condemned the document for what were perceived to be its restrictive and anti-democratic implications.

Coincidentally, at the height of this controversy, the government called a 'snap' election and, perhaps predictably, with public attention already focused on the core curriculum for schools, education became an election issue. The opposition Labour Party pledged to 're-open' the discussion and to extend the opportunities for consultation and participation. Labour won the election on 14 July 1984 and the new Minister of Education announced that the review of the core curriculum for schools would be re-opened and would involve wide public discussion.

The Committee to Review the Curriculum for Schools was set up by the Minister in November 1984. During the following year, a series of issue booklets were distributed to stimulate and focus public discussion. In this phase of the review, more than 21,500 responses were received from individuals and groups, including students, parents, school committees, boards, teacher organizations, Maori and Pacific Island groups and community education organizations. A draft report was released in August 1986 and a further 10,000 responses were received. The final document, entitled *The Curriculum Review*, was released in March 1987. It has subsequently been lauded by the political 'left' while invoking strong criticism from the 'right' for its 'liberal and costly' proposals.

The Curriculum Review is a 128 page policy document divided into two main sections. The first section sets out the policy and the second is largely descriptive of the review process itself. Considered as a whole, the document is constructed within an ideological framework of liberal humanism which enables the text to be read in different ways by readers who occupy different social locations. Belsey describes the main assumptions upon which such a framework rests:

> The ideology of liberal humanism assumes a world of non-contradictory (and therefore fundamentally unalterable) individuals whose unfettered consciousness is the origin of meaning, knowledge and action. It is in the interests of this ideology above all to suppress the role of language in the construction of the subject, and to present the individual as a free, unified autonomous subjectivity.
>
> (Belsey 1980: 67)

Within this kind of ideology, policy texts such as *The Curriculum Review* are constructed as determinate representations (i.e. they claim to convey intelligible relationships between elements of social reality). Hence, the document opens with a statement which focuses on the individual learner and projects an image of social harmony surrounding the institution of schooling.

> The learner is at the heart of all educational planning. Learning is the distinctive purpose of schools. Learning happens best when there is an active partnership of students, teachers, families, and the community.
>
> (*The Curriculum Review* 1987: 8)

The document asserts that a national common curriculum should 'be given status by regulation' and that 'each school have responsibility to develop a school curriculum which is consistent with the national common curriculum'. In other words, the document presents simultaneously proposals which can be interpreted as representing *both* centralization and decentralization of control. There is a strong emphasis on school and community based planning of the curriculum while, at the same time, it is stated that each school's curriculum 'must be agreed to by the schools' managing body, and approved by the district senior inspector' (p. 21). Nowhere in the document is the possibility of conflicts of interest discussed and the fundamental contradiction between autonomy and control is not addressed directly.

One of the central tasks for the critical analysis of a document such as *The Curriculum Review* is a deconstruction of its text which focuses on the processes of its production as well as on the organization of the discourses which constitute it and the strategies by which it masks the contradictions and incoherences of the ideology that is inscribed in it. The process of deconstruction of policy texts is an objective process because such texts contain within themselves an implicit critique of their own values.

The values that are central to *The Curriculum Review* are explicitly presented within the 15 basic principles upon which the national common curriculum is to be developed. These principles signify an ideal set of conditions which prescribe that the curriculum shall be: common to all schools; accessible to every student; non-racist and non-sexist; able to ensure significant success for all students; whole; balanced; of the highest quality for every student; planned; co-operatively designed; responsive, inclusive, enabling, enjoyable. These values presuppose the existence of a social context in which it is possible for all individuals to gain maximum fulfilment – a society which is non-competitive and where unlimited resources can be distributed to all on an equal basis. Such a society, of course, does not exist outside the liberal-humanist ideology within which it is conceived. The implicit critique of this ideology is signified by the document's total lack of any specific reference to a social context in which there are major structural inequalities and where there is fierce competition for finite resources. Nowhere does this document contain language which would draw the attention of the reader to the current fiscal crisis, the unequal distribution of power or the economic imperatives of a segmented labour market. The internal contradiction is brought into sharp focus by the small section of the document presented under the heading 'Economic Implications'. Here it is stated that:

> Some of the resources needed to implement the recommendations of this review already exist; others will need to be developed, and some of these have considerable financial implications.
>
> (*The Curriculum Review* 1987: 20)

This can be read as an *understatement* which draws attention to the impossibility of achieving what the 15 principles prescribe. Such a reading however, which is a deconstruction of the text's explicit meaning, requires a new process of production of meaning by the reader.

The above example serves to illustrate how the process of deconstruction can be used in the analysis of a policy document such as *The Curriculum Review.* This process needs to distance itself from the imaginary coherence of the text, examining its discourse and viewing it not as a vehicle for communicating 'information' or transmitting 'a plan of action', but as an ideologically constructed product of political forces. Because it is unable to produce a coherent and internally consistent representation of a contradictory social world, the policy text, in spite of itself, embodies incoherences, distortions, structured omissions and negations which in turn expose the inability of the language of ideology to produce coherent meaning. Deconstructive analysis would focus on the process of production of the text as well as on the organization of the discourses which constitute it and the linguistic strategies by which it masks the contradictions and incoherences of the ideology that is inscribed in it. The purpose of deconstructing policy texts is to ascertain their actual and potential effects upon readers, rather than to establish the intended meaning of their authors. As Belsey points out:

> The aim is to locate the point of contradiction within the text, the point at which it transgresses the limits within which it is constructed, breaks free of the constraints imposed by its own realist form. Composed of contradictions, the text is no longer restricted to a single, harmonious and authoritative reading. Instead it becomes *plural*, open to re-reading, no longer an object for passive consumption but an object of work by the reader to produce meaning.
>
> (Belsey 1980: 104)

Empirical evidence of a policy document's plurality of meaning can be readily obtained from an examination of the comments made about it by various categories of reader. The widely differing comments made about *The Curriculum Review*, for example, by representatives of teachers' and parents' organizations, politicians, various conservative (and liberal) pressure groups and, most notably, The Treasury, demonstrate the wide spectrum of interpretations that such a text can elicit. The aim of discourse analysis is not to prove which of these readings is *correct* but to consider them *all* as evidence of the text's inherent ideological ambiguities, distortions and absences. In this way, it is possible to penetrate the ideology of official policy documents and expose the real conflicts of interest within the social world which they claim to represent.

Conclusion

In surveying the field of policy analysis a decade ago, Dye suggested that it was a weakness of such analysis that it concentrated 'primarily upon activities of governments, rather than the rhetoric of governments' (Dye 1976: 21). What were needed, however, were methods appropriate to this new task. This article has gone some way towards outlining an alternative approach to the analysis of policy documents based on theories of discourse.

References

Althusser, L. (1969) *For Marx*, trans. B. Brewster (London: Penguin).

Barthes, R. (1977) 'The death of the author' in *Image-Music-Text* (Glasgow: Fontana/Collins). (Originally published in French.)

Belsey, C. (1980) *Critical Practice* (London: Methuen).

Bourdieu (1977) 'The economics of linguistic exchanges', *Social Science Information*, 16(6), pp. 645–68.

Burton, F. and Carlen, P. (1979) *Official Discourse* (London: Routledge & Kegan Paul).
Codd, J. A. (1985) 'Images of schooling and the discourse of the state' in J. Codd, R. Harker and R. Nash (eds) *Political Issue in New Zealand Education* (Palmerston North: Dunmore Press), pp. 23–41.
Dror, Y. (1971) *Design for Policy Sciences* (New York: Elsevier).
Dye, T. R. (1976) *Policy Analysis* (Alabama: University of Alabama Press).
Fay, B. (1975) *Social Theory and Political Practice* (London: Allen and Unwin).
Foucault, M. (1972) *The Archaeology of Knowledge* (London: Tavistock).
Foucault, M. (1980) 'Two lectures', in C. Gordon (ed.) *Power/Knowledge: Selected Interviews and Other Writings 1972–1977* (Brighton: Harvester Press), pp. 78–108.
Frye, N. (1957) *Anatomy of Criticism* (Princeton: Princeton University Press).
Gordon, I., Lewis, J. and Young, K. (1977) 'Perspectives on policy analysis', *Public Administration Bulletin*, 25, pp. 26–35.
Gould, S. J. (1981) *The Mismeasure of Man* (London: Penguin).
Ham, C. and Hill, M. (1984) *The Policy Process in the Modern Capitalist State* (Brighton: Harvester Press).
Hirsch, E. D. (1967) *Validity in Interpretation* (New Haven: Yale University Press).
Lasswell, H. (1951) 'The policy orientation', in D. Lerner and H. Lasswell (eds) *The Policy Sciences* (Stanford: Stanford University Press), pp. 3–15.
Lyas, C. (1973) 'Personal qualities and the intentional fallacy', in G. Vesey (ed.) *Philosophy and the Arts* (London: Macmillan), pp. 194–210.
Macdonell, D. (1986) *Theories of Discourse* (Oxford: Blackwell).
Offe, C. (1984) *Contradictions of the Welfare State* (London: Hutchinson).
Ogden, C. K. and Richards, I. A. (1923) *The Meaning of Meaning* (London: Routledge & Kegan Paul).
Renwick, W. L. (1986) *Moving Targets* (Wellington: NZCER).
Report of the Committee to Review the Curriculum for Schools (1987) *The Curriculum Review* (Wellington: Government Printer).
Review of the Core Curriculum for Schools (1984) (Wellington: Department of Education).
Rose, N. (1979) 'The psychological complex: mental measurement and social administration', *Ideology and Consciousness*, 5, pp. 5–68.
Saussure, F. (1974) *Courses in General Linguistics* (London: Fontana/Collins). (Originally published in French 1916.)
Shuker, R. (1987) *The One Best System* (Palmerston North: Dunmore Press).
Simonson, H. P. (1971) *Strategies in Criticism* (New York: Holt, Rinehart and Winston).
Smart, B. (1983) *Foucault, Marxism and Critique* (London: Routledge & Kegan Paul).
Thompson, J. B. (1984) *Studies in the Theory of Ideology* (Cambridge: Polity Press).
Wimsatt, W. and Beardsley, M. (1954) 'The intentional fallacy', in W. K. Wimsatt (ed.) *The Verbal Icon* (London: Methuen), pp. 3–18.
Wittgenstein, L. (1953) *Philosophical Investigations*, trans. G. E. M. Anscombe (Oxford: Blackwell).

11 Community, philosophy and education policy

Against effectiveness ideology and the immiseration of contemporary schooling

Michael Fielding

University of Sussex Institute of Education

Source: *Journal Education Policy*, 15 (4), 397–415, 2000.

Introduction

We are facing a multiple crisis within this country, a crisis of intellectual and imaginative nerve that currently afflicts policy makers, teachers in schools and the research community alike. We remain prisoners of an outmoded intellectual framework and a properly zealous political will; taken together they present a well-intentioned, if mistaken, symbiosis and as a consequence our demise is likely to deepen rather than disperse. Just as school effectiveness and school improvement articulate the moribund categories of a frightened, unimaginative society so the aspirant hegemony of the technologies of teaching provide a classroom equivalent which will do more damage more quickly and more widely than its institutional predecessor.

The contention of this paper is that an alternative perspective exists and it is now both appropriate and urgent that we give it our collective attention. The alternative for which I am arguing centres round the centrality of community in human affairs in general and in education in particular and takes as its starting point the work of the Scottish philosopher, John Macmurray, one of the great unsung figures of twentieth-century British philosophy.[1] In Section 1 *Community, Emancipation and Inclusion*, I outline Macmurray's account of community tracing his key philosophical distinctions which give it such a welcome emancipatory, inclusive edge. Section 2 *Understanding the Relationship between the Functional and the Personal: On The Integrity of the Personal*, picks up on Macmurray's outstanding work on the relationships between society and community, the functional and the personal, and in extending it I begin my own defence of the standpoint of the personal in education and my critique of the current instrumentalist hegemony under which much of our intellectual life and our current educational practice presently suffer. The section which follows (*Interrogating*

Two Sites of Education Policy: Applying a Personalist Framework) seeks to explore the efficacy of an interrogative framework against which current and future education policy might be judged. In its final section (*Why Effective Policies Won't Work*) the paper concludes with a renewed attack on the impotence and irrelevance of school effectiveness in serving the needs and aspirations of education and a reaffirmation of the importance and necessity of community.

Community, emancipation and inclusion: on the central importance of John Macmurray

One of the reasons that Macmurray's account of community is both profound and persuasive lies not merely in his willingness to provide a philosophical account of a difficult and challenging notion, but also in the remarkable coherence of his undertaking. In contrast to the lack of proper philosophical engagement with the notion of community itself which, surprisingly, seems to be a feature of much of the debate about communitarianism (see Fraser and Lacey 1993) Macmurray's articulation of community draws as much on the realms of ontology, axiology, and epistemology as it does on the more commonly encountered fields of ethics, philosophical psychology, and social and political philosophy.

At root Macmurray's account of community is coterminous with his account of what it is to be and become human. In providing an account of the one you must inevitably be providing an account of the other because our being as persons is essentially mutual. For Macmurray:

> The self is one term in the relation between two selves. It cannot be prior to that relation and equally, of course, the relation cannot be prior to it. '*I*' exist only as a member of the '*you and I*'. The self only exists in the communion of selves.
>
> (Macmurray 1933: 137)

or, as he put it nearly 30 years later in the second of his Gifford Lectures:

> We need one another to be ourselves. This complete and unlimited dependence of each of us upon the others is the central and crucial fact of personal existence... Here is the basic fact of our human condition.
>
> (Macmurray 1961: 211)

Whilst this essential mutuality of human being and becoming, this relational, dynamic account of the self provides a welcome contrast to the atomistic individualism which continues to figure so pervasively in the management of our 'common sense' it is not, of course, unique to Macmurray. Where his account does become particularly interesting is, firstly, in his wider account of human association and, secondly, in his articulation of both the philosophical and psychological principles of community.

Whilst Macmurray's commitment to a plural, embedded account of human being is common to what might be loosely termed the communitarian tradition of social and political thought, what sets him apart from many within it is his insistence that we are not primarily social beings; rather, we are, first and foremost, communal beings. In other words, the categories 'social' and 'communal' pick out importantly different distinctions, with the latter as more fundamental than the former.

Functional and personal relations: society and community

There are two main strands to Macmurray's account of community; firstly, a contextual or relational account which locates community within the broader nexus of human association and, secondly, an internal account which articulates a set of constitutive philosophical principles.

Central to Macmurray's contextual account of community is his two-fold distinction between functional and personal forms of human relations. Broadly speaking, functional relations characterize those kinds of encounter we have with each other that are instrumental, encounters in which we enter into relations with each other in order to get something done, in order to achieve particular purposes. Examples of functional relations would include buying an item in a shop, or working to produce goods and services, which you then sell. Your relationship with those from whom you buy items or to whom you sell your services is defined by the purpose embedded in that encounter and when the transaction is completed your relationship ends. In functional relations your engagement with others is partial and specific: partial in the sense that it does not draw on a whole range of attitudes, dispositions and capacities which you do in fact possess and use in other circumstances; specific in the sense that what is deemed appropriate or necessary in the exchange is circumscribed by its constitutive purposes, by the roles which shape the form and conduct of the encounter. For Macmurray, functional relations are typical of society; society is, in fact, an organization of functions.

In contrast to functional relations of society, personal relations of community are not aspectival, task specific or role defined; rather they are expressive of who we are as persons. Whereas functional relations are defined by their purposes, personal or communal relations have no purposes beyond themselves: purposes are *expressive* of personal relations, not constitutive of them. Macmurray's preferred example to illustrate the differences between functional and personal relations is friendship. Friendship does not consist of common purposes. If you ask what the purpose of a friendship is, the asking of the question implies that it is not a friendship at all, but rather a relationship that, despite having the veneer of friendship, in fact has ulterior motives or instrumental reasons for its existence. In a friendship the common purposes arise from the care and delight in each other. If you care for someone you want to do something for them and with them, and the mutuality of those intentions give rise to the practical ground of its shared reality. In a co-operative, functional relationship typical of society, if you change the purposes you dissolve the unity; in a communal relationship of friendship, far from the change of purposes dissolving the relationship, it both maintains and enriches the unity.

Finally, it is important to stress that whilst society and community, the functional and the personal are distinct they are nonetheless necessary to each other, but not of equal importance.

> We become persons in community, in virtue of our relations to others. Human life is inherently a common life. Our ability to form individual purposes is itself a function of this common life . . . Community is prior to society.
>
> (Macmurray 1950: 56)

Philosophical and psychological principles of community

Having located community within the wider framework of human association and established its pre-eminent importance, Macmurray then approaches his second task which is to examine the constitutive philosophical principles of community and it is here that his contribution has particular resonance. Here at last is an account of community that takes us beyond the residual, but unsatisfactory, core of belonging and significance and provides us with an emancipatory grounding from which we are able to critique empirical examples of community that suffocate rather than nourish human well-being.

Macmurray argues that there are two fundamental philosophical principles of community; they are the principle of freedom and the principle of equality. He suggests not only that freedom and equality are central to any adequate understanding of community or fellowship, but that these two principles have a mutually reinforcing relation with one another. His view is that:

> equality and freedom, as constitutive principles of fellowship, condition one another reciprocally. Equality is a condition of freedom in human relations. For if we do not treat one another as equals, we exclude freedom from the relationship. Freedom, too, conditions equality. For if there is constraint between us there is fear; and to counter the fear we must seek control over its object, and attempt to subordinate the other person to our own power. Any attempt to achieve freedom without equality, or to achieve equality without freedom, must, therefore be self-defeating.
>
> (Macmurray 1950: 74)

Freedom for Macmurray is freedom to be ourselves, something we can only do in and through our relations with others, and only in certain kinds of relations. Friendship or community 'reveals the positive nature of freedom. It provides the only conditions which release the whole self into activity and so enable a man [*sic*] to be himself totally with out constraint' (Macmurray 1950: 73).

Likewise, equality, understood in a personal rather than a functional sense, is enriching rather than diminishing: 'It is precisely the recognition of difference and variety amongst individuals that gives meaning to the assertion of equality' (Macmurray 1938: 75).

The psychological principles of community provide an important complementary dimension to the philosophical principles of freedom and equality. For community to become real the mode of relation characterized by freedom to be and become ourselves in and through relations of personal equality, must take place within the context of certain dispositions and intentions towards other persons. Community is neither constituted nor maintained by organization. It relies on motives which sustain the personal relations of its members: 'It is constituted and maintained by mutual affection' (Macmurray 1961: 158). It is about human beings caring for one another reciprocally.[2]

In taking stock of Macmurray's account of community it is perhaps worth reflecting on the nature of the insights he offers. Firstly, it is clear that community consists in certain kinds of relations between human beings, relations in which we encounter each other in both our vulnerability and our creative capacity as persons. Secondly, there is a rich and detailed account of why community is essential to our development as persons. Thirdly, the twin principles of freedom and equality which provide the philosophical foundations of community spell out a set of conditions which are corrosive of community as an exclusive or oppressive set of relations. Macmurray's principle of community thus rules out of court many examples of community in a sociological sense which are diminishing or destructive of human flourishing. His account is deeply emancipatory. Fourthly, the philosophical principles of community are partnered by a psychological account, which indicated the dispositions necessary for its realization.

Macmurray's articulation of a philosophical principle of community seems to me to be of prime importance because it gives us a powerful philosophical tool with the capacity to take us far beneath the surface of particular instances to the core of human association and not only decide the degree to which they are, in reality, true to the principles of community, but also help us work together to enhance its further development. In the end, community is not fundamentally about place, time, memory, or even the belonging or significance found in close relationships. Community is rather the reciprocal experience people have as persons in certain kinds of relationships; it is an experience of being that is alive in its mutuality and vibrant in its sense of possibility. Community thus turns out to be adjectival, not substantival; it is not a group of people, nor is it the mere fact of a relationship; rather it is the shared, mutuality of experience that is constitutive of it. Community is a way of being, not a thing. Community is a process in which human beings regard each other in a certain way (love, care, concern for the other) and in which they relate to each other and act together in mutuality as persons, not as role occupants. Furthermore, that mutuality is informed by the values of freedom (freedom to be and become yourself) and equality (equal worth) which condition each other reciprocally.

Understanding the relationship between the functional and the personal: on the integrity of the personal

John Macmurray's work on community is compelling in its insights for a whole range of reasons outlined earlier. There is, however, a further reason for advocating the significance of Macmurray's work on community and that concerns his commitment to providing a companion account of the relationship between the functional and the personal, between society and community, and, thus, within the context of this paper, between such things as school effectiveness and transformative education, between a school as a learning organization and a school as a learning community, between teaching as a technical undertaking and teaching as a personal encounter.

The functional in and for the personal

The broad outline of Macmurray's position on these matters is that ontologically, socially, and economically/politically the two forms of human association – that is, the functional and the personal (ontology), organization and community (social philosophy), the economic/political and the communal (political philosophy) – are distinct. In exploring the relation between the two, Macmurray goes on to make three further points. Firstly, whilst the functional and the personal are distinct, they are, nonetheless of differential importance; the personal is prior to and more important than the functional. Secondly, though the personal is more important than the functional, it cannot do without it any more than the functional can do without the personal; they are, in fact, necessary to each other. Thirdly, they are in constant tension thus making it extremely difficult to establish 'a right and satisfactory relation between them' (Macmurray 1941a: 1) either at the macro level of society or the micro level of individual living.

The functional life is for *the personal life.* With regard to the first strand of the argument, that is, that the functional and the personal are inextricably linked, but not of equal importance, Macmurray's position was that all functional, that is to say, social, political, and economic activity must be brought within the compass of human well-being and not the other way around. Writing nearly 60 years ago he insisted that 'The whole complex of organised social co-operation for economic and political ends has no value in itself. Its value lies only in its contribution to the personal life of men and women' (Macmurray 1941a: 2), a point reiterated in the second volume of his Gifford Lectures in ways which are (regrettably) still poignant: 'an economic efficiency which is achieved at the expense of the personal life is self-condemned, and in the end self-frustrating... the economic is for the sake of the personal' (Macmurray 1961: 187, 188). In sum then, the first and arguably the most important step in his exposition of the relation between the functional and the personal is to establish that, despite their inextricable unity, they 'are not co-ordinate. The personal is primary and the functional is secondary... The meaning of the functional lies in the personal and not the other way around... The functional life is *for* the personal life' (Macmurray 1941b: 822).

The resonance of this position for all aspects of education seems to me both profound and wide-ranging. At the most fundamental level it forces us to ask what schools are for and, in so doing, it helps to reclaim a truth that is no longer obvious or understood; namely, that schools are primarily educational institutions. Whilst they do, of course, have important functional dimensions to their work, like socializing young people and ensuring the country is equipped to compete economically, it is the specifically educational character of schooling that should provide both the end and the means of its accomplishment. To raise questions about the human purposes of our policy and our practice at macro and micro levels seems to me especially important at a time when the initial plausibility of substantial and sustained pressure for raising attainment sweeps aside questions and queries as if they were all regressive remnants of a self-serving educational establishment. We live in especially dangerous times: the elevation of half-truths into unblinking national imperatives blinds us to the counter-truths of the halves that remain hidden by the very clarity which, following Gloucester in Shakespeare's *King Lear*, cannot see because it cannot feel. Consequently, despite much goodwill and even greater effort we are driven by laudable confidence and latent confusion towards educational failure. Targets may be reached and scores may rise, but as long as we remain within the remit of a functionally conceived undertaking they will do so despite, rather than because of, the policies and practices which attended them. Whether our students will be better educated is not a question that can be properly understood, let alone answered with any conviction, so long as we persist with the wearisome superstition of audits and the interminable tyranny of targets which feature so prominently in the current mantra of school effectiveness and school improvement. We are asking the wrong questions for the wrong reasons and the answers we get tell us less than we wanted and more than we understand.

The personal life is through *the functional life.* The second step in the argument is equally compelling: just as the functional life is *for* the personal life, so 'the personal life is *through* the functional life' (Macmurray 1941b: 822). Community is not about some ethereal disengagement from the world or about sitting around feeling endlessly well-disposed towards each other. If community is to be a lived reality, rather than a pretence or an illusion, it must express itself in action: it only becomes real '– only gets hands and feet – when in our daily work we provide for one another's needs and rejoice that we are doing so' (Macmurray 1941c: 856).

Summing up the philosophical underpinning of the interrelationship between the functional and the personal in our daily lives, Macmurray suggests that, having acknowledged the primacy of the personal over the functional, the reconciliation of the two can best be understood by holding three further points together:

> They are opposites, with a tension between them. They are inseparable and limit one another. They are essential to one another and form a unity. Any attempt to fuse them or absorb one into the other will fail because they are opposites. Any attempt to separate them will fail because they limit one another. Any effort to run them parallel with one another without relating them will break down because they form an essential unity.
>
> (Macmurray 1941a: 5)

Thus far, it seems to me that Macmurray has been concerned to do two things: firstly, and most importantly, to establish the primacy of the personal over the functional; secondly, to not merely acknowledge, but also celebrate the necessity of the functional and in so doing ground the notion of community in the soil of real human action and engagement, rather than allow it to float freely and inconsequentially in the ambience of wistful and merely sentimental aspiration. Both undertakings are hugely important: the first provides a more than adequate counter to the considerable dangers of the technicist delusions from which we continue to suffer as a society in general and within education in particular; the second provides an equivalently demanding requirement of those who are inclined to shelter behind an easy rhetoric of care, namely that the rigour of community, the rigour of the personal, is more, rather than less, demanding than its more familiar counterparts in either the intellectual disciplines or the now ubiquitous and insistently dreary discourse of performativity.

This last point bears some emphasis. Those of us within education who argue for the importance of community and for the importance of seeing the functional as the servant of the personal are often assailed by accusations of some kind of marshmallow parochialism that is typically undemanding, too often condescending, almost always woolly and consequently a betrayal of the immediate lives and future prospects of students who are suffocated rather than liberated by practices that are more congenial to teachers than they are useful to their students. Certainly it is true that there have been times when the rhetoric of care has fed rather than challenged those perceptions. If my care for you as a student remains at the level of disposition and makes no demands on you through difficult intellectual and interpersonal encounters, then it does, indeed, deserve the contempt to which I have just alluded. However, the failure of specific instances, or the indulgences of a particular era should not be extended to the underlying perspective itself. In the insistence that the personal is through the functional Macmurray provides us with a philosophical corrective to the kind of idealistic and unreal travesty of the standpoint of community which has sometimes been evident, not just in education, but in the wider context of social and political action. The functional is, and always will be, necessary because it is through the functional that the personal, the standpoint of community becomes real and authentic. What I go on to argue in the next part of this paper is, firstly, that whilst the functional is necessary to the personal, it is also true that the personal is *foundational* and that, within the current hegemony of the functional, it is particularly important to reveal the *personal in the functional.* Secondly, when the functional comes under the aegis of the personal, that is, when the functional is *expressive of* the personal, it is both transformed and transformative.

On the necessity of the personal: revealing the personal in the functional

My own reading of Macmurray suggests that the two further points to which I have just alluded are consistent with his line of argument and extend his position in ways which are only implied, hinted at, or partially developed in his work. Rather than focusing on the relation of the functional to the personal and the functional in the personal, they concern the place of the personal *in* the functional; what I call the necessity of the personal.

To recap and extend: the first of my two additional points argues that the personal is foundational or necessary in the sense that the functional depends upon the personal in ways which are insufficiently acknowledged; it is, after all, people who are performing particular tasks and not machines or slaves and it is the qualities, capacities, and dispositions of people as persons, not merely as role occupants that enable the functional not just to prosper, but to exist at all. My second additional point argues, not only that the functional is predicated on some minimalist notion of the personal, but that if we are to conduct our lives in ways which are both fulfilling and productive then adopting a standpoint of the personal transforms the functional in ways which have as much to offer those who are interested in utility alone as those who prefer to see utility within the context of a more wide-raging account of human flourishing. In effect, what I argue is that if we commit ourselves to a personalist framework what we accomplish is likely to be both more productive and more fulfilling that could be achieved within a purely functional remit.

Personal as foundational. Whilst making a strong case for the foundational importance of the personal is, of course, what Macmurray's work is primarily about, what I want to bring out here is the particularity of its application in the domain of daily interaction. The view for which I am arguing is that functional enterprises and undertakings cannot even get started, cannot get off the ground in anything like a sustained way without the help of the personal. In other words, *the personal is foundational*; it is not a kindly add-on, or an optional humanistic frill; without it the functional has no soil in which to flourish.

There is evidence in Macmurray's writing, particularly from his work in the 1940s, that he supported a view of the personal as foundational in similar ways to those for which I am arguing. The first example concerns the vulnerability of purely functional relations in times of stress or difficulty. Self-interested or myopically functional behaviour devoid of any intention of personal relation runs into difficulty once the perceived pay-offs of that co-operation begin to wane. The unity is therefore superficial and fragile, until and unless it begins to move in the direction of personal relation. This is also the case, though perhaps to a lesser degree, when times are not so tough. Macmurray suggests that even in normal contexts 'it is much less clear that functional co-operation is quite independent of the more personal forms of relationship . . . The more positive the personal interest the easier, *ceteris paribus*, the co-operation must be' (Macmurray 1942: 189). My second example, taken from a complementary passage in an earlier work, points strongly to a more foundational view of the personal *in* the functional. It suggests that because human beings are by their nature communal, rather than merely social or functional beings, unless they are constrained and constantly refocused on the instrumental task in hand, the unity of co-operation inevitably gives rise to the wider more inclusive unity of community:

> Set a group of people to work together on a common task, *with* one another, *for* one another, and they tend to become a community . . . the tendency to community is the fundamental human motive, and is always present, even when its effect is inhibited, whenever men [*sic*] come into contact.
>
> (Macmurray 1943: 11)

Sailing with the current of this line of thinking I want to tack more deliberately towards a destination which recognizes the foundational importance of the personal, certainly in any kind of educative encounter, and most probably in any kind of purposive human interaction. It is absolutely clear to me from my own experience as a teacher and a parent, as it is from my reading of Macmurray, that the functional presupposes the personal in ways which are as obvious as they are hidden. Systems and roles which dominate our educational arrangements socialize and institutionalize us into ways of seeing and behaving which tend too often to mark a retreat from the personal. And yet in education the personal is always both the starting point and the end point of our endeavours, and properly so, since education is immediately and ultimately about being and becoming more fully human. It is this understanding to which parents return again and again. It is this understanding which many children share too. Hence the resonance of the contribution from a respondent in a television studio discussion about the importance or otherwise of formal schooling when she insisted that:

> once you went to school you went to school with the attitude where you expect the teacher to be responsible for *you* and to look after you and there was a bit of yourself that you gave to them, a *very large* bit and if they didn't take that bit and treat it properly, or stamped on it . . . or perhaps if you lived in a country where your colour made a difference, that could be devastating for you as a child.
>
> (BBC 1992)

It is this understanding to which Macmurray refers when he argues that:

> We, the teachers are persons. Those whom we would teach are persons. We must meet them face to face, in a personal intercourse. This is the primary fact about education. It is one of personal relationship . . . We may ignore this fact; we imagine that our task is of a different order, but this will make no difference to what is actually taking place. We may act as though we were teaching arithmetic or history. In fact we are teaching people. The arithmetic or the history is merely a medium through which a personal intercourse is established and maintained.
>
> (Macmurray 1949)

I have argued earlier that the functional is *for the sake of* the personal and that the personal is *through* the functional. I am further arguing here that the personal is not only *foundational*, but residually so. By our very nature as human beings, the personal provides our preferred starting point and whilst we are inclined to forget this we should not only remember it, but also be aware that the personal remains a persistent presence in even the most severely functional of environments. For those who are inclined towards my argument, that agreement carries with it, if not an obligation, then at least an invitation towards engagement: in the current climate of unremitting outcome measures it seems to me that the requirement to reveal the personal in the functional is paramount. Not only will it help us to understand ourselves and the way we conduct our lives a little better, it may remind us to ask questions about what it is all for, even if the answers are not always as we would wish.

The personal as transformational. My second suggestion is that, not only is the personal *foundational*, the functional *for the sake* of the personal and the personal articulated *through* the functional, but the functional *within* the personal is itself transformed. My point takes its cue from the kind of argument Michael Ignatieff develops with such poetic elegance in his *The Needs of Strangers* where he asks us to imagine circumstances where a health professional helps an old person from their flat into the ambulance taking them to day care. Here it is not the bare accomplishment of taking someone's arm that is important; rather, 'It is the manner of giving that counts and the moral basis on which it is given' (Ignatieff 1984: 16). It seems to me that the underscoring and illumination of the transformative power of the personal has widespread significance, not least in the field of education and in extending insights of writers like Macmurray and Ignatieff I would wish to argue for a six stage dialectic (see Figure 11.1). In working through the structure of my argument I look in particular at how it might be instantiated within the context of pedagogy.

The first stage of a pedagogy within the dialectic of the personal, primarily concerns the teacher, and exemplifies the expressive dimension of the personal. Here the argument is largely instrumental or functional and suggests that within the context of the personal there is a deepening and widening of skills and an increasingly discriminating use of them. The teacher's care for the other, for the student, makes her more attentive to the details and appropriateness of the functional, of the pedagogy. The impetus of the personal leads to an intensification and differentiation of the functional, not to its diminution. Such attentiveness speaks not only of experience and situational awareness, but above all, of care, not just in its formal, professionally required sense, but essentially and necessarily, in its authentic dispositional sense. In sum, the first step of my argument is that within the dialectic of the personal a teacher's pedagogic skills and talents are heightened and developed precisely because of their felt care for their students, because of the essentially centripetal nature of their care.

The second stage, still primarily within the ambit of teacher action, forms a transformative bridge to the third stage which is mainly concerned with the response of the learner. This transformative bridge concerns the transformation of

1. THE EXPRESSIVE DIMENSION
   Deepening and Widening of Skills and their increasingly Discriminating Use
   The Instrumental Argument
   - The teacher's care for the other makes her/him more attentive to the detail and appropriateness of the functional.
   - The impetus of care leads to the intensification and differentiation of the functional, not its diminution.
2. THE TRANSFORMATIVE BRIDGE
   From the Deployment of Skills to the Rigour of Care
   The Transformational Argument
   - The skills the teacher uses are transformed from mere skills to expressions of care.

   Transformative Agency
   - Being transformed the skills-as-expressive-of-care become agents of transformation.
3. THE RESPONSIVE DIMENSION
   - Because the functional is expressive of the personal, its power to gain the learner's interest is enhanced – 'This person cares about me, is attending to me as an individual . . .'.

   Recognition of Expertise
   - The demonstration of the teacher's interest through the disposition of care, the enhanced and detailed use of skills and passion for what is being taught engenders confidence and prompts engagement.
4. THE BOND OF MUTUALITY
   Doing It For Yourself and For Your Teacher
   - The student does not wish to let the teacher down.
   - The student takes pride and delight (for self and/or for others) in increased powers of understanding, skill, and achievement.

   Doing It For Your Students and For Yourself
   - The student's teacher is their strongest advocate and their fiercest critic.
   - The teacher also applies the intensity and authenticity of those demands to her own work as teacher of this (and other) students.
5. THE DIALOGIC DIMENSION
   Mutual Learning
   - A shared sense that both student and teacher are learning with and from each other.
6. EDUCATION AS TRANSFORMATIVE COMMUNITY
   Hope for the future
   - A shared sense that education is expressive of positive human agency and shared hope in the future.

Figure 11.1 The dialectic of the personal within the context of education.

the functional into the more-than-functional precisely because of its location within a creative dispositional context of care. This is not to say that as a teacher I am doing more than 'delivering' the curriculum: it is not about something that I add on to 'delivery'; I am not 'delivering' it at all. The metaphor is entirely inappropriate. To describe or conceive of the daily encounters of education as a 'delivery' process is either to profoundly misunderstand the nature of education, or, in an equally profound way, to utterly betray it. The extended dexterity or capacity of the teacher is transformed by the context of the personal. The skill and attention to detail is no longer a functional act: it is expressive of care, and in being perceived as such it engenders confidence and trust, not just in the student to whom it is directed, but in the teacher herself. Here, the essentially dialogic nature of teaching begins to be felt by the teacher, not just acknowledged tacitly or merely intellectually. In offering teaching as an expression of care the particularities of its further development wait upon the learner's response.

There is one further characteristic of this bridging stage that needs to be mentioned here. It is that, not only are the pedagogic skills transformed by their personal context, being transformed they become the agents of further transformation. It is precisely the metamorphosis of the functional within the personal, from a manifestation of professional duty into, if not a loving, then certainly a caring act that triggers the response in the learner.

The third stage of the personal dialectic engages with its responsive dimension. The transformational presence of the personal has within it the pull of reciprocity; it invites a response; it is, if not inveterately educative, then invariably engaging in ways which bring out in the learner a generosity of spirit and a willingness to contribute in some way. Because the functional is expressive of the personal its power to gain the learner's interest is enhanced. The learner responds both to the teacher's interest in and care for them as a person and to the teacher's heightened pedagogical commitment and more visible expertise. Thus in the previously cited television discussion about what was important to them about school education one participant said:

> It's the caring that I found. I had two very good teachers that I can remember now and I hold them up as models because they inspired me to look at the environment. I became a designer and I value those experiences of handling materials.
>
> (BBC 1992)

When asked how those teachers did that he replied:

> By showing; by cajoling me; by taking a personal interest in me, not just in the subjects I was doing, but in my wider life.
>
> (BBC 1992)

The fourth stage is characterized by a bond of mutuality exemplified by another participant in the same discussion who, because she 'felt that the teacher cared about me and that helped me a lot', also felt a sense of regret when, on occasions, she failed to live up to the shared expectations that developed.

> I felt I'd let the teacher down and I would strive to do better. And they made this known to me. It was like, if you love someone you chasten them. That kind of way they would make it known to me. They'd look at me, as though, 'How could you do this?' and then I would . . . It made you feel good. It made you feel that you were valuable and if you are valuable you begin to act in a valuable way and valuable in that sense was achieving.
>
> (BBC 1992)

What comes through so vibrantly here is the heterocentric nature of the care, of not wanting to let yourself or your teacher down, a concern which in different circumstances would be mirrored by a delight and pride in your achievement for yourself, maybe for others, and certainly for your teacher. Within this phase of the dialectic of the personal there are also consequences for the teacher. Not only is she the learner's strongest advocate and fiercest critic; there is also a strong sense of the necessity of a strenuous, creative mutuality in which the teacher's demands on the student apply equally strongly to her own pedagogic work. There is a hugely important distinction here between practices of care that are unidirectional, condescending, or dependency-oriented and those that are the agent of further personal and professional development of the teacher as much as the learner (see Fielding 1999b).

The penultimate stage – the dialogic dimension – develops that two-way relationship in a more overtly dialogic way to include a mutuality, which involves learning with and from each other. There is reciprocity here which extends the relationship in ways that begin, on occasions, to transform the roles, which have inevitably informed the articulation of the personal: thus learners also become teachers, and teachers learners.

It might be argued that the sixth stage of the personal dialectic – education as transformative community – is not properly speaking a stage, but rather a context which informs all the others and which is enhanced and deepened as they progress. Indeed, it is perhaps best regarded in that multi-faceted way – as an aspiration, a means of proceeding and an increasingly encountered reality. It is a concrete manifestation of a belief that education is as at once a profoundly personal undertaking, that is to say one that is ultimately about human being and becoming, and also an undertaking that is, if not utopian, then infused with hope. It is about a shared sense that education is expressive of positive human agency and shared hope in the future of human kind. It is about education as transformative community.

Before briefly pointing to the resonance of the dialectic of the personal in a variety of contexts, I need to make it clear that what I have just described is not intended to demean or disregard the importance of functional interactions that teachers and students have on a day-to-day basis, nor is it to suggest that the experience of transformative community, or indeed the stages that precede it, can become the reality for all of us all of the time. Rather it is intended to both offer an articulation of the demanding nature of the reality of the personal in teaching and learning and a celebration of its transformative power. It is to suggest that the world is like this some of the time, and that if we are concerned to educate rather than merely school young people, that it ought to be and could be like it more of the time. As I shall argue shortly, if we are to be subject to a new hegemony which reduces pedagogy to the mere technologies of teaching, we will not only betray our vocation as teachers committed to the education of young people, we will diminish, not enhance, our economic productivity.

Interrogating two sites of education policy: developing an emancipatory community framework

Whilst the primary intention of this paper has been to articulate a more satisfactory notion of community than current thinking has thus far produced and to explore in a more exacting way what a philosophical account of the relationship between community and related notions might look like, there remains the further step in the enquiry which begins to formulate a philosophically informed intermediate resource on which current and future education policy might draw.

Whilst such an undertaking might sensibly and desirably be tackled at considerably more length than a single, short section of this paper allows, nonetheless, my hope is that something provocative and useful might be sketched out or hinted at in such a way as to make engagement by others both possible and fruitful. My intention is to approach this task in two ways: firstly, to articulate a manageable, if rather compressed, series of questions which might provide an interrogatory framework that reflects the philosophical groundwork of the paper; secondly to illustrate the framework in action by focusing briefly on two sites of education policy.

Towards an emancipatory community framework

In seeking to apply Macmurray's insights to the arena of social and educational policy it is possible to formulate a set of double imperatives which provide a powerful interrogative basis for a communal, person-centred critique of existing arrangements, and suggestions for future possibilities (see Figure 11.2). The two imperatives articulate the emancipatory and person-centred strands of his thinking outlined in Sections 1 and 2 above. These strands can in turn be understood through the formulation of a double question designed to probe what might be called the personalist credentials of the practices under consideration.

One way of articulating such a schema would be to suggest that the person-centred imperative provokes two questions. Firstly, 'Is the technical or functional for the sake of the personal, for the sake of community?' (the personal interrogative). Secondly, 'Is the technical/functional informed by and expressive of the personal?' (the ends–means interrogative). The emancipatory imperative suggests a third and fourth question: 'How does the principle of freedom inform the relations between those involved?' (the libertarian interrogative); and 'How does the principle of equality inform the relations between those involved?' (the egalitarian interrogative).

The Person Centred Imperative

The Personal Interrogative

1. Is the technical or functional for the sake of the personal?

The Ends–Means Interrogative

2. Is the technical/functional informed by and expressive of the personal?

The Emancipatory Imperative

The Libertarian Interrogative

3. How does the principle of freedom inform the relations between those involved?

The Egalitarian Interrogative

4. How does the principle of equality inform the relations between those involved?

Figure 11.2 Towards an emancipatory community framework.

By way of illustration I have taken two examples, one at the macro level of schools as institutions and the other focusing on target-setting as experienced at the micro level of teacher-student encounter. I activate the four interrogatives via one or two questions and in each instance I contrast functionally dominated approaches with person-centred practices.

Schools as educational institutions. In applying the *personal interrogative*, in asking whether schools as sites of required functional activity are also dedicated to the education of persons, we might usefully ask questions of, for example, the school's admission policies and the public articulation of its purposes and curriculum. Is the school so anxious to attract a particular kind of student that, despite the obligatory and often meaningless linguistic gesture about realizing students' full potential, its public persona is knowingly and persistently targeted at academic achievement or social selection? Or is the school's engagement with its community a celebration of its diversity and a commitment to providing wide-ranging experience? Is the curriculum narrowly conceived and effectively delivered? Or is the curriculum wide-ranging and flexible in its aspirations and constructed together in ways, which are as demanding as they are imaginative?

We might also ask questions of its public spaces. Are the barren expanses of corridor and concourse devoid of students' work or replete with the slick or the ready-made indicative of a narrowness of view and a poverty of feeling? Or are public spaces more than mere conduits of movement, places which delight in the creativity and courage of those whose work it displays and, wherever possible, through the simplicity of carpet or the thoughtfulness of design, contexts which invite deliberation and dialogue, rather than the din and damage of indifference?

In applying the *ends/means interrogative*, in asking if the functional is informed by and expressive of the personal, we might ask questions of the school's communication systems and practices at all levels. Is the school one which relies on written communication, often impersonally generated in formulaic formats (however bright and however bold) which betray no specific knowledge or genuine care of those to whom it is addressed and whose approach to accountability is compendious, paper-based, and inimical to dialogue? Or is the school one which values personal encounter, often in contexts outside the school, and always in ways which speak of personal knowledge, informed and detailed concern? Is the school one which sees transparency and flexibility and the necessity of dialogue as the democratic alternative to market accountability?

We might also ask how the school values those whom it serves. Is it a school which has a rewards system which is narrowly conceived, predominantly rewarding of those whose backgrounds and living circumstances are more favoured, and largely extrinsic in its motivational dynamic? Or is it a school which is wide ranging in its sense of what is valuable, imaginative in its means of valuing those achievements, inclusive in its actual practice, as encouraging of intrinsic motivation as of extrinsic reward, and both personal and communal in its lived articulation of delight?

In applying the *libertarian interrogative*, in asking how the principle of freedom informs the relations between those involved in the life of the school, we might ask questions of the systems and practices which shape the quality and nature of the interactions between staff and students. Is it a school which extends the communicative distances between students and staff through the language of address, the required conduct of automatic encounter, the spaces which are forbidden, the frequency of separate provision, and the innumerable other articulations of institutional living? Or is it a school in which staff and students address each other by their first names, which encourages students and staff to relate to each other as persons as much as it requires behaviour informed by an understanding of roles, and which has shared or equivalent provision with regard to the daily necessities of social living?

We might also ask an equivalent set of questions of relations between staff and staff. Is this a school where hierarchy dominates the modes of encounter, inhibits the willingness to raise matters of real importance and equivalent inconvenience, and increasingly balkanizes the institutional culture? Or is it a school where an open and rich collegiality encourages and extends mutual professional exchange and increasingly moves the school from a learning organization towards the creation of the school as a learning community?

In applying the *egalitarian interrogative*, in asking how the principle of equality informs the relations between those involved in the life of the school, we might ask questions of ways in which student perspectives are viewed and utilized and ways in which leadership is practised and understood amongst staff. In line with the current interest in consulting students on an increasingly wide range of matters we might ask questions about the extent to which students are seen as sources of data rather than agents of their own transformation. Is this a school in which students views are sought by staff, for staff purposes, to which the students either do not have access or with which they are denied the opportunity to debate and engage? Or is this a school in which students have the opportunity to become researchers of matters of concern to them, work in partnership with staff, engage in dialogue about recommendations for action, and subsequently become part of the joint implementation and embedding of new practices?

In line with new developments in school improvement we might also ask questions about the opportunities for leadership within the school. Is this school one in which occasions for leadership are confined to those whose status and position are assumed to entail those capacities? Or is this a school in which leadership is seen as potentially open to all, in which opportunities are offered within emerging development structures and one in which leadership is reconceptualized round notions of communal commitment rather than individual discretion?

Target-setting. In applying the *personal interrogative*, in asking whether target-setting[3] at the level of individual encounter within schools is, in fact, dedicated to the education of persons, we might usefully ask questions concerning the origins of new structures and newly focused conversations. Is this a school in which the impetus for the development of target-setting lies primarily in the emergence of league tables and government requirement, the nature of the questions asked is instrumentally conceived, and individual attainment made significant largely through its capacity to improve a comparative picture of the school's attainment?

Or is this a school where conversations with students about attainment and aspiration have always been driven by concern for them as individuals, where the nature of the questions asked is concerned with action but not confined to a narrow understanding of its remit, and where individual attainment has ipsative rather than comparative significance?

The *ends/means interrogative*, asks if the functional is informed by and expressive of the personal. In the case of target-setting it prompts questions to do with the nature of achievement and the disposition of care exemplified in the kinds of questions asked and the manner in which they are put. Is this a school in which the kinds of things targeted are confined to a narrow notion of what is desirable, in which the questions are more often generic, detached from or tangential to the real concerns and aspirations of the student, and asked in a way which is inattentive to or ignorant of personal detail? Or is this a school in which achievement is widely conceived, in which questions are expressive of an integral concern for and detailed knowledge of the uniqueness of the individual student, and one in which the manner of asking is genuinely attentive rather than a disguised form of teacherly assertion?

In applying the *libertarian interrogative*, in asking how the principle of freedom informs the relations between those involved in the target-setting conversations, we might ask questions concerning the shaping of the agenda and the opportunity to raise difficult issues. Is this a school in which the target-setting conversations are dominated by the teacher's agenda, by the teacher's perceptions of what needs to be done, by the teacher's management of the conversation itself? Or is this a school in which target-setting conversations are informed by the felt concerns of both parties, in which understanding emerges from dialogue as often as it precedes it, in which both parties have the confidence and the courage to raise difficult issues, in which the course of the conversation is a genuinely joint endeavour?

In applying the *egalitarian interrogative*, in asking how the principle of equality informs the target-setting process, we might ask questions of the extent to which mutual learning figures as a significant element. Is this a school in which the process is conceived and executed on the assumption that its true purpose is instructional, the learning unidirectional, and the most appropriate manner monologic? Or is this a school in which target-setting is seen as supportive of the student's learning, but in so doing turns out to be enabling of the teacher's learning too; learning about the student, learning from the student, learning with the student, learning about the process of learning and the teacher's role in it? Is this a school in which target-setting is predicated on the teacher's capacity to listen, to be receptive as much as the student's capacity to do these things?

Stepping back from the current intensity with which target-setting is being advocated and pursued, it seems to me that questions structured round the four interrogative impulses which articulate the essence of a personalist perspective are especially important in the light of recent developments. Work in the field is now beginning to encounter students expressing doubts about the genuineness of their school's interest in their progress and well-being as persons, as distinct from their contributions to the school's league table position. The overriding instrumentality of conversations makes listening difficult: attentiveness is overdirected; clues for meaning are trodden underfoot in the scramble for performance; dialogue disappears as reciprocity retreats under the sheer weight of external expectation; contract replaces community as the bond of human association (Fielding 1999a).

Why effective policies won't work

The intention of this paper has been to argue for an account of community, which is both emancipatory and inclusive, and expressed in the form of a philosophical principle. The intention has also been to provide a theoretical articulation of the difficult, but crucial, interrelation of society and community, of the functional and the personal, without which any adequate theory of human development cannot begin to make headway. In passing, I have also argued against those intellectual frameworks and understandings which seem to me inimical to human flourishing and it is to those dangers, which currently appear so emphatically and so mistakenly at the forefront of much current thinking in so many aspects of educational endeavour, to which I now wish to briefly turn.

The power and poverty of effectiveness ideology

I have suggested elsewhere (Fielding 1997) that school effectiveness and school improvement are seriously flawed. What this paper has sought to demonstrate is that one of the major reasons for its intellectual demise and its unintended practical dysfunction is its insistence on beating the drum of a crude and dispiriting pragmatism that refuses to recognize the stupidity within an essentially moral field of endeavour such as education of an undifferentiated insistence on 'what works'. Its thin, measurement-driven notion of schooling too easily marginalizes concerns for wider, more profound aspirations for the development of persons; and education itself is refashioned in ways which make the call for community seem weak, undemanding and vague. As Stephen Ball has recently reminded us: 'Quality and effectiveness are not neutral mechanisms. They do not simply improve education, they change it. What education is, what it means to be educated are changed' (Ball 1996). Perhaps most serious of all, there is a tendency in outcomes driven thinking to ignore or marginalize discussion about the integral relationship between the means and the end, between what it is we are supposed to be doing and how we go about doing it (Tierney 1993: 69, 79). 'Effective policies'[4] will not work, can never work, precisely because the narrowness and strength of their instrumental preoccupations force them to destroy or prevent the very unity which makes policies simultaneously educational and practically viable. The whole point of education is that we deepen and extend our understanding of the inextricable unity of means and ends; not that we tear them apart in pursuit of goals which should be the servant and not the master of our efforts and aspirations.

The same kind of danger threatens from the apparent rise of technicist models of pedagogy, which have received so much attention of late. If we deprive teaching of its wider human purposes, if personal encounters are reduced to functional exchanges, teaching will become unpleasant, unproductive, unsustainable, and utterly without joy or educational justification. Nearly 50 years ago Macmurray came to similar conclusions:

> No technical training in educational methods can ever be a substitute for (certain human qualities), however unexceptionable the methods may be in themselves. Education is not and cannot ever be a technical activity. The attempt to turn would-be teachers into technicians by teaching them classroom tricks is as stupid as it is ineffective... Here I believe is the greatest threat to education in our society. We are becoming more and more technically minded: gradually we are falling victims to the illusion that all problems can be solved by proper organisation: that when we fail we are doing the job in the wrong way, and that all that is needed is 'know how'. To think thus in education is to pervert education. It is not an engineering job. It is personal and human.
>
> (Macmurray 1958)

Just as effective policies are bound to fail, so too are those which elevate the technical over the personal or seek to disconnect the two. Macmurray's work helps us to understand why this is so. They will fail because they violate the integrity of the personal on which education depends. The lineaments of that integrity suggests five interrelated truths: firstly, that the personal is foundational; secondly, that the functional is for the sake of the personal; thirdly, that the personal is through the functional; fourth, that the context of the personal transforms the functional, the functional thus becoming expressive of the personal; finally, that the functional in and for the personal expresses the joy and hope of human community.

On the necessity of community

Community works and the necessity of creating community together remains absolute. To attempt anything less is to invite profound and pervasive failure – not failure to be efficient, effective, or even a leader in the economic field, but failure to understand the most basic and enduring of human truths, failure to understand what Macmurray calls the first priority in education.

> The first priority in education – if by education we mean learning to be human – is learning to live in personal relation to other people. Let us call it learning to live in community. I call this the first priority because failure in this is fundamental failure, which cannot be compensated for by success in other fields; because our ability to enter into fully personal relations with others is the measure of our humanity. For inhumanity is precisely the perversion of human relations.
>
> (Macmurray 1958)

Notes

1 I have chosen to focus almost exclusively on the work of John Macmurray for three main reasons. Firstly, his work seems to me to be especially poignant and relevant to the dilemmas we are currently facing. Secondly, his insights have an enduring, profound quality that take us well beyond the vicissitudes of the present: he is one of the great philosophical figures of the twentieth century. Thirdly, my hope is that those writers within the field of education who are concerned with the nature of community (a) from the standpoint of philosophy (e.g. Kathleen Abowitz, Nick Burbules, Jane Roland Martin, Nel Noddings, Richard Pring, Ken Strike) and (b) from the standpoint of a wide-ranging, interdisciplinary project (e.g. Antony Bryk, David Clark, Judith Warren Little, Karen Seashore Louis, Deborah Meier, Mary Ann Raywid, Thomas Sergiovanni and Ted Sizer) will prefer an account to which they can bring their own understandings and enthusiasms rather than one which peppers the text which interminable brackets and citations so aptly and insightfully dubbed (by Bernard Crick) 'the ugly carapace of footnotes'. Intellectual intrusions and attributions, are often too general to be of much use to readers unfamiliar to the field or too dubious in their specificity for those steeped in the literature; they are refreshingly absent from Macmurray's own writing.

2 A fuller account of the psychological principles of community than space permits would make reference to Macmurray's insistence that both love and fear are present and necessary in relations of community. The key point is that fear must be subordinated to love. (See Macmurray 1961: 158 ff.)

3 This small section on target-setting draws on material developed in more detail elsewhere (see Fielding 1999a).

4 I realize there is an apparent contradiction here since part of what it means for a policy to be effective is precisely the fact that it does work, that it does deliver. The inverted commas round 'effective policies' point to the special sense in which I am using 'effective' here, that is, policies imbued with the outcomes-driven myopia of contemporary effectiveness ideology.

References

Ball, S. J. (1996) Recreating Policy through Qualitative Research: A Trajectory Analysis, American Educational Research Association Annual Conference, New York.

BBC (1992) Schooling Recollected, in BBC LEAO 4 *Quality in Schools* Video – Interview with John Humphries.

Fielding, M. (1997) Beyond school effectiveness and school improvement: lighting the slow fuse of possibility. *Curriculum Journal*, 8(1), Spring, 7–27.

Fielding, M. (1999a) Target setting, policy pathology & student perspectivees: learning to labour in new times. *Cambridge Journal of Education*, 29(2), June, 277–87.

Fielding, M. (1999b) Radical collegiality: affirming teaching as an inclusive professional practice. *Australian Educational Researcher*, 26(2), August, 1–34.

Fraser, E. and Lacey, N. (1993) *The Politics of Community: A Feminist Critique of the Liberal-Communitarian Debate* (Hemel Hempstead: Harvester Wheatsheaf).

Ignatieff, M. (1984) *The Needs of Strangers* (London: Chatto & Windus).

Macmurray, J. (1933) *Interpreting the Universe* (London: Faber).

Macmurray, J. (1938) *The Clue to History* (London: Student Christian Movement Press).

Macmurray, J. (1941a) Persons and Functions, Outline Document for a series of radio talks submitted to the BBC, 19 September, Unpublished.

Macmurray, J. (1941b) *Two Lives in One.* Persons and Functions – III *Listener*, 36(675), 18 December, p. 822.

Macmurray, J. (1941c) *The Community of Mankind.* Persons nd Functions – IV *Listener*, 36(675), 24 December, p. 856.

Macmurray, J. (1942) Freedom in the Personal Nexus, in R. N. Anshen (ed.), *Freedom: Its Meaning* (London: Allen &Unwin), pp. 176–93.

Macmurray, J. (1943) *Foundations of Economic Reconstruction* (London: National Peace Council).

Macmurray, J. (1949) Principles of Personal Culture: (1) The Integrity of the Personal The First 1949 Joseph Payne Memorial Lecture, College of Preceptors, 1 November, Unpublished.

Macmurray, J. (1950) *Conditions of Freedom* (London: Faber).

Macmurray, J. (1958) Learning to be Human, Moray House Annual Public Lecture, 5 May, Unpublished.

Macmurray, J. (1961) *Persons in Relation (The Form of the Personal Vol 2* Gifford Lectures 1953–54) (London: Faber).

Tierney, W. G. (1993) *Building Communities of Difference* (Westport, CT: Bergin & Garvey).

12 Towards a view of policy analysis as practical reason

Fazal Rizvi

University of Illinois, Urbana-Champaign

Source: *Journal of Education Policy*, 1 (2): 149–62, 1986.

Policy analysis is a relatively new industry, going back no more than 30 years. However, even in this short time, it has come to hold a key position in modern public administration. In the last five years educational authorities throughout Australia have appointed policy analysts, assuming their role to be of crucial significance. Invariably policy analysts hold important positions close to the places where decisions are explored, made and evaluated. The work of policy analysts has become part of the institutional apparatus that is instrumental in determining and legitimizing policy choices.

So what is policy analysis? According to its orthodox formulation, a formulation I shall refer to as the technological conception, policy analysis is social scientific research conducted in order to assist rational policy-making (Lindblom and Cohen 1979). It is this research which, it is claimed, adds a measure of rationality to the hurly burly of policy-making. By providing objective evidence, such research supposedly helps counteract the special pleading and selfish sectional interests that might otherwise seem to dominate the political process. It could be said that policy analysis, viewed as a technology, has an 'underlabourer's' job to the more upfront activities of policy development and implementation. Policy analysts are social scientists trained to reason and collect data about social processes in careful and rigorous ways, and to provide information to policy-makers about such things as the likely options and possible consequences of various policy choices. Policy analysis is thus viewed as *applied* social research.

What is distinctive about this technological conception of policy analysis, viewed as applied social science, is the belief that while it has normative implications, in so far as it can indicate to the policy-maker the 'most efficient' course of action to take to achieve a particular goal, it is not qualified to judge the rationality or legitimacy of the goal itself. The task of the policy analyst is thus seen in instrumental terms. S/he can advise policy-makers about the *technically* most efficacious course of action to adopt in order to implement a political decision, but, *qua* policy analyst, s/he is not permitted to judge that decision. Policy analysis thus can tell policy-makers what *can* be done; it is *not* qualified to say what *should* be done. No amount of actual or possible events can, according to this view, determine what state of affairs *ought* to exist. It is this categorical distinction between 'is' and 'ought' which leads Dye (1981: 6) to suggest that 'it's important to distinguish *policy analysis* from *policy advocacy*'. Insisting that the primary concern of policy analysis is with explanation rather than prescription, Dye argues (1981: 6–7):

> *Explaining* the causes and consequences of various policies is not equivalent to prescribing what policies governments ought to pursue. Learning why governments do what they do and what the consequences of their actions are is not the same as saying what governments *ought* to do, or bringing about changes in what they do. Policy advocacy requires the skills of rhetoric, persuasion, organization, and activism. Policy analysis encourages scholars and students to attack critical policy issues with the tools of systematic inquiry. There is an implicit assumption in policy analysis that developing scientific knowledge about the forces shaping public policy and the consequences of public policy is itself a socially relevant activity, and that such analysis is a prerequisite to prescription, advocacy and activism.

Policy analysis is thus given by Dye and others an exclusive function, unrelated to substantive moral and political concerns. The tools of policy analysis are moreover thought to be applicable to all policy contexts, be it engineering or education. It is this assumption which no doubt explains why so many educational policy analysts depend for their understanding of educational problems on theories and methods which are borrowed wholesale from economics, political science and sociology. As Prunty (1984: 35) points out, 'to engage in the wholesale purchase of general theories of policy is to accept the assumption that immutable principles govern policy-making in educational organizations that equate with those in any other organizational context' and yet educational problems are located in contexts which are formed by moral considerations in the way other organizational contexts may not; and to assume that educational problems can be resolved in some generalized way is to ignore the particular moral dimensions which are constitutive of the processes of education – that is, curriculum, evaluation and pedagogy.

In this paper I want to argue that the technological conception of policy analysis is fundamentally mistaken. It is based on philosophical assumptions which cannot be sustained. In particular I maintain that the fact-value distinction upon which the technological conception is based is epistemologically incoherent; and that questions of moral value which lie at the heart of all educational problems *can be* rationally debated and assessed, and that they therefore should not be excluded from the province of educational policy analysis.

The technological conception of policy analysis is embedded in a highly influential tradition in the philosophy of social science. It is linked to what Shils (1980: 20) refers to as the technological picture of social science, a view which emphasizes social science's ability to manipulate and control social environments; a view resting on the presumption that just as natural science has been effectively used to win control over the physical environment, so too could scientific techniques be used to discover general laws of social processes so that it is possible to win control over the human environment. To do this, it is claimed social science must be scrupulously value-neutral and free from any form of subjectivity.

In historical terms, the technological conception of policy analysis can be said to have arisen from within the empiricist tradition. Perhaps the clearest account of this tradition can be found in Hume's writings. Hume (1888) considers reason to be the faculty with which we are endowed that enables us to grasp logical relationships between concepts and propositions. The only rationality concerning practical ends that is possible, Hume maintains, is the rationality that is concerned with determining the ways of achieving particular ends. Hume's primary interest is, therefore in showing reason to be lacking the power his predescessors, the rationalists, took it to have.

Hume's view concerning the limited applicability of reason depends on the sharp distinction he draws between 'ideas' (a notion intended to cover both concepts and propositions) and 'passions' (a notion roughly equivalent to our broad notion of value).

> The understanding exerts itself after two different ways, as it judges from demonstration of probability; as it regards the abstract relations of our ideas, or those relations of objects of which experience only gives us information.
>
> (Hume 1888: 413)

This clearly suggests that there are only two ways in which understanding can operate: the first depends on the analysis of concepts or the employment of deductive reasoning; the second involves the discovery and application of causal statements based, according to Hume, on observed regularities, that is, inductive reasoning. Reason is thus restricted to apparently limited activities of comparing ideas and discovering matters of fact, to deduction and induction. This implies that in making decisions about practical ends, we are confined to reasoning deductively about them and using causal knowledge to ascertain the means of achieving their satisfaction. But the ends themselves may not be derived from reason, the idea of reason being essentially theoretical. Hume maintains that 'moral distinctions are not derived from reason'. Moral and practical ends cannot, in principle, be affected by the operations of reason, for these are notions which are, for Hume, objects of one's passions. Our passions are original essences:

> original facts and realities compleat in themselves and implying no reference to other passions, volitions or action.
>
> (Hume 1888: 458)

So, to suggest that reason can conflict with or control the passions is misleading. Indeed, concludes Hume (1888: 416): ' 'tis not contrary to reason to prefer the destruction of the whole world to the scratching of a man's finger'.

During this century no other sociologist has popularized this Humean tradition more than Max Weber (Weber 1949). Like Hume, Weber maintains that there is a logical disjunction between statements of facts and statements of value. Impressed with the 'manipulative success' of the natural sciences during the late nineteenth century, Weber wished the study of social relations and human behaviour to be 'scientific', believing this to be in principle possible. The view of science to which Weber subscribes involves a general acceptance of the essential features implicit in the positivist philosophy of science developed during the Vienna Circle days. These features include: the drawing of a distinction between discovery and validation; support for the deductive-nomological account of explanation; a belief in a neutral observation language as the proper foundation of knowledge; a commitment to the 'value-free' ideal of scientific knowledge; and a belief in the methodological unity of the sciences. Weber holds that only the sphere of 'facts' is properly the subject-matter of science, whether physical or social, for only facts and not values are ascertainable by the observational methods of science. For him, only the problems of what phenomena exist in the world, what law-like relations hold between them and what explains these relations, constitute the legitimate sphere of 'facts'. In contrast, Weber considers value-judgements to be assertions of the 'satisfactory or unsatisfactory character of phenomena', their 'desirability' and 'undesirability', subjects on which science cannot make pronouncements (Weber 1949: 10).

The Weberian doctrine of value-freedom is in many ways parallel to the Humean account of the limits of rationality. Both Weber and Hume emphasize that empirical sciences cannot establish values since no evaluative conclusions can ever be deduced or derived from factual assertions. For Hume, values are original states of mind; for which he uses the general term 'passions'; they are not objects of reason. Weber similarly regards values as entirely a matter of 'choice or compromise'; there are no rational or empirical (scientific) procedures of any kind which could provide us with rational decisions. Just as for Hume reason can function in a limited fashion in practical discourse, so for Weber empirical social science can perform a variety of functions relative to practical value decisions. Weber stresses the limitations of 'rational or empirical science' in the following terms:

> (1) the indispensable means and (2) the inevitable repercussions, and (3) the thus conditioned competition of numerous possible evaluations in their practical consequences, are all that an empirical discipline can demonstrate with the means at its disposal. Even such simple questions as the extent to which an end should sanction unavoidable means, or... how conflicts between several concretely conflicting ends are to be arbitrated, are entirely matters of choice and compromise. There is no (rational or empirical) scientific procedure of any kind whatsoever which can provide us with a decision here. The social sciences which are strictly empirical sciences, are the least fitted to presume to save the individual the difficulty of making a choice...
>
> (Weber 1949: 18–19)

Accordingly, social science can specify the means to a certain end, it can tell one what one is able to do in certain circumstances; it can provide information that might be relevant for the acceptance of rejection of values (though it cannot provide any criteria of relevance); it can estimate the cost of consequences (intended or unintended) of holding certain value positions; and it can analyse the relationship between various value positions. But while a person's practical ends (or attitudes) can of course provide the explanations of his or her actions, there is no set of ends that has a privileged status as rational.

It has been argued so far that the technological conception of policy analysis is embedded in the empiricist tradition, represented most clearly by Hume and Weber. A central claim belonging to this tradition is the proposition that facts and values are logically distinct. Putnam (1981) argues that during this century so pervasive has the belief in the fact-value distinction come to be that it can appropriately be referred to as 'a cultural institution'. In recent years, however, there have been signs of discontent among social scientists generally but policy analysts in particular. Following developments in post-empiricist philosophies of science and social sciences, there is no longer the conviction that generalizations in social science can be entirely value-free. Many policy analysts have expressed their disappointment in admitting that it may not be possible to have the truly scientific knowledge of social processes that was so enthusiastically promised by positivist social researchers. Rein (1983: 84) claims that a review of leading policy journals – such as *Policy Review*, *Policy Science* and *Public Policy* – reveals that while not all mainstream analysts have abandoned the idea of value-neutrality, there are signs of considerable discontent and disillusionment with the concept as a realisable ideal.

There is yet another front on which the technological conception of policy analysis has been subjected to a great deal of criticism. It has been argued that the questions of means and ends, procedural and substantive values, cannot be as easily separated as the empiricists like Hume and Weber thought. Fay (1975), for example, has argued that the key notion in the technological conception of policy analysis is 'efficiency', and that the idea of the 'most efficient means to a given end' is not entirely free of evaluative import. The very emphasis on efficiency, at the exclusion of other virtues such as thoroughness, creativity, imagination, and education indicates that a particular value is already presupposed as more worthwhile than others (Fay 1975: 50).

Despite the recognition of these practical and epistemological problems, the technological conception of policy analysis remains as popular as ever among administrative theorists and educational administrators alike. The model of reasoning about practical matters which is implicit in this conception means that there continues to be an insistence upon a division of labour between policy advocates and policy analysts. While the value-neutrality thesis is often denied, the most fundamental of all empiricist ideas, the view that it is impossible to reason about ultimate policy decisions, the moral ends, is seldom questioned. Gripped by the propaganda of the so-called 'naturalistic fallacy' (Moore 1903), policy analysts continue to conceive of their task as one which does not involve making substantive moral judgements.

So while the idea of value-neutrality of social research is now beginning to be discredited, most policy analysts continue to subscribe to a somewhat naïve account of practical discourse derived from empiricist epistemology. This account is governed by a distinctive set of metaphysical presuppositions. It is a view, clearly articulated by both Hume and Weber, which announces that there is no such thing as moral cognition or knowledge. According to this view, knowledge requires a real object set over against the knowing subject, but since there is no objective moral reality, moral utterances cannot be *known*. A corollary of this view is that moral judgements, since they lack cognitive content, lack truth-status. Non-cognitivism, as this view has now come to be known, can thus be characterized as involving the assertion that individuals are ultimately morally autonomous – that is, they are free to form their own moral opinions in their own way, regardless of the presence of any distinctive set of facts. So while the 'revisionist' enlightened policy analysts are prepared to accept that value-neutrality of social research is, in practical terms, an unachievable ideal, they nevertheless hold fast to the view that morality is an individual matter, originating in personal consciousness. Even such 'enlightened' philosophers of educational administration as Hodgkinson (1978) argue that values are a function of the individual's choice or preference.

The non-cognitivist view of moral discourse implicit in the technological conception of policy analysis has in recent years begun to be subjected to a great deal of criticism – not that these criticisms, confined as they are to academic journals in philosophy, have had any great effect on the way policy analysis has developed and flourished! Many of the philosophical criticisms of non-cognitivism have revolved around the claim that it is a doctrine which promotes moral irrationalism. Kolnai (1977: 31) has, for example, argued that since it places moral notions beyond the reach of criticism, non-cognitivism amounts to a 'suicide of thought'. Another influential rationalist critique of non-cognitivism can be found in Iris Murdoch's ethical writings (1970). More recently, Wiggins (1976) has presented a strongly argued phenomenological critique in which he draws attention to the subjective consequences of embracing an ethical theory of the non-cognitivism type. He objects to the idea that our moral thinking can be logically isolated from that part of our mental life which is regulated by external reality. Wiggins maintains that at a phenomenological level, the sense of the moral value of what we are doing cannot be independent of objective considerations. On the contrary, he argues, the human will 'picks and chooses, deliberates and weighs concerns. It craves objective reasons; and often it could not go forward unless it thought it had them' (Wiggins 1976: 341).

MacIntyre (1981) has recently explored the social consequences of non-cognitivism. MacIntyre argues that non-cognitivism entails a picture of the social world which can be characterized as nothing but a meeting place for individual wills, each with its own set of attitudes and preferences. He insists, moreover, that this picture has the effect of obliterating any genuine distinction between manipulative and non-manipulative social relationships. While the social, moral and political critiques of non-cognitivism presented by such philosophers as Kolnai, Murdoch, Wiggins and MacIntyre certainly weaken the non-cognitivism case, in what follows a more debilitating critique is attempted. It is argued that non-cognitivism is an epistemologically incoherent thesis.

At the metaphysical level, non-cognitivism is a doctrine which derives its plausibility from an implicit acceptance of empiricism. Empiricism is a contentious term, but for the purposes of this paper empiricism can be understood as a school of thought which embodies a number of related suppositions. First, the empiricist subscribes to a certain specific view of language: he sees language as an *instrument* for the communication of thought. According to the empiricist, thought is conceived as historically and logically prior to its expression in words. Second, the empiricist understands natural language on the model of a 'scientific calculus'. That is, once meanings of words have been fixed in definitions, there is no possibility of rational disagreement about their correct application. Third, empiricism involves the belief that we can define our terms in any way we like, but once this has been done it is the configuration of objects in the world which determines the truth-value of propositions, independently of any mediation by us. The objects exist in the world prior to the construction or deployment of any theory. Fourth, empiricism implies that all our evidence for the truth or falsity of propositions is derived from our senses; that is, the ultimate authority for any rationally grounded belief which is not analytic resides in sensory experience. Finally, empiricism involves, following Hume, a belief that 'sense data' constitutes a source of information from which we *infer* how things are in reality. These suppositions lead the empiricist to a distinctive view of knowledege. S/he acknowledges as real and objective only those entities which are ultimately reducible to experimental sciences.

Even this somewhat simplified account of empiricism is sufficient to show how non-cognitivism gains its plausibility. According to the empiricist, truth-value can only be assigned to those entities which impinge directly upon our senses. But since the non-cognitivist does not admit moral entities as being part of the 'fabric of the world', s/he cannot admit the idea of immediate 'non-inferential' experience which might be constitutive of a moral proposition. Mackie (1977) has thus argued that 'if there were objective values, they would be entities or qualities of a very strange sort, utterly different from anything else in the universe. Correspondingly, if we're aware of them, it would have to be by some special faculty of moral perception or intuition, utterly different from our ordinary ways of knowing everything else' (Mackie 1977: 15). Not finding G. E. Moore's argument concerning the existence of non-natural properties convincing, Mackie concludes that moral judgements cannot be truth-functional. Mackie's argument is, of course, circular, as Lovibond (1983: 20) has pointed out, for it rests on the assumption that our 'ordinary way of knowing' is in fact determined in accordance with the epistemological restrictions of empiricism.

Indeed it is these empiricist restrictions which give rise to the so-called fact-value distinction. At one level, the distinction involves a belief in two separable regions of discourse but at another deeper level it embodies an assumption that there are two modes of judgements, two distinguishable kinds of human mental activities – one passive and the other active. In our capacity as describers of the world we passively 'read off' what is displayed to us by our senses in accordance with a pre-specified set of rules, while in our capacity as judges of value we are active in the sense that we construct our own individual emotional, motivated expressions without any determinate reference to external reality. The assumption of these distinct activities of the mind provide the non-cognitivist with the basis for the alleged opposition between the cognitive and the expressive functions of language. Supposedly, there are those statements with which we describe states of affairs, and then there are those judgements with which we express our feelings, emotions and other non-cognitive states. It is this dualism about meaning which underlies the empiricist view, so central to the technological conception of policy analysis, that there can be no objectively valid inference from descriptive premises to a practical conclusion.

A philosopher who has systematically questioned the whole idea of comparisons between different regions of discourse or between two allegedly distinct aspects of mental activity is Wittgenstein. In the *Philosophical Investigations* and elsewhere in his later work, Wittgenstein rejects empiricist assumptions regarding language as both naïve and false. He offers us instead a homogeneous or 'seamless' conception of language. In his later work, Wittgenstein abandons his previous normative notion of propositions and argues that all language-games are of 'equal value', in the transcendental sense of *Tractatus*. In the *Investigations*, he denies that any reference to some allegedly neutral idea of objective reality is necessary in determining what can count as a proposition, and what can therefore have truth-value. In what follows it will be argued that, freed from the epistemological restrictions of empiricism by a Wittgensteinian vision of language, it would indeed be possible to restore rationality to moral language, language which is so inextricably linked to all forms of policy discourse. A rehabilitation of the notions of truth, objectivity and rationality in moral discourse would moreover enable us to view policy analysis in a different light – not as technological reason but as practical reason.

Wittgenstein's criticisms of the empiricist view of language are embodied in two main propositions. First, Wittgenstein denies the logical priority of thought over the language in which it is made manifest; that is, he repudiates the instrumental conception of language which posits a relation between two logically distinct entities: thought and language. For Wittgenstein, a distinction between thought and language lacks coherence, for thought is logically inseparable from its physical manifestation in language and that language itself arises only in the context of a collective life. Second, Wittgenstein rejects the 'calculus' model of natural language (Wittgenstein 1975: 25). He sees natural language instead as an organic growth of human culture. On Wittgenstein's view of language the use of signs is conceived, not on a model suggested by natural science, but by a model suggested by art. Wittgenstein argues that with words we *do* things; words have pre-eminently a practical character. Rejecting the empiricist idea that with language we merely communicate our thoughts, Wittgenstein claims that the goal of language is essentially practical; namely, that with language we are able to participate in various manifestations of human forms of life. All language-games, for Wittgenstein, are essentially practical.

Highly reminiscent of the metaphysical position of Marx is Wittgenstein's insistence that consciousness is from the beginning a social product, which is both historically and conceptually prior to the thoughts that individuals might have (Rubinstein 1981). Wittgenstein sees language as a social institution which is grounded, like other institutions, in the shared way of life of a community. For him, it is our *acting* which lies at the bottom of language-games (Wittgenstein 1977: 204). The full significance of this claim lies in Wittgenstein's account of 'following a rule' (Wittgenstein 1974: 139–242). There he argues that all linguistic behaviour is guided by rules and that rules should properly be regarded as normative, or action-guiding.

Rules are rules in the sense of regulations; rules which may be violated, disobeyed, enforced and so on. They specify which combinations of words make sense in which linguistic or extra-linguistic contexts. According to Wittgenstein, many, perhaps most, of what he calls rules are also unformulated. They are nonetheless *public.* That is, they manifest themselves in the spectrum of human practices.

That it is logically impossible to have private rules is a proposition Wittgenstein explores in what has become known as his 'private language' argument (Wittgenstein 1974: 269). A 'private language' is characterized by Wittgenstein as the sort of language people imagine can be used to refer to the owner's private sensations. It is a language which, in principle, cannot be learned or understood by anyone other than the user. The coherence of the private language user's claim to have given a name to a sensation is dependent upon the ability to connect some sign with a particular sensation in a regular, that is, rule-governed way. The existence of a rule is dependent upon the presence of distinguishable behaviours which constitute rule-following and rule-breaking. The 'private-language' user must be able to determine whether the rule for matching up sensations has been followed or broken. But such a determination requires appeal to some external or independent standard. It is just this type of appeal which is, in principle, not available to the 'private-language' user. Whatever the private language user does is correct and thus the concepts of correctness and correctly following a rule become vacuous. It follows that any behaviour which can be termed rule-following should necessarily be discernable as such by others. It is the nature of rules to be common and public in this way. Wittgenstein concludes that there is no such thing as a private rule. The private language user's claim to have given meaning to a word by correlating it in a rule-governable way with some sensation is therefore incoherent.

Given these insights about the nature of language, the distinction between regions of discourse at the metaphysical level becomes spurious. Instead of confining the descriptive function to those parts of languages that deal with a natural scientific subject-matter, Wittgenstein's view of language allows that function to pervade all regions of discourse, irrespective of content. Equally, given the practical character of language, the expressive function of language also comes to pervade language in its entirety. In other words, 'fact' and 'value' *coalesce* – 'value' is thus reabsorbed into the real world from which the non-cognitivist theory expelled it. The non-cognitivist view that moral utterances have an entirely private character cannot survive the challenge of Wittgenstein's private language argument.

The denial of the fact-value distinction at the metaphysical level would, according to Wittgenstein, reside in the lack of any distinction between those of our beliefs which are *actually true* and those which are merely *held true by us*. No such distinction can survive the recognition that some *human* authority has to *decide* the claim of any proposition to be regarded as actually true. This also means that the objective validity of a piece of reasoning is always, at the same time, something of which human beings are subjectively, but collectively, persuaded.

The empiricist thinks of a perceptual judgement as involving a matching up of sentences with sensory inputs. Wittgenstein argues that, on the contrary, a perceptual judgement is a function of human linguistic practice, and not of some neutral fidelity to some supposed 'hard data' of individual awareness. The alternative to the theory which makes sensory evidence the ultimate rational basis of knowledge is the view that renounces altogether the idea that such a basis is needed, which holds, in other words, that knowledge *can stand without foundation*. The non-foundational view of knowledge of course does not involve rejecting the very idea of the rational justification of beliefs and actions. What is does imply, however, is that the process of justification is not regulated by the concept of an absolute or rationally grounded end point (such as sensory evidence), but instead is relative to socially specific contexts.

So the notion of justification – whether theoretical or practical – is interwoven within a total system of behaviour of a community. The context of the language-game of seeking justification is itself defined by human culture. Beyond a normatively defined limit of reasonableness, there is no point in seeking justification, for here, according to Wittgenstein, we can only respond, 'this is simply what I do' (Wittgenstein 1976b: 309). Wittgenstein argues that talking about objectivity rests not upon an alleged rational foundation in our sensory experience but upon certain material facts, facts which are linked to the 'natural history' of language-users. Indeed, logic itself 'belongs to the natural history of man' (Wittgenstein 1976a: 49). As Lovibond (1983: 40) correctly observes, 'Wittgenstein's conception of language' incorporates a non-foundational epistemology which displays the notions of objectivity (sound judgement) and rationality (valid reasoning) as grounded in *consensus* – theoretical in the first place, but ultimately practical'.

We should be warned that Wittgenstein is not advocating an idealist portrait of the world, one which presents itself simply as a function of the perceiver, in which the facts of the world are irrelevant to human thought. Wittgenstein argues that (1976b: 352):

> Do I want to say, then, that certain facts are favourable to the formation of concepts; or again unfavourable? And does experience teach us this? It is a fact of experience that human beings alter their concepts, exchange them for others when they learn new facts; then in this way what was formerly important to them becomes unimportant and vice versa.

In contrast to the idealist picture, Wittgenstein emphasizes the interaction of subject and object. The notion of the interaction here is appropriately characterized as *dialectical.* As Pitkin (1972: 114) puts it: 'Wittgenstein... attempts to hold a dialectical balance between mutual influences of language and the world.' Phillips (1977: 86) similarly speaks of 'Wittgenstein's recognition of the dialectical relationship between nature and language'.

We are now in a position to see how the non-foundational view of knowledge suggested by Wittgenstein's later work undermines the non-cognitivist view of moral discourse. The non-cognitivist accepts the empiricist view which separates off a privileged class of beliefs, deemed to possess ultimate rational foundations, the facts, from an inferior class not supposed to be thus founded, the values. Wittgenstein's view of language, on the other hand, implies a rejection of this dichotomy. As Lovibond (1983: 42) has pointed out the Wittgensteinian homogeneous conception of the relation between language and the world can be understood, by comparison with the empiricist view, either as a 'levelling up' of evaluative discourse *vis-à-vis* scientific discourse, or as a 'levelling down' of the latter relative to the former. Wittgenstein however would reject any a priori discussion of the content of our thought such that, on the one side, we get a region where certain norms of argument cannot be disputed by the individual without risking the charge of irrationality; and on the other, an acceptance of the current consensual norms as arbitrary. Wittgenstein's views imply therefore that it is just as reasonable to speak of the rationality of *moral* questions as it is to speak about, say, the physical environment. Moral reasoning is thus restored to parity with scientific language on the strength of its answerability to similarly public cannons of evidence. What is now acknowledged as legitimate reasoning takes place against a background of shared assumptions and, ultimately, shared practice. Even mathematical rationality, insists Wittgenstein, turns out to consist in nothing more than conformity to the consensual norms of valid reasoning which happen to apply within an appropriate field.

Wittgenstein's private language argument clearly implies that non-cognitivism, when asserted at the metaphysical level, is an incoherent doctrine. For the private language argument leads us to the conclusion that since words have meaning for an individual only in so far as he is a participant in a system of shared activities, he can only conceptualize the conduct of his moral life in the terms laid down by some real system of moral institutions. The idea that the individual may have his own 'intellectual-authority' norms would seem incoherent in the light of Wittgenstein's demonstration that epistemological norms are necessarily public. To regard a given class of judgement as intelligible is to accept that there exist certain rules which are implicit in a community's linguistic and other social practices, and which are 'upheld' in a quite material sense by the sanctions which the community can bring upon deviant individuals. This much clearly follows from Wittgenstein's claim that any objective discourse, regardless of its content, is grounded in a tacit consensus within the speech community – in agreements 'initially in judgements but ultimately in actions', actions which are constitutive of a *form of life* (Wittgenstein 1974: 241). Objective discourse, on this view, consists in adoption of a publicly accessible perspective on the world. It is a form of human activity in which, as a matter of logic, we cannot participate unless, we are prepared to acknowledge certain tacit intellectual authorities.

The Wittgensteinian insight that obedience to a rule consists in conformity to a practice implies that there is an essential role for *historical continuity* in securing a meaningful life for individual persons. Human perception, whether moral or of any other kind, is historically informed, because language-games are grounded in a *form of life*, that is, a shared and continuous practice. Human beings develop their consciousness by inserting themselves into historically specific practices, by imitating other human beings, initially in a tacit manner, but later, in some circumstances, self-reflectively and critically. This position again is in contrast with non-cognitivism because non-cognitivism is a thesis which implies that we bring moral order into our lives by the exercise of an autonomous will – a mysterious decision-making power with no discernable historical roots. Moral judgements are seen by the non-cognitivist as both *asocial* and *ahistorical.* On a Wittgensteinian view, in contrast, we acquire our capacity for moral judgement by actively engaging ourselves into the historical processes of using moral language and participating in human language-games. Instead of having isolated moral existences we find morality in human practices, intellectually and practically integrated into the community to which we belong.

Wittgenstein's view of moral language has much in common with the Hegelian tradition, as represented in the ethical writings of Bradley (Norman 1983). In his essay 'My Station and its Duties' Bradley rejects the false dilemma between absolute (ahistorical) morality and a relativist view of morality. He argues (Bradley 1927: 189–90):

> A morality which was *not* relative would be futile . . . At any given period to know more than he did, man must have been more than he was; for a human being is nothing if he is not the son of his time; and he must realize himself as that, or he will not do it at all . . . Morality is 'relative', but is nonetheless real. At every stage there is the solid fact of a world so far moralized. There is an objective morality in the accomplished will of the past and present.

Like Bradley, Wittgenstein's views would seem to suggest that concepts of non-instrumental value – whether in morals or politics – are available for our use only in so far as we can 'find ourselves' in the specific range of social practices which happen, historically, to 'lie at the bottom' of moral discourse within the community to which we belong. Rationality, including moral rationality, is embedded in social relations – it is the social institutions which display the Hegelian 'objective mind', and as such have a semantic value. The question of what moral rationality consists in now presents itself as a *historical* question. This question is historical in the sense that one can only judge the rationality of practical judgements by inspecting the actual social institutions which inform one's life.

Given this Wittgensteinian understanding of moral discourse and moral rationality, what might moral argument consist in? Clearly a formula such as the one suggested by Hare's account of practical syllogism (Hare 1952) would be an inappropriate model for the entire range of moral arguments. Instead, moral arguments simply involve the presentation of certain information about a particular event which provides sufficient grounds for action, the criteria for what might constitute sufficient grounds being themselves contextually specific, and indeed contestable. We garner moral information directly from the scene that meets our eyes when we turn them in a particular direction: we do not make moral inferences from information of a non-moral kind; we simply *describe* the moral significance of the situation. In this way, there is no major premise of a practical syllogism suppressed, for in presenting a moral picture of a situation, 'nothing is concealed' (Wittgenstein 1974: 435), or at any rate, 'what is hidden . . . is of no interest to us' (Wittgenstein 1974: 126). There is, moreover no distinctive faculty which helps us describe moral reality. We simply describe what we see from the moral point of view. Moral judgements or prescriptions are thus regarded as non-inferential. This implies that moral assessment of a situation is best understood, for example, on the model which suggests a weighing up of the consequences of possible actions in terms of their effect on human beings.

To provide an argument to support a particular policy decision, we would simply describe those features of an event in a given context which are connected to our historically specific conception of what is morally right or practically fitting. There is nothing mysterious about describing from a moral point of view, in much the same way as there is nothing strange about describing mountains from the point of view of current theories in geology. Both descriptions are intelligible only in the context of language-games informed by our form of life. When challenged to further justify our descriptions we are sometimes able to, but ultimately we simply say, '*this* is how I think, *this* is how *we* act. *This* is how we talk about it' (Wittgenstein 1976b: 309).

It might be suggested that the view of moral rationality presented in this paper is linked inherently to the interests of conservative ideology. Such a suggestion might be thought to follow from the emphasis Wittgenstein places upon historical continuity and upon tacit 'agreement in judgement' about social practices. It might be argued that since Wittgenstein cannot see language functioning without a degree of uncritical acceptance of existing practices, he lends support to those who wish to maintain 'old traditions', traditions which have historically served to reproduce unequal power relations. In what follows, it will be argued that such a reading would indeed be a misrepresentation of Wittgenstein's later philosophy.

It is true that Wittgenstein argues that human personality is acquired by imitating other human beings in a community. The kind of imitation here is, by its very nature, uncritical. Such an uncritical imitation is thought by Wittgenstein to be essential in learning to 'talk', and until we can talk we cannot think at all, critically or otherwise. In *On Certainty* Wittgenstein argues that we cannot doubt everything, for the language in which doubt is couched itself has to be accepted. For Wittgenstein critical thought itself rests on the condition that there is a system of beliefs for which no further grounds are offered. Moreover even the language-game of criticism is always grounded in cultural presuppositions which are held tacitly. Criticism, if it is extreme, furthermore carries the inherent danger of isolating the critic from the network of social relationships which helps construct a conception of rationality for him in the first place. As Lovibond (1983: 110) points out, Wittgenstein's non-foundational theory of knowledge certainly suggests:

> a certain measure of conservatism, or gradualism, in respect of theory-change imposed on us by the material exigencies of 'finding our way about'. Our ability to do this depends not only on the internal coherence of our behaviour as individuals, but also on the sustainability of our relation to existing social institutions.

Equally, however, Wittgenstein's later philosophy has a radical element to it as well. It reaffirms the view that the use of language is an aspect of *human* behaviour and that this implies the importance of the genuinely philosophical task of self-examination of our ways of talking and thinking, and ultimately acting. Lovibond argues that to gain a reflective awareness of the practical character of language is 'to loose one's innocence with respect to participation in language-games' (Lovibond 1983: 117). The proposition 'words are also deeds' (Wittgenstein 1974: 546) implies that we stop thinking of language as primarily a medium in which we *copy* reality, and that we come to recognize the organic connection of each individual language game with a specific culture, historically evolved.

Wittgenstein's view of language also enables us to appreciate that both objectivity and subjectivity are present in moral discourse. Each time we describe the objective world, under whatever aspect, we in fact identify ourselves with the institutions which are associated with those language-games. All reports on experience thus become potentially morally significant. This is because our use of the particular words constitutes an act which exhibits our commitment to the scheme of values implicit in that vocabularly. With this understanding comes the recognition that linguistic practices depend for their survival on the continuing will of individuals to participate in them. Within the bounds of physical possibilities, nothing constrains our choice of how to live or what language-games to maintain. Those who recognize this participate in any existing way of life with the realization that their participation will henceforward appear under the aspect of moral *complicity.* To have 'a reflective understanding of the practical character of language is to come to see oneself as morally implicated in the form of life in which one participates' (Lovibond 1983: 129).

However, to assume that Wittgenstein demands complicity to *all* existing language-games is to grossly misunderstand this thought. For nothing Wittgenstein says rules out criticism. All he insists is that even the canons of criticism are governed by historically specific rules, and that forms of extreme subversion of values run the risk of severing themselves from all available modes of 'sound' judgement. So there is nothing problematic in Wittgenstein's view of language about combining a practical commitment to a particular form of life with a reflective awareness of its replaceability by a different one. Values are grounded in a form of life, but forms of life are not static; they arise organically out of our personal experiences of participation in the relevant social practices. Any organically dynamic form of life necessarily encompasses the values which govern the thought of rational dissenters as well as those which govern the thought of the orthodox; it incorporates institutions which are dedicated to diverse, and often competing, ends. Importantly too, however, there are 'agreements in judgement' regarding canons of criticism between the orthodox user of language and the dissenter for there to be any kind of communication between them at all. Nor are the canons of criticism so complete that they cannot be resisted and contested.

This account of rational criticism restores a role for an individual as a critic of the values and policies expressed in the public life of his community. This is done without abolishing the notion of moral rationality altogether, by giving individuals complete 'freedom' of moral and political judgement which they possess in the non-cognitivist picture. The critic becomes the immanent critic in relation to his forms of social life. Through the immanent critique of social institutions linguistic communities undergo a development of the kind termed 'dialectical'. By enhancing a self-consciousness about the workings of language we are in a position to explore how things might be different. An examination of the tacit presuppositions of language-games allows for the possibility that rules governing those language-games might in fact be changed. A consequence of this process might be that the criteria of sound reasoning might themselves be different at the end of the process from what they were at the beginning. In *On Certainty* Wittgenstein provides us with an image to better understand this dialectical process. There he asks us to think of the river bed which shifts, or is eroded over a period of time, though in relation to the water passing over it we think of it as static (Wittgenstein 1977: 96–7). Rules of socially meaningful behaviour change over time – there is a development and decay of specific configurations of intellectual authority. Thus if I happen to live through the historical transition from one form of life to another, my assessment of the initial form of life will be different at the beginning of the process than it will be at the end. Importantly too, there cannot be a neutral standpoint outside historical locations from which we can deliver judgements about the relative merits of each form of life.

What implications does all this have for the notion and practice of policy analysis? It is clear that the technological conception of policy analysis, based as it is on the assumption of a categorical fact-value dichotomy, is radically misconceived. The whole notion of value-neutrality is, in Wittgenstein's view of language, incoherent. Technological conception of policy analysis is no less connected to values than any other conception. In practising policy analysis we are guided by a set of rules which is governed by moral considerations inherent in specific historical locations.

Even if we assume moral values to be inapplicable in certain policy contexts we nevertheless make a significant moral choice. Of all policy contexts education, in particular, is 'shot through' with moral considerations. With a recognition that education is a system of cultural transmission which serves to simultaneously maintain, disguise and legitimate the interests of particular groups within the social system, we begin to see how problems of curriculum, evaluation and pedagogy cannot be resolved unless we pay due attention to the questions of moral values involved. A policy analysis in education which sets moral questions aside, places them outside its province, is bound to be inadequate.

Wittgensteinian thought allows us to restore notions of truth, rationality and objectivity to our moral vocabulary from which they were expelled by the non-cognitivists. We *can* and *do* know a good deal about virtues and goals and this knowledge is no less empirical. Perhaps we can now view policy analysis as practical reason in the Aristotelian sense of the term.

Practical reason (*phronesis*) is, for Aristotle, the ethical and political reflection, self-understanding, that helps the citizens of a free society practice the ethically good life (see MacIntyre 1981). Wittgenstein's view of language implies an assertion of the primacy of moral practice over both social and moral theory. Policy analysis would then be the practice of ethically informed reflection relative to specific social and historical conditions. We have to begin from where we are, but *first* we have to determine where that is. We need to place less emphasis on the generality of our explanations. We need to moderate what Wittgenstein calls our 'contemptuous attitude towards the particular case' (Wittgenstein 1975: 18). Policies must be examined in the particular contexts in which they are formulated and sustained. Educational policy must be fundamentally *educational*, and not transplanted from other policy areas.

With a Wittgensteinian understanding of language we become aware that 'words are deeds too'. This recognition implies that we as humans do have the power to view the world, and act upon it, differently. Self-reflection of this kind is indeed empowering, for it enables us to become ethically aware of the forms and the consequences of our linguistic practices. With this empowerment arises the possibility that we can undertake a radical reconstruction of those objectionable institutions in which the moral spirit of our community is currently embodied. It would seem that educational policy analysts are in an ideal position within administrative organizations to promote such self-reflection and reconstruction of educational institutions which they are urgently in need of.

References

Bradley, F. (1927) 'My station and its duties' in *Ethical Studies*, 2nd Edition (Oxford: Oxford University Press), pp. 160–213.
Dye, T. R. (1981) *Understanding Public Policy* (Englewood Cliffs, NJ: Prentice-Hall).
Fay, B. (1975) *Social Theory and Political Practice* (London: George Allen & Unwin).
Hare, R. M. (1952) *The Language of Morals* (Oxford: Oxford University Press).
Hodgkinson, C. (1978) *Towards a Philosophy of Administration* (Oxford: Blackwell).
Hume, D. (1888) *A Treatise on Human Nature*, translated by L. A. Selby-Bigge (Oxford: Clarendon Press).
Kolnai, A. (1977) *Ethics, Value and Reality* (London: Athlone Press).
Lindblom, C. and Cohen, D. (1979) *Usable Knowledge* (New Haven, CT: Yale University Press).
Lovibond, S. (1983) *Realism and Imagination in Ethics* (Oxford: Blackwell).
MacIntyre, A. (1981) *After Virtue* (London: Duckworth).
Mackie, J. (1977) *Ethics: Inventing Right and Wrong* (Harmondsworth: Penguin).

Moore, G. E. (1903) *Principia Ethica* (Cambridge: Cambridge University Press).
Murdoch, I. (1970) *The Sovereignty of Good* (London: Routledge & Kegan Paul).
Norman, R. (1983) *The Moral Philosophers* (Oxford: Oxford University Press).
Phillips, D. L. (1977) *Wittgenstein and Scientific Knowledge* (London: Macmillan).
Pitkin, H. (1972) *Wittgenstein and Justice* (Berkeley, CA: University of California Press).
Prunty, J. (1984) *A Critical Reformulation of Educational Policy Analysis* (Geelong: Deakin University Press).
Putnam, H. (1981) *Reason, Truth and History* (Cambridge: Cambridge University Press).
Rein, M. (1983) 'Value-critical policy analysis' in D. Callahan and B. Jennings (eds) *Ethics, The Social Sciences and Policy Analysis* (New York: Plenum Press).
Rubinstein, D. (1981) *Marx and Wittgenstein* (London: Routledge & Kegan Paul).
Shils, E. (1980) *The Calling of Sociology and Other Essays on the Pursuit of Learning* (Chicago, IL: University of Chicago Press), pp. 83–112.
Weber, M. (1949) *The Methodology of the Social Sciences* (New York: The Free Press).
Wiggins, D. (1976) 'Truth, invention and the meaning of life', British Academy Lecture, *Proceedings of the British Academy* (London: BA).
Wittgenstein, L. (1974) *Philosophical Investigations* (Oxford: Blackwell).
Wittgenstein, L. (1975) *The Blue and Brown Books* (Oxford: Blackwell).
Wittgenstein, L. (1976a) *Remarks on the Foundations of Mathematics* (Oxford: Blackwell).
Wittgenstein, L. (1976b) *Zettel* (Oxford: Blackwell).
Wittgenstein, L. (1977) *On Certainty* (Oxford: Blackwell).

13 Critical inter/multicultural education and the process of transnationalization

A view from the semiperiphery*

Stephen R. Stoer and Luiza Cortesão

University of Oporta, Porto, Portugal

Source: *Journal of Education Policy*, 10 (4): 373–84, 1995.

Introduction

Three influential Portuguese education policy-makers recently wrote, 'Education is the privileged mechanism for the preservation and affirmation of national identity, for the transmission of moral and civic values and for taking on the challenge of economic development and the modernization of society' (Grilo *et al.* 1992: 11).

Given that both the crisis of the welfare state and the crisis of the nation-state have been attributed, in some way, to globalization and the crisis of Fordism (where the major agents of the restructuring process have been multinational firms), one wonders to what extent education has been affected by this process of transnationalization. In what way does it still make sense to talk about the contribution of schooling to the formation of national identity? Stuart Hall (1992), in talking about 'national cultures as "imagined communities"', suggests that there is occurring a dislocation of national cultural identities as a result of the globalization process. Or may it be that state schooling is the last refuge of resistance to the transnationalization process?

While we cannot satisfactorily respond to all of the questions raised above in an article of this nature, we would like, in the first part of this paper, to question the substance of the continuing claim that 'education is the privileged mechanism for the preservation and affirmation of national identity', particularly in the light of what has been termed Portugal's semiperipheral condition. In the second part of the article, we would like to suggest that critical inter/multicultural education may be seen, in an epoch of transnationalization, as a challenge to the formation through schooling of national and minority identities as a result of its preoccupation with 'the construction of new identities (subjectivities) in a globalized world' (Albrow and Eade 1994). We conclude by arguing that critical inter/multicultural education in a semiperipheral country like Portugal will need to articulate the integration of subjectivities in the school with the goal of modernization of providing guarantees for citizenry through schooling.

Rhetorical mass schooling and its contribution to the formation of national identity

Theories on the development of mass schooling from a world system perspective (see, for example, Boli *et al.* 1985; Boli and Ramirez 1986; Ramirez and Boli 1987; Soysal and Strang 1989) have emphasized its contribution to what is termed the 'construction of the polity':

> The interstate system evolved from a loose collection of centralizing monarchies that espoused divine-right ideologies to a highly interdependent set of national states, that invoked 'the nation' as the overriding justification for state action... *Transforming the masses into national citizens* became a standardized feature of the state-orchestrated nation-building process; utilizing state-sponsored mass schooling to achieve this political end became a routinely accepted *modus operandi.*
>
> (Ramirez and Boli 1987: 13; cited in Araújo 1993: 70, emphasis added)

Soysal and Strang (1989) have referred to this process of transformation, in southern European countries like Portugal, as a *rhetorical* construction of education. 'States (in southern Europe) were quick to formulate compulsory schooling, but unable to pursue it in actual schooling' (cited in Araújo 1993: 71).

Indeed, looking back over the history of mass schooling in Portugal, we find a curious mixture of precociousness and frustration. For example, in spite of the fact that Portugal was one of the first European countries to establish the principle of compulsory schooling, 'which came to be formulated in the Reform of Rodrigo de Fonseca on the 7th of September, 1835, was suspended in December of the same year, but renewed once again with the reform of Passos Manuel on November 17, 1836' (Sampaio 1978: 11), the illiteracy rate among the population at the turn of the century was extraordinarily high (in 1900, 66 per cent of all men and 82 per cent of all women). Mass schooling advanced slowly, in Portugal, throughout the twentieth century. One social analyst (Mónica 1978: 39–40) has argued that mass schooling developed during the Salazarist dictatorship (1928–68) as a stringent form of social control, particularly of the 'masses' – either through the socialization of 'untamed children' or through the inculcation, in those remaining, of 'a full consciousness of their dignity as proud members of the (Portuguese) nation'. Through its contribution to promoting 'Portuguese pride', the school constituted a powerful ideological device which depended upon the existence of an undifferentiated populace ('the people'). The Salazarist phrase 'proudly alone', in a Europe and in a world that rapidly distanced themselves from a stagnating Portugal, became symbolic of dictatorial social control (Cortesão 1981). However, in spite of the effort made to mould young minds, the percentage of all children aged 6 to 10 in school in 1940 did not exceed, according to Mónica, 42 per cent (while in fact probably only about 37 per cent actually undertook schooling).[1]

With respect to secondary schooling, Portuguese sociologist Sérgio Grácio has noted (1986) that vocational options ('ensino técnico e industrial') expanded considerably during the 1950s and the 1960s, thus permitting the construction of what Grácio has termed a 'mitigated meritocracy' (to the extent that the construction of a full meritocracy was heavily constrained by the undemocratic nature of the political régime). However, it is doubtful if one can rigorously refer to mass schooling at the secondary level in Portugal during the 1960s or 1970s, or even during the decade of the 1980s. In fact, it was only in 1967 that six years of schooling became compulsory, and, further, it was only with the publication of the recent 'Lei de Bases' (*General Education Law of 1986*) that such compulsory schooling was extended, not to nine years of schooling, but to 15 years of age.

In addition to Portuguese colonialism and the censorship of the *Estado Novo*, both of which played important roles in the *rhetorical* construction of mass schooling in Portugal, two constant thorns in the side of the Portuguese education system have been the problems of a frequent inability to translate policies into practice, and a lack of resources. In fact, these (often inter-related) problems are not specific to the education system, but refer to the state generally. They have become recognized as problems in large part because public expectations have been generally stimulated with regard to what a 'successful' Portugal should be. This means that Portugal is obliged to try and live up to its history as one of the first and most successful European colonizing powers, with a national life dominated by memories of her former glory, and by the benefits and the much more important costs of attempting to retain elements of that empire and its associated glory. It also means that Portugal's strategic location on the European continent and its proximity to the consumer and cultural centres of Europe are now, and have been, exceptionally important factors in determining the country's future.

The two problems referred to above may be seen as inherent in the nature of the Portuguese state (and society), which in Wallerstein's term (1981) can be designated as *semiperipheral*. In the light of this theory, mass schooling in Portugal owes a good part of its rhetorical nature to its semiperipheral condition. Portuguese sociologist Boaventura Sousa Santos (1985b: 872) has characterized this condition as an 'articulated discontinuity between capitalist relations of production and relations of social reproduction'. Basically, this means that there exists 'a delay with regard to capitalist production relations but consumption standards are equivalent to those in centre countries'. A first important effect of this 'articulated discontinuity' is the fact that 'the strength of the state (in Portugal) does not easily convert itself into the legitimation of the state (as occurs, generally, in centre countries)' (pp. 872–3).

A second important effect of this 'articulated discontinuity' is the existence of 'social layers and fractions of class located alongside and below the working class and functioning as social supports for this same class'. Other writers, including

Wallerstein (1983, 1984), have referred to this phenomenon as the existence of a 'semiproletariat' (with regard to Portugal, see Pinto 1985, 1988). Effectively, one of the characteristics of Portugal's position on the periphery of Europe is the process of mutation through which peasant/rural groups are passing. Until relatively recently, Portugal had a sizeable primary sector, based largely on a subsistence economy. However, from the 1960s onwards, rural/peasant groups began organizing 'strategies for abandoning traditional (agricultural) work' (Almeida 1986: 381; Stoer and Araújo 1992a), due mainly to the increasing penetration of capitalist social relations of production into the countryside and to the perception, by these same groups (coupled with new consumption standards 'imposed' from the outside – often by way of emigration and by the mass media) that their way of life, based on agriculture, was becoming increasingly unviable. Thus rural/peasant groups have increasingly sought work off the land, often in small factories/shops or in civil construction. Agricultural work has consequently become mainly part-time for these groups, normally occupying early morning or late afternoon hours and the weekend.

The results for Portuguese mass schooling of the two effects referred to above are first, a constant and necessary effort to legitimate education policies, which often includes appealing for justification of policies through their recognized approval by international organizations (OECD, World Bank, European Commission),[2] and secondly the existence of a dynamic, initially based on social class, which has produced an important gap between rural and 'semirural' culture and the culture of the school. This 'gap' inevitably penalizes children and youth from rural and semirural zones of the country (see Stoer and Araújo 1992a). Thus, traditionally, Portugal appears to have experienced relatively weak formation of national identity through mass schooling (suggesting that there have existed other mechanisms in 'traditional' Portugal for this task – certainly an inviting theme for another article). In this sense, one may argue that rhetorical mass schooling in Portugal (with only a rhetorical 'transformation of the masses into national citizens') has encouraged what one might term 'the rhetorical construction of citizenship'.[3]

National identity and schooling as national administration

Alvin Gouldner, writing in the early 1970s on sociology and the Welfare State, refers to the new middle class as an increasingly national, *administrative*, class in the USA.

> The educated, bureaucratically employed, and highly mobile middle classes have a dwindling localistic attachment and a narrowing base of power on the *local* levels, which could provide them with the economic and political leverage to effectuate urban reform. They must, in consequence, seek a remedy not on the local but the national level.
>
> (1973: 47)

The implication for social reform is that

> The locus of reform initiatives and resources is increasingly found on the level of national politics and foundations, rather than in the political vitality, the economic resources, or the zealous initiatives of élites with local roots... As the locus of reform efforts moves upwards from the local to the national level, the conception and meaning of social reform changes. The urban reforms being sought by this new middle class are now aimed at the reform of a community to which they are less tied by complex interests, urbane pleasures, or by a round of familiarizing daily activities. It is not 'their' community that they now wish to reform – for their suburbs are decent enough as they view them. ... Social reform now becomes an effort largely motivated by bland political appraisal, removed economic calculus, prudent forecasting, or a sense of pity and sympathy that becomes increasingly remote as it loses rooting in daily experience and encounter. The community to be reformed becomes an object, something apart from and outside the reformer. ... Social reform now becomes a kind of engineering job, a technological task to be subject to bland 'cost-benefit' or 'system-analysis'. The rise of the welfare state then means the rise of the uninvolved reformer: it means the rise of reform-at-a-distance.
>
> (1973: 46–8)

The modernization process in Portugal, although occurring at a time when the Welfare State itself is being called into question as a form of social regulation,[4] has involved, in Gouldner's terms, a move of teachers – as members of the new middle class – from the local to the national level. Teachers in Portugal have, as have their counterparts in centre countries, generally moved their place of residence from the 'local community' to the suburbs of the larger cities.[5] They have also become part of a national (administrative) class, in the sense that they not only observe the rules and directives of national administration, but also in the sense that they largely identify themselves with a principle of equality of educational opportunity which guides their practices on the basis of a rational orientation that insists on assessing competences acquired and not on different (i.e. local) social and individual characteristics (although, as we pointed out above, there is some doubt as to the eficacy of this principle with regard to teachers' educational practices). Thus, apart from their perception of Portugal as a socially and culturally homogeneous country, teachers refuse, in principle, to recognize difference, above all within their classrooms (and perhaps less so with regard to the school in the wider sense), so as not to let it interfere with what is seen as a universal teaching/learning process (Cortesão and Pacheco 1992; Stoer and Araújo 1992a,b; Cortesão and Stoer 1995b). As one would expect on the basis of Gouldner's assessment, the effect of teachers' monocultural orientations is a tendency to reduce qualitatively different local circumstances and realities, to local 'disturbances'.

Thus, the modernization process in Portugal has promoted increased emphasis on national identity and its consolidation through schooling administered at the national level. This process has constituted a major component of the detraditionalization (in Giddens' sense, 1990) of Portuguese society. Another major component has been modernization as *an inherent part of globalization*, that is, an orientation towards full integration in the European Union (which Portugal joined in 1986) that has provided an impulse for the deconstruction of schooling as the preservation and affirmation of national identity. We have attempted to combine these two components in the notion of the *simultaneous crisis and consolidation of mass schooling in Portugal.*

Modernization in an epoch of globalization: the simultaneous crisis and consolidation of mass schooling in Portugal

The crisis of mass schooling is clearly related to the crisis of Fordism and the so-called youth crisis (youth unemployment). Historians and pedagogues, like Jacky Beillerot in France (1982) and António Nóvoa in Portugal (1987), have referred to the end of what they call the 'pedagogic century'. The crisis of mass schooling has to do, in large part, with its incapacity, up to now, to satisfactorily resolve (in legitimation terms) the question of social and cultural inequality. Even further, it has to do with the actual *promotion* of inequality within the school. Interesting in this respect are Wallerstein's comments on the subject:

> The major social mechanism created presumably to allocate individuals to occupations by virtue of talent rather than descent – the educational system – in fact functions only among the 'free' laborers, and even for them primarily as a way of maintaining descent lines by making exceptions for the very few (co-optation of bright individuals from the working classes) and thereby justifying the castle-allocation for the remaining vast majority. The justification is now more subtle and effective than that of redistributive systems: instead of the inevitability of fate or the will of God, caste-allocation is claimed to be the consequence of the application of human reason. Each individual is said to have a status he has achieved, rather than one ascribed to him.
>
> (1984: 154–5)

Portuguese sociologist Santos (1988) has suggested, ironically, that although one cannot find either Fordism or the welfare state in Portugal the symptoms of both their crises are remarkably present. Indeed, in recent times, youth employment has appeared – and is increasing, a form of 'new vocationalism' in education, directly related to 'productivist' education policy, has been documented (Stoer *et al.* 1990), a *Coordinating Secretariat for Programmes of Multicultural Education* has been set up by the Ministry of Education, and both the terms *globalization* and *social exclusion* have become part of the vocabulary of official social policy.

As referred to earlier on, the consolidation of mass schooling in Portugal is presently underway, having received an additional impulse from the ongoing national education reform process initiated in the latter half of the 1980s. As one would expect, at an official level, it is the discourse associated with traditional modernization ideology that has been the main official promoter of the consolidation of mass schooling in Portugal (Correia *et al.* 1993). Like the three Portuguese educators referred to at the beginning of this article (Grilo *et al.* 1992), official promoters of modernization see mass schooling as making a crucial contribution to the formation of national identity:

> The modernization process as a whole will always have in mind the need to reinforce national identity, as a permanent reference both in the study of our history and in the effort to renew and to promote the progress of Portuguese society.
>
> (*Programme of the XII Constitutional Government: Chapter 2, Education*, 1991)

However, the very fact that the modernization process is occurring at a time, in Portugal, when the effects of globalization as a phenomenon are evermore present has led 'private' promoters of modernization to make such statements as the following:[6]

> One understands that modernization is, essentially, a process by way of which one reformulates and recognizes different sectors of activity (with particular emphasis on economic and financial affairs) in the framework of an open society, with an economy subject to a rapid process of internationalization and (increasingly) integrated into a strongly competitive market.
>
> (Lopes *et al.* 1989: 255)

The central problems of both Portuguese economy and society, according to these same authors, are to know how to deconstruct 'the traditional and very persistent characteristics which have blocked our possibilities for modernization', and to know how to stimulate 'new relationships, new institutional and organizational frameworks, new strategic aims that correspond to new world and European frameworks' (1989: 11). 'Resistance to change' is seen by these authors as either irrational (a result of 'human inertia') or as based on the 'national' and, as such, suicidal in the new world climate. Raising the educational level of the population is considered the best way to combat such 'resistance':

> Increasing the education level of the population is, in the medium range, the way that may best counterbalance resistence to the integration process, since it allows citizens to better understand what is at stake while at the same time it widens the possibilities of entrance onto the labour market.
>
> (p. 251)

At the same time, a strategy should be adopted which guarantees that schooling serves the modernization of *all* of Portuguese society:

> Such a strategy should, on the one hand, promote an education of the Portuguese which respects the human being and which emphasizes the values which characterize Western democratic societies, and, on the other, train the professionals ... indispensable to development and the modernization of the economic, social and cultural structures of Portuguese society.
>
> (p. 61)

Although there may be much to object to in this updated version of modernization theory, the implications of it for mass schooling in Portugal appear to be clear. The modernization process in Portugal, conditioned by the simultaneous crisis and consolidation of mass schooling, provokes the simultaneous deconstruction of schooling as the preservation and affirmation of national identity and its very promotion in these same terms in order to preserve national and civic (based on representative democracy) values. Mass schooling's contribution to the modernization process is therefore, on the one hand, the promotion of a 'culture of schooling' (in a still very much semirural society) and other measures which guarantee that universal access to official schooling is not mere rhetoric (thus the appearance in the recent educational reform of measures aimed at tighter control of school attendance, the provision of transport and school meals to get – and keep – children/youth in school, and a multicultural educational programme aimed mainly at drawing teachers' attention to the 'special characteristics' of mainly Gypsy and African ethnic groups). On the other hand, mass schooling tries to respond to the crisis of schooling through measures that either promote new forms of provision (e.g. Portugal's *Escolas Profissionais*, in many ways similar to England's City Technology Colleges) or that involve both the local and the supranational communities as 'partners' in the elaboration and implementation of education policy.

Inter/multicultural education as a challenge to the preservation and affirmation of national identity

As seen above, the production of citizens through mass schooling for the nation-state continues to be considered, at least at the level of official discourse, an essential task of schooling in a European country which reassumed representative democracy only 20 years ago and which still sees the majority of its youth leave school before 15 years of age. In addition to works by theorists of modernization, a critical author such as Balibar, in recent works on ethnicity, nationalism and racism in Europe, has argued that, indeed, mass schooling is crucial to the production of the nation-state itself (Balibar 1991; Balibar and Wallerstein 1991). However, in manufacturing 'citizens', schooling also produces what Balibar terms *fictive ethnicities*. These are made up of mere 'subjects' who permanently remain citizens-in-development. These 'subjects' (the 'other', which in the context of Europe are minority subjects without the political rights of citizens)[7] are inherent to the production of the nation-state because the preservation and affirmation of national identity depend on contrast with, and difference from, the 'other' for their own construction.

Critical inter/multicultural education has developed, in part, as a challenge to this process, on the basis of the argument that subjectivities also have the right to a place in schooling. This may be seen to have occurred as part of a tendency to challenge the apparent triumph of instrumental rationality in the twentieth century and its 'smashing' of the subjectivity of social actors (Touraine 1990). Critical inter/multicultural education, as part of a social movement aimed at restoring the role of social actors, has argued that subjacent to the notion of subjectivities in the school is the structuring proposition of a form of citizenship based on participative democracy (McCarthy 1990). That is, cultural diversity is not only seen as a source of wealth for (instead of as an obstacle to) the teaching/learning process but also as a means of turning visible socio-cultural differences within the school in order to promote equality of opportunity based on school success (and not on mere access).

This argument is posed in contrast to another which sees the formation of (national) citizens through schooling as linked basically to the structuring propositions of citizenship based on representative democracy. Here the promotion of cultural homogeneity in the classroom is considered important in order to guarantee and to facilitate the transmission of national culture in official schooling. Cultural identity tends to be seen as fixed and based on an indisputable historical heritage. Official schooling should prepare citizens for the ongoing modernization process.

We want to argue that the relationship between producing citizens and producing subjectivities through schooling may be characterized by an unstable and permanent oscillation between the concepts of representative and participative democracy. Although it is the former that is hegemonic, the latter may be seen to grow in a process where the social actor gains increasing social control over his/her environment. It may also be seen as implying the recognition of the education system, in the words of Sousa Santos,

> as a cluster of social relations which occupies an intermediate position (between capital and labour, and which is lacking in structural autonomy), . . . heterogeneous in its internal composition due to the fact that it joins together elements from all, or most, structural places (namely, [i] the household place, [ii] the workplace, [iii] the citizenplace, and [iv] the worldplace).
>
> (1985a: 311–12)

Thus, the education system (in the words of Margaret Archer 1991) reflects, refracts, and even resists the effects of a contradictory development of the structural places, and its position with respect to these changes over time (e.g. the fact that with the birth and development of mass schooling the school has changed its position from one close to the workplace – learning to labour in the rural family unit and/or the factory school during the industrial revolution – to another clearly identifiable with the citizenplace).

In accordance with the arguments we have presented, the challenge to the preservation and affirmation of national identity through schooling, expressed through the appearance and development of inter/multicultural education, is double: on the one hand, the restructuring of the development process has led to the construction of citizenship based on representative democracy at levels that go beyond the nation-state (e.g. the role of schooling – European education – in the construction of the European Union through its contribution to the production of a system of cultural representation – the concept of being European); on the other hand, the idea – and the attempted concretization – of the contribution of schooling to the production of subjectivities (i.e. the recognition and legitimation of difference in schooling) signifies that there has been a qualitative change in the development process itself. Both the restructuring of the development process and the qualitative change in its nature have been attributed, in varying degree (Harvey 1989; Giddens 1990; Beck *et al.* 1994), to the phenomenon of globalization and the associated phenomena of the crisis of Fordism and its mode of state regulation and the technological 'revolution' in information and communications.

Globalization, as Giddens (1990) has pointed out, implies the linking of social and regional contexts in the form of networks extended across the earth's surface. As a result, there occurs an intensification of world social relations which subjects localities to factors delocated in terms of both time and space. Local activities thus take on a new dimension; they become simultaneously global.

> Globalisation expresses the increasing role of 'action at-a-distance' in human social affairs. In other words, to an increasing degree, our lives are influenced by activities and happenings that occur at a great distance from us. ... Globalisation can be ... defined as the intensification of worldwide social relations which link distant localities in such a way that local happenings are shaped by events occurring many miles away and vice versa.
>
> (Giddens 1990: 18, 64)

The fact that local transformation becomes part of globalization means not only that the modernization process challenges the traditional role of the nation-state in this process, but also that a renewed stress on cultural identity may alter the relation between the global and the local. Thus, as Giddens puts it, citing Daniel Bell, 'in circumstances of accelerating globalisation, the nation-state has become "too small for the big problems of life, and too big for the small problems of life"' (1990: 65).

The consequences of globalization for the modernization process are embedded in the presuppositions of critical inter/multicultural education: local, often 'traditional', culture cannot be seen as 'resistance to change' and mass schooling will inevitably construct multiple inter-connected identities (local, national, global).

We put the stress on *critical* inter/multicultural education because as part of globalization and the transnationalization process (felt particularly strongly at this moment in Europe where, as Hall points out (1992), the 'building' of Europe involves both its construction as a political entity *and* as a system of cultural representation) inter/multicultural education may conceal, as a legitimation effect, the trajectory of capitalism in this same process. Authors such as Bullivant (1981) and McCarthy (1990) have provided critiques of pluralist – 'benign' – inter/multicultural education which confuses 'life styles' with 'life chances' and which divides society into separate spheres of structure and culture, thus prematurely eliminating from analysis delimitations based on social class. Also, seeing critical inter/multicultural education as an inherent part of the transnationalization process does not mean denying its response to the negative effects of spacial/geographical alterations mainly under Fordism (Katznelson and Weir 1985). It does mean, however, a qualitative change in its content – for example, adding the 'noise', as McCarthy puts it (1990), of multidimensionality – and in its effects, for 'globalisation effectively means that societies now cannot be seen as systems in an environment of other systems, but as sub-systems of *the larger inclusive world society*' (M. Albrow cited in Smart 1994: 152).

Critical inter/multicultural education and the simultaneous crisis and consolidation of schooling in Portugal

On the basis of action-research carried out in Portuguese schools over the past five years,[8] it has become clear to us that citizenry cannot be reduced to subjectivity, nor can subjectivity be reduced to citizenry. Mass schooling, we would like to argue, in a semiperipheral country like Portugal still has an important contribution to make to the task of the consolidation of basic social and human rights through the 'construction of the polity'. At the same time, our work has convinced us that citizenry promoted by the school can be enriched through the integration in the school of the complexity of subjectivities. 'Cultural bilingualism', for example, may play an important role in contributing to the strengthening of personal and group self-images (which are the products of subjectivities) that would facilitate the taking on of citizenship or in making 'subjects' less fictive. The role of critical inter/multicultural education appears, in this light, as a challenge to the formation through schooling of national and minority identities. New identities, in a globalized world, that are both 'multiple' and 'hybrid', possibly based on what Albrow and Eade (1994) term 'personal/actor competence in constructing and manoeuvring identity', interact with national identity.

The challenge for a country like Portugal involves articulating the integration of subjectivities (in the construction of new identities) with modernization's promise of guaranteeing basic citizenry. Such articulation implies transforming 'rhetorical citizenship' into actual, lived, citizenship (where, indeed, moral and civic values give life to basic social and human rights – and obligations) while at the same time extending such citizenship to the local, supranational and global levels. This simultaneous crisis and consolidation of schooling in Portugal may provide interesting effects with regard to the quality of schooling produced through a successful articulation of citizenship and subjectivity. For example, in our work which has had as one of its main objectives reinforcing local cultures inside a school oriented on the basis of the principle of equality of educational opportunity, an attempt has also been made to make educational agents of both the school and community aware of the proximity of the school to the 'citizenplace' (i.e. the rights and duties inherent to official mass schooling). In other words, our emphasis on identifying and developing *cultural rights* has occurred simultaneously with the consolidation of *basic social and human rights*. Might it be that there is a potential in this interaction (e.g. seeing problems in all their complexity rather than seeing them in a compartmentalized way) that can give added value to Portugal's (semi)peripheral – in the European context – specificity?

Notes

* An earlier version of this paper was presented at the 13th World Congress of the International Sociological Association, Bielefeld, July 1994.

1 Candeias (1994) has referred to the very rhetorical nature of mass schooling in Portugal as having created a national identity based on illiteracy.

2 Santos (1991a) has referred to Portugal's entry into what is now the European Union as 'Portugal's construction of itself as an *imaginary core country*'.

3 Indeed, Stoer and Araújo (1992b) argued that rather than an internalization of basic human and social rights through mass schooling there has occurred a 'bureaucratization' of these same rights which has frequently included only *formal* loyalty to and identification with the principle of equality of educational opportunity.

4 Although Portugal's 1st Republic (1911–26) set many of the principles for modernization in Portugal, it was only in the 1970s, particularly after the April Revolution of 1974, that the term assumed its entire dimension. For an interesting critical analysis of the state and modernization in Portugal during the period 1974–88; see Santos (1990).

5 This affirmation needs more research particularly with regard to primary school teachers. Some insights into the implications of the move itself may be ascertained from works by Mónica (1978), Nóvoa (1987) and Araújo (1993).

6 Interesting to note is that the 'official' and the 'private' promoters of modernization are often the same persons. Tentatively, this suggests that considerations of a predominantly political nature guide the actions (and words) of the former, while the latter are more market-bound.

7 Here the Portuguese case is interesting, for the Portuguese tend to be simultaneously 'citizens' and 'subjects' within the European space. See Trindade and Mendes (1993) for some basic information on Portugal as both an immigrant and a migrant country.

8 We are referring to two action-research projects for which we were directors carried out in four Portuguese schools between 1989 and 1994 *(Projecto Educação Inter/Multicultural* and *Projecto Educação e Diversidade Cultural: para uma sinergia de efeitos de investigação*, Cortesão and Stoer 1995a).

Bibliography

Albrow, M. (1990) Introduction, in M. Albrow and E. King (eds) *Globalization, Knowledge and Society* (London: Sage), 3–13.

Albrow, M. and Eade, J. (1994) Constructing new identities in a globalized world, paper presented at the twelfth *World Congress of Sociology*, Bielefeld, July.

Almeida, J. F. de (1986) *Classes Sociais nos Campos* (Lisbon: Instituto de Ciencias Sociais).
Araújo, H. C. (1993) The construction of primary teaching as women's work in Portugal (1870–1933), unpublished PhD thesis, Open University.
Archer, M. (1991) Sociology for one world: unity and diversity. *International Sociology*, 6(2), 131–48.
Balibar, É. (1991) *Es gibt keinen staat in Europe*: Racism and politics in Europe today, *New Left Review*, 186, 5–19.
Balibar, É. and Wallerstein, I. (1991) *Race, Nation, Class: Ambiguous Identities* (London: Verso).
Beck, U., Giddens, A. and Lash, S. (1994) *Reflexive Modernization* (Cambridge: Polity).
Beillerot, J. (1982) La *Société Pédagogique: Action Pédagogique et Controle Social* (Paris: Presses Universitaires de France).
Boli, J. and Ramirez, F. (1986) World culture and the institutional development of mass education, in J. Richardson (ed.) *Handbook of Theory and Research for the Sociology of Education* (New York: Greenwood), 65–90.
Boli, J., Ramirez, F. and Meyer, J. (1985) The origins and expansion of education, *Comparative Education Review*, 29, 145–70.
Bullivant, B. M. (1981) *The Pluralist Dilemma in Education* (Sydney: Allen & Unwin).
Candeias, A. (1994) A situação educativa Portuguesa: raízes do passado e dúvidas do presente, *Análise Psicológica*, 4(11), 591–607.
Correia, J. A., Stoleroff, A. D. and Stoer, S. R. (1993) A ideologia da modernização no sistema educativo em Portugal, *Cadernos de Ciencias Sociais*, 12/13, 25–52.
Cortesão, L. (1981) *Escola e Sociedade, que Relação?* (Porto: Edições Afrontamento).
Cortesão, L. and Pacheco, N. (1992) O conceito de educação intercultural: interculturismo e realidade Portuguesa, *Inovação*, 4, 2–3, 33–44.
Cortesão, L. and Stoer, S. R. (1995a) *Projectos, Percursos, Sinergias no campo da Educação Inter/Multicultural: Relatório Final* (Fundação Calouste Gulbenkian/Junta Nacional de Investigação Científica: Final Report).
Cortesão, L. and Stoer, S. R. (1995b) Inter/multicultural education on the European (semi)periphery: notes on an action-research project in four Portuguese schools, *European Journal of Intercultural Studies*, 6(1).
Giddens, A. (1990) *The Consequences of Modernity* (Cambridge: Polity).
Gouldner, A. W. (1973) *For Sociology* (London: Penguin).
Grácio, S. (1986) *Política Educativa como Tecnologia Social* (Lisbon: Horizonte).
Grilo, E. M., Emídio, M. T. and Silva, J. J. R. Fraústo da (1992) Algumas considerações sobre as reformas da educação, *Colóquio Educação e Sociedade*, 1, October, 11–27.
Hall, S. (1992) The question of cultural identity, in S. Hall, D. Held and T. McGrew (eds) *Modernity and its Futures* (Cambridge: Polity/Open University Press), 273–316.
Harvey, D. (1989) *The Condition of Postmodernity* (Cambridge: Blackwell).
Katznelson, I. and Weir, M. (1985) *Schooling for All: Class, Race and the Decline of the Democratic Ideal* (New York: Basic).
Lopes, E. R., Grilo, E. M., Nazareth, J. M., Aguiar, J., Gomes, J. A. and Amaral, J. P. do (1989) *Portugal, o Desafio dos Anos 90* (Lisbon: Presença).
McCarthy, C. (1990) *Race and Curriculum: Social Inequality and the Theories and Politics of Difference in Contemporary Research on Schooling* (London: Falmer).
Mónica, M. F. (1978) *Educação e Sociedade no Portugal de Salazar* (Lisbon: Presença).
Nóvoa, A. (1987) *Le Temps des professeurs* (Lisbon: Instituto National de Investigação Científica).

Pinto, J. M. (1985) *Estruturas Sociais e Práticas Simbólico-Ideologicas* (Oporto: Edições Afrontamento).

Pinto, J. M. (1988) Scholarisation: rapport au travail et transformation des pratiques sociales, in A. Custódio Gonçalves, A. Teixeria Fernandes and C. Lalive. d'Epinay (eds) *La Sociologie et les Nouveaux Défis de la Modernisation* (Oporto: Association Internationale des Sociologies de la Langue Française).

Programme of the XII Constitutional Government, Chapter 2: Education (1991) (Lisbon).

Ramirez, F. and Boli, J. (1987) The political construction of mass schooling: European origins and worldwide institutionalization, *Sociology of Education*, 60, 2–17.

Sampaio, J. S. (1978) Insucesso escolar e obrigatoriedade escolar em Portugal, *Análise Psicológica*, 2, 2.

Santos, B. S. (1985a) On modes of production of law and social power, *International Journal of the Sociology of Law*, 13, 299–336.

Santos, B. S. (1985b) Estado e sociedade na semiperiferia do sistema mundial, *Análise Social* (Lisbon), 87–89, 869–903.

Santos, B. S. (1988) O social e o politico na transição post-moderna, *Comunicação e Linguagens*, 6/7, 25–48.

Santos, B. S. (1990) O *Estado e a Sociedade em Portugal* (1974–88) (Porto: Afrontamento).

Santos, B. S. (1991a) *State, Wage Relations and Social Welfare in the Semiperiphery: The Case of Portugal* (Coimbra: Oficina do Centro de Estudos Sociais).

Santos, B. S. (1991b) Subjectividade, cidadania e emancipação, *Revista Crítica de Ciencias Sociais*, 32, 135–91.

Smart, B. (1994) Sociology, globalisation and postmodernity: comments on the 'Sociology for One World' thesis, *International Sociology*, 9(2), 149–59.

Soysal, Y. and Strang, D. (1989) Construction of the first mass education systems in nineteeth-century Europe, *Sociology of Education*, 62, 277–88.

Stoer, S. R. (1983) The April Revolution and the contribution of education to changing 'Portuguese Realities', PhD thesis (Milton Keynes: Open University).

Stoer, S. R. (1986) *Educação e Mundança Social em Portugal: 1970–80, uma década de transição* (Oporto: Afrontamento).

Stoer, S. R. (1992) A Reforma Educativa e a Formação Inicial e Contínua de Professores em Portugal: perspectivas inter/multiculturais, in A. Nóvoa e T. S. Popkewitz (eds) *Reformass Educativas e Formação de Professores* (Lisbon: Educa).

Stoer, S. R. (1994a) O Estado e as Políticas Educativas: uma proposta de mandato renovado para a *Escola Democrática, Revista Crítica de Ciencias Sociais*, 40.

Stoer, S. R. (1994b) Construíndo a Escola Democrática através do 'Campo da Recontextualização Pedagógica', *Educação, Sociedade & Culturas*, 1, 7–27.

Stoer, S. R. and Araújo, H. C. (1992a) *Escola e Aprendizagem para o Trabalho num País da Semiperiferia Europeia* (Lisbon: Escher).

Stoer, S. R. and Araújo, H. C. (1992b) Basic human and social rights and the democratic school on the European (semi)periphery. Paper presented at the Eighth *World Congress of Comparative Education*, Prague, 8–14 July.

Stoer, S. R. and Dale, R. (1987) Education, state and society in Portugal: 1926–1981, *Comparative Education Review*, 31(3).

Stoer, S. R. and Stoleroff, A. D. (1988) Education, travail et état: du Fordisme aux nouvelles technologies, in A. Gonçalves *et al.* (eds) *La Sociologie et les nouveaux defis de la modernisation* (Oporto: Faculdade de Letras).

Stoer, S. R., Stoleroff, A. D. and Correia, J. A. (1990) O novo vocacionalismo na politica educativa em Portugal e a reconstrução da lógica da acumulação, *Revista Crítica de Ciencias Sociais*, 29, 11–53.

Touraine, A. (1990) A critical view of modernity. Paper presented at the twelfth World Congress of the International Sociological Association, 9–13 July, Madrid.

Trindade, M. B. R. and Mendes, M. L. S. (1993) Portugal: a profile of intercultural education, *European Journal of Intercultural Studies*, 4(2), 59–65.

Wallerstein, I. (1981) The rise and future demise of the world capitalist system: concepts for comparative analysis, in R. Aya, H. Alavi and T. Shanin (eds) *The Sociology of Developing Societies* (London: Macmillan).

Wallerstein, I. (1983) *Historical Capitalism* (London: Verso).

Wallerstein, I. (1984) *The Politics of the World-Economy* (Cambridge: Cambridge University Press).

14 Macroecological reforms as a strategy for reducing educational risks associated with poverty

John A. Kovach

Pennsylvania State University, Delaware Country Campus, Media, PA

Source: *Journal of Education Policy*, 13 (2): 167–78, 1998.

Throughout most current literature on reform needs to alleviate the risks associated with poverty, there is a growing awareness that educational reforms must address the larger context within which schools function if outcomes for poor children are to be improved. The whole Ebonics movement and debate could be seen as one attempt to link schools and schooling to the cultural context of groups that have been socially and politically excluded in our society. However, beyond attempts to link schools to community services through increased coordination of social service and health-related delivery systems, there seem to be few strategies for educational professionals to seriously effect change in the macroecological context within which schools are embedded. This paper briefly examines the ways in which risks associated with poverty threaten to undermine even the best-designed school improvement measures. It will be argued that most current approaches for reducing risks associated with poverty cannot be effectively brought to scale. Macroecological reforms are put forth as a powerful strategy for achieving necessary changes at the political and economic structural levels of the community and larger society. Last, prospects for successfully applying this strategy to bring about change in the near future are considered.

US children: bearing the burden of poverty in the 1990s

In the 1960s, a period of sustained economic growth and relative prosperity, Michael Harrington's *The Other America* provided the impetus for Presidents Kennedy and Johnson to launch the 'War on Poverty'. In the 35 years since, the level of poverty among children and youth has actually worsened; now, almost one in four US children is officially considered poor. Ironically, this has occurred even though the US economy has become almost twice as productive (Children's Defense Fund 1992). Further, the issue of poverty has increasingly become one of disparity among races; although two-thirds of the poor children in this nation are white, African–American children are three times as likely as white children to be poor, while the rate for Latinos is almost as high. Half of all African–American youth are poor, as are just over 40% of Latino children. Partially as a result of these high child-poverty levels, schools are confronted with a seemingly endless barrage of daily problems from teen pregnancy to high levels of violence, to children who cannot learn owing to serious physical, social or emotional difficulties. These problems have been the catalyst for dozens of social, health and special education initiatives, but the insistent growth and depth of poverty tends to sabotage even the best-designed school improvement measures.

Poverty and schools

Today's schoolchildren from poor families are at risk on several different levels. Many poor children receive inadequate nutrition during critical years of brain growth, placing them at risk of 'cognitive deficits' that may manifest as learning disabilities when they reach elementary-school age (Physicians Task Force on Hunger in America 1985). Levine and Havighurst (1989) claim that 75% of over 100,000 new cases of mental retardation diagnosed each year are related to poverty. It is also estimated that 20% of all handicapped children would not be handicapped if their mothers had at least *one* prenatal examination in the first trimester of pregnancy; more than one-fifth of all pregnant women receive no medical care during this critical period (Select Committee on Children, Youth and Families 1988). Health risks among poor children also include iron deficiencies and increased exposure to hazards such as lead paint and tuberculosis. In combination, these factors may contribute to decreased performance in school and impaired cognitive development.

An additional threat to the development of poor children is the epidemic of perinatal substance abuse. Although drug abuse can affect children from all social classes, poor children are most likely to be born with deficits resulting from maternal drug use during pregnancy (Chasnoff 1987; NIDA 1995). The risks associated with poverty, then, begin even before birth. This reality can do much to undermine the effectiveness of school-level programmatic attempts to deal with these risk factors.

Accompanying the physical problems of poor children, significant problems also result from emotional deprivation. Drug abuse by poor mothers, working poor single-parent families, an inadequate patchwork system of after-school care, and disappearing community resources for the emotional development of young children leave many children in the streets or as latchkey children; these children are more likely to drink alcohol, use drugs, smoke cigarettes and contract sexually transmitted disease (Select Committee on Children, Youth and Families 1988). They are three times more likely than children supervised by adults to be involved in accidents, engage in delinquent behaviour or be victimized (National Crime Prevention Council 1996).

In sum, poor children are at increased risk for drug abuse, have elevated dropout rates, experience higher rates of teen pregnancy, are more apt to have discipline problems in school, and show generally lower performance in all academic areas, especially reading and maths achievement (Kovach 1991).

As poverty rises in urban neighbourhoods, both children and young adults are more likely to witness a homicide or know someone with syphilis or AIDS; they are more likely than other children and youth to be victimized by crime of all sorts, to receive inadequate health care, and to suffer from a host of physical, psychological and social problems. Many of these results stem, at least partially, from the fact that the USA leads the industrialized world in childhood poverty rates (Johnson *et al.* 1991).

The combined effect of these risk factors is a marked achievement gap between poor children and national norms. Yancey and Saporito (1994) have shown that the mean reading score of a school can be predicted by the aggregated rates of childhood poverty and the various epidemiological problems found in the catchment area from which a school draws students. In addition, many of these children suffer from severe learning problems related to low self-esteem, stressful life experiences and inadequate or highly fragmented patterns of social service and health care delivery. These problems are intensifying as we approach the next millennium.

The larger problem of inequality

Any policy initiative seeking to reduce risks associated with poverty must contextualize poverty within the structure and functioning of economic and political institutions in the USA, where the stratification of social classes is characterized by gross levels of inequality which is growing worse. Even though many educational professionals, and certainly most mainstream politicians, conjure a reality of boundless opportunities and social mobility, the USA is, among all industrialized nations, the country with the largest disparity between rich and poor (Barlett and Steele 1992).

Viewed critically, poverty is simply one facet of the problem of growing inequality. The operating logic of the US economic system guarantees that, at any given time, a sizeable proportion of the population will be in an extremely deprived position. To focus on specific risks associated with poverty, such as poor performance in school, high teen pregnancy rates or dropout rates, obscures the reality that the economic system would not have a productive place for these students from poverty families even if they all graduated from college with honours. It is important, then, to call into question the popular understandings of where the primary responsibility for perpetuating the cycle of school failure relative to risks associated with poverty really resides. Educational professionals must take these larger economic and social contexts seriously if they are to offer long-term solutions. For this reason, it is imperative that any policy initiatives applied in the schools that are directed towards improving schooling for poor children must be evaluated critically; this means that we must ask 'who benefits?'. These questions must be addressed from a perspective that makes the interests and benefits to different social classes very clear. We must consider which structures that are instrumental in the oppression of poorer groups of Americans are affected and which are not by various approachs. If policy initiatives do not employ this type of class analysis and approach, it is very likely that they will miss their intended audience and be ineffective on a large scale.

Unfortunately, the dominant approach to analysing and understanding school achievement problems has been to employ a pathological analysis, in which difficulties faced by students and teachers are conceived as existing within and caused primarily by 'deficits' or 'diseases' in students or their families. This view of poverty sees the poor as being the source of a problem that actually has its roots in the societal structure. Initiatives based on such a conceptualization are doomed to failure because they miss the point that poverty is a structural aspect of the economic system. Without structural change, real and significant change, poverty and all the risk factors associated with it cannot be eliminated.

Many researchers and policy makers continue to operate as though the social structural reality is an inalterable. As a result, schools tend to reinforce the dominant view of poverty as a problem that is separate and distinct from the problem of gross inequality in American society. In the end, educational researchers, teachers and school administrators continue to focus on the poor and their supposed deficits such as low educational attainment levels, incomplete training or the lack of a match between training and available jobs, low intelligence or lack of virtue as causes rather than symptoms of poverty. And curiously enough, as inequality has grown worse and it has impacted on a host of problems in the schools, institutions such as the US Department of Education's Office of Educational Research and Improvement (OERI) – which is of great influence in educational innovation and policy making – have spent the past decade providing heavy funding for researchers and national research and policy centres that focus on the 'positives' in the urban landscape, while at the same time suggesting that larger social structural factors are 'inalterable' (e.g. Wang and Walberg 1985; Wang 1992; Wang *et al.* 1993, 1995; Wang and Gordon 1995). In the end, such funding serves to strengthen the hegemony of an understanding of risk factors associated with poverty which divorces poverty from the larger problem of growing inequality in the USA. Policy initiatives which are based on such an understanding tend to focus on dropouts and at-risk students as an educational problem, and one that has primarily an educational solution. The approach of such initiatives tends to focus on the micro level of fixing schools, the poor children in those schools or the families of these children. Perhaps this is why many policy makers have been frustrated by decades of federal education research and development enterprise that has had very little impact on education practice (Vinovskis 1993).

The irony here is that these same educational research, policy and planning structures that promote this myopic paradigm for addressing risks associated with poverty could also provide the ready-made framework and organizing nucleus for implementation of a coordinated, nationally based, progressive strategy for effecting significant structural change in local communities and on a national level. Slavin (1996) recently made such a suggestion with a call for 'design competitions' where the federal government would solicit structures and design prototypes for education in much the same way that it does when ordering a piece of equipment to perform a specific task or function. Of course, school reform models are not jeeps (Slavin 1996), but the implication is that existing federal structures could provide a nucleus for significant change directed towards a clearly specified end or goal.

The problem of microperspectives and approaches

Put most succinctly, the prevailing perspective – conceptualizing the locus of solutions for the problems of poor children as resting within the school or families – is thought to lead to limited solutions that cannot be scaled up beyond the level of an individual school. Researchers and social reformers who focus on family factors emphasize the need to expand preschool classes for disadvantaged children or suggest that more education/job training programmes are needed for the mothers and fathers of these children (Taverne 1995). Others who focus on the family propose increasing birth control knowledge among the poor with additional forms of assistance and family support (Gilbert 1981). Some researchers have built mini-empires over the past decade – heavily subsidized by federal funding – by emphasizing the fact that some poor children are successful even though they are surrounded by a wasteland of limited opportunity structures, poor parenting, deficient educational and cultural resources, and a general lack of a community supportive of educational achievement and success (Masten 1989; Masten *et al.* 1990; Wang and Gordon 1995). Such approaches focus on the deficiencies of poor children and their families, while leaving unattended the larger problem of cultural and political disenfranchisement.

Researchers who emphasize school factors when examining risks associated with poverty seek solutions in new approaches to educating poor students. These reformers call for a radical restructuring within the schools, along with a new and more powerful curriculum for the poor (Council of Great City Schools 1987; Wang and Walberg 1988; Wang 1989; Freedman 1994; Wang and Reynolds 1995). These approaches reinforce the view that education is the primary cause of our economic problems and that educational reform is the universal panacea (Apple 1996).

Other reformers believe that compensatory educational programmes can provide an even start for children from poor families. Such a view seems to be one of the driving forces behind the Okland School Board's decision to recognize Ebonics as the primary language of poor African–American children in that urban school district. Given the extremely concentrated nature of US poverty in the 1990s, this approach would appear to be sorely lacking. Almost a decade ago, a national evaluation of Chapter 1 students concluded that the programme, which provides funds to 70% of all US elementary schools, was not working. A wealth of literature from the past ten years indicates that these compensatory programmes have resulted in only small gains in reading and maths, and that these gains did little to offset such children's large learning deficiency (Anderson 1977; Kennedy 1987; Kovach 1991). To expect results different from these past examples of attempts at remediating the effects of poverty and economic and political isolation of a large segment of the American population seems naive at best.

In the end, most educational initiatives for addressing the risks associated with poverty have been misguided by perspectives that locate the causes of poverty within poor children, their families or the schools. Instead, what is needed is an approach that frames the question in a new way, that recognizes poverty as a political problem involving power struggles at many different levels. Poverty is a structural problem, inherent in our economic system along with unemployment and underemployment. Therefore, to deal with risks associated with poverty, educational professionals must be involved in the larger struggle for structural – that is, political and economic – change. Here is where an understanding of macroecological reforms as a strategy for addressing serious structural change is critical.

Macroecological reforms as a strategy for change

If educational professionals are to effectively address the risks associated with poverty, what is needed is a strategy for undermining the basic structure and functioning of our economic and political system. Such reforms have been referred to as *macroecological reforms* (Bartelt 1995a,b; Wang and Kovach 1996). Macroecological reforms are efforts that are realistic in the sense that they are both feasible and acceptable given the current political and economic climate, but are also designed to contribute to a long-range agenda of serious structural change. True macroecological reforms undermine the structures of power and privilege for the few, which are the antithesis of liberal democracy and community self-determination (Apple 1996). Macroecological reforms can simultaneously be directed towards removal of barriers to educational equity for poor children, and towards change at the larger social structural level. Such reforms would force educational and community policy makers to consider the social impact and human factors related to economic change and restructuring. Ultimately, to effect significant structural change and concomitant change in the education of poor children, macroecological reforms must be designed to increase the power people have over their own lives and reduce the power of corporations and those with money, they should be realized at the level of political struggle where the average person is politically engaged – state government, county government and city government; last, they must relate to the needs of people in their everyday lives (Carnoy and Shearer 1980).

A critical question becomes one of determining who the major players will be in such a movement for structural change and how the existing framework of education policy structures and institutions might provide resources and a foundation for such change. In our view, the impetus for such change must arise from a coalitional group of teachers, parents, school administrators, community agencies and activists who work together, through progressive organizations, to provide coordinated social services and transform the schools from what has been described as a disconnected non-system (Schorr and Schorr 1988; Levy and Copple 1989) into an institution that is vitally connected to the community and larger society as an active agent of social change (Kovach 1995). But to go beyond the community level and truly become the impetus for national-level change, policy planning structures such as OERI, working with national educational associations and progressive caucuses of local teachers' unions, must provide the coordinating framework for a larger movement for change. These national educational policy and planning groups could have a tremendous impact because of their financial/funding influence over a large community of researchers, policy planners and implementors. The bottom line is that organizations such as OERI represent a hegemonic force in the educational community through the funding of large national initiatives such as the Regional Educational Laboratory Network, and national research centres.

Coalitions, partnerships and alliances for progressive change

The political activism and agenda for change in the schools and larger society that is being suggested here is too big a job for educational professionals to tackle alone. That is why it is critical to establish organizations that solidify partnerships and coalitions among schools, community groups and groups with a national agenda for change. The types of partnerships and coalitions in which schools must be engaged are ones which solidify and centralize political power. Teachers, parents, students and school administrators must work within centralized – but democratic – political groups and organizations that are linked to larger movements for working-class power and control. This is why the resources and support of existing policy organizations are so crucial in the strategy for macroecological reforms which is being unfolded here.

This need to be involved in larger political groups and movements is difficult for some educational professionals to understand, particularly because their perspectives have been conditioned by the successful efforts of independent grass-roots organizations of the 1960s and early 1970s which resulted in measures such as the Education for All Handicapped Children Act. However, although the economic expansion of the 1960s allowed power and federal monetary support to filter down to this grassroots level, the structural changes and economic realities of the 1990s have diffused the power and removed the monetary support of most of these community groups and organizations. The problem of today is finding an appropriate political model for solidifying these disparate groups and for organizing those who have been effectively excluded from the political process.[1]

An immediate agenda

Understandably, most educational professionals want to know what must be done right now. They want concrete plans for action. In answer, there certainly are reforms that need to be undertaken immediately, which could be developed into what have been described as macroecological reforms that would support significant structural change in the future. First, there should be no misunderstanding about the implications of educational professionals taking an activist stance. To focus on needed structural change does not mean that nothing can be done within the schools to affect poverty. Schools can become involved in trying to reduce the concentration of poverty in poor neighbourhoods through projects and partnerships that give a voice to people living in these areas, reducing their social and political isolation and disenfranchisement. Schools need to support public and private ventures aiming to create needed jobs in the inner city. School administrators need to develop desegregation plans that include ways to reduce the isolation and concentration of the poor (economic segregation) both across schools in a district as well as *within* individual schools (Kovach 1996). It must be recognized, though, that such programmes and plans, in themselves, will not eliminate poverty and related risk factors that are structural in nature; there must be a long-range agenda for structural change built into any reforms instituted in the schools. This is why the attention directed towards macroecological reforms is so critical. Mentoring programmes, for example, are important, but if they are to be effective they must be linked to political struggle aimed at creating real opportunities for the future of these children. The focus on segregation and stratification within our schools, too, is an important issue relative to educational equity, but it cannot be remedied without addressing the reality of segregation and stratification in the workplace.

Other reforms that could help to undermine the current structure of power and privilege include long-neglected concerns for meeting the educational needs of poor, and especially minority, children:

1 *Elimination of tracking at all levels of the educational pipeline.* Thirty years' worth of research indicates the inequities perpetuated by tracking (Kariger 1962; Brookover *et al.* 1965; Jones *et al.* 1972; Connell 1973; Trimberger 1973; Heyns 1974; Oakes 1985, 1992; Bastian *et al.* 1986). For poor students as well as racial minorities, the elimination of tracking would have an immediate positive effect. Recent studies suggest that this effect would be marked in suburban schools as well as in urban ones (Rigsby *et al.* 1994).
2 *Elimination of all standardized tests.* Again, the educational research literature is rife with examples of the class bias of standardized tests. It seems that their continued use relates more to hegemonic needs related to bureaucratic organization in schools as well as in larger society (Mensh and Mensh 1991).
3 *Restructuring schools to give teachers and principals more flexibility.* Many schools that have adopted internal restructuring models during the past decade have discovered that the success or failure of such reforms hinges upon increased empowerment of teachers and principals (Reese 1986). If reforms are to empower those with the least political voice in our culture, it is imperative that educational professionals in schools that serve poor students have a maximum amount of flexibility in order to adapt quickly to the needs and concerns of the community that they serve.
4 *Elimination of the practice of ability and age grouping in elementary grades.* Any type of hierarchical educational policy or practice in a society which is as deeply stratified and unequal as the USA cannot help but contribute to educational inequities for poor children. There is simply too much literature which demonstrates the benefits of cross-age/grade tutoring and group

learning for elementary students to justify the continued use of rigid ability or age-grouping practices (Wang and Walberg 1985, 1988; Wang *et al.* 1993; Osin and Lesgold 1996).

5 *Providing a preparatory year ('grade 13') for minority students entering college.* Even though most colleges and universities have attempted to establish fairly well-developed remedial education and tutoring programmes for academically ill-prepared students, it still is the case that minority students, who are disproportionately poor, are those least likely to finish college. A post-high school preparatory year would serve to 'prep' these students in order that they could begin their higher education on a more equal footing with more privileged students and thus increase their chances of academic success.
6 *Increasing the number of minority teachers.* There is an across-the-board need for poor and minority students to have strong role models not only in the early and high school years, but in their higher education experiences as well. The importance of these role models is demonstrated in much of the recent literature on nurturing resilience in children at risk due to poverty (Masten 1989; Masten *et al.* 1990).
7 *Providing quality out-of-school educational experiences for poor minority students.* Wang and Reynolds (1995) have suggested that out-of-school educational experiences are extremely important for the overall development of poor children. This is one area where school–community connections can be built rather easily, thus providing a base for further organizing and action.
8 *Abolition of remedial and 'pull-out' classes in favour of keeping students of mixed abilities together in the classroom.* Educational segregation and the inequities which are its result begin, quite often, with remedial and pull-out classes that are disproportionately filled with children from poor families (McBay 1989). Such programmes have been shown to exacerbate and reinforce risks associated with poverty (Oakes 1985, 1992; Kovach 1991).

None of these measures should be seen as an end in itself. Instead all should be seen as reforms that are aimed at transforming current educational ideology and expectations. In time, such reforms can begin to effect change on a larger structural level if they are successful at undermining the rationality which supports current ideology. For this reason, it is very important for educational professionals to be connected to community groups as well as to national organizations that have a long-range agenda which can be attached to these immediate reform measures.

Regardless of the level (i.e. micro or macro) at which educational professionals choose to become involved in the change process, they must learn that politics does matter. Meier *et al.* (1989) note that a particular deficiency of educational policy analysts and policy makers has been their ignorance of the role that politics plays in determining public policy. Educational professionals must be actively involved from the beginning of initiatives to ensure that the problems they experience are defined in ways that result in policies that impact on schools positively while effecting change in the larger society. Such policies could win wide public support and backing if they were based on traditional American ideals related to work and the American work ethic. The focus on the right to a job that pays a living wage would, no doubt, find wide appeal among the vast majority of working Americans who have experienced deterioration in their real wages and economic security owing to shifts in the social contract over the past 20 years (Rubin 1996). In social, economic and historical terms, the time for such an approach, involving the effective utilization of macroecological reforms, is theoretically ideal.

Conclusion: positive prospects for structural change

As we move towards a new millennium, the entrenchment of poverty in America makes it imperative for educational professionals to develop a new strategy for confronting risks associated with poverty. In the past, liberal education reformers have simply called for increased social programmes or more reforms within the schools to deal with risks associated with poverty. But the structural nature of poverty necessitates that educational professionals develop an understanding of more sophisticated political strategies for bringing about significant social change that extends beyond the walls of the school. Ultimately, such strategies must address the larger problem of growing inequality in the USA and very real shifts in the social contract that has existed between workers and employers since the beginning of this century. The strategy for change suggested here involves educational professionals working in a coordinated and connected manner, within schools, their communities and on a national level, to undermine and change ideological structures that support growing economic inequality in the USA.

As we approach the year 2000, there is a unique mix of political discontent and continuing flat economic growth that sociologists suggest could provide the objective circumstances required for significant social change over the next decade (Berlet 1995; Kovach 1996). Deteriorating social and economic conditions have impacted not only on the inner cities, but on suburban and rural areas as well, while the foundation of fundamental institutions is weakening. Economic 'downsizing' and the 're-engineering' of the workplace have created a polity that continues to demonstrate its disdain for the status quo by favouring candidates who present themselves as political 'outsiders'.

This swing to the Right, though, while suggesting that the public is alienated from 'politics as usual', can also be seen as a window of opportunity for serious structural change. In many states, the current economic situation is resulting in a fiscal crisis coupling flat or declining state revenues with growing social welfare expenses. The result in states such as Pennsylvania has been the election of governors who try to relieve the state's fiscal obligation to schools by supporting privatization or voucher initiatives. This situation puts increased pressure on educational professionals and schools. However, declining state revenues for education, and the continuing deterioration of the larger social fabric, could become a positive force that will pressure educational reformers to translate the current knowledge base and apply it within the context of a larger, more sophisticated understanding of the change process. A coordinated approach, in which the actions of coalitional community groups are united with progressive organizations on a national level advancing an agenda that is focused on traditional American values related to work, could serve to link educational professionals with the broader community, thus building on the very real collective power and strength of educational professionals united with a public that has been culturally and politically disenfranchised. The result could be precisely what most educational professionals desire – to effect progressive change and increased life-chances for all children and youth.

Note

1 A hopeful sign of possibilities for change is that for the first time in US history, the country now has an official Labor Party which announced its existence at its founding convention in June 1996. This political party, which will not attempt to run candidates for at least the next two years, thus enabling it to focus its resources on building a national organizational base, is supported by the leadership of nine major international unions. Its existence means the USA is no longer the only industrialized Western nation without a labour party to represent its working people. It also means that an organizational structure is being built that could unite agents of change from a community to a national level. Such a structure could become an extremely powerful political voice for change if educational professionals and their unions were connected through its organizational auspices.

References

Anderson, R. (1977) The effectiveness of followthrough: what have we learned? Paper presented at the Annual Meeting of the American Educational Research Association, Washington, DC.

Apple, M. (1996) *Cultural Politics and Education* (New York: Teacher's College Press).

Barlett, D. and Steele, J. (1992) *America, What Went Wrong?* (Kansas City: Andrews & McMeel).

Bartelt, D. (1995a) The university in community development: a common cause. *Metropolitan Universities: An International Forum*, 6 (3), 15–28.

Bartelt, D. (1995b) The macroecology of educational outcomes, in L. Rigsby, M. Reynolds and M. Wang (eds), *School/Community Connections: Exploring Issues for Research and Practice* (San Francisco, CA: Jossey-Bass), 159–91.

Bastian, A., Fruchter, N., Gittell, C. and Hoskins, K. (1986) *Choosing Equality* (Philadelphia, PA: Temple University Press).

Berlet, C. (1995) *Eyes Right: Challenging the Right-wing Backlash* (Boston, MA: South End Press).

Brookover, W., Leu, D. and Kariger, R. (1965) Tracking. Unpublished manuscript, Western Michigan University.

Carnoy, M. and Shearer, D. (1980) *Economic Democracy, the Challenge of the 1980s* (New York: Pantheon Books).

Chasnoff, I. (1987) Perinatal effects of cocaine. *Contemporary OB/GYN*, 27, 163–79.

Children's Defense Fund (1992) *The State of America's Children* (Washington, DC: CDF).

Connell, R. (1973) *Schools and Social Justice* (Philadelphia, PA: Temple University Press).

Council of Great City Schools (1987) *Challenges to Urban Education: Results in the Making* (Washington, DC: Author).

Freedman, S. (1994) *Exchanging Writing, Exchanging Cultures: Lessons in School Reform from the United States and Great Britain* (Cambridge, MA: Harvard University Press).

Gilbert, L. (1981) Parenting counseling. *Counseling Psychologist*, 9 (4), 5–68.

Heyns, B. (1974) Social selection and stratification within schools. *American Journal of Sociology*, 79, 1434–51.

Johnson, C., Miranda, L., Sherman, A. and Weill, J. (1991) *Child Poverty in America* (Washington, DC: Children's Defense Fund).

Jones, J., Erickson, E. and Crowell, R. (1972) Increasing the gap between whites and blacks: tracking as a contributory source. *Educational and Urban Society*, 4, 339–49.

Kariger, R. (1962) The relationship of lane grouping to the socioeconomic status of the parents of seventh-grade pupils in three junior high schools. Doctoral dissertation, Michigan State University. *Dissertation Abstracts*, 23, 4586.

Kennedy, M. (1987) *The Effectiveness of Chapter I Services* (Washington, DC: US Government Printing Office).

Kovach, J. (1991) Risks associated with poverty: an analysis of problems and reform needs of urban schools, in M. Wang, M. Reynolds and H. Walberg (eds), *Handbook of Special Education: Research and Practice*, Vol. 4 (New York: Pergamon Press), 199–215.

Kovach, J. (1995) Decreasing educational segregation in urban schools: the role of inclusive education and the need for structural change. *Applied Behavioral Science Review*, 3 (2), 165–75.

Kovach, J. (1998) Decreasing educational segregation in urban schools to reduce risks associated with poverty: current reform needs. *Journal of Poverty*, 2 (1), 79–100.

Levine, D. and Havighurst, R. (1989) *Society and Education* (Boston, MA: Allyn & Bacon).

Levy, J. and Copple, C. (1989) *Joining Forces: A Report for the First Year* (Alexandria, VA: National Association of State School Boards).

McBay, S. (1989) *Education that Works: An Action Plan for the Education of Minorities* (Cambridge, MA: Quality Education for Minorities Project).

Masten, A. (1989) Resilience in development: implications of the study of successful adaptation for developmental psychopathology, in D. Cicchetti (ed.), *The Emergence of a Discipline: Rochester Symposium on Developmental Psychopathology*, Vol. 1, 261–94.

Masten, A., Best, K. and Garmezy, N. (1990) Resilience and development: contributions from the study of children who overcome adversity. *Development and Psychopathology*, 2, 425–44.

Meier, K., Stewart, J. and England, R. (1989) *Race, Class, and Education: The Politics of Second-Generation Discrimination* (Madison, WI: University of Wisconsin Press).

Mensh, E. and Mensh, H. (1991) *The IQ Mythology* (Carbondale & Edwardsville, IL: Southern Illinois University Press).

National Crime Prevention Council (1996) *Latchkey Children: Young Children at Home Alone* (Washington, DC: Author).

Nida (1995) Survey profiles first data on drug use during pregnancy. Washington, DC: National Institutes on Drug Abuse *Notes* (January/February).

Oakes, J. (1985) *Keeping Track: How Schools Structure Inequality* (New Haven, CT: Yale University Press).

Oakes, J. (1992) Can tracking inform practice: technical, normative and political considerations. *Educational Researcher* (May), 12–21.

Osin, L. and Lesgold, A. (1996) A proposal for the reengineering of the educational system. *Review of Educational Research*, 66 (4), 621–57.

Physicians Task Force on Hunger in America (1985) *Hunger in America: The Growing Epidemic* (Middletown, CT: Wesleyan University Press).

Reese, W. (1986) *Power and the Promise of School Reform* (New York: Routledge).

Rigsby, L., Stull, J. and Morse-Kelly, N. (1994) School performances: complicating explanatory models by incorporating race and gender. Paper presented at the annual meeting of AERA, New Orleans.

Rubin, B. (1996) *Shifts in the Social Contract: Understanding Change in American Society* (Thousand Oaks, CA: Pine Forge Press).

Schorr, L. and Schorr, D. (1988) *Within our Reach: Breaking the Cycle of Disadvantage* (New York: Anchor Books).

Select Committee on Children, Youth and Families (1988) *Children and Families: Key Trends in the 1980s* (Washington, DC: US Government Printing Office).

Slavin, R. (1996) Design competitions: a proposal for a new federal role in educational research and development. *Educational Researcher*, 26 (1), 22–8.

Taverne, A. (1995) Parent training in interactive book reading: an investigation of its effects with families at risk. *School Psychology Quarterly*, 10 (1), 41–64.

Trimberger, E. (1973) Open admissions: a new form of tracking? *Insurgent Sociologist*, 4, 29–43.

Vinovskis, M. (1993) *Analysis of the Quality of Research and Development at the OERI Regional Educational Laboratories* (Washington, DC: US Department of Education).

Wang, M. (1989) Accommodating student diversity through adaptive instruction, in S. Stainback, W. Stainback and M. Forest (eds), *Educating all Students in the Mainstream of Regular Education* (Baltimore, MD: Paul Books), 228–39.

Wang, M. (1992) Achieving school success for all students, in K. Haring, D. Lovett and N. Haring (eds), *Integrated Life Cycle Services for Persons with Disabilities: A Theoretical and Empirical Perspective* (New York: Springer-Verlag), 122–52.

Wang, M. and Gordon, E. (1995) *Educational Resilience in Inner-city America, Challenges and Prospects* (Hillsdale, NJ: Erlbaum Associates).

Wang, M. and Reynolds, M. (1995) *Making a Difference for Students at Risk: Trends and Alternatives* (Thousand Oaks, CA: Corwin Press).

Wang, M. and Walberg, H. (1985) *Adapting Education Strategies, Building on Diversity* (Berkeley, CA: McCutchan).

Wang, M. and Walberg, H. (1988) Four fallacies of segregationism. *Exceptional Children*, 55 (2), 128–37.

Wang, M., Haertel, G. and Walberg, H. (1993) Synthesis of research: what helps students learn. *Educational Leadership*, 51 (4), 74–9.

Wang, M., Haertel, G. and Walberg, H. (1995) *Effective Practices and Policies: Research and Practitioner Views* (Philadelphia, PA: National Center on Education in Inner Cities at Temple University).

Wang, M. C. and Kovach, J. A. (1996) Bridging the achievement gap in urban schools: reducing educational segregation and advancing resilience-promoting strategies, in B. Williams (ed.), *Closing the Achievement Gag: A Vision to Guide Change in Beliefs and Practice* (Philadelphia, PA: Research for Better Schools), 9–24.

Yancey, W. and Saporito, S. (1994) *Urban Schools and Neighbourhoods: A Handbook for Building an Ecological Database.* Research report to the Office of Educational Research and Improvement, National Center on Education in the Inner Cities, Temple University Center for Research in Human Development and Education.

15 Renovating educational identities

Policy, space and urban renewal

Kalervo N. Gulson

Charles Strut University, Australia

Source: *Journal of Education Policy*, 20 (2): 141–58, 2005.

Introduction

Educational policy change occurs in particular spaces. Whilst human geography has a long history of using space to analyse public policy, there is little focus in the sociology of education on analysing relationships between spaces and educational policy changes. Nonetheless, some studies do locate educational change in terms of spatial factors such as place and globalisation (Kenway *et al.* 2001; Thomson 2002) or explicitly use theories of space within a theoretical framework (Ball *et al.* 1995; Ball *et al.* 1998; Gulson 2002; Taylor 2002; Armstrong 2003; Dillabough 2004). Others, such as Butler and Robson (2003a,b), position space as central when analysing connections between educational change and urban change. I consider these types of studies to be crucial delineators in the current use of space in education policy sociology; part of what Ball (1994b) calls 'an "applied sociology" which engages with "real world" issues' (p. 171). Nevertheless, there is still much work to be conducted, specifically exploring the links between urban change and educational policy change. Additionally, in education policy sociology, following arguments in human geography, 'space' needs further theorising as a term and analytical tool. These concerns are at the forefront of this paper.

This paper analyses a specific Blair New Labour government educational policy initiative, the *Excellence*[1] *in cities* (EiC) partnership in the inner London Borough of Tower Hamlets. First, I propose a framework for a spatialised policy analysis that explicitly links space and policy. Second, I use this framework to analyse the Mondale EiC Action Zone, within the Tower Hamlets EiC, examining relations between urban change and educational policy change. I point to the degree to which space is a focus in education policy change and the cogency of a spatialised policy analysis.

Proposing a spatialised policy analysis

Tools such as 'contexts of policy' (Bowe *et al.* 1992) and 'policy cycles' (Howlett and Ramesh 1995) usefully allow an analysis of educational policy change.

Building on these tools I would like to propose an explicitly spatial form of policy analysis; a *spatialised policy analysis.* This follows, in part, Richardson and Jensen's (2003) call for a 'practice and cultural orientated understanding of the spatiality of social life' (p. 8), particularly public policy, using a 'cultural sociology of space' (p. 8). I also heed Whitty's (2002) call for the sociology of education to recognise the wider contexts within which, and through which, educational policy change takes place. I pay attention to the interaction of policy and the everyday practices of populations that shape, and are shaped by, physical locations, particularly cities.

In constructing the theoretical framework for this paper I draw on post-structural notions of power, discourse and the subject (Foucault 1980, 1994; Clegg 1989). I consider policy a discursive practice in which there are struggles over the production of truth (Bowe *et al.* 1992; Ball 1994a). These struggles are seen as happening through time and space; that is giving credence to temporality and spatiality (Massey 1999). This credence is implicit in the notion of socially constructed spaces.

> Spaces . . . may be constructed in different ways by different people, through power struggles and conflicts of interest . . . spaces are socially constructed, and . . . many spaces may co-exist within the same physical space . . . suggest[ing] the need to analyse how discourses and strategies of inclusion and exclusion are connected with particular places.
>
> (Flyvbjerg and Richardson 1998: 9–10).

However, space is not only produced by social relations it is also a producer of social relations (see Lefebvre 1991). As Massey (1993a) argues, space is socially constituted, and the social is spatially constituted. This occurs across a multitude of geographical scales as a 'multi-scale rearticulation of space' (Perry and Harding 2002: 848). Consequently, and importantly, for the study of urban areas and educational policy change, this position also permits the reconfiguring of the relationship between global processes and local mediations. Thus, I follow Smith (2001) in holding a key analytical predicate that 'cities, local states and community formations are not bounded self-contained entities' (p. 168). Rather, the local, national and transnational are mutually constitutive. Therefore, my approach is, in part, an:

> analysis of sociocultural, political, and economic networks situated in the social space of the city, with an awareness that the social space being analysed might usefully be understood as a translocality, a fluid cross-border space in which social actors interact with local and extra-local institutions and social processes in the formation of power, meaning and identities.
>
> (Smith 2001: 174)

This approach allows for educational policy change to involve processes and places;[2] a perspective particularly useful in envisioning schools as multiple and contradictory sites with porous borders. A policy analysis that is explicitly spatial takes note of elements outside the school gates, part of the place in which policy is 'done', as well as inside schools. The following outlines how this form of analysis might work in practice.

Methodology

This study brings together a range of research approaches including ethnography (see Hammersley and Atkinson 1995; Smith 2001) and elements of critical policy analysis (see Ball 1994a; Taylor *et al.* 1997). I also use photographs as part of a visual ethnographic approach (Pink 2001).

As part of my doctoral work I undertook a 'snapshot' study of the Mondale EiC Action Zone in Tower Hamlets during the balmy months of January and February 2003. A range of key stakeholders including education policy advisors, corporate employees, public sector employees, school administrators, teachers, students and community workers were interviewed. Data was generated from these interviews, relevant policy documents, photographs and field observations. All participant names used in this paper are pseudonyms. I use the actual names of all other places and organisations unless otherwise stated.[3]

Tower Hamlets EiC partnership and Mondale EiC Action Zone

According to the 2001 Census the Mondale (pseudonym) area is one of the most deprived within Tower Hamlets (Office of National Statistics 2001). Importantly, for this paper, the Mondale area is physically isolated with major arterial roads providing a barrier between it and the surrounding areas, including the adjacent 'Docklands', or more specifically, the Canary Wharf area of Tower Hamlets.

In March 1999 the Department for Education and Skills (DfES) incorporated the Tower Hamlets Local Education Authority (LEA) into an EiC partnership. EiC is a 'key policy initiative for redressing educational disadvantage and under-performance in…schools located within the most deprived urban areas in England' (Stoney *et al.* 2002: 1).[4] The focus of EiC is on raising standards as:

> Successive governments have failed to resolve the educational problems of the major cities. Standards have been too low for too long. Raising standards in order to lift opportunities for our children is the key priority for the Government.
>
> (DfES 2003b)

There are only two criteria for a LEA to be integrated into an EiC partnership: 24% or more students receiving Free School Meals (FSMs), and the LEA is in a city or conurbation (DfES 2003a). Tower Hamlets LEA had 62% of students eligible for FSMs (Tower Hamlets Local Education Authority 2003) and it is located in East London. EiC has six strands of which EiC Action Zones are one (DfES 2004). The Mondale EiC Action Zone is one of the three EiC Action Zones in Tower Hamlets EiC. EiC Action Zones are derived from, and in some cases supplant, Education Action Zones (EAZs), a policy initiative launched by the Blair government in June 1998. EAZs combine secondary and primary schools with an emphasis on private/public sector involvement in education (see Gamarnikow and Green 1999; Dickson and Power 2001; Power and Gerwitz 2001). At the time of the study[5] the Mondale zone incorporates a number of primary schools and a secondary school under one administrative structure. The Mondale zone is a partner with, among other public sector organisations, the Urbanmoney Finance Group (pseudonym), a transnational company with offices in Canary Wharf.

Urban renewal and educational policy change

In this section I apply a spatialised policy analysis to the Tower Hamlets EiC partnership and particularly the Mondale EiC Action Zone. The analysis is in two parts and yields some valuable insights into educational policy change in a neo-liberal state, notably that physical locations are significant enabling and disabling factors within neo-liberal policy-making. In the first part, I identify EiC as a spatial policy that positions disadvantaged urban areas, such as Tower Hamlets and in particular the Mondale area, as deficient in terms of educational standards. The proximity of Canary Wharf is accorded a 'real' and symbolic significance in the everyday life of the Mondale area. In the second part of the analysis, I identify the processes by which Canary Wharf is used as a strategic part of the Mondale zone's aim to raise educational standards. This strategy uses Canary Wharf as an enabling focus for Mondale students' aspirations. I see this as people 'on-the-ground' appropriating a physical location and positioning it in discourses of educational achievement and the life aspirations of students. I also identify some disabling elements of this appropriation. This interaction between places, standards and aspirations I term the *educational renovation of identity.*

EiC, the Mondale zone and the physical environment

The EiC partnership initiative is unequivocally spatial in the targeting of urban areas using the school based poverty indicator of FSMs. Policy and place concern EiC as the DfES intends it to complement other urban renewal programmes 'funded through the Single Regeneration Budget, New Deal for Communities and the Neighbourhood Regeneration Strategy' (Office for Standards in Education 2003: 6). The Mondale EiC Action Zone works in partnership with government and nongovernment agencies associated with such urban renewal funding streams. Ms Talon, a member of the Tower Hamlets EiC partnership, sees these partnerships as allowing the Mondale zone to say:

> 'I'm coming from the state but I'm part of this whole community' that whole perspective...Can the [Mondale] zone go in and sort out problems that are happening on the [social housing] estates? No they can't and that's not their

> function…[B]ut there are always [other] sort of things to be gained, if… they…also work with those people for whom [working on estates] is their prime work.
>
> (Ms Talon, Tower Hamlets EiC)

The Mondale zone is conceptualised as part of, rather than detached from, the 'community'. Therefore, I would like to suggest a spatialised policy analysis be required to interpret a spatial policy that gives primacy to the relations between the worlds that exist inside and outside of the school gates. This relocates the reading of a policy process to the place where the policy is enacted and examines the interactions of people, place and policy.

A spatialised policy analysis recognises the Mondale area as adjacent to the radical urban development of the Docklands, or more specifically Canary Wharf. This development is a hyperbolic representation of urban renewal practice with a huge influx of government funds and global capital since 1987. It is a financial centre to complement, if not rival, the City of London. In creating the Docklands, including Canary Wharf, the total investment of public funds between 1981 and 1996 was £2041 million. This was in addition to £6227 million of private sector funds, resulting in a total of £8268 million over 15 years (Foster 1999). Development and public and private investment continues apace. This influx of capital has created, and is creating, a lifestyle precinct with shopping, bars and apartments that surround the financial hub of the development (for an overview of these changes see Foster 1999).

Canary Wharf has the tallest buildings in London, housing global banks such as HSBC and Urbanmoney Finance Group and, as can be seen in Figures 15.1 and 15.2, these physically dwarf the Mondale area. Figure 15.1 reveals the view of the Wharf from outside a Mondale zone primary school, with social housing in the foreground. Figure 15.2 is taken at the 'border' of Mondalc and Canary Wharf. Both photographs graphically illustrate the overwhelming sense of imposition created by the disparate spatial scales of the Mondale and Canary Wharf areas.

Figures 15.1 and 15.2 Looking towards Canary Wharf from a Mondale zone primary school; and Canary Wharf dwarfing the Mondale area's senior college.

The relative scales of renewal exacerbate this imposition. Public investment has been limited in the other areas of Tower Hamlets outside the Docklands, including Mondale. Best scenario estimates place total investment in urban renewal at £15 to £20 million a year. This equates to approximately £400 million over 20 years, significantly lower than total investment in Canary Wharf (see Leaside Regeneration Ltd 2003; Neighbourhood Renewal Unit 2004). What is missing in the rest of Tower Hamlets, and particularly in Mondale, is substantial private as well as public investment. This results in a significant contrast between areas. Ms Gerrard, a senior executive of a Mondale zone primary school points to the differences between the everyday environment of the Mondale area and the pervasive presence of Canary Wharf, asserting that:

> the quality of the housing stock and the quality of amenities, in the whole of [Mondale]... had been allowed to deteriorate and of course that has a direct impact on... the people who live here and the people who want to live here, so anybody who could get out had got out really and [Mondale] was gradually being left with either people who had no where else to go, or people who were being shipped through. And there was a very... big feeling of being very close to a... centre of wealth, and yet having no access to it at all, and almost it having a really detrimental effect on the area.
>
> (Ms Gerrard, Mondale zone primary school)

The deteriorating local housing operates as a peripheral concern to the ongoing renewal associated with Canary Wharf. Similarly, Mr Cole, a Mondale zone board member, refers to the disparity of physical size and wealth. He identifies a key characteristic of the Mondale area being:

> the location next to Docklands, Canary Wharf... wherever you are [in Mondale] you see it, and the divide if you like between the money that exists there and the lack of things that are [in Mondale is clear]. Although again I would argue that over the last few years... there are a whole number of exciting initiatives in [Mondale] about regenerating the area in the broader sense.
>
> (Mr Cole, Mondale zone)

Through the development of limited private and public sector partnerships this 'broader sense' includes education. The educational work of the Mondale zone unfolds in an area where there are conspicuous differences between the everyday perspective from the Mondale area and that from Canary Wharf. These differences are obvious in Figures 15.3 and 15.4. Figure 15.3 shows the benign outlook from Canary Wharf towards Mondale. Workers and residents in, and of, Canary Wharf are visually unaware and, thus, can choose to be unconscious of the Mondale area, except perhaps those that look down upon the area from office towers. However, Figure 15.4 illustrates that the Mondale residents are not afforded the same choices.

Figures 15.3 and 15.4 The view of Mondale from Canary Wharf; and Canary Wharf from near one of the zone schools.

For the population of the Mondale area Canary Wharf is a constant presence, 'a foreign body' according to Mr Cole. This 'body' may well be embedded in the minds of the young as Ms Fowler, an ex-senior executive of the Mondale zone secondary school, outlines how young students include Canary Wharf when asked to paint or draw their area. Similarly, Mr Azad, a Bengali worker with the Mondale Social Housing Action Group (pseudonym), reflects that:

> I think the young people . . . I mean eight-year-olds, nine-year-olds, they realise this stark contrast between where they live and . . . when they look through a window they see all these really fancy tall buildings, they realise it, but they are unable to understand.
>
> (Mr Azad, Social Housing Action Group)

This proximity can also have negative effects on some Mondale residents' quality of life. Ms Lampard, a member of the Mondale Social Housing Action Group, claims that urban renewal in Canary Wharf has meant that people in the south Mondale area:

> have had their summer and everything else blighted by the noise from [Canary Wharf] . . . most people around here have done nothing for the last 20 years, but put up with huge construction. At one point we could say we were living on the biggest construction site in Europe. We lost 500 homes to make way for it; 500 social homes.
>
> (Ms Lampard, Social Housing Action Group)

The contiguity of the ongoing Canary Wharf building developments to Mondale is manifest in Figures 15.5 and 15.6. The social housing in the foreground of Figure 15.5 ends at the arterial road in Figure 15.6. The Canary Wharf developments are significant backgrounds in both photographs. In Figure 15.6 arterial road is a barrier between the two areas that reinforces the social and economic divide of wealth and poverty. As all of the photographs and participant viewpoints exemplify,

Figures 15.5 and 15.6 Social housing in south Mondale with Canary Wharf in the background. A main road forms a physical division between Mondale and Canary Wharf.

Canary Wharf is a constant reminder of this divide, its late twentieth-century facade dominating the vista of the Mondale area. The consistently radical growth of Canary Wharf is juxtaposed with incremental urban renewal in the Mondale area. The built environment is an allegorical and real reproduction of societal inequality.

The buildings of Canary Wharf are jointly symbols of capital and renewal and the embodiments that reinforce the disadvantage of the adjacent areas. A more affluent and expansive life is but a step away. However, the size of that step is substantial; in effect this 'life' is a world away for, as Ms Gerrard suggests, in Mondale there is 'a very . . . big feeling of being very close to a . . . centre of wealth, and yet having no access to it at all'. She contends that this results in a 'stressed community', and due to this stress, the role of schools is to:

> make sure that we look at people in the context of this very stressed community . . . It's stressed because . . . we are socially and economically quite divorced from the rest of Tower Hamlets, and particularly . . . Docklands. Not even as far away as Docklands, there's . . . [a] whole business community just across the [road] there, but it's not really part of our children's experience, but you know [it] ought to be.
>
> (Ms Gerrard, Mondale zone primary school)

The Tower Hamlets EiC partnership and the Mondale EiC Action Zone are faced with both the challenge of raising standards and the challenge of mitigating a physically imposing representation of social division. The EiC initiative targets areas, such as Mondale, that have populations that are both economically and educationally 'lacking'. Canary Wharf, as symbol and 'reality' constantly reinforces the relative deprivation of the Mondale area. Thus, in this spatialised policy analysis the relations between people and places have significant import when looking at education policy changes. Whilst Ms Gerrard claims the 'Docklands' is 'not really part of our children's experience', to the contrary I suggest that Canary Wharf plays a significant part in their lives and I argue below that the

Mondale zone strategically uses Canary Wharf as part of the drive for higher academic standards. The transforming, through hyperbolic urban renewal, of existing space such as Canary Wharf affects metaphorically, and literally, adjacent areas and consequently populations and schools.

Standards, places and aspirations: the educational renovation of identity

In this section I identify the practices by which physical location weaves into discourses of educational achievement and life aspirations for populations in disadvantaged areas. This identification connects the EiC discourse of educational standards to the constructing of student aspirations, and examines the relationship between this connection and Canary Wharf. I argue that people involved in schooling in Mondale refer to Canary Wharf as part of a strategy to raise educational standards, and that this points to the *enabling* and *disabling* effects of a discursive positioning of policy, people and place.

As noted above EiC aims to raise educational standards in urban areas of disadvantage. However, it is a spatial policy that ignores the specifics of local contexts. As a policy representation it lacks engagement with the particular social and visual inequalities that characterise Mondale. In all places in which EiC is implemented it targets the aspirations of students and as such is an initiative that:

> tackles the particular problems facing children in our cities . . . it aims to raise the aspirations and achievements of pupils and to tackle disaffection, social exclusion, truancy and indiscipline and improve parents' confidence in cities.
> (DfES 2003b)

This is certainly a lot to ask of education (Jones 2003). Nevertheless, this approach reflects the way a number of participants draw links between educational achievement, aspirations and the alleviation of poverty. As Mr Bellamy, a senior executive of a Mondale zone primary school, states the purpose of the zone is:

> to raise levels of achievement . . . within the school, so that the children leaving here will gain better qualifications and be able to share in the prosperity, cause there are . . . jobs available around here. But people from around here haven't gone on to further education, so haven't been able to get the well-paid jobs, [they've] been getting the service jobs. So I think long term you'll have a better-qualified community and a more prosperous community.
> (Mr Bellamy, Mondale zone primary school)

This fits neatly within New Labour's discursive approach to education and social exclusion. Schooling, standards and social inequality form part of what Jones (2003) calls the 'success against the odds' assumption that raising academic standards will address social inequalities (p. 171). Redressing social exclusion becomes an individual responsibility (Jones 2003). Alexiadou argues that this is part of 'official discourses' that:

> establish a causal relationship between social exclusion/inclusion (as a condition, and so, located within the realm of consumption) and educational success (again, as a form of differential consumption of educational opportunities). In doing so, these discourses tend to ignore or marginalise the effects of governance structures on the production and distribution of opportunities (educational, employment, etc.).
>
> (Alexiadou 2002: 73)

As part of these 'official discourses' the position of EiC, and some people in the Mondale zone, is that individual students who achieve higher educational standards will escape poverty. Ms Talon reinforces this link between individual achievement and 'quality of life'. She states that the focus of the Mondale zone should be on the students rather than improving quality of life for:

> the thing . . . the zone must focus on [is] . . . its pupils . . . and the key is to look at what . . . is preventing those pupils from really taking hold of their learning opportunities and running with them and opening up their horizons and aiming for everything and anything. That's . . . the key question that the zone must always ask itself . . . It is not [the zone's] remit to actually . . . have as their main focus improving the . . . quality of life in that area. It isn't, it should impact on that by driving at the children and sometimes I think perhaps there is a . . . misunderstanding.
>
> (Ms Talon, Tower Hamlets EiC)

This belief in individual students being able to take 'hold of their . . . opportunities' reflects a faith in the outcomes of meritocracy. Consequently, aspirations are presented as a practice through which students will be encouraged, and able, to achieve higher educational standards. The equating of aspiration with success displaces other educational processes that may act as barriers to achievement, such as those affected by race or gender. Accordingly it is conceivable that students can become members of any employment group by 'aiming for everything and anything'. For example, Ms Kewell, a community relations manager with Urbanmoney Finance Group muses:

> there's no reason if they're given the background these [Mondale students] cannot become our employees and our customers and our clients . . . there's no reason why they just can't rise above [the class system] if given the proper kind of background and education.
>
> (Ms Kewell, Urbanmoney Finance Group)

For Ms Kewell, the right 'background' is the exposure to the practices of high finance that students may learn through an ongoing engagement with a company over their school lives, an engagement encouraged by New Labour's emphasis on the public/private relationship.

Now, I am not disputing the possibility, or desirability, of Mondale students achieving high academic results. Furthermore, I am not disputing the role of aspiration and dreams, and the significance of hope, in the lives of young people. However, what I am suggesting is the discursive assumptions underpinning these factors need further interrogation. This interrogation can be undertaken in relation to Canary Wharf for in Mondale, the 'opening up' of student horizons is paralleled by the remaking of the adjacent area into Canary Wharf. As I argued above Canary Wharf is an imposing presence in, and of, the Mondale area. As Ms Fowler reflects:

> in a way you can't not be aware of the physical environment. The fact, that all . . . the children in [the zone secondary school] . . . they have got around them [is] . . . Docklands, where all the money is. And they've got the DLR and they've got a little patch of green, and the school itself doesn't have any green . . . and the primary schools don't.
>
> (Ms Fowler, ex-Mondale zone secondary school)

Figures 15.7 and 15.8 illustrate the closeness of Canary Wharf to the Mondale secondary school. Figure 15.7 depicts social housing that is adjacent to the school, whilst Figure 15.8 shows the view of Canary Wharf from the side of the school. These depictions, in conjunction with Mrs Talon's reference to 'huge areas of richness [that Mondale students] cannot tap into', further highlight the importance of these contrasting places.

Spatialising the discourse of standards develops the relationship between policy, educational achievement, aspirations and place. A spatial approach to policy accepts the multiple subject positions of people, with a 'self' constituted by 'multiple, incomplete and partial identities, formed in historically specific relation to the different social spaces people encounter, move through and inhabit

Figures 15.7 and 15.8 Mondale EiC Action Zone Secondary School on left and social housing on the right; the school on the left, Canary Wharf and the wall separating the Docklands Light Rail from the school on right.

over time' (Smith 2001: 131). Further, aspirations may be seen as relative. As Goldthorpe (1996) suggests, working class and middle class parents may have similar aspirations for their children in regards to say further education, but these students do not end up in the same places. However, it is not that working class aspirations or ambitions are deficient, but 'that variations in the courses of action that are actually taken arises from the fact that, in pursuing any given goal from different class origins, different "social distances" will have to be traversed' (Goldthorpe 1996: 490). Additionally, places are processes that do not have simple boundaries counterpoising the local with the outside. Conceiving of places in this way means that:

> Places do not possess singular but multiple contested identities. Place-making is shaped by conflict, difference and social negotiation among differently situated and at times antagonistically related social actors, some of whose networks are locally bound, others whose social relations and understandings span entire regions and transcend national boundaries.
>
> (Smith 2001: 107)

Thus, social actors in Mondale, from a variety of subject positions, with a variety of 'situated knowledges' (Keith 1997), actively participate in the negotiation of place. This construction affects the relations between place and students. Those people with a role to play in the Mondale zone, from the DfES, the local schools, community workers and employees of transnational companies will see Canary Wharf in different ways. Eade (1997) suggests that the Docklands operates as a type of parallel space. For example, he notes that: 'A general impression is created of an area which was socially and economically deprived before "redevelopment." What does not emerge within this picture are the counterclaims to urban space constructed by diverse sections of those relying largely on manual work jobs and small business' (p. 138). These parallel spaces can be conceived in terms of educational achievement and aspiration with some people who see Canary Wharf as enabling, whilst others see it as disabling.

For those that see Canary Wharf as enabling, it provides a, or the, focus of success and security for students in Mondale to aspire. Ms Talon claims that:

> Our kids now see Canary Wharf as an opportunity, but in some areas like Mondale I don't think they think of it as realistic yet that they can actually aspire to hold one of those high flying paid jobs up there . . . [B]ecause it's a generation thing isn't it? Each one becomes more able to see themselves . . . being able to take opportunities that present [themselves].
>
> (Ms Talon, Tower Hamlets EiC)

The presence of Canary Wharf provides the symbolic and concrete representation of intended aspiration and achievement. However, as Ms Talon notes, resonating with Goldthorpe above, aspirations and achieving these goals are different things.

Nonetheless, and significantly, Canary Wharf is a constant presence positioning successive generations of students. This is evident in the current cohort of young people. Mr Azad, who also runs a homework class on a mostly Bengali estate, considers that:

> the older guys, the 16-year-olds and 18-year-olds, they . . . want to work in big offices. They want to do all these great things but they don't . . . have the confidence to do it . . . all their life they've been told, 'oh, you're no good, you don't want to work in offices, you'd probably suit a factory or a supermarket or wherever'. So a lot of them have really, really low self-esteem. . . . They want to . . . work in big offices, they want to make a name for themselves, or they want to be in good positions, earn good money, but it's just, they feel, the necessary . . . pre-requisites, aren't there . . . It's a stark contrast. We're only just behind the Docklands business community and a lot of people do want to be in . . . those big buildings, but they just don't have the confidence. . . . One of [the Action Group's] aims is to . . . foster that confidence, and make them . . . believe they can achieve great things, but it will take hard work, but we're here to help you, that's what we do.
>
> (Mr Azad, Social Housing Action Group)

Again, the individual student, with confidence and aspiration, will be able to improve their educational achievements. Canary Wharf represents, and provides, particular types of employment that may be read as 'successful'. Phrases such as 'wearing suits', 'working in an office' and 'work in a big office', used by many of the people when discussing student aspirations, posit these aspirations as part of a *white-collaring* of the student population; that is aspiring for white-collar jobs in the financial centres on Canary Wharf. However, I would like to point to some possible dilemmas that these aspirations pose for students.

The EiC partnership and the Mondale zone aim to raise standards through the involvement of parents. Ms Talon sees parents as a crucial part of the EiC Action Zone's work; however, she also sees these parents as 'lacking' in an educational sense. Parental involvement is necessary in order for parents to learn how to be 'better' partners in their children's education (see Standing 1999; Simpson and Cieslik 2002). Similarly, the Mondale zone frames 'key barriers to achievement' within 'parental attitudes to education', 'lack of positive involvement' and other similar factors (Mondale Small Action Zone 2001: 5). Other participants in the study identify groups of parents who are 'deficient' in understanding the practices and positioning of education and schooling. These groups include migrant Bengali parents from Bangladesh's rural areas and white 'Indigenous' working class parents. The 'deficiency' of parents ostensibly puts their children at an educational disadvantage. Gerwitz (2001) asserts that within New Labour education policy there is a rhetoric of disadvantage, a pathologising of working class families and communities as deficient. As such, New Labour's project is to convert working class parental practices, in relation to schooling, into a set of selected middle class parental practices. At the level of the Mondale zone, there is certainly a tension between aspiring for white-collar jobs, improving educational standards and the actual conditions of students' everyday lives. To achieve in this discursive frame means to acknowledge deficiencies in family and culture.

Furthermore, even if these students do achieve academically, there is some doubt that the focus of aspiration, Canary Wharf, will actually provide 'high finance' and 'high-paid' type employment. The enabling view of Canary Wharf points to the opportunities available due to its position as a key 'node' in the knowledge economy. Within this economy a distinction is made between those people able to access, and retrain, for highly skilled work, and those people that are in less skilled or unskilled labour (Jones 2003). The latter people form a body of manual workers that are often dismissed in talk of knowledge economies (Massey 1994), but play a crucial, yet derided, role as 'knowledge support workers'. These 'knowledge support workers' include those in cleaning, administrative functions and retail. This employment distinction forms part of a 'dual-economy' (Ball *et al.* 2000: 282), in which there has been an increase in high end employment and a concomitant rise in employment for workers with little or no formal credentials. However, the latter will work in highly unstable and underpaid sectors of the workforce. As Sassen suggests:

> Corporate culture collapses differences, some minute, some sharp, among the different sociocultural context into one amorphous otherness, an otherness that has no place in the economy, that holds the low-wage jobs that are, supposedly, only marginally attached to the economy. It therewith reproduces the devaluing of those jobs and of those who hold the jobs . . . The corporate economy evicts these other economies and its workers from economic representation, and the corporate culture represents them as the other. What is not installed in a corporate centre is devalued or will tend to be devalued.
>
> (Sassen 2000: 175)

Many of the Mondale students may become 'knowledge support workers' rather than knowledge workers. Ms Viduka, a member of the local senior college, notes that Canary Wharf provides many jobs for the graduates of Tower Hamlets school and university graduates. However, they are 'mostly in service industries, so that's retail, that's what most of the job's over there are that don't require [one] to be a global graduate'. She reflects that:

> it looks to me like the local graduates who've been to local unis . . . who are then employed after graduation, they're going into first entry jobs, that are not very high paid, in the admin or something . . . [W]ith just a degree now you can't command a high level job, and a lot of those big Canary Wharf companies, for their graduate jobs they're looking for the global milk

round...The bigger ones are looking at Harvard, Yale, Oxbridge, the Ivy League in the States or the Russell group of universities, they're looking in that market.

(Ms Viduka, Local senior college)

The Canary Wharf companies demonstrate a sense of 'farsightedness' in which they look past the educational landscape of Mondale and Tower Hamlets to the 'global milk round' when searching for employees for 'high level' positions (Beratan 2004, personal communication).[6] This process of international recruitment is complemented by a new form of higher education, 'sensitive to the need to prepare graduates to enter global workplaces, graduates who are confident in their capacity to move across national boundaries and to relate to a diverse range of cultural practices and traditions' (Henry *et al.* 2001: 151). Furthermore, this farsightedness parallels what I noted above as the unconsciousness of the Mondale landscape for many in Canary Wharf. Farsightedness results in certain aspirations being 'imaginary' and beyond reach and others as 'real' and achievable. That is, the 'office' aspirations are plausible within the frame of 'knowledge support workers' rather than knowledge workers. This framing is what underpins the practices of linking aspirations and educational achievement.

Furthermore within the discursive framing of the EiC policy it does not especially matter if these aspirations are realised as long as it fits with the focus on the individual as part of neo-liberal educational policy-making. Raising standards is the key focus for the Tower Hamlets EiC partnership. As one strand of the EiC partnership the Mondale zone also has a role to play in raising standards. One practice in which the students in Mondale are encouraged to undertake this process is through reference to Canary Wharf. That is, Canary Wharf is a strategic element of the EiC strategy in Mondale, and is a symbolic and real representation of what students can do, if they achieve in school. Canary Wharf, the jobs, the lifestyle and so forth, becomes a part of the aspirations of the students of Mondale. To obtain these jobs or lifestyles students need to raise their educational standards. Whether the aspirations are realised or not is relatively unimportant in terms of the overall policy goal of raising standards. What is paramount for the state is that students are focused on this goal. In this discourse, physical location operates as an enabling device.

The spatial significance of this can be understood through the relation of Mondale students' subjectivities to educational and physical change. However, naming the spatial relations of this focus perhaps requires a different vocabulary from educational change. Similarly, commonly used terms such as educational reform and educational restructuring are inadequate in this context. In thinking, talking and writing about space we need to use terms that have an appropriate resonance. I would like to suggest that *renovation* is a term with spatial resonance that is cogent with a spatialised policy analysis. Renovation can be considered in the following way. Students are required to focus on raising standards. Canary Wharf sits as a convenient representation of worthy aspirations for students. To undertake this journey towards educational achievement students may have to recognise that their parents are deficient in terms of understanding educational processes and practices. Here physical location operates as a disabling device. Students are placed in the invidious position of acknowledging deficiency and striving towards a goal that may or may not be achievable. Regardless, the individual carries the responsibility for renovating themselves. As such I term this interaction between standards, aspirations and place as an *educational renovation of identity.*

Conclusion

The relationships between policy, schooling, place and space in urban environs are complex in which educational policy change is situated within, and commensurate with, urban change. As I have argued a spatialised policy analysis allows for an exploring of policy acknowledging space as a crucial enabling and disabling element in unpacking educational policy change, such as EiC, in neo-liberal states. The EiC policy is a spatial policy that has two key elements. One requires the EiC Action Zones, like the Mondale zone, to work with partners in the local area. This recognition of a wider context of education, of social disadvantage, or poverty, as a factor in educational achievement is in tension with the second element. This is the focus on education, and the individual, as the key to address social exclusion. The process of the *renovating* educational identities suggests that it is cheaper for the state to work on the renovation of identities than it is to address structural inequalities. It acts as a panacea for populations in disadvantaged areas. By making this point I am not intending to denigrate the work of schools and community organisations in the area. Rather, I am pointing out that students can aspire to something that concurrently reinforces the social divide. If students do not achieve, it is their fault, or they are culpable, something Gillborn and Youdell (2000) note as the move towards individual responsibility for failure. Furthermore, if these students 'fail' their own situation is reinforced by the Canary Wharf embodiment of aspiration constantly on the landscape. The encouraging of students to *renovate* themselves allows the state to absolve itself of responsibility to address issues of structural inequality, whilst still arguing that it is tackling social exclusion.

Acknowledgements

An earlier draft of this paper was presented at the *American Educational Research Association* Annual Meeting, San Diego, 12–16 April 2004. I would like to thank Gregg Beratan and Stephen Ryan for their incisive and constructive comments on this paper and Colin Symes for suggesting the idea of educational renovation. Thank you also to the two anonymous referees for their constructive comments on an earlier version of this paper.

Notes

1 'Excellence' is a term that is used to name or describe other DfES policies. They speak to the notion of excellence within a frame of choice and diversity in schooling provision rather than a focus on excellence in comprehensive schooling.
2 I acknowledge that space and place are considered differently by writers such as Harvey (1993), Massey (1993b) and Smith (2001). However, for the purposes of this paper, space and place will be used interchangeably.
3 In empirical work places and people are often easily identified. 'Insiders' can identify people quite easily. 'Put simply, giving anonymity through pseudonyms to sites and people often does not work' (Walford 2002: 98). Rather, researchers claim anonymity to facilitate access and more 'free' talking about contentious issues. However, there may be more questionable motives around allowing researchers to write with less accuracy or hide weak claims behind pseudonyms. Further, pseudonyms make any site 'just like another site' thus allowing implicit claims of generalisability to be made (Walford 2002). Nonetheless, when obtaining the consent of participants I raised the possibility that an insider may be able to identify particular people, and I have endeavoured to protect the identities of people by removing the specifics of their positions. However, by using photographs I create a conflict between anonymity and complete disclosure of place. Specific places are a crucial part of this study and photographs of places are an integral component of the work but they also provide instant identification markers. Similarly, the use of national census data may also allow for a fairly simple identification of place. In fact, the notion of anonymity seems to oppose my argument that spaces and places matter in policy. These are tensions that I attempt to grapple with in my forthcoming dissertation.
4 It should also be noted that it is equally about reassuring the middle classes about inner city government schooling (see Whitty 2002; Gulson 2004 – PhD University of Maquarce dissertation).
5 EiC Action Zones may add schools into the zone subject to the approval of the EiC partnership and the DfES (DfES 2004).
6 Gregg Beratan raised this notion of 'farsightedness' at the *American Educational Research Association* annual meeting in San Diego, 12–16 April 2004, at the awful hour of 8.15 am. I thank him for his perceptivity at this early hour.

References

Alexiadou, N. (2002) Social inclusion and social exclusion in England: tensions in education policy, *Journal of Education Policy*, 17(1), 71–86.

Armstrong, F. (2003) *Spaced out: policy, difference and the challenge of inclusive education* (London, Kluwer Academic Publishers).

Ball, S. J. (1994a) *Education reform: a critical and post-structural approach* (Philadelphia, Open University Press).

Ball, S. J. (1994b) Some reflections on policy theory: a brief response to Hatcher and Troyna, *Journal of Education Policy*, 9(2), 171–82.

Ball, S. J., Bowe, R. and Gerwitz, S. (1995) Circuits of schooling: a sociological exploration of parental choice in social class contexts, *Sociological Review*, 43, 52–78.

Ball, S. J., Maguire, M. and Macrae, S. (1998) 'Race', space and the further education market place, *Race, ethnicity and education*, 1(2), 171–89.

Ball, S. J., Maguire, M. and Macrae, S. (2000) Space, work and the 'new urban economies', *Journal of Youth Studies*, 3(3), 279–300.

Bowe, R., Ball, S. J. and Gold, A. (1992) *Reforming education and changing schools: case studies in policy sociology* (London, Routledge).

Butler, T. and Robson, G. (2003a) *London calling: the middle classes and the re-making of inner London* (Oxford, Berg).

Butler, T. and Robson, G. (2003b) Plotting the middle classes: gentrification and circuits of education in London, *Housing Studies*, 18(1), 5–28.

Clegg, S. R. (1989) *Frameworks of power* (London, SAGE Publications).

Department for Education and Skills (2003a) *EiC: excellence in cities: FAQ*. Available online at: http://www.standards.dfes.gov.uk/excellence/faq/?faq=#FAQ2 (accessed 28 July 2003).

Department for Education and Skills (2003b) *Excellence in cities*. Available online at: www.standards.dfes.gov.uk/excellence/ (accessed 19 May 2003).

Department for Education and Skills (2004) *EiC overview*. Available online at: http://www.standards.dfes.gov.uk/sie/eic/EiCOverview/ (accessed 26 May 2004).

Dickson, M. and Power, S. (2001) Education action zones: a new way of governing education?, *School Leadership and Management*, 21(2), 137–41.

Dillabough, J. (2004) Representations of female homelessness and youth poverty in Canada: global political economies, classification struggles and epistemic posturing, paper presented at the *American Educational Research Association Annual Meeting*, San Diego, CA, 12–16 April.

Eade, J. (1997) Reconstructing places: changing images of locality in Docklands and Spitalfields, in: J. Eade (Ed.) *Living the global city* (London, Routledge), 127–45.

Flyvbjerg, B. and Richardson, T. (1998) In search of the dark side of planning, paper presented at the *Planning Theory Conference*, Oxford Brookes University.

Foster, J. (1999) *Docklands: cultures in conflict, worlds in collision* (London, UCL Press).

Foucault, M. (1980) *Power/knowledge: selected interviews and other writings 1972–1977, volume 1* (Brighton, The Harvester Press).

Foucault, M. (1994) *Power: essential works of Foucault 1954–1984, volume 3* (London, Penguin).

Gamarnikow, E. and Green, A. G. (1999) The Third Way and social capital: education action zones and a new agenda for education, parents and community?, *International Studies in Sociology of Education*, 9(1), 3–21.

Gerwitz, S. (2001) Cloning the Blairs: New Labour's programme for the re-socialization of working class parents, *Journal of Education Policy*, 16(4), 365–78.

Gillborn, D. and Youdell, D. (2000) *Rationing education: policy, practice, reform and equity* (Buckingham, Open University Press).

Goldthorpe, J. H. (1996) Class analysis and the reorientation of class theory: the case of persisting differentials in educational attainment, *British Journal of Sociology*, 47(3), 481–505.

Gulson, K. N. (2002) *Education, policy, space: the policy process and the Lowlands*, unpublished M.Ed thesis, Macquarie University, Sydney.

Hammersley, M. and Atkinson, P. (1995) *Ethnography: principles in practice* (London, Routledge).

Harvey, D. (1993) From space to place and back again: reflections on the condition of postmodernity, in: J. Bird, B. Curtis, T. Putnam, G. Robertson and L. Tickner (Eds) *Mapping the futures: local cultures, global change* (London, Routledge), 3–29.

Henry, M., Lingard, B., Rizvi, F. and Taylor, S. (2001) *The OECD, globalisation and education policy* (Oxford, Permagon).

Howlett, M. and Ramesh, M. (1995) *Studying public policy: policy cycles and policy subsystems* (Oxford, Oxford University Press).

Jones, K. (2003) *Education in Britain: 1944 to present* (Cambridge, Polity Press).

Keith, M. (1997) Conclusion: a changing space and a time for change, in: M. Keith (Ed.) *Geographies of resistance* (London, Routledge), 277–86.

Kenway, J., Kelly, P. and Willis, S. (2001) Manufacturing the global locality, customizing the school and designing young workers, in: J. Demaine (Ed.) *Sociology of education today* (Basingstoke, Palgrave), 119–41.

Leaside Regeneration Ltd (2003) *Leaside SRB4: year 5 delivery plan 2002–2003* (London, Leaside Regeneration Ltd).

Lefebvre, H. (1991) *The production of space* (Oxford, Blackwell).

Massey, D. (1993a) Politics and space/time, in: M. Keith and S. Pile (Eds) *Place and the politics of identity* (London, Routledge), 141–61.

Massey, D. (1993b) Power-geometry and a progressive sense of place, in: J. Bird, B. Curtis, T. Putnam, G. Robertson and L. Tickner (Eds) *Mapping the futures: local cultures, global change* (London, Routledge), 59–69.

Massey, D. (1994) *Space, place and gender* (Cambridge, Polity).

Massey, D. (1999) Negotiating disciplinary boundaries. *Current Sociology*, 47(5), 5–12.

Mondale Small Action Zone (2001) *The Mondale small Education Action Zone* (London, Mondale Small Action Zone).

Neighbourhood Renewal Unit (2004) *Neighbourhood renewal fund allocation.* Available online at: http://neighbourhood.gov.uk (accessed 20 March 2004).

Office for Standards in Education (2003) *Excellence in cities and education action zones: management and impact* (London, OFSTED Publications Centre).

Office of National Statistics (2001) *Neighbourhood statistics: statistics by area.* Available online at: http://neighbourhood.statistics.gov.uk/area_select_fs.asp?nsid=false&CE=True&SE=True (accessed 5 March 2004).

Perry, B. and Harding, A. (2002) The future of urban sociology: report of joint sessions of the British and American Sociological Associations, *International Journal of Urban and Regional Research*, 26(4), 844–54.

Pink, S. (2001) *Doing visual ethnography* (London, SAGE Publications).

Power, S. and Gerwitz, S. (2001) Reading education action zones, *Journal of Education Policy*, 16(1), 39–51.

Richardson, T. and Jensen, O. B. (2003) Linking discourse and space: towards a cultural sociology of space in analysing spatial policy discourses, *Urban Studies*, 40(1), 7–22.

Sassen, S. (2000) Analytic borderlands: economy and culture in the global city, in: G. Bridge and S. Watson (Eds) *A Companion to the city* (Oxford, Blackwell), 168–80.

Simpson, D. and Cieslik, M. (2002) Education Action Zones, empowerment and parents, *Educational Research*, 44(2), 119–28.

Smith, M. P. (2001) *Transnational urbanism: locating globalisation* (Oxford, Blackwell).

Standing, K. (1999) Lone mothers' involvement in their children's schooling: towards a new typology of maternal involvement, *Gender and Education*, 11(1), 57–73.

Stoney, S., West, A., Kendall, L. and Morris, M. (2002) *Evaluation of excellence in cities: overview of interim findings* (London, Excellence in Cities Evaluation Consortium).

Taylor, C. (2002) *Geography of the 'new' education market: secondary school choice in England and Wales* (Hampshire, Ashgate).

Taylor, S., Rizvi, F., Lingard, B. and Henry, M. (1997) *Educational policy and the politics of change* (London, Routledge).

Thomson, P. (2002) *Schooling the rustbelt kids: making the difference in changing times* (Stoke on Trent, Trentham Books).

Tower Hamlets Local Education Authority (2003) *Achieving against the odds: the challenge.* Available online at: http://www.towerhamlets-pdc.org.uk/policies.php?id=12 (accessed 21 May 2003).

Walford, G. (2002) Why don't researchers name their research sites?, in: G. Walford (Ed.) *Debates and developments in ethnographic methodology* (London, JAI), 95–106.

Whitty, G. (2002) *Making sense of education policy* (London, Paul Chapman Publishing).

16 Power, pedagogy and persuasion

Schooling masculinities in the secondary school classroom

Lynn Raphael Reed

University of the West of England, Bristol

Source: *Journal of Education Policy*, 13 (4): 501–17, 1998.

Introduction

At this political and historical juncture it seems apposite to re-evaluate our theories and perspectives as educationalists committed to social justice. As the discourse of individualism, competition and the unfettered market are replaced with talk of communities, stakeholding and 'zero tolerance' of dissent from the project to create a fairer society, we have an important new culture of influence to engage with. The crucial task facing us, in the interest of children and of social justice, is to,

> rebuild a shared discourse in which critical social scientists can speak to policy makers and teachers about *new ways* of reconceptualising the *old problem* of schooling, social differentiation and inequality.
>
> (Mac an Ghaill 1996: 164)

In this we need to take account of the dominant educational discourses currently influencing conceptualizations of 'justice' and 'fairness' in schooling as well as to acknowledge the limitations of existing theorizations. Specifically, in relation to gender and social justice, we need to deconstruct the discursive complex around the 'underachieving boy', whilst revisiting the adequacy of our ways of thinking about issues of masculinity and schooling. In particular, my argument in this paper is that we need to explore this through a praxis-orientation to enquiry into classroom actions, pedagogic experience and identity formation – for teachers, pupils and researchers. In this we need to acknowledge the significance of unconscious as much as conscious processes, and the importance of the emotions.

The genealogy of my interest

My interest in developing this area of research arises out of my own experience and my way of conceptualizing the issues, my epistemological stance, requires some explication. I believe this is a theorized study referencing the personal

(Grumet 1990) within which I seek to reveal the often invisible robes of the researcher, including some elements of the refracting lens of my own identity (Raphael Reed 1996). In training to be a secondary school teacher in the early 1980s I sought to move away from a purely academic engagement with ideas on culture, social reproduction and sociology of knowledge that I had engaged with in my studies in social anthropology, linguistics and sociology of education. On the assumption that inequalities are perpetuated but may also be challenged through the processes of life in school, I was keen to engage as a teacher in the practice of combating the class-based, racist and sexist values which I saw predominating in society.

For my first appointment I sought out a testing context and went to work in an all-boys secondary school in East London with a reputation for its pioneering work on anti-sexist and anti-racist work with boys (Askew and Ross 1989). It was a school that was closely associated with the London Institute of Education and represented a particular manifestation of the Inner London Education Authority (ILEA) culture of the late 1970s.

It was a huge shock – emotionally and physically. I immediately found that my commitment to political values and positions associated with equal opportunities and social justice did not automatically make my practices as a teacher anymore effective. Indeed, I struggled long and hard, individually and in collaboration with others, to build a practice that seemed to 'work' more effectively at engaging students productively in the learning process (and it *was* 'effective' in the sense demanded so vociferously today; pupils in my classes and department gained GCSE results in line with national standards and contrary to the poor results from many other departments in the school). This entailed the establishment of certain social relations in the classroom; the development of cognitive and literate processes in dialogic contexts for learning that gave meaning to cultural respect rather than tolerance (Shor and Freire 1987). Painfully I learnt the significance of what, on returning to academic work, I found identified as poststructuralist perspectives on social justice and schooling: people's need to define and take ownership of their own identities; that identities are multiple and fluid with hegemonic and non-hegemonic influences at play; that dilemmas and contradictions constantly remain significant in adopting the stance of a critical pedagogue (Luke and Gore 1992; Anderson and Herr 1994; Rizvi 1994).

In particular I experienced tensions and difficulties around being a white woman of middle-class origin working with working-class boys in a multi-ethnic inner city all-boys school: so many moments of 'difference' to negotiate. Models of how to work in an emancipatory way with girls do not easily transfer across the gender divide, and dilemmas created by working from a radical or feminist perspective with pupils whose masculine identities in school may manifest as domineering, disruptive and misogynist, illuminate some significant limitations to existing perspectives on gender work in schools and unproblematized notions of critical pedagogy. I struggled with contradictions of power circulating through processes and positionings of domination/subordination between adult/child, male/female, teacher/pupil, black/white.

As a consequence of this experience I identify the following as crucial and difficult questions to address:

- how can teachers build relationships and practices with boys in school across multiple spectrums of difference, in ways that promote 'voice' and ownership but do not validate oppressive attitudes or ways of relating to each other?
- what pedagogic practices in such contexts can achieve raised levels of achievement whilst promoting principles of gender equity and social justice? What happens when you take on the first of these aims whilst forgetting the second?
- how does such work draw upon and shape the emotional landscape and identity work of teachers as well as pupils?
- what institutional and policy contexts and what landscapes of meaning are prerequisite to supporting such developments?
- what theories and perspectives on social justice best articulate what we want to achieve, whilst providing a meaningful language for understanding the messiness of our experience of real schools and classrooms?

These are questions which my own research seeks to address. However, before I turn to my own work, I wish to examine a range of perspectives on gender, social justice and education.

Social justice, gender and education

Dominant discourses on social justice and education

In order to develop a meaningful perspective on social justice and the education of boys, it is useful to review the use of concepts of social justice in relation to education in general and to identify some significant elements of recent education policy directions of the British Labour Government. We need culturally and historically specific perspectives brought to bear here since, as Rizvi and Lingard argue (1996: 11):

> In policy discourse, the idea of social justice has practical significance and needs therefore to be articulated in terms of particular values, which while not fixed across time and space, nevertheless have to be given specific content in particular struggles for reform.

This will allow us to situate our argument about the education of boys in relation to the challenges of the current era.

Definitions of social justice, of course, vary, as Sharon Gewirtz notes in this issue. Rizvi and Lingard (1996) in their analysis of traditions of social justice in the Australian Labour Party identify three traditions: the 'liberal-individualist' tradition, in a classic Rawlsian perspective, which stresses the basic criteria of protection and promotion of maximal liberty for individuals, without infringing the liberty of others, and a commitment to fairness of distribution of social goods, adopting compensatory affirmative action measures to 'remove barriers, arising from unequal power relations and preventing equity, access and participation' (Rawls 1971: 60); the 'market-individualist' tradition, influenced by the ideas of Nozick (1976) with an emphasis on the mechanisms of acquisition and the justice of the competition, to ensure entitlement to an individual's 'just deserts'; the 'social-democratic' tradition, derived from Marx and focusing on state intervention to fulfil fundamental human needs. For the Australian Labour Party, they identify the tensions within their 'symbolic commitment to justice... trapped within its wider concern with the restructuring of the Australian State towards a more market-driven political economy' (p. 12). In this context they suggest:

> The view of social justice now emerging in the form of a consensus is a contradictory amalgam of Rawlsian redistributive principles and Nozickian entitlement theory.
>
> (18–19)

Whilst the historical, political and cultural context of the New Labour Government in Britain is in many respects different, there are some important similarities in this fusion of perspectives, with the additional attempt to redefine an authoritarian definition of social democratic justice. This is evident in the first education White Paper of this government's term of office, *Excellence in Schools* (DfEE 1997) where the significance of the market, the widescale support for managerialist tendencies and the influence of consumerism can all still be detected, but now combined with an increased role for LEAs as accountable for school improvement targets and results in their localities and a strong interventionist steer from the centre. Talk of 'accountability' and 'standards' and proposed measures to ensure fair distribution of the social good of educational credentials against the scourge of social deprivation, and rewards and penalties as the 'just deserts' for individual effort, permeate the policy text. However perhaps more striking is the specificity of political rhetoric used in attempting to cohere fealty around the standard of 'standards', particularly the permeation of masculinist and bellicose language and imagery (see also Mahony and Hextall 1998). We are asked to join the Government 'crusade', to use 'tough love', send in 'hit squads', have 'zero tolerance of failure' and silence the 'doubts of cynics and the corrosion of the perpetual sceptics'.

Taking issue with this agenda in current times feels increasingly risky since raising doubts is so easily caricatured as whinging by trendy teachers or politically correct researchers. Yet serious concerns remain. The validity of the evidence used to prove poor or falling standards in numeracy and literacy has been questioned (Reed *et al.* 1995; Webster *et al.* 1996; Burton 1997) and a recent report by Peter Robinson from the Centre for Economic Performance, LSE (1997) argues on the basis of longitudinal data from two surveys that social class, parental interest and peer group pressure are the main factors in determining levels of numeracy and literacy and that pre-school education, class size, teaching methods, homework policy and streaming have little impact.

Further, concern has been raised by the lack of positive attention in the White Paper to anti-racist educational strategies in teacher education and schools, and the potential for suggested teaching methods and institutional practices to increase inequality of experience and of outcome:

> The White Paper simply continues the long tradition of locating the problem not with the schools but with the pupils. It should be seeking to transform a system which is underachieving in relation to black pupils, not instigating policies which could make matters worse.
>
> (Klein 1997)

Finally the positioning of teachers in this document is problematic, with stated support for teacher professionalism (through establishing a General Teaching Council, teacher fellowships and advanced professional qualifications) undermined by a disempowering tendency to overregulate, inspect and penalize teacher practices (through continuing curriculum control, ongoing testing, more stringent OfSTED measures of teacher performance and fast-track interventions when teachers or schools are perceived to be 'failing'). This continued erosion of teacher autonomy in the name of accountability and standards is unlikely to stem the tide of teachers seeking to leave the profession, or students avoiding teaching as a career, or to promote a positive approach to teacher professional development. Jane Kenway, writing recently on the influence and effects of technical rationality on gender reform policies in Australia (1997: 335) identifies the consequences of privileging teacher accountability over teacher professionalism:

> Clearly, accountability mechanisms produce a very different emotional dynamic. They position teachers in a non-dialogical relationship to policy makers in what Foucault (1977) might call a confessional mode of self-regulation and self-monitoring. And as such, they implicitly infantilise teachers and imply they do not understand, cannot be trusted, must be shamed into good practice and will be blamed if change does not occur. It is predictable that emotional responses to this will not be positive, particularly if one takes into account the broader political context of recent times involving major educational restructuring, a 'mean and lean' approach to supporting teacher development for change, and reform fatigue on the part of teachers.

I will return later to how such an atmosphere and culture amongst teachers and schools might be impacting upon their work with boys in school. What appears evident from a preliminary analysis of this policy document is that its notion of social justice has many similarities with the understanding that Rizvi and Lingard (1996) suggest dominates the Australian Labour Party. It is a distributive notion of social-justice (Troyna and Vincent 1995), articulated in this particular context through the politics of a Labour Party keen to demonstrate its tough and realist neo-social democratic credentials.

Perspectives on gender and social justice in education

Having looked at the influence of distributive concepts of social justice in relation to education in general and identified some significant elements of the education policy directions of the British Labour Government, I now want to briefly review recent perspectives on gender, social justice and education, ending with a critique of the dominant discourses around the educational underachievement of boys and their effects on policies and practices, acknowledging that,

> any discussion of educational in/equality... needs to be understood as enmeshed within and suffused by other more dominant discourses.
>
> (Weiner *et al.* 1997)

Weiner *et al.* (1997) map out the parallel discourses in education in general and those around gender and education. They identify five significant periods since the Second World War (see Figure 16.1). From the point of view of developing a perspective on gender, social justice and the education of boys, it is important to note, as Skelton (1997) does that boys were always there in those gender analyses

Historical period	**Prevalent discourses of education**	**Prevalent discourses of gender and education**
1940s & 1950s	equality of opportunity – IQ testing (focus on access)	weak (emphasis on equality according to 'intelligence')
1960s & 1970s	equality of opportunity – progressivism/mixed ability	weak (emphasis on working-class male disadvantage)
1970s to early 1980s	equality of opportunity – gender, race, disability, sexuality etc. (focus on outcome)	equal opportunities/anti-sexism (emphasis on female disadvantage)
late 1980s & early 1990s	choice, vocationalism and marketisation (focus on competition)	identity politics and feminisms (emphasis on femininities and masculinities)
mid-1990s	school effectiveness and improvement (focus on standards)	performance and achievement (emphasis on male disadvantage)

Figure 16.1 Discourses of education and gender.

Source: G. Weiner, M. Arnot and M. David 1997.

and projects of the 1970s and 1980s. However, with the exception of a few feminist studies (Heward 1988; Askew and Ross 1989) they were not the focus of enquiry.

In looking for analyses of masculinities in education that we might usefully draw upon, we need to look at studies influenced by the work of Connell (1989, 1995). Such work stresses an important shift away from a sex-role socialization thesis about the significance of gender towards a post-structuralist interest in the non-unitary nature of the subject and the contingent nature of identity formation. Masculinities within this are seen as socially constituted and constituting, with 'relations of alliance, dominance and subordination' (Connell 1995: 37) between hegemonic and non-hegemonic forms of masculinity. Exploration of external relations, but also internal psychological spaces and the interplay between the shifting dimensions of 'race', class gender and sexuality, become the focus of enquiry. Within this schools are seen as,

> complex gendered and heterosexual arenas. Within this reconceptualised focus, the school's institutional, material, social and discursive practices are all salient features in the making of student subjectivities: including student selection, subject allocation and stratification, disciplinary modes of authority, instruments of surveillance and control and the web of gendered and sexual student–teacher and student–student social relations.
>
> (Mac an Ghaill 1994: 4)

However, despite the significant contribution of such an analysis to our understanding of what schools are 'doing' in the construction and perpetuation of masculinities, what remains is the urgent task of deconstructing the dominant public and policy educational discourses around the 'underachieving boy', discourses largely unaffected by the academic perspectives on masculinities and schooling. This is not an argument over whether male educational underachievement exists or not: its 'reality' is a measure of its productivity in reshaping the landscape of educational policies and practices and there is considerable evidence of its current effects (Arnot *et al.* 1996; EOC and OfSTED 1996; Morris 1996). Rather, it is an attempt to deconstruct the elements of signification at a particular historical juncture and as part of a specific genealogy, accepting that,

> the reality represented does not determine the representation or the means of representation. Instead, the process of signification itself gives shape to the reality it implicates.
>
> (Henriques *et al.* 1984: 99)

Full critiques have been elaborated elsewhere (Raphael Reed 1997; Weiner *et al.* 1997) but let me highlight some terms and implications of the debate. Despite evidence of continuing gender in/equality for girls through the social relations of schooling and life chances post-16, the promoted wisdom is that boys are now the disadvantaged sex and that,

> the failure of boys and *in particular white working class boys* is one of the most disturbing problems we face, within the whole education system.
>
> (C. Woodhead quoted in the *Times Educational Supplement*, 15 March 1996)

The vital significance of social class identified here is elsewhere articulated with 'race' through a concern for the high exclusion rate affecting African Caribbean boys. Such differentiation however appears to be elided in the increasing industry generating inservice materials and events to look at 'improving boys' performance' and school development plans which target resources at 'raising the achievement of boys' with boys as an undifferentiated mass.

In these arenas two influential explanatory paradigms are regularly deployed to explain the pattern of academic achievement by gender in the years of compulsory schooling. The first draws upon a crude version of cognitive psychology and theories of innate difference (BBC 1994; Hannan 1996) with the claim that predominant classroom practices favour the reflective and language-rich approach to learning of girls and seriously disadvantage boys, who are naturally poorer at things which require reflection and carefully thought-through organization and sequential planning.

To some extent, this represents part of a shift in the dominant individualist pedagogic perspective, building on Piagetian pre-occupations with the emergence and activation of innate developmental stages, and heavily influenced by the work of Howard Gardner on multiple intelligences (Gardner 1993). The related interest in 'accelerated learning strategies', reflected again in popular inservice courses and LEA and school development plans of the moment (Smith 1995) provides a rearticulation of child-centred pedagogy, where the teacher is responsible for identifying and matching individual pupil learning needs by preferred learning style, or by failing to do so being responsible for pupil failure (Walkerdine 1984). This way of looking at classroom experience is fundamentally apolitical and asocial; gender as a social practice is replaced by idiographic descriptions of learner orientations, with gendered preference embedded in the brain.

Combined with a call to make the curriculum more relevant in content to boys' interests (e.g. using football scores to teach maths), this discursive element may well lead to a further masculinization of teaching styles and classroom environments, particularly in secondary schools, although also in primary classrooms required to teach in more didactic and structured ways (phonics-based approaches to literacy; whole-class inculcation of mathematical rules, etc.). One could see this as a reinforcement of hegemonic masculinity through the form of pedagogy, privileging rationality and the 'mastery of reason' as individual power, over emotional and intuitive connectedness through social and linguistic practices (Walkerdine 1988).

The second explanatory paradigm rests upon simplistic notions of the significance of social role. Increasing male unemployment and particularly high rates of unemployment amongst black and working-class young men are used to explain boys' disaffection with schooling and young men's oppositional stances as well as the growing incidence of psychosocial disorders, although Rutter and Smith (1995) argue that some of the most popular theories of causation between sociological factors and increasing incidence of psychosocial disorders amongst young people are not supported by reliable evidence and that further research is urgently needed.

Linked to this perspective, and arising from a sex-role socialization thesis about the creation and sustenance of gender identity, is anxiety about the lack of positive male role models for boys. This is articulated most clearly in relation to African Caribbean boys where deficit theories still predominate through a crude sociological proposition that absent black fathers in the home must be substituted for by positive black role models in the classroom (Holland/Channel 4 1995; Jeffreys and Bradley 1995; Parry 1995) and that African Caribbean boys suffer from over-domination by the black matriarch in the family. Overall, most reports assume that boys consider it 'uncool' to be successful at school (Williams 1995) with schoolboy cultures unmediated by work-orientated male models or unsupported by family aspirations and standards. Engaging the support of Premier club footballers in after-school study centres is supposed to help.

Such a perspective on the 'problem' leads to particular educational solutions, themselves potentially problematic. The intervention of black male mentors into primary schools has been criticized by some for diverting attention away from institutionalized racism, and for undermining the integrity of female teachers, including black teachers and mothers (Hutchinson and John 1995). One school in Rochdale established a mentoring scheme for boys to shadow business people in industry, so that 'boys will see what being busy and organised at work really means' (Haigh 1995). This included being picked up by a male manager at 6.45 am to attend a business meeting over breakfast, a questionable and highly gendered practice to emulate and one which reasserts traditional hegemonic notions of masculinity. The idea of returning to a 'self-discipline through authoritative male practices' is equally evidenced in recent suggestions that what badly behaved and unmotivated boys need is a compulsory period in the cadet corps (Harding and Fairhall 1997). Hegemonic masculinity itself is not seen as part of the problem.

This articulation of regulation and surveillance has wider significance when put together with suggestions of curfews for young troublemakers, home–school contracts on behaviours and fining parents for their children's (sons') misdemeanours (Home Office 1997). It points to the discursive repositioning of family and state responsibilities at a time when family poverty remains a critical issue for more than one in five children in school, and family child welfare and support services are being cut back by cash-strapped local authorities.

In terms of gender and social justice perspectives this dominant discursive complex on male underachievement can be seen to have worrying implications:

- equity is conceived of *only* in terms of the distribution of the social 'goods' of academic credentials.
- at the same time it provides a re-articulation of child-centred individualist perspectives on pedagogy, divorced from social context, and used to discipline

teachers – particularly female teachers (primary school teachers, English teachers and SEN teachers) – for their failure to meet boys' needs.

- it provides a medium for the reassertion of particular forms of hegemonic masculinity built around social and pedagogic practices of 'discipline' and structure (through social roles and identities, orientations to learning, curricular focus, forms of knowledge, etc.) that will affect teachers and pupils alike.
- in promoting social deficit theories about African Caribbean and white working-class families, and shifting responsibility and blame towards those sectors of society for behaviours and performance of their boys and young men, it provides important validation for increased surveillance and regulation of these social groups. Situated within this, mothers are blamed in a number of contradictory ways: for dominating or neglecting their sons; for undermining the male role by becoming the principal wage-earner; for generating family poverty by staying on welfare and not getting out to work.
- it legitimates the appropriation of resources to support an agenda of prioritizing boys and suggests that the issues affecting girls are all resolved.

As Weiner *et al.* (1997: 15) note:

> What is evident is that new educational discourses have silenced demands for increased social justice *for girls and women*, characterised by increasing resistance to policies and practices focusing specifically on them.

When articulated with the managerialist culture prevalent in many schools, the effects of this re-prioritization of the 'male' becomes even more potent. The report of Arnot *et al.* (1996: 133) for the EOC identified:

> One of the most worrying features to emerge from the research has been the evident continuing dominance of white male cultures in school and LEA hierarchies. A quote from a male headteacher usefully illustrates the perceptions of LEA management held by some, as: 'grey suited men running the authority in a paternalistic rather than partnership sort of way' with 'blunt autocratic reputations' and with 'uncomfortable, defensive, dismissive, sceptical (and) hostile' responses to gender issues.

The impact of the school effectiveness and improvement culture, where issues of social justice have been assimilated into the imperatives of performance targets and standards, has also in some cases reinforced the feeling of teachers that there is a masculinist agenda at work. One female secondary school teacher in discussion with me illustrated this graphically:

> I feel really down at the moment. My purse was stolen in class. My finger is bleeding and I don't know why. Thing around me aren't working or keep getting lost. I feel invaded somehow. I really *feel* it, you know, inside... The new Head of Faculty (X) has come from a middle class school and has a particular style

> that seems to be acceptable or encouraged in an 'Improving School'. We are being asked all the time to put ourselves right in the faces of kids, *all the time*... Like (X), he is always shouting, and angry and aggressive. I just can't do that... I *won't* do that. I don't want to nag and nag... and it just doesn't work. I always thought it was to do with relationships. Having and building and keeping relationships going with the kids. And if someone comes into my classroom and takes a 'snapshot' picture maybe they might say I'm not being demanding enough; I'm not being pushy enough. But I'd say... 'You can't do that. You can't make judgements without seeing how things happen over time'. I end up being not 'all there' because I don't want all to be there.

Such accounts urge us to continue an analysis and intervention that makes sense of the current articulations of masculinities and schooling from a gender critical perspective. In this we need a perspective on social justice, gender and the education of boys, that relates to the pressing concerns of teachers, pupils and schools.

Towards conceptualizing a feminist perspective on social justice in the education of boys

In this section I want to draw on the work of Young (1990), Shaw (1995), Connell (1993), Kenway (1997) and Kenway and Fitzclarence (1997) to articulate some important elements of a way of thinking about the issues of social justice, gender and boys. I then want to begin to discuss a framework for enquiring into classroom cultures and interactions between teachers and boys, taking classrooms themselves to be complex, fluid and non-unitary.

Iris Marion Young's work (1990) is regularly referred to in discussions of education and social justice (see, for example, Gewirtz 1998) because of her insightful critique of the limitations of a distributive theory of justice. This critique highlights two things. Firstly, that by focusing on the distribution of goods we fail to notice the other relevant factors influencing this pattern of distribution, including structural inequalities, institutional processes and the separation of the private from the public sphere (Fraser 1987; Pateman 1988). Secondly, that by broadening distribution to cover not only material goods but also goods such as self-respect, opportunity, power, honour, etc. we reify these things, suggesting they are fixed and static, and we thereby avoid looking at social processes (Young 1990: 25).

Seeing social justice as more than just a matter of distribution of material goods, and identifying the centrality of relational and diverse dynamics and actions, allows us to identify a more meaningful framework for defining and evaluating the macro and micro political conditions of social in/equality. This framework includes focusing on 'actions, decisions abut actions, and provision of the means to develop and exercise capabilities' (Young 1990: 16) within which 'Oppression and domination... should be the primary terms for conceptualising injustice' (pp. 8–9).

Looking at these elements around the education of boys in school rather than narrowly concentrating on just their access to academic credentials, immediately opens up a richer vein of enquiry. It also allows us to consider the experience of girls, boys and teachers on the same plane of analysis, since oppression and domination may be experienced by each or all of them in different ways at different times and in different contexts.

One immediate question that is raised by associating oppression with the experiences of boys in school, is whether boys are in fact oppressed, or not. Accepting, as given, the diversity of masculinities and 'boyness' in school, it is nevertheless the case that adults interested in theories of social justice, including some feminists, will only take a justice perspective on those groups of boys perceived as disadvantaged and 'oppressed' by virtue of their structural location as part of another category: working-class, black, gay, etc. Quite rightly, there is suspicion of the capture of political attention by the totalizing claim that 'boys' are disadvantaged (see the discussion earlier of the discourses on male underachievement). But disadvantage and oppression are not the same thing. White middle-class heterosexual boys may be advantaged by their access to material and cultural capital as well as their identification with hegemonic masculinity, yet, as children, schooled in an education system permeated by 'poisonous pedagogy' (Kenway and Fitzclarence 1997), may suffer from both powerlessness and violence in relation to adults; two of the five 'faces of oppression' identified by Young where 'the presence of any of these five conditions is sufficient for calling a group oppressed' (Young 1990: 64).

This is not confined to specific instances of child abuse or aberrant behaviours of a few individuals. Alice Miller reminds us that many child-rearing practices privilege the adult over the child resulting in the loss of an authentic sense of being alive (Miller 1987) and the very tenets of hegemonic masculinity require repression, displacement and denial. Both Walkerdine (1985) and Kenway and Fitzclarence (1997) identify how:

> At this stage of Western history, hegemonic masculinity mobilises around physical strength, adventurousness, emotional neutrality, certainty, control, assertiveness, self-reliance, individuality, competitiveness, instrumental skills, public knowledge, discipline, reason, objectivity and rationality. It distances itself from physical weakness, expressive skills, private knowledge, creativity, emotion, dependency, subjectivity, irrationality, co-operation and empathetic, compassionate, nurturant and certain affiliative behaviours. In other words it distances itself from the feminine and considers the feminine less worthy.
>
> (Kenway and Fitzclarence 1997: 121)

Such values and meanings are communicated not only through the explicit content of the curriculum, but through the hidden curriculum and dominant form of pedagogy, expressed through logocentric and rationalist control as well as autocratic and insensitive forms of behavioural management. The consequences are significant. Both Iris Marion Young (1990) and Jenny Shaw (1995) stress the destructive outcomes when fear of the 'other' or anxiety about maintaining a separate identity, at an unconscious level, drive actions and interactions. Shaw suggests that such processes explain the attachment boys make to certain subjects as 'transitional objects' and their fear of loss of self in subjects identified with the 'feminine' and emotions. She also postulates that gender issues become more significant and problematic in schools, with more repression of 'difference', anxiety about the 'other', and 'psychic and emotional stress' (for teachers as well as pupils) in correlation with increased general levels of anxiety. Increased surveillance, regulation and testing, as identified earlier in this paper, all have the potential to do just that.

This analysis suggests a completely different agenda on social justice, gender and the education of boys to that identified under the rubric of performance outcomes and standards. Elements of this agenda are expressed by Kenway and Fitzclarence (1997: 125):

> If schools implicitly subscribe to and endorse hegemonic versions of masculinity, particularly in their more exaggerated forms, then they are complicit in the production of violence. If they fear 'the feminine' and avoid and discourage empathetic, compassionate, nurturant and affiliative behaviours and emotional responsibility and instead favour heavy-handed discipline and control then they are complicit. If they seek to operate only at the level of rationality and if they rationalise violence then they are complicit. If they are structured in such a way as to endorse the culture of male entitlement and indicate that the needs of males are more important than those of females then they are complicit. If they are repressive in their adult/child relations and do not offer adolescent students in particular opportunities to develop wise judgements and to exercise their autonomy in responsible ways, then they are complicit. If they operate in such a way as to marginalise and stigmatise certain groups of students then they are complicit…it is our view that interventions which do not attend to all these matters will be limited in their effects.

However, the actions and arenas that schools should explore in order to address these issues are not entirely clear. Connell (1993: 18) argues that,

> education is a social process in which the 'how much' cannot be separated from the 'what'.

In part this is about revealing and deconstructing the epistemological influences determining subject content; in part it is about discussing principles of curricular justice to guide developments. For Connell such principles include: the need to ensure that the interests of the least advantaged are advocated including compensatory programmes as much as counter-hegemonic projects across the spectrum of difference, without falling into relativism; the democratic principle of participation, active citizenship and decision-making for students combined with an entitlement to a common curriculum; the need to acknowledge and advocate change as part of an historical perspective on the production of equality. Salisbury and Jackson (1996) suggest a range of curricular approaches to working with adolescent boys that fulfil in many senses the criteria specified by Connell whilst addressing boys' fear, anxieties and displacements, which may be expressed in violent or prejudicial ways. In part, it is about challenging the increasingly rational curriculum content, as much as acknowledging the support that teachers need to engage with such difficult issues.

Of course, in many respects, this is entirely out of step with the times. Kenway (1997: 334–5), remarking on the difficulties of what to do in practice in education to promote gender equity, singles out the general absence of attention to emotions, even in periods of time when explicit gender reforms were high on the agenda in Australia:

> Since their inception government policies for gender reform have not had much to say about the emotions involved in either being an agent for change or in teacher development . . . gender reform policies are hyper-rational; they not only minimise or ignore the emotional and psychic field of schooling generally, they also tend to ignore and repress the emotions which they themselves generate . . . It is my view that the theories which inform gender reform and the feminist pedagogies which arise from them must now come to include such concepts as pleasure, nurturance, pain, blame, shame, risk, investment and fantasy. However, in times characterised by hyperrationality and emotional repression on a wide cultural scale, such a focus is unlikely in policy circles at least.

A theory on social justice and the education of boys that drew upon the work of Young, Shaw and Connell, as sketched out above, would have the potential to encompass the emotional and psychic dimensions of schooling as they affect both teachers and pupils.

However, in order to take this out of the academy and into schools in a way that is meaningful we need to do a number of things. Firstly, we need to gather and reflect back into schools accounts of how teachers *feel* about the complex work of teaching, including the challenges and frustrations of working against the grain of masculinist schooling. Such stories are tremendously revealing of the circulatory nature of sexualized and racialized power and oppression across and between the different subject positions in a classroom, and allow us to own the pain:

> There are the tensions between issues of gender and ethnicity which often feel difficult to handle. Sometimes I feel the need to resist or challenge antagonism, not from a position of white authority but from a position of feminist outrage, you know. 'How dare you treat me like shit. You say to me that you feel like you're being treated like shit, stop treating me the same!' I've found ways of bringing that out. I don't think that I do it very well, but I try to make it part of the explicit agenda – which is to talk about power and to point out how different people in different ways in social relations in the

> world become the objects of power – players in a game of power that structures relationships unequally in the world, and that people carry that within them in ways that reproduce inequality and reproduce hurt. They are showing in school their emotional reactions to the abuses of power, but so am I and I feel that they need to see that. There is lots of bad language between them, often to do with mothers, and particularly around sexuality, and I let them know how that makes me feel as a woman and a mother. I bring my gendered self into the arena and I think it's important that they see that.
>
> (Transcript quoted in Raphael Reed 1995: 83–4)

Secondly, we need to enquire into the effects of the ordinary processes of schooling from the perspective of boys, including how those processes affect their engagement with learning. One part of this is to look at boys' own orientations to learning in specific pedagogic contexts, and their responses to the articulations of hegemonic masculinity in those pedagogic contexts. In my current research project[1] I am attempting to do just that. The study is based in an inner-city mixed comprehensive, tracking the learning experiences and orientations in the core subjects of maths, English and science of ten boys in a single tutor group as they move between Years 8 to 10. Whilst their cultural and ethnic backgrounds are diverse, they might all be identified as working class. Their personalities, peer group friendships and positions in the school are also diverse, as are their levels of attainment. None of them has been excluded for any length of time, nor are any of them identified on the special educational need register. Half of them have been identified as 'underachieving' by the school and the school itself is under increasing pressure to improve performance. Almost all staff express feelings of stress and unhappiness.

Through a combination of structured and unstructured observation, group discussions and individual interviews, personal construct interviews, selections of samples of work and assessments, and recordings of classroom talk, I am attempting to build up a situated case study account of the learning careers of ten boys who are prime candidates for the focus of current gender anxieties. Parallel to this I am conducting unstructured life history interviews with their teachers to see how masculinist aspects of schooling situated in the current climate of education and the specific culture of the school together with working with boys impact upon their own identity formation and how they represent their own gendered teacher identities and careers including their values and orientations to pedagogy.

In attempting to refine an appropriate framework for systematic observations of learning orientations in classrooms, to complement my fieldnotes from participant observation, I have adapted a useful framework of enquiry drawn from Webster *et al.* (1996) (Figure 16.2), renaming the quadrants and the axes (Figure 16.3). Whilst designed to focus on literacy events, the definition of 'literacy' proposed by the original authors includes subject specific and multiple literacies and I agree with the premise of the authors that 'literacy is the learning curriculum in schools'. In addition I am recording specific languages of authority, control and instruction, and am moving on to record the dialogue of boys at work in the class. This framework

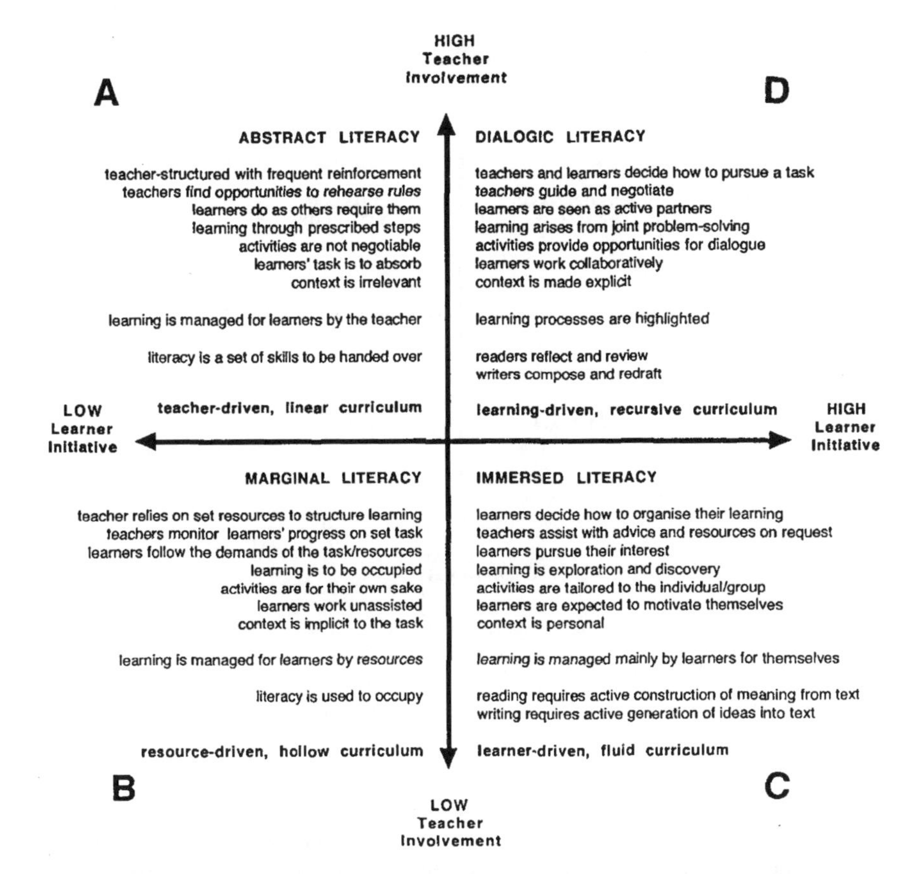

Figure 16.2 Framework of teacher–learner proximation: literacy learning through interaction.

Source: Adapted by M. Reed from Webster, A., Beveridge, M. & Reed, M. (1996) *Managing the Literacy Curriculum*, London: Routledge.

supports observation of the non-explicit aspects of masculinist pedagogy in social context and the detail of individual boys' responses, without oversimplifying the complexity of classroom actions. It also helps to focus on the actions and interactions of boys who are *not* disruptive or visible in the classroom, those normally 'hidden from gaze' (Gordon *et al.* 1997). It is important to recognize that no single lesson takes place in just one quadrant, and that teachers and pupils may be operating in different quadrants at any one time. Observations at each event of two boys and the teacher unsurprisingly reveal different scripts of experience of the lesson.

Details of the data are in the process of being analysed and remain to be fully reported, but interesting issues are beginning to emerge as evidenced. For example, and very briefly, Matthew and Robert are two boys in the top set for maths working with John, a very traditional male teacher who maintains a classroom environment where there is virtually no pupil initiative or autonomy encouraged

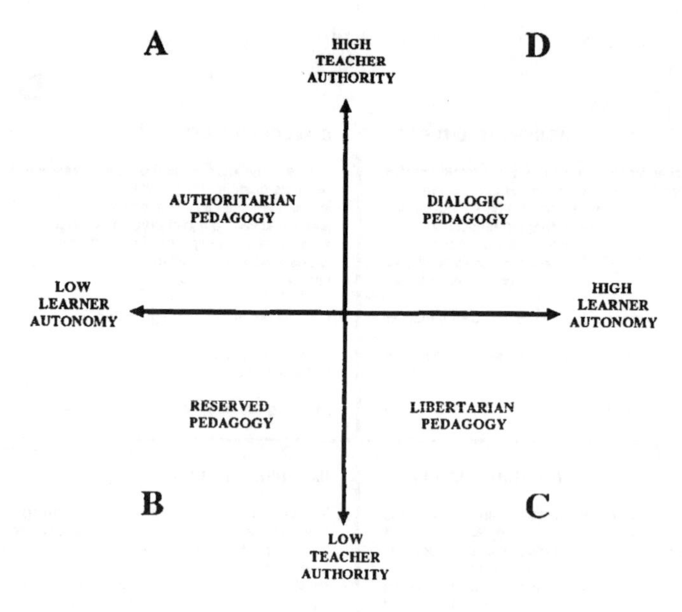

Figure 16.3 A framework of teacher–learner interaction.

Source: Based on Webster *et al.* 1996.

or allowed. They rate him highly as a teacher and remain on task and compliant for virtually the whole lesson. In a subsequent interview Matthew said:

> yeh . . . I think he is a really good teacher. He makes things really clear and he doesn't mess around with group work, and you always feel like you are learning something. I don't think women make good teachers. They're too soft and flappy.

Significantly, Sally, their English teacher, operates in a mixed ability setting predominantly in quadrant C. Their attention to task in the lesson is sporadic and their levels and attainment far lower than in maths. By contrast, two other boys in the study, Ryan and Danny, also in the top set for maths are in a mixed-ability English classroom with Diane who operates skilfully across quadrants for specific reasons, including promoting interactions in Quadrant D. Perhaps unsurprisingly, their SATs results in English match their SATs results in maths.

More interestingly perhaps, the teachers concerned in discussing with me their particular orientations to teaching, each articulated, without explicitly using the term 'social justice', a distinctive perspective on social justice and education. John talks of effort and rewards, and categorizes pupils almost entirely on the basis of their 'ability' and willingness to work; Sally talks of liberties, freedoms and self-determinations and in personal construct definitions of the pupils in her class adopts a varied, idiosyncratic and individualistic set of categorizations; Diane talks of responsibilities and social processes and categorizes pupils predominantly by learning needs and social skills. Only Diane recognizes explicitly that gender is an important factor in the classroom.

In undertaking a crude school effectiveness evaluation of these three teachers, one would say that John and Diane were 'effective' and Sally was not. However, even from this brief fragment of research material we can see how much such an analysis misses. Gendered relationships to school subjects here are mediated through specific pedagogic contexts. Ways of thinking about social justice appear to affect what goes on inside particular classrooms, as much as informing how to evaluate the qualitative and quantitative outcomes.

Conclusions

In this paper I have attempted to sketch out the elements of a perspective on social justice and the education of boys that resists the colonization of concern about them through the discourses of school effectiveness and underachievement. In doing this I have critiqued the presumptions of the distributive paradigm of social justice, and attempted to analyse its influence on recent education policy, specifically the first White Paper of the New Labour Government, *Excellence in Schools.* I have then briefly reviewed recent perspectives on gender, social justice and education, ending with a deconstruction of the composition of the 'underachieving boy'. Finally, in turning to look at an alternative feminist perspective on social justice issues in the education of boys I have drawn on the work of Iris Marion Young, Jenny Shaw, Bob Connell and Jane Kenway to identify important elements of such a perspective. These include:

- that oppression and domination should be the primary terms for conceptualizing social in/justice, rather than adopting distributive paradigms
- that we need to research actions and contexts, including decision-making procedures, division of labour and culture
- boys as children, even those advantaged by social class or synergy with hegemonic forms of masculinity, experience powerlessness and violence as a consequence of the predominance of 'poisonous pedagogy' in schooling
- psychic anxiety and displacement is related to fear of the 'other', represented in control of the 'female'. Anxiety associated with gender is an integral part of schooling
- ownership of the emotions is an important part of a new social justice perspective.

In conclusion I suggest that we need to take these understandings back into schools and connect with the lived experience of teachers and pupils: firstly by researching the emotional and psychic landscapes of teaching and learning, and secondly, by seeing how particular pedagogic frameworks, whilst raising examination performance, can either promote or undermine a social justice perspective on the education of boys. On this, more empirical work remains to be done.

Note

1 'Working with Boys'; three year ethnographic and life history project, funded by the Faculty of Education, University of the West of England, Bristol.

Bibliography

Anderson, G. L. and Herr, K. (1994) The micropolitics of student voices; moving from diversity of bodies to diversity of voices in schools, in C. Marshall (ed.), *The New Politics of Race and Gender* (London: Falmer), 58–68.

Arnot, M., David, M. and Weiner, G. (1996) *Educational Reforms and Gender Equality* (Manchester: Equality Opportunities Commission).

Askew, S. and Ross, C. (1989) *Boys Don't Cry: Boys and Sexism in Education* (Buckingham: Open University Press).

BBC (1994) The future is female. *Panorama*, 24 October, BBC1.

Burton, L. (1997) Contempt for evidence. *Forum*, 39(1), 10–12.

Christensen, C. and Rizvi, F. (eds) (1996) *Disability and the Dilemmas of Education and Justice* (Buckingham: Open University Press).

Connell, R. W. (1989) Cool guys, swots and wimps: the interplay of masculinity and schooling. *Oxford Review of Education*, 15(3), 291–303.

Connell, R. W. (1993) *Schools and Social Justice* (Toronto: Our Schools/Our Selves Education Foundation).

Connell, R. W. (1995) *Masculinities* (Cambridge: Polity Press).

Department for Education and Employment (1997) *Excellence in Schools* (London: HMSO).

Equal Opportunities Commission and Office for Standards in Education (1996) *The Gender Divide: Performance Differences Between Boys and Girls at School* (London: HMSO).

Fraser, N. (1987) Women, welfare and the politics of need interpretation. *Hypatia: A Journal of Feminist Philosophy*, 2, 103–22.

Gardner, H. (1993) *Frames of Mind; The Theory of Multiple Intelligences,* 2nd edn (London: Fontana Press).

Gewirtz, S. (1998) Conceptualising social justice in education: mapping the territory. *Journal of Education Policy*, 13(4), 469–84.

Gordon, T., Holland, J., Lahelma, E. and Tolonen, T. (1997) Hidden from gaze: problematising action in the classroom. Paper presented at the BSA annual conference, Power/Resistance, University of York, April.

Grumet, M. (1990) Retrospective: autobiography and the analysis of educational experience. *Cambridge Journal of Education*, 20(3), 321–5.

Haigh, G. (1995) Not for wimps. *Times Educational Supplement*, 6 October.

Hannan, G. (1996) *Improving Boys' Performance*, INSET materials, G. Hannan.

Harding, L. and Fairhall, D. (1997) Labour repels lads' army, *Guardian*, 24 January.

Henriques, J., Hollway, W., Urwin, C., Venc, C. and Walkerdine, V. (1984) *Changing the Subject* (London: Cassell).

Heward, C. (1988) *Making a Man of Him* (London: Routledge).

Holland, S. (1995) *Frontline*, Channel 4, 13 September.

Home Office (1997) *No More Excuses: A New Approach to Tackling Youth Crime in England and Wales* (London: HMSO).

Hutchinson, M. and John, G. (1995) Enter the role model. *Guardian Education*, 26 September.

Jeffreys, D. and Bradley, L. (1995) They're poisoning our kids: the new rap backlash, *Independent*, 31 July.

Kenway, J. (1997) Taking stock of gender reform policies for Australian schools: past, present and future. *British Educational Research Journal*, 23(3), 329–44.

Kenway, J. and Fitzclarence, L. (1997) Masculinity, violence and schooling: challenging 'poisonous pedagogies'. *Gender and Education*, 9(1), 117–33.

Klein, G. (1997) Excellence . . . but for whom? *Guardian Education*, 12 August.

Luke, C. and Gore, J. (1992) *Feminisms and Critical Pedagogy* (London: Routledge).

Mac an Ghaill, M. (1994) *The Making of Men: Masculinities, Sexualities and Schooling* (Buckingham: Open University Press).

Mac an Ghaill, M. (1996) Sociology of education, state schooling and social class: beyond critiques of the New Right hegemony. *British Journal of Sociology of Education*, 17(2), 163–76.

Mahony, P. and I. Hextall (1998) Social justice and the reconstruction of teaching. *Journal of Education Policy*, 13(4), 545–58.

Miller, A. (1987) *The Drama of Being a Child and the Search for the True Self* (London: Virago).

Morris, E. (1996) *Boys will be Boys? Closing the Gender Gap* (Labour Party Consultation Document).

Nozick, R. (1976) *Anarchy, State and Utopia* (Oxford: Blackwell).

Parry, O. (1995) What's sex got to do with it?, *Guardian Education*, 5 September.

Pateman, C. (1988) *The Sexual Contract* (Stanford, CA: Stanford University Press).

Raphael Reed, L. (1995) Reconceptualising equal opportunities in the 1990s: a study of a radical teacher culture in transition, in M. Griffiths and B. Troyna (eds), *Antiracism, Culture and Social Justice in Education* (Stoke on Trent: Trentham Books), 77–97.

Raphael Reed, L. (1996) Re-searching, re-finding, re-making: exploring the unconscious as a pedagogic and research practice. Paper presented at the British Educational Research Association Conference, University of Lancaster, September.

Raphael Reed, L. (1997) Troubling boys and disturbing discourses on masculinity and schooling: a feminist exploration of current debates and interventions around boys in school. Paper presented at the Gender and Education Conference, University of Warwick, April 1997.

Rawls, J. (1971) *A Theory of Justice* (Cambridge, MA: Belknap Press).

Reed, M., Webster, A. and Beveridge, M. (1995) The conceptual basis for a literacy curriculum, in P. Owen and P. Pumfrey (eds), *Children Learning to Read: International Concerns*. vol. 41: *Emergent and Developing Readers: Messages for Teachers* (London: Falmer), 161–80.

Rizvi, F. (1994) Race, gender and the cultural assumptions of schooling, in C. Marshall (ed.), *The New Politics of Race and Gender* (London: Falmer), 203–17.

Rizvi, F. and Lingard, B. (1996) Disability, education and the discourses of justice, in C. Christensen and F. Rizvi (eds), *Disability and the Dilemmas of Education and Justice* (Buckingham: Open University Press), 9–26.

Robinson, P. (1997) *Literacy, Numeracy and Economic Performance* (London: LSE, Centre for Economic Performance).

Rutter, M. and Smith, D. (1995) *Psychosocial Disorders in Young People: Time Trends and their Causes* (London: Wiley).

Salisbury, J. and Jackson, D. (1996) *Challenging Macho Values: Practical Ways of Working with Adolescent Boys* (London: Falmer Press).

Shaw, J. (1995) *Education, Gender and Anxiety* (London: Taylor and Francis).

Shor, I. and Freire, P. (1987) *A Pedagogy for Liberation* (New York: Bergin and Garvey).

Skelton, C. (1997) Feminism and research into masculinities and schooling. Paper presented at the Gender and Education Conference, University of Warwick, April.

Smith, A. (1995) *Accelerated Learning in the Classroom* (Basingstoke: Network Educational Press).

Troyna, B. and Vincent, C. (1995) The discourses of social justice in education. *Discourse: Studies in the Cultural Politics of Education*, 16(2), 149–66.

Troyna, B. and Vincent, C. (1996) The ideology of expertism: the framing of special education and racial equality policies in the local state, in C. Christensen and F. Rizvi (eds), *Disability and the Dilemmas of Education and Justice* (Buckingham: Open University Press), 131–44.

Walkerdine, V. (1984) Developmental psychology and the child-centred pedagogy: the insertion of Piaget into early education, in J. Henriques, W. Holloway C. Urwin, C. Venn and V. Walkerdine (eds), *Changing the Subject: Psychology, Social Regulation and Subjectivity* (London: Methuen), 153–202.

Walkerdine, V. (1985) On the regulation of speaking and silence: subjectivity, class and gender in contemporary schooling, in C. Steedman, C. Urwin and V. Walkerdine (eds), *Language, Gender and Childhood* (London: RKP), 203–40.

Walkerdine, V. (1988) *The Mastery of Reason: Cognitive Development and the Production of Rationality* (London: Routledge).

Webster, A., Beveridge, M. and Reed, M. (1996) *Managing the Literacy Curriculum* (London: Routledge).

Weiner, G., Arnot, M. and David, M. (1997) Is the future female? female success, male disadvantage and changing gender patterns in education, in A. H. Halsey, P. Brown and H. Lauder (eds), *Education, Economy, Culture and Society* (Oxford: Oxford University Press).

Williams, E. (1995) Lapped by girls. *Times Educational Supplement*, 14 July.

Young, I. M. (1990) *Justice and the Politics of Difference* (Princeton, NJ: Princeton University Press).

17 Framing justice

Challenges for research

Terri Seddon

Monash University, Clayton, Victoria

Source: *Journal of Education Policy*, 18 (3): 229–52, 2003.

In 1998, *Journal of Education Policy* published a special issue on social justice and education policy. This collection highlighted the importance of studies of social justice not just in their own right but because they provide a powerful window on contemporary education reform. Such research sheds light onto the way the social organization of education is accompanied by distinctive patterns of justice and injustice. It also creates a context for more methodological debate about the way research on social justice is framed and what this means for our understandings and conceptualizations of education and society.

In this paper, I take up this special issue invitation to debate the issues of conceptualization through the medium of specific research on social justice. It has been prompted by my growing unease at the apparent research commonsense evident in much English and Australian policy sociology in relation to contemporary neo-liberal education reform. There is now an abundance of such research which describes the neo-liberal reform of education on a quasi-market model and decrys the impact these changes have had for social justice (Ball *et al.* 1996; Marginson 1997a; Whitty *et al.* 1998). While this research is usually robust in design and interpretation, its accounts sometimes read in a rather immiserationist way (Haug 1984). The narrative of reform seems bleak, preoccupied with increasing social misery. In such analyses, it is almost as if neo-liberalism in education drives towards injustice in a more or less straightforward fashion, relatively uninterrupted by agency or contradiction. Not surprisingly, they lead to judgements that neo-liberal education is unjust.

While my own research leads me to be sympathetic to these arguments that neo-liberalism has changed education in ways that have increased injustice, I am uncomfortable with their unmitigated bleakness. It raises questions about the kinds of evaluative judgements that are being made in this research and the evidence base on which such judgements are made. For instance, what conceptions of justice and practical justice ethics are assumed in such evaluations? How are justice practices contextualized and in relation to what socio-historical horizon?

How does the conceptualization of social change influence the evaluation by signifying some rather than other social practices? And, as a result, what evidence is admitted? As Sen (1999: 54–6) argues, evaluative judgements about different justice principles depend upon the particular information that is seen to be decisive. The specification of decisive information in any process of judgement is contingent upon the conceptualization of social justice, that is what is seen to count as 'justice' and the empirical data that is taken to be evidence (or an appropriate proxy or indicator) of such justice.

My aim in the paper is, then, to orchestrate a specific dialogue around social justice in education in order to open up questions about ways of understanding social justice and contemporary education reform. I argue that there is a need for us, as researchers in policy sociology, to sharpen our theoretical and empirical focus by clarifying where there is continuity and where there is change in the patterns of justice and injustice in contemporary education. In the process, the paper worries at the relationship between conceptualization and contextualization, the way we research contemporary history as both outsiders and insiders in processes of social change, how these issues shape our engagement with the empirical world, and what we select as evidence to support our arguments and judgements.

I develop my case in this paper by engaging with two of Gewirtz's research papers. The first is Gewirtz's (1998) contribution to the social justice special issue of *JEP* The second is her application of the justice principles developed in the *JEP* article in a social justice audit. This audit is presented in her recent book, *The Managerial School* (Gewirtz 2000). It draws on data generated through a series of ethnographic studies in London schools to evaluate the justice of neo-liberal education reform or, in Gewirtz's terms, 'post-welfarist' education.

I have used these pieces as a kind of protagonist in this paper because, taken together, they go much further than most education research in articulating the basis for evaluative judgements about justice in contemporary education. The strength of Gewirtz's work lies, first, in its explication of the justice principles that constitute the normative basis for her evaluative judgements and, secondly, in its innovative application of an audit technology to justice judgements against these normative principles. The effect of the audit procedure is to encourage more than usual transparency in the way evidence is selected and used in relation to the justice principles as a basis for making justice judgements. While recognizing the limitations in using just two pieces of Gewirtz's overall body of work and the consequential dangers of overstatement and/or reification, I believe that there are benefits in building on this audit and its explicit methodology. Specifically, these two papers provide a valuable opportunity to unpack the processes that lead to Gewirtz's judgement that there has been an overall decline in justice in post-welfarist schooling and to ask questions about the way social justice is being framed and evidence used.

The paper is organized in three main sections. First, I outline Gewirtz's position, her justice principles and the social justice audit that she conducts. I set this evaluation of social justice in a post-welfarist context against a parallel case: a short vignette drawn from my own research on post-welfarist reform in

Australian education. The second section of the paper presents the vignette and my own commentary on the patterns of justice and injustice in this post-welfarist education context. Setting the two evaluations of justice within post-welfarism against one another provides a basis for clarifying the dissonances between the two analyses. In the final section of the paper, I explore the way judgements about social justice have been framed in the two cases and how this framing shapes what is seen as decisive information in justice judgements.

Before embarking on the analysis, it is important to emphasize that my own research, its theoretical resources, and its commitment to social justice comes from very much the same intellectual stable as Gewirtz and the wider policy sociology research community. I am not approaching this analysis as an external critic with a political motivation to undercut either ethnographic research or inquiries into social justice. Instead, the paper has been written with a view to productive debate on social justice and change in education within the policy sociology community.

Post-welfarism in English schools: a social justice audit

Gewirtz is well known for her research on market reform in English education under successive conservative and, now, Labour governments. With Ball, Whitty and others, she has undertaken substantial ethnographic research in schools to document and critique the impact of marketization on the work of schools, and the work-life of students, teachers and principals. This work has led the way in putting the English narrative about neo-liberal reform in education at the forefront of international research.

In *The Managerial School*, Gewirtz (2000) draws on this ethnographic research to argue that the particular pattern of market liberal reform in education represents a new 'post-welfarist' educational settlement and something of a break from the institutional and discursive practices of the prior, post-World War 2, welfarist settlement. She uses her data from a sample of London schools as evidence to support this case for a new settlement and to highlight the implications of the disjuncture in values, institutional practices, and expectations on students, teachers and managers in these schools. Finally, she makes a strong case for analysis that recognizes the obdurate social structuring of education rather than being too preoccupied by either a 'celebration-of-indeterminacy' (p. xi) post-modern approach or a technicist, problem-solving, school improvement approach. Analysis, she argues, must attend to the systematic patterning of social relations and the way these relations structure both persistent social dynamics such as systematic state agency in education (Dale 1989), and the persistence of particular social inequalities.

My own research has followed a parallel path to that marked out by Gewirtz. I fully endorse the call for analysis of social structures and the significant role of the state in shaping education as a social technology of population management, and economic and social development (Seddon 1993). My work has also used the concept of settlement (Centre for Contemporary Cultural Studies 1981) as a basis for theorizing the historicity of education and its particular patterns of continuity and change (Seddon 1988). Building on these broad ontological and epistemological assumptions, I have investigated neo-liberal reform in Australia, particularly in Victoria. However, this research has moved outside the domain of school education to encompass vocational education and training and its diverse learning sites in Institutes of Technical and Further Education (TAFE), community and private providers workplaces and community settings. This research considers the justice implications of neo-liberal reform not only in terms of distributive and relational justice, but also in terms of the way restructuring re-shapes people's capacity to act. In this respect, I have found it helpful to draw on both Marxist notions of praxis and the development literature and its concepts of capacity-building and capability (Seddon 2000; Seddon and Cairns 2001). This development literature builds on an Aristotelian justice ethic that complements the distributive-relational justice framework but offers a more grounded conceptualization of social justice (Sen 1999). It re-works the language of freedom, participation and choice, and re-presents them in terms of capacity and capability. This ethical discourse steps back from abstracted universalism to affirm, in quite practical ways, politics over economics and to accommodate cultural pluralism and contextual diversity (Yeatman 1994; Nussbaum 1999; Ackerly 2000).

Given the parallels in our research agenda, it is not surprising that there are many convergences in our research analyses. However, the different empirical contexts in which we work, coupled with different nuances in conceptualization, do create dissonances. It is these issues that I address below.

In *The Managerialist School*, Gewirtz (2000) argues that the school reforms of the 1980s and 1990s have established a 'post-welfarist' settlement in education, replacing the older welfarist settlement that was institutionalized in the period after World War 2. As she notes, post-welfarism entails 'New Right-inspired' market reforms that coalesced into distinctive 'sets of languages, meanings, assumptions, values and institutional forms, practices and relationships' (p. xi). These institutional and discursive practices differed significantly from the prior welfarist settlement. Its formal commitments to Keynesian economics and distributive justice were replaced by commitments to market democracy and competitive individualism. Bureaucratic organization and those who worked within them, bureaucrats and professionals, were seen to be a source of problems rather than solutions.

In an innovative step, Gewirtz uses her detailed research on the effects of market reform to conduct a social justice audit, assessing post-welfarist policy and reform outcomes against a social justice framework that acknowledges both distributive and relational justice. She argues that social justice should not just be conceptualized in terms of the way goods are distributed through society, but it should also attend to the 'nature and ordering of social relations, the formal and informal rules that govern how members of society treat each other both on a macro-social and micro-interpersonal level' (Gewirtz 2000: 140). Gewirtz argues that Young (1990) provides a robust conceptualization of social justice that moves beyond the traditional focus on distribution. It brings into view another dimension of justice related to the way social relations structure society, including forms of co-operation, the way people relate to one another and confer dignity and respect within relationships. Rather than just considering what people have, it turns attention to how what people do is structured by institutional rules, by their social position constituted within institutionalized relations, and by the recursive effects of doing and having on their lives. It draws attention to Young's 'five faces of oppression': exploitation, marginalization, powerlessness, cultural imperialism and violence. And, because this notion of relational justice is framed by a clear conception of modes of oppression, it provides some basis for understanding social justice in a way that can inform the direction and content of collective action.

In the *JEP* article, Gewirtz (1998) uses these insights to identify five key questions that need to be addressed in making an assessment of social justice:

How, to what extent and why do education policies support, interrupt or subvert:

- Exploitative relationships (capitalist, patriarchal, racist, sexist, disablist, etc.) within and beyond educational institutions;
- Processes of marginalization and inclusion within and beyond the education system;
- The promotion of relationships based on recognition, respect, care and mutuality, or produce powerlessness (for education worker and students);
- Practices of cultural imperialism? And which cultural differences should be affirmed, which should be universalized and which rejected; and
- Violent practices within and beyond the education system.

(Gewirtz 1998: 482)

Judging the research findings from post-welfarist contexts against these questions provides a basis for auditing post-welfarism in terms of social justice. This audit reveals substantial relational as well as distributional *injustice.* Gewirtz (1998: 154) sums up this analysis saying:

> that the post-welfarist policies of successive Conservative administrations in the 1980s and 1990s have exacerbated educational injustices, both distributional and relational, in various ways. In particular, it would seem that: educational resources have effectively been redistributed away from the most vulnerable and towards the most privileged groups of children in society; exploitation of teachers has been intensified; working-class students, particularly boys, and some racialized groups of students have been increasingly marginalized; and opportunities to develop 'pedagogies of recognition' and to undermine the culturally imperialist practices of schools have been heavily circumscribed.

I am sympathetic to the assessment that justice has been a casualty in neo-liberal reform, but my own research leads me to query the way social justice is being evaluated in this study; the way judgements hinge on specific conceptions and horizons for social justice theorizing. Let me illustrate this claim using a short counter-narrative, a vignette that is contextualized in the politics of neo-liberal reform in Australia, specifically Victorian, vocational education.

Post-welfarism and social justice in Australian vocational education

A vignette

> A car manufacturer, about 1993. Serrated factory roofs stand black against a blue dusk sky. Hard light in some windows; glare of furnaces in others. My destination: a brightly lit classroom where men from the melt line had come, after their shift, for literacy classes. The 15 or so ranged in age, spoke many different languages. For some, English was a real struggle. The teacher, an experienced adult educator, knew nothing about cars or technicalities of metal production and fabrication.
>
> This class provided a programme of training qualifying these learners for the competency-based Vehicle Industry Certificate. One man arrived with a briefcase containing the trappings of literate culture – pens, paper, staples, whiteboard markers, hole puncher. The rest were casually dressed but clean. In the first week, they had come straight from 8 hours on the melt line but from then on they had showered and changed before coming to class. 'Sometimes the smell of aftershave is overpowering' the teacher laughed.
>
> The teacher engaged the men in discussion of their work, drawing out and affirming what they knew as a basis for developing language practices. She worked with the engineers to gain technical understandings to integrate into her teaching materials, but she also arranged for the men to meet and talk with the engineers. The melt-line men crossed invisible boundaries between the shopfloor and technical staff to access and appropriate engineers' technical expertise.
>
> The day I attended, the class discussed technicalities of alloy production, using this process to build up a vocabulary and understand the linkages between their work practices and the overall production process. The teacher used the language of the workplace to describe industrial processes. The class spoke and wrote these words, demonstrated them using materials from the plant, looked at fabrication failures, considered how failure rates might be reduced. Those with poor English spoke in their own languages and were translated by their same-language peers. The teacher asked if anyone had a whiteboard marker. The man with the briefcase visibly swelled with pride and took a couple from his briefcase for her. Another younger man was asked to explain the metal failure in a part but was reluctant, hanging his head, too shy to talk. Friends encouraged him, but no, and the teacher moved the discussion on.

About 9 weeks later, I returned to that class. It was 'presentation night'. Each learner had investigated a particular aspect of the production processes and, that night, they presented their research reports and recommendations to management as well as their peers. The project required them to use whatever resources they could find, observing their own and other's work practices, visiting associated sections in the plant, discussing the issues with staff with relevant experience or expertise. Their task was now to report their investigation, outlining what they had done, their findings, and, on the basis of this assessment, their recommendations for improvements in the production process. There was an air of excitement, especially with middle managers sitting in the desks. The reports were presented orally, with supporting overheads. I particularly remember the man who was unwilling to speak just 9 weeks before. He stood up and delivered his report. 'And', he said, standing straight and looking directly at the middle managers sitting in the desks, 'my recommendations for management are . . . '.

This vignette is one window on Australian vocational education in the 1990s when social justice was undercut by the retreat from equality of opportunity and the opening of access through market arrangements. This period was, for some, a dark era when policy conferred 'a dignity and social power' on training that was 'scarcely merited' (Marginson 1997b: 203). It certainly marked a distinctive pattern of policy intervention in Australian education that was also evident world-wide. It has been widely described as a period in which many of the social justice gains in education and training within the Keynesian welfare state were rolled back by market fundamentalism (Robertson 1996; Whitty *et al.* 1998; Gewirtz 2000).

However, let us pause here. Rather than slipping too easily into the research commonsense that these changes drive straightforwardly towards increasing injustice, let us consider what is going on in more detail.

Contextualization

In analysing this vignette, I assume arguments about the shift from an industrial to an informational economy and the growing significance of knowledge, culture and creative capacity at work. These structural and discursive changes provide the preconditions for a new settlement in education. They represent the period of crisis that is both the prelude and outcome of relatively stable institutional arrangements that are, never-the-less, riven with contradictions (Centre for Contemporary Cultural Studies 1981). In this changing social environment, knowledge is increasingly central to economics, and identity and culture are central to cultural change (Castells 1998). These developments challenge Australia's sense and practice of nation, rooted in a monocultural colonial history based upon indigenous dispossession and realized through a centralized statist social order. It is these economic and cultural dynamics, shaped and driven by global developments, that frame a critical contemporary education policy question: how to govern in a way that addresses the challenges of our time but without falling back into monocultural practices of nationhood? Specifically, how does governance accommodate cultural pluralism?

Education[1] as a generic social institution is recognized as a key means of addressing the challenges of knowledge economy and innovation, cultural pluralism and governance. Education has always been structured to tackle these dynamics because its primary capacity is to shape learning (Connell 1995). This priority underpins patterns of action and concrete social structures and organization. It works by developing capacities for social practice that are realized through both individual development and the development of collective capacities for action. Learning creates individual and collective property. It supports responsible participation in work, citizenship and lifeworlds (New London Group 1996).

Yet education, as a social institution, has also been problematized by these broad social changes. For over 100 years, public schools in Australia promised equality of opportunity for all, providing for those children who could not access schooling on a user-pays or faith basis. In practice, this meant equality of starting points: equal opportunity to participate in mainstream school education through the compulsory years and to compete for educational success in academic curriculum and examinations which constituted the pathway to university (Marginson 1997a). In the compulsory years, there was open access to a state-funded school which provided a standardized programme of curriculum and assessment on an equivalent resource base that included trained teachers. Despite comprehensivization, curriculum retained a dualist structure. A bookish academic curriculum, based on that institutionalized in private schools, was available for those students deemed good with their heads (Collins 1992). Others, deemed good with their hands, accessed a technical and pre-vocational curriculum which provided some training for work. Equality of opportunity after the compulsory years was seen largely in terms of the academic pathway which offered access to better employment, and, for some, university education and professional-managerial occupations. The technical pathway just led out of school. While there were apprenticeships and technical education available for some, this was heavily biased towards boys and towards skilled employment. There was no recognition of other formal or informal post-school learning opportunities (Seddon and Deer 1992).

Since the 1960s, these old patterns of state-provided educational provision have become fragmented as cultural pluralism compounded divisions between, and within, public and private schooling. In the 1970s, there were efforts to extend equality of opportunity through the recognition of cultural difference. This generated its own cultural conservative backlash, the standards debate and 'back to basics' movement. In the mid–1980s, these agendas were overtaken by the assertion of market principles and a retreat from equality of opportunity. Asserting access and choice, governments reconfigured education on a market basis, increased access through user-pays, and naturalized attendant inequalities. Individual investment in education was presented as a way of shedding risk of unemployment, but it increased overall inequalities in society (Teese 2000).

Access to education increased but on a declining resource base, undermining the functionality of education, loading social and economic costs onto those who could least sustain them, and creating an increasingly intolerant cultural environment where victims were blamed for their disabilities and disadvantages (Marginson 1997b).

Since the later 1990s, there are some signs that the wheel of public policy may be turning again. Preliminary rethinking in relation to the Washington Consensus and its commitment to market fundamentalism, and struggles around the question of global governance, is beginning to reweight public policy (Stiglitz 2002). The emergent model gives somewhat more weight to 'social development', emphasizing participation over access, active agency over passive dependency, and choice over supply. This reworking of neo-liberal market policies is rooted in growing recognition that (a) the globalization of informational capitalism prioritizes knowledge resources which depends upon social investment in knowledge production and learning; (b) economic productivity is contingent on social and cultural resources (trust, social capital, resources of identity, community development); and (c) the market and community, by themselves, cannot ensure conditions for optimal development. There remains an important role for the state (Beem 1999). Its role, according to Sen (1999: 18), is to sponsor activities that support social and community development and enable individuals to develop and realize their capabilities so that they 'can lead the lives they value, and have reason to value'.

This development discourse frames an integrated reform agenda that affirms 'mutually beneficial exchanges, the working of social safety nets, of political liberties, . . . of social development' (Sen 1999: 35). Education is central. It is identified as the means to social, economic and civic participation, and personal growth that realizes 'capabilities'. These are not potentials (capacities) but 'functionings'; the practical realization of a person's chosen way of life. They depend not only upon individual and organizational capacity-building but also on the construction of conducive contexts, from which 'unfreedoms' (Sen 1999) or constraints have been removed, and within which potentials can be realized in practical action (Seddon and Cairns 2001).

Rhetoric is, of course, cheap, and 'social development' can be framed in different ways (Levitas 1998). What kinds of social justice issues are raised by the vignette?

Justice practices in workplace learning

Structural issues Neo-liberal training reform did increase access to learning. There was no prior educational provision for workers at the operative-level (Brown and Rushbrook 1995). Yet, in 2002, the vocational education and training Student Outcomes Survey reported 20% of graduates were undertaking training to gain skills for work and most of these are likely to be working towards Certificate 2 or 3 qualifications, like the Vehicle Industry Certificate (National Centre for Vocational Education Research 2002: 6–7). The melt-line men would never have received such learning support and literacy education under the old dualist educational structure. They would have just left school and taken a job. They would never receive credentialled training which recognized their skills and enabled transferability of employment. Yet, some of them were well educated in their own countries. It was lack of English and prejudice that restricted their labour market opportunities. Having missed school learning pathways, there was only limited English-classes for migrants to extend their education. School-based equality of opportunity systematically excluded many people, like the melt-line men, often for no fault of their own.

The men clearly gained from literacy education. There were spin-offs in terms of individual learning, personal self-affirmation and growth, and company benefits. This learning was not trivial, although the legacy of the academic–vocational dualism implies that 'training' is always instrumental, mindless, 'undignified'. This mind set is entrenched on both sides of the academic–vocational divide. Unease at VET in schools is one expression of this attitudinal barrier to change (Lasonen and Young 1998); conceptions of work in TAFE that affirms 'hand work' and downplays 'head work' is its vocational education counterpart (Seddon and Malley 1998). However, vocationalism does not by its nature erode solid learning or the kind of open-ended inquiry prized in academic learning contexts; it depends on how vocational learning is orchestrated (Dewey 1925; Billett 2001a,b).

Opening up the training market through the 1990s emphasized 'customer service'. This orientation had costs, especially where market demand became the only criteria for programme viability, but it also encouraged attention to learners. Positive and negative incentives focused educators on student progression, learning processes, support structures and transitions, rather than on organizational and knowledge maintenance in closed systems. The melt-line workers benefited from such customer focus in having carefully contextualized learning programmes rather than submitting to generic programmes taken off the shelf. This kind of provision was available because the car company could contract training providers of their choice and they had approached a training provider which emphasized and marketed careful contextualization of learning as part of its educational approach to training. Without training reform, the melt-line men would have had no access to such training and the training provider, with its highly skilled adult educator, would have had no access to the men.

Training reform, then, gave force to the notion of 'pathways'. On the one hand, the pathway metaphor linked learning to qualifications and career opportunities. On the other hand, it encouraged a quite physical understanding of learning as movement through different learning spaces within which different kinds of learning encounters occur. The metaphor persists as a way of thinking about educational structure in terms of learner flows. As the Victorian Kirby Report (2000: 8) says, 'the focus of provision must be on the needs of young people, not the institutions'.

The focus on learner flows permits a reconsideration of educational structure. It highlights the way learners flow through different sites and the kinds of learning they gain and require at each. Research indicates that many young people enjoy a mixed mode of work and learning, and they package their learning profiles in terms of their preferred mix of work, social activity, relationship-building, and education in line with their future aspirations (Dwyer and Wyn 1998). However, there are marked regional and social disparities in young people's pathways, opportunities, and outcomes (e.g. Lamb 1998; Teese 2000). These are not new disparities and inequalities; they were firmly established by 100 years of dualist educational provision and the longer history of social inequality. They were central to the construction of the post-war welfare state and framed contestation around gender, ethnicity, and race through the 1970s and 1980s (Shaver 1993). The challenge in thinking about educational justice is to avoid recreating the old head–hand structure of education, or formalizing closed-in second-class pathways that offer only parochial or dead-end outcomes. Re-structure, then, depends upon renegotiating content.

Curriculum issues The old head–hand division of curriculum regulated the distribution of 'official knowledges' to learners in different educational sites (Apple 2000). This meant that different culturally specific and variously validated and authorized representations, or knowledge practices, were made available to different kinds of people. Such validation and authorization does not just depend upon academic processes, but also includes other culturally specific processes of knowledge codification and endorsement embedded in the social practices of other particular groups (Farrell 2001).

In this differentiated knowledge bazar, some students did academic school subjects, loading up with content so as to demonstrate the academic performances that provided recognition and positional goods in a literate culture. Others did technical and vocational learning tending towards skills development that also gave admission, albeit to different communities. The hierarchy of knowledge correlated with the hierarchy of social power. Some knowledge was the key to greater social and occupational opportunities. They tended to be textually mediated knowledge practices that also permitted more complex and less context-specific understanding. Yet, as the melt-line class suggests, it doesn't have to be that way.

The melt-line men accessed engineers' knowledge and appropriated it in a way that would not have been possible under the old dualistic curriculum structures. They gained powerful knowledge and it showed in their questions, their confidence, their bearing. These new understandings of the technical characteristics of alloys and production processes did not replace their previous ways of thinking but gave them a language, a set of concepts, a grasp of context and sense of relationships that enabled them to organize their understandings, frame questions, identify problems and solutions, and to conceptualize recommendations. The technical knowledge extended their existing conceptual capacities.

These extended conceptual capacities are important in a context of change. Traditionally, education skilled and disciplined individuals for relatively settled workplaces, citizenries and communities but, now, these are changing. If learning is to support individuals, it must enable learners to reconfigure and produce knowledge and skills that are appropriate to changing contexts and to the different cultural repertoires that are found in them. Building these capacities requires access to established and systematized knowledge resources and also to the metalanguage they provide, enabling learners to grasp concepts, relationships and processes of meaning making, representation and knowing, and to put them to work (New London Group 1996: 72).

These capacities give 'access to knowledges' a different complexion. Research shows that abstracted school subjects have always been exclusionary but powerful (Teese 2000). Concrete practical knowledges have been accessible but opened less doors. The melt-line workers engaged with abstract knowledges in practical contexts, and they were supported as they learned to manipulate the concepts and build their own conceptual understandings of the practical processes of production. Integrating abstract and concrete representations of the world permitted not only understanding but also action: problem-identification, theorizing explanations, conceptualizing solutions, presentation of ideas and framing recommendations.

Such learning combines head and hand knowledge. There is no doubt that it requires opportunities to engage with different knowledge, and to understand differences in knowledge quality – such learning is not a content-free-zone. However, the outcome is a dynamic engagement that has the potential to develop further rather than ossifying into fixed and blinkered conceptions. Such learning permits greater flexibility in understanding and the generation of new ideas, insights, and explanations. Learning becomes a practical constructivist process of meaning-making. It is a process in which knowledge is co-produced as the learner engages with knowledge sources to realize both new meanings and new representations (Lusted 1986). It underpins practical wisdom.

This processual conception of curriculum opens up the kinds of resources that can be used as knowledge sources and ways of engaging with them. In academic schooling, the emphasis was on appropriating abstracted knowledge, using heuristics to manage masses of detail, seeing patterns, and, as learning advanced, identifying discontinuities, developing critique and questions. In more processual learning, the emphasis is on working with knowledge resources and knowledge practices to generate new meanings, understandings and questions. Learning resources do not have to be formalized academic knowledges but can also include experience, practical activities, social situations, all kinds of media products. In a sense, a key task of learning is to develop the skills of intellectual work that provides engagement with both abstract and concrete knowledge sources as a basis for action rather than just appropriating knowledge as property. Friere (1972) made this point long ago.

The trend, evident in the melt-line class, towards reconfiguring learning as a practical and dynamic process is parallelled in many other contexts. These range from the highest academic qualifications (e.g. professional doctorates) (Lee *et al.* 2000), through school education (e.g. Education Queensland 2000) to good vocational educational, as in the melt-line class (Sefton *et al.* 1994). There is much to commend this trend as a basis for curriculum development. It builds on existing curriculum, but actively undercuts the head–hand dichotomy by creating a rich, action-oriented, problem-based learning agenda. Moreover, it addresses cultural diversity in productive ways, providing opportunities for learners to acknowledge and work with difference as a basis for realizing productive diversity at work, civic pluralism, and rich multi-layered lifeworlds (New London Group 1996: 71).

Yet, through the 1990s, the curriculum trend went in the opposite direction. Rather than celebrating open-ended learning that could sustain intellectual skill development and risk-taking, conceptual flexibility, and the capacity to innovate, outcomes were pre-specified in increasingly fine detail, monocultural teaching programmes and standards implemented. Competency-based training (CBT) pressed vocational education towards narrow and fragmented behavioural outcomes defined in relation to current, rather than future, industry needs. The end-of-school Victorian Certificate of Education was cut back to affirm an exam format, and age-old school subjects were reasserted as Key Learning Areas.

Two points here. First, there is no doubt that good vocational teachers, like the teacher working with melt-line workers, worked around the CBT specification to support rich learning that was attuned to good occupational practice (Billett *et al.* 1999). In this factory classroom, the teacher aimed to develop 'holistic competence' that gave learners broad understandings, a sense of linguistic processes, and personal empowerment rather than being driven by 'tick-a-box' behavioural competencies. And this kind of good practice is evident in all other sectors of education where educators are resisting the hollowing-out of education's core institutional practices as much through innovation as defensive tactics (Seddon 2000).

Secondly, what underpins these curriculum politics is judgements about what knowledge – cultural content – is of most worth. Cultural diversity makes it increasingly difficult to assert that the cultural resources of one group – conservative educational or vocational interests – are the best and that everyone should be inducted into them, irrespective of the success or failure of the induction, or the relevance of these knowledge resources in a changing world. However, it is also unhelpful to proliferate specialist knowledges based on special interests and identities. This only encourages tribalism and cultural fragmentation.

This dilemma provides another argument for learners developing a metalanguage to capture knowledge processes and, through that, developing a capacity to produce, transact and judge knowledge. It is a traditional idea – submitting knowledge to the 'tribunal of reason'. While this is not a simple notion, and as Saul (2001) argues, reason must be tempered by other ways of knowing there is a sense that the capacity to consider knowledge claims on the basis of evidence and argument is an important protection in a democratic society.

As these points suggest there are real problems with the head–hand divisions of knowledge and their social effects. These historic consequences are accentuated as justice and social problems in contemporary 'knowledge society'. An educational structure for 'new times' cannot support the re-development of such dualistic education, but it also cannot mean a lack of engagement with content. Rather, it requires curriculum that (a) gives access to diversified knowledge resources (including traditional academic and practical knowledge, experience, practical action and media products) by orchestrating learners engagement in sites where different culturally specific representations and knowledge practices are located, not only as abstracted representations but also embedded in practical action (like getting to melt-line workers to talk with engineers); (b) develops capacities for intellectual work in relation to these knowledge resources that sustain knowledge production, critique, communication, and validation, as well as opportunities to use these knowledge practices; and (c) builds an appreciation of and capacity for reason, evidence and argument, and the importance of these processes in judging knowledge quality. Realizing this specification of curriculum depends, however, on the availability of appropriate infrastructural resources and processes: pedagogy, assessment, teacher development and organizational development.

Infrastructural supports As the vignette implies, the teacher's work was a key element in making the worker's learning possible. Given the opportunity for the melt-line men and the teacher to work together, the teacher orchestrated social learning activities that made the integration of head and hand knowledges and the development of a meta-language, possible. It involved creating sites where learners could engage with new knowledge sources, developing strategies to drive the learning process, giving support when they took the risks necessary for learning, encouraging them and recognizing them as intellectual workers (e.g. by recognizing one man as someone who *would* carry whiteboard markers). It also meant being a knowledge-source in her own right and engaging with the learners and pushing them along in her core knowledge areas. This is relationship-building at its best: challenging, caring, guiding and cajoling. This pedagogy, orchestrating the learning contexts, contents, processes, relationships and performances, is fundamental to learning.

Yet, market reform in both school and vocational education and training marginalized teachers. It excluded them from decision-making; tightly controlled their work through work redesign on inadequate funding, as well as through control technologies like CBT; and in VET eroded the qualifications base in the occupation. Now, with an ageing workforce and indications of poor quality training provision (including fraud (Schofield 2000)), there is slow recognition of the need to rebuild the skill base and re-acknowledge the value of professional responsibility as a quality mechanism in education (Malley *et al.* 1999).

Assessment (especially when tied directly to funding) is a critical incentive in learning. Defining what is assessable defines what must be learned; using what is measurable as the assessment unduly narrows curriculum. CBT drives vocational education in a behaviourist direction where underpinning knowledge is disregarded (Rumsey 1997). Academic assessment drives school and university education towards an abstracted, cognitive, and individualistic mode of learning that has been shown to be discriminatory (Teese 2000), and a poor preparation for people dealing with change (Rumsey 2001). Both are inadequate by themselves – even industry bodies are recognizing this (Ballenden 2001). Teachers do not structure curriculum and pedagogy in contradiction to assessment and credentialing processes. This would disadvantage learners and professional responsibility would not permit it. The melt-line workers could learn lots because the competencies were treated as a minimum required for the certificate. With this in hand, there was scope for more extended learning.

The teacher at the car plant was not a conventional technical teacher formed within the academic–vocational binary and oriented to technical skill-formation. Rather, she was an 'applied adult educator' who practiced integrated learning that combined development of knowledge and skills, enhanced literacy practices, and personal relationship-building. The teacher could do this work because of her social and cultural formation, and also because she embodied appropriate knowledge resources. These knowledge resources did not include the engineers knowledge, although she did re-work what she gained from the engineers as classroom materials. Her knowledge related to pedagogy, assessment, creating sites for social learning, working with difference and social justice.

The teacher worked alone in her class, but, in reality, she was the front-line for a wider educational organization: a small training provider. Her work would not have been possible without the infrastructure provided by that organization, the managers and office staff that worked within it, other teachers with whom she engaged, and the public funds used to support this training. Beyond this infrastructure were wider supports: the car company that purchased workforce training, the training market, the policy context that made all this happen. Some of this infrastructure constrains practice: the deskilling effects of CBT and training reform; attrition of experienced teachers which withdraws knowledge resources from the public education and training system; and persistence of funding based on contact hours, which does not acknowledge the developmental and pedagogical work that underpins good learning (Billett *et al.* 1999; Malley *et al.* 1999). These contextual features all depend upon the exercise of embodied knowledge – lots of people using their capacities to problem-solve and implementing strategies that are intended to make a difference in training reform. They can only be changed through changes in people and their work practices, creating both the practical capacities required to support learning and the political and organizational will to re-organize contexts so that functionalities that support learning can be realized. It depends not on social justice in the abstract but on lived justice within the social practices at every level of everyday life – from immediate face-to-face relations in classrooms to the highest levels of government. Let me now consider these two analyses of social justice under post-welfarism.

Evaluating justice judgements

Evaluative judgements are always framed conceptually and empirically. In *The Managerial School*, Gewirtz (2000) uses a distributive-relational conception of social justice to interpret empirical data on English school education and comes to the view that post-welfarist schooling is unjust. In the vignette discussed here, the empirical base lay in vocational education and, specifically, in the shadow-world of adult learning in industry contexts. This is hardly the realm of popular education, but, equally, it is not what the Centre for Contemporary Cultural Studies termed 'unpopular education' (CCCS 1981).

The evaluation of social justice was conducted within a similar distributive-relational framework to that used by Gewirtz, but embellished by a closer focus on the lived justice associated with changing capacities to act within localized settings. Pressing this evaluative framework beyond assessment of policy to the micro-level permits some assessment of localized praxis or, in development-speak, change rooted in enhanced capacity and capability and realized through individual and organizational development.

Capacities to act were assessed not in relation to some fixed standard, like Year 12 completion or examination success, but in terms of those actor's life contexts. The melt-line man was affirmed when he could provide the whiteboard marker. The man who reported had found his voice and used it to speak back to management. The teacher, in a marketized context, tailored her ways of working to this specific policy and learning context. Within it she was able to develop creative pedagogic practices which touched not only the men from the melt-line, but also other workers, shop stewards, company management, the men's union, and, because of the success of this programme, the wider vocational education and training practice and policy. Within the concept of relational justice, such practices could be said to address powerlessness, facilitate contestation of exploitative relations, and address the kinds of cultural imperialism that occurs when teachers disregard what learners already know and the knowledge of worth to them. And yet, these justice practices are occuring within a post-welfarist context.

There are certainly questions that should be asked about the kinds of capacities that are being built here (Lawn 2001). Does such capacity-building contribute to the formation of a more individuated, self-regulating society or to a social order in which there is greater scope for participation and self-determination? What is the social and political difference in these linguistic representations? It is true that this programme operated outside what is commonly regarded as mainstream educational structures and the teacher could not be a member of the teachers' union because she worked in a 'private' training provider (despite receiving 70% of the budget from government, in the form of contestable not recurrent funding). Yet, this programme was fully endorsed and supported not just by the company but also by the metalworkers union to which the melt-line men belonged. However, to accept this positioning of the melt-line men as a particular category of learners outside the horizons of the conventional education and training system is to simultaneously accept and privilege the institutional and discursive framing of welfarism with its historic commitment to school education. And, clearly, welfarist education as an institution had long ago marginalized these melt-line men.

My point is that, while Gewirtz social justice audit is premised upon a similar conception of social justice, it comes to somewhat different judgements. Gewirtz's view that post-welfarist education is unjust only partially matches my own judgement: that post-welfarist education is unjust in some respects. There is evidence of increased inequality in terms of some aggregate patterns of access, content, control and recognition, but there are also aggregate data that show increased access albeit to less well resourced provision, except where private funding is available. Such data are evidence of changing opportunities for learning that do enhance both individual and collective capacities to act.

I would argue that such enhanced capacity to act is a kind of justice practice, a principle of justice. Its consequences are not particularly evident at the level of conventional aggregate effects, such as academic achievement, although they are more evident in some recent attempts to assess outcomes in terms of participation and equity (e.g. PISA). It is difficult to be sure what the longer term impact of these changing individual and collective capacities to act might be, although, as in welfarism, most educators justify individual learning on the assumption that if you can change people's hearts and minds, you ultimately have an effect on society. In my experience, the belief that education makes a difference persists amongst teachers, whether they are working in welfarist or post-welfarist contexts, or in a school or in the vocational sector. Adult educators, in particular, demonstrate a clear understanding of the way their educational work contributes to praxis and social change. Whatever the long-term implications of these changing capacities to act, the issue is that, within the melt-line, men's particular post-welfarist educational environment there is not only evidence of social justice but evidence of an increase in justice practices compared to that which occurred within welfarist education.

These differences in the two evaluations of social justice are, as Sen (1999) suggests, a consequence of the different information judged to be significant by each of the evaluator's. These judgements about what counts as important information are contingent upon the complex conceptualizations that layer upon one another to define relevant evidence of identifiable justice ethics within specific educational contexts which are themselves being shaped by the wider dynamics and lived processes of social change. Indeed, I was motivated to write this paper because of the conceptual dissonance I experienced when reading *The Managerial School* and the way the conceptual layering converged with and diverged from my own assumptions about the world.

It is clear that this dissonance is not just an individual matter but, rather, raises questions about the framing of research on social justice and in policy sociology. It appears as the development of what I have termed a research commonsense about neo-liberal education reform. This research commonsense is a particular framing of neo-liberal education reform which retains certain taken-for-granted assumptions about the relationship between policy discourse and policy effects; about the historicity of education systems and the continuing validity of welfarist institutional and discursive horizons (especially the privilege accorded to school education); the framing of evidence, and the way the researcher's understanding of social change influences what is taken as a decisive indicator of justice. I consider each of these in turn.

The relationship between policy discourse and policy effects

There is now substantial education research which analyses neo-liberal education policy and its marketizing trajectory, and maps its policy effects within education and training institutions and those who work and learn within them. This has involved significant attention to the disjunctures between the writing and reading of policy, with considerable ethnographic evidence showing that participants renegotiate policy in its enactment. Yet, despite these conceptual and empirically evident disjunctures, the overall tenor of these analyses is of loss.

The case of the melt-line men provides, I hope, an indication of the roots of my unease at these kinds of interpretations. My own research on the impact of neo-liberal reform in Australian education certainly confirms some of these trends, but it also reveals neo-liberal reform to be much more contested and double edged than is sometimes suggested. It is also dynamic. There have been shifts in the way the state is orchestrating its reform agenda, driven by both large-scale historical dynamics and practical politics. Free market discourse is increasingly tempered by the recognition of the distinctive role of the state. While market mechanisms remain, they are being re-worked towards goals that are more alert to social development and the importance of co-operation rather than competition. In Victoria, at least, the education debate is focused more on participation than privatization.

These developments are shaped by defensive strategies aimed at protecting education and social justice, as well as by innovative developments that are re-working and re-norming educational practice without letting go of fundamental justice commitments (Angus and Seddon 2000). The effect is to contest as well as re-sediment 'sets of languages, meanings, assumptions, values and institutional forms, practices and relationships' (Gewirtz 2000: xi), including those related to social justice. In making this claim, I do not want to overstate the importance of voluntaristic struggles or minor variations in state practices. Yet, equally, I do not want to discount them entirely.

There is a genuine research question here about the way social structure and obdurate practices of possession/dispossession and domination/subordination interface with the kind of indeterminacy celebrated in post-structural analysis. There is no doubt that unequal social relations persist. The state pursues its structural agenda, but not in a consistent or coherent way. The empirical picture is of small steps, difficult to judge without the benefit of hindsight, but likely to be both gains and losses. Theoretically, this practical interface between structure and indeterminacy has long been recognized. For Touraine (1981), these small steps are what constitutes social movement. Or, in other lexicons, class struggle (Marx 1976b), creative destruction (Schumpeter 1934), or the 'dissolution–renovation' dynamic in Marx's (1964) more historical writings. However, while such metaphors at least name the practices that constitute this interface, it is less clear how the mundane and discrepant practices of everyday life coalesce beyond tactics and strategies into social movement (Skeggs 1997).

The historicity of education and social justice

To my (Australian) eye, the institutionalization of educational practice has been in crisis since the 1960s when teachers, parents and various other social groups contested the centralization and monoculturalism of state authority within education and asserted their claim for recognition and voice. There is little sign of this crisis of institutionalization abating and this means that, as a researcher, I assume continuing slippage and contestation around discursive and institutional practices of educational justice. Whether or not the current re-sedimenting of institutional and discursive practices within education leading to the institutionalization of markets and managerialism in a new settlement is an open question. Its resolution will depend on hindsight and the construction and conceptualization of historical narratives. Whether, with time, this new settlement will be termed 'post-welfarist' is also open to question. While it is useful to name the constellation of recent changes in education, I think that 'post-welfarism' is too referenced to the past; a past that is located within school education, a past that is particularly English, and a past that institutionalized a particular and limited conception and practice of social justice.

My point is that the object of analysis – education and social justice – is a moving target. The historicity of these social dynamics and their effects needs to be acknowledged. This acknowledgement is evident in parts of *The Managerial School*, but, in the audit, Gewirtz (2000) makes judgements and then constantly qualifies them in historical terms. What does one make of such qualifications? Saying that education under post-welfarism is unjust in distributive and relational terms, but that this is not to say that welfarism was innocent of injustice, tells us little. To say that welfarist and post-welfarist education is unjust, but to different degrees, also adds little to our understanding of how social justice is being re-worked practically in the messy and uneven transition from welfarism to post-welfarism. There is a truckload of evidence of injustice within welfarist education – this was the bread and butter of sociology of education for decades (Centre for Contemporary Cultural Studies 1981; Crouch and Heath 1992), but where is there continuity and where is there change in the pattern of justice and injustice in the two regimes? Is it possible for the post-welfarist educational settlement to have *no* justice practices at all?

Gewirtz argues that the institutional and discursive frames of education have shifted with the institutionalization of post-welfarist provision. Might this mean that what we should 'see' as justice practices have shifted too because they are embedded in, rather than abstracted from, educational practice and its institutionalization? One of the limitations of audit technologies is the way an audit framework is set up by abstracting historically specific practices from their institutional locations and then ajudicating other historically specific practices against them. Perhaps it is this technologization that shapes what is seen as social justice in line with justice practices under welfarism. The implication is that welfarism predisposes us to see justice in particular practices which are premised upon specific welfarist constellations and interpretations of justice principles. Assessing the practices that are commonplace within post-welfarist contexts against the welfarist reference points will almost inevitably reveal reduced justice. Yet, in such an analysis, the judgement of injustice within post-welfarist education could be seen as an artefact of this process of abstraction within the audit technology. Equally, the way injustice under welfarism is noted as a simple qualification to the judgement about post-welfarism may also be a consequence of the assumptions embedded in the audit technology.

The framing of evidence

The conception of social justice that is embedded within the audit technology will influence what is 'seen' and counted as social justice, and what is taken to be decisive evidence of justice practices. In *The Managerial School*, the focus on distributive and relational justice leads to an assessment of justice practices in terms of who has what and how relationships are orchestrated and ordered within social relations and institutions. Yet, other justice ethics alert us to further dimensions of justice and injustice. For instance, libertarian ethics, along the lines articulated by Nozik, are significant in post-welfarist education. It is this kind of conception of social justice that provides a moral justification for market reform and the privileging of property rights and market freedoms. It means that, in post-welfarist education, there will always be dilemmas around the concept of 'freedom'. However, as Gale (2000) argues, the affirmation of freedom is important in education because it highlights instances where, for example, individuals are unable to exercise their talents and develop their capacities (rather like the melt-line men prior to training reform). In this sense, the concept of 'freedom' converges with Gewirtz's marginalization as an injustice. However, freedom within the libertarian ethic also encourages a retributive and punishment orientation that falls most heavily on those who infringe other's (property) rights and (market) freedoms. It is also used against those who don't conform to prevailing market norms – including those professionals, bureaucrats and schools that are said to be 'failing' young people who are at risk of social exclusion. What counts as justice is framed by the justice ethics selected and the way that particular ethical discourse reveals and obscures educational practice.

What counts as decisive evidence of social justice is also framed institutionally and in time and space. It is significant that *The Managerial School*, like most education research, treats school education as the conceptual horizon for inquiry. The story of the melt-line men troubles the assessment of social justice precisely because it is the story of a social group to whom significant injustice has already been done because of the way school education was institutionalized – both as a provision for the young, excluding adults, and as a provision based on academic and, therefore, class traditions. Post-welfarism has problematized the traditional boundaries of school education and, while it does enhance distributive injustice in some respects, it has also enhanced distributive justice in others. This is relevant not just in terms of access to learning but also in relation to the codification and valuation of knowledge. Market reform, particularly through the critique of universities, has problematized traditional knowledge hierarchies and the processes of codification and valuation upon which they depended (e.g. Gibbons *et al.* 1994). It has also encouraged a diversification of provision both in form and content, spilling over from the traditional frames of welfarist school education to enable provision that is more attuned to specific identities (Seddon 2001). In a closed system, like traditional school education, it is relatively easy to see these developments as incidental to the main game: there may be greater choice in school subjects, but the selective mechanisms still operate as they always have (Teese 1981, 2000). However, in a more open system, in which boundaries are more porous and new learning spaces are opening up inside and outside traditional education and training, the social significance of these developments and their relationship to traditional social hierarchies are less clear. It is possible, as Gale and Densmore (2001) suggest, that these challenges to the institutions of knowledge codification and the diversification of curricula do mark some sort of shift away from the justice practices of welfarism and that alternative justice practices are possible.

The time/space framing in the social justice audit is not addressed in detail. In *The Managerial School*, Gewirtz (2000) claims wide applicability for her analysis of post-welfarist education on the grounds that data from her research sites, London schools, is the experience of 'an archetypically post-welfarist environment' (p. xii) that will be familiar to other schools in England and other countries where similar reforms have occurred. Just as Gewirtz downplays the institutional frames of school education in her assessment of social justice, she also disregards the institutional frames of England. Yet, England is renowned for its 'exceptionalism' (Anderson 1964; Hutton 1996), its historically weak state and powerful local networks, its market pre-occupations and its celebration of a post-aristocratic amateur culture (Seddon 1996). In English education, autonomy from the unitary central state was orchestrated through the welfarist partnership, so that the influence of central government on schools and teachers was mediated by Local Education Authorities. These features are very different in Australia where there is a federal structure of government and yet a highly centralized statist tradition of education orchestrated through the State, rather than Commonwealth level of government. In this context, the impact of the central state is mediated by State and Territory governments. Within States, with weak local networks, a highly centralized mixed economy educational model has long been institutionalized with strong utilitarin pre-occupations and a pragmatic increasingly 'can-do' culture (Musgrave 1992).

These contextual variations highlight the distinctiveness of different education systems and the importance of their historicity. It also underscores the significance of comparative analysis, not so much as a basis for systemic description but as a stimulus to methodological debate which encompasses conceptualization and ways of understanding, and also issues related to the conscious and unconscious shaping of the research process.

Theorizing social change and the evidence of justice admitted

A central issue in such methodological debate is the question of how understandings and experience of social change influences research practice. In the conduct of any research, there is a tension between the research process and the practical experience of living inside complex historical change. Research rightly uses distance and abstraction in order to reveal social structuring, historical trends and patterns of injustice. However, such research interpretation can never be entirely disconnected from the researcher's socio-cultural positioning and from the everyday practices and politics of work-life. In managing insider–outsider insights, the researcher must be clear and reflective about the way research practice is being shaped as the lived point of connection between historicity, sedimented outcomes and social structures. How one conceptualizes this point of connection as a working theory of social change is critical for contemporary social analysis because it determines the kind of information that is selected in or excluded from the process of reaching evaluative judgements.

It is difficult to see distributive and relational justice in the present, at the moment when the day-to-day waves of continuity and change actually break. In every contemporary context, there are a range of justice ethics in play and this creates dilemmas in ethical practice. For instance, within welfarism there was a convergence between distributive justice and utilitarianism. The degree of convergence is context-dependent and can have a profound effect on lived justice practices, privileging the assessment of consequences over the priority accorded to rights. This makes sense in practical ways, particularly when there is serious material deprivation. What should come first: needs that must be addressed as a matter of life and death, or rights and liberty? The diversity of ethical discourse also means that there are real linguistic complexities within particular sites. Terms like 'freedom', 'rights', 'utility' can mean many things and can operate at quite different levels of analysis. Without a detailed sense of either the features or contextualization of these different justice ethics it becomes difficult to 'see' and 'read' justice practices in different social contexts or to disaggregate the different justice ethics that become muddled up and integrated into everyday practice (Gale 2000).

These processes of change and continuity and the muddle of justice ethics can be lived in different ways. Sennet (1998: 29–30) suggests, for instance, that current pressures for flexibility and the disorganization of time means that people commonly live change in a quite contradictory way. On the one hand, there is a kind of drifting experience in which events seem to be beyond control and, on the other, resistance to this flux leads people to become trapped in a defensive but static assertion of fundamental values. He argues that what is missing in this polarity is a narrative that permits and gives shape to the forward movement of events and time. It raises questions about the narrative structure informing the two evaluations of social justice and how they are contextualized. Is it, perhaps, that Australian utilitarianism and education politics predispose me to tell the melt-line men's story as a story of innovation? Is it also that the lived experience of central government challenge to education's relative autonomy in England influences English policy sociology interpretations of English post-welfarist education?

Such insider–outsider issues have implications for the selection of evidence of social justice because the interface between the lived experience and conceptualization of change shapes what is seen as change and continuity, and the meaning accorded to these different developments. The social justice audit, in *The Managerial School*, focused its assessment of post-welfarist justice practice by setting ethnographic data against a particular set of justice principles. This assessment is inevitably retrospective in character. Data already available are considered *post hoc*, permitting a distanced judgement about the effects of policy when one has the advantage of hindsight. Yet, the pre-conditions for this analytical maneouvre rest up a determination of what is significant in terms of continuity and change, and this is likely to be influenced by experience as well as research. As the analytical distance between past and present is reduced, the clarity of vision that is possible through retrospective analysis receeds and the researcher is required to make judgements about what counts or not in the lived muddle of justice ethics, meanings and practices that constitute every contemporary context. In the context of regime change, such abstraction and assessment of significance is doubly hard because meanings and practices can be read as differentially referenced to the imperatives of welfarism and post-welfarism. In 'new times', then, assessment of justice will mean moving beyond the consideration of conventional policy effects, social structures and established patterns of agency within familiar institutional horizons. It means identifying information that is indicative of justice practices: in the context of ambiguous justice ethics and diverse patterns of accommodation, resistance and innovation; in the way people mobilize and respond in different contexts; and in the discursive politics and silences which contest particular ways of knowing and coalesce as 'structures of feeling' (Yeatman 1994; Jones 1999).

Of course, these methodological issues cannot be deciphered on the basis of just a journal article and book chapter. Yet, there are differences in the data sources used to judge justice in the two cases. The implication is that, while the ethnographic data that Gewirtz uses in her social justice audit provides important insights into these social practices of change as well as the policy effects of post-welfarism, a different working theory of social change can justify the inclusion of other data as decisive evidence of justice practice. In the Australian vignette, for instance, further ethnographic data focused on individual patterns of practice within institutional constraints, and opportunities revealed justice practices rooted in individual and collective capacity and capability. They illuminated the way people negotiate regime change on a day-to-day basis and their scope for living the life they value. Political arithmetic research contributes by monitoring the brute movements of people, patterns of activity, and opinion within social systems, and revealing where individual movement is being repatterned within regime shifts, as in the data relating to the take up of Certificate 2 and 3 level training as a consequence of training reform. Such data provide a picture, albeit crude and approximate, of what is happening at the critical moment when present becomes past and can begin to shed light on emerging structures of feeling and the tentative first steps of collective mobilization.

Conclusion

This paper has used a small vignette to raise questions about the social justice audit conducted by Gewirtz and, more generally, about the way research in policy sociology is framing studies of post-welfarist education conceptually and empirically. Conceptually, I am troubled by the theory of social change that appears to inform and shape the analysis of post-welfarism. Empirically, I think it is important to assess both the generality and localism of the English narrative of post-welfarist reform in education in a globalizing world and also diversify the kinds of information that can be considered decisive in assessing justice. The analysis leads to a series of conclusions about both social justice and research.

Turning to social justice, my view is that there are no necessary connections between post-welfarism and social justice. To suggest as much implies a level of over-determination which I don't think the evidence sustains. It, therefore, does not seem appropriate to talk of an 'archetypal post-welfarist environment' which is somehow applicable across contexts, especially given the complexities of globalism. It seems more appropriate to conceptualize the way justice practices are embedded, contested and reworked within the shifting institutional and discursive frames of education as a social institution – and increasingly this is much more than school education (Lawn 2001). The social organization of learning that is the fundamental feature of education as an institution is constituted within the 'dissolution–renovation' dynamics of social movement; the processes of educational formation that arise from systematic structuring within social relations and the distinctively patterned manifestations of state agency; and the day-to-day practical politics of social actors working and learning in and around different educational spaces. What is generalizable and specific in these different contexts, and what is changing and what is continuous, is a matter for debate and systematic research.

The implication of this analysis is that social justice in education hinges on the way contexts, access, content and control are institutionalized and regulated within the dynamic interplay of obdurate social relations and voluntaristic social action which is willed for and worked for. The Centre for Contemporary Cultural Studies (CCCS 1981) made this point long ago. However, as the story of the melt-line men suggests, these social justice hotspots in education are realized in different, contextually specific ways. They take different forms as a consequence of both the historical legacies within particular societies and cultures and the ongoing struggles for social justice in an unequal world. The point is that, while the structures for justice persist, their form and content is historically and spatially specific. Such historicity need not imply a 'celebration-of-indeterminancy' approach (p. x) but, rather, encourages a conceptualization of social change that is premised on praxis and recognizes not only the 11th Fuerbach Thesis, but also the 3rd. The 3rd thesis explicitly addresses the relationship between social change, learning and the role of the educator. It concludes not by affirming the educator, but by stressing the importance of understanding and engaging with 'revolutionising practice' that arises in the coincidence of changing circumstances and human activity (Marx 1976a: 618–19).

These issues clearly have implications for research in policy sociology. Gewirtz is right to assert the importance of structural determination and the role of the state in shaping education and its justice practices. However, in recognizing obdurate social structures, the task of research is also to document, interrogate, and critique historicized social practices (the 'revolutionizing practice') to reveal social movement and the processes through which it is realized in the everyday practices that move from past to present and future. Given this conception of social change, I find it counter-intuitive to imagine any historical period that only realizes injustice in education, for every period brings its own forms of justice and injustice. While the explication of the audit technology may partially account for Gewirtz's findings, I think there may also be value in reflecting further to refine the conceptual and empirical basis of the interpretation, its explicit and less obvious frames of reference, its designation of decisive information as evidence of justice, and, hence, its conceptual and empirical limits.

Acknowledgements

I thank John Freeland, Trevor Gale, Sharon Gewirtz, Jenny Ozga, Colleen Ryan, Pat Thompson and an anonymous reviewer for their valuable contributions in the development of this paper.

Note

1 'Education' is used as a generic institutional term to describe the organizational field concerned with learning across the population. It includes formalized provision through schools, TAFE Institutes, universities, community providers, and other private providers. It also increasingly encompasses informal learning contexts in community settings and workplaces.

References

Ackerly, B. A. (2000) *Political Theory and Feminist Social Criticism* (Cambridge: Cambridge University Press).

Andeerson, P. (1964) Origins of the present crisis, *New Left Review*, 144, 26–53.

Angus, L. and Seddon, T. (2000) The social and organisational renorming of education, in T. Seddon and L. Angus (eds) *Reshaping Australian education: beyond nostalgia* (Camberwell: Australian Council for Educational Research).

Apple, M. (2000) What postmodernists forgot: cultural capital and official knowledge, in H. Lauder, P. Brown, A. Stuart Wells and A. H. Halsey (eds) *Education: culture, economy and society* (Oxford: Oxford University Press), pp. 595–604.

Ball, S. J., Bowe, R. and Gewirtz, S. (1996) School choice, social class and distinction: the realization of social advantage in education, *Journal of Education Policy*, 11, 89–112.

Ballenden, C. (2001) Skills for the 21st century: the limits of training packages, in F. Bevan, C. Kanes and D. Roebuck (eds) *Knowledge demands for the new economy*, Vol. 1 (Brisbane: Centre for Learning and Work Research, Griffith University).

Beem, C. (1999) *The necessity of politics: reclaiming American public life* (Chicago, IL: University of Chicago Press).

Billett, S. (2001a) *Learning in the workplace: strategies for effective practice* (Sydney: Allen and Unwin).

Billett, S. (2001b) Workplace pedagogic practices: participatory factors in localised arrangements, in F. Bevan, C. Kanes and D. Roebuck (eds) *Knowledge demands for the new economy*, Vol. 1 (Brisbane: Centre for Learning and Work Research, Griffith University).

Billett, S., McKavanagh, C., Beven, F., Hayes, S., Angus, L., Seddon, T., Gough, J. and Robertson, I. (1999) *The CBT decade: teaching for flexibility and adaptability* (Adelaide: National Council for Vocational Education Research).

Brown, M. and Rushbrook, P. (1995) Bringing in the operative: case studies in work-based training and micro-economic reform, in F. Ferrier and C. Selby Smith (eds) *Economics of education and training 1995* (Canberra: Australian Government Publishing Service).

Castells, M. (1998) *The end of millennium* (Cambridge: Blackwell).

Centre for Contemporary Cultural Studies (1981) *Unpopular education: Schooling and social democracy in England since 1944* (London: Hutchinson).

Collins, C. (1992) The academic curriculum, in T. Seddon and C. E. Deer (eds) *A curriculum for the senior secondary years* (Hawthorne: Australian Council For Educational Research).

Connell, R. W. (1995) Education as transformative work, in M. Ginsburg (ed.) *The politics and culture of educators work* (New York: Garland).

Crouch, C. and Heath, A. (1992) *Social research and social reform: essays in honour of A. H. Halsey* (Oxford: Oxford University Press).

Dale, R. (1989) *Education and the state* (Milton Keynes: Open University Press).

Dewey, J. (1925) *How we think: a restatement of the relation of reflective thinking to the educative process* (Carbondale, IL: Southern Illinois University Press).

Dwyer, P. and Wyn, J. (1998) Post-compulsory education policy in Australia and its impact on participant pathways and outcomes in the 1990, *Journal of Education Policy*, 13, 285–300.

Education Queensland (2000) New basics project: Technical paper, Http://Www.Education.Qld.Gov.Au/Corporate/Newbasics/, visited 23 July 2001.

Farrell, L. (2001) The new work order, *Pedagogy, Culture and Society*, 9(1), 57–74.

Freire, P. (1972) *Cultural action for freedom* (Harmondsworth: Penguin).

Gale, T. (2000) Rethinking social justice in schools: how will we recognise it when we see it? *International Journal of Inclusive Education*, 4, 253–69.

Gale, T. and Densmore, K. (2001) *Just Schooling* (Milton Keynes: Open University).

Gewirtz, S. (1998) Conceptualising social justice in education: mapping the field, *Journal of Education Policy*, 13, 469–84.

Gewirtz, S. (2000) *The managerial school* (London: Routledge).

Gibbons, M., Limoges, C., Nowotny, H., Schwartzmann, S., Scott, P. and Trow, M. (1994) *The new production of knowledge: the dynamics of science and research in contemporary societies* (London: Sage).

Haug, F. (1984) Marx and work: the immizeration discourse or the logic of ruptures and contradictions, in S. Hanninen and L. Paldan (eds) *Rethinking Marx* (Berlin: Argument).

Hutton, W. (1996) *The state we're in* (London: Vintage).

Jones, K. (1999) In the shadow of the centre-left: post conservative politics and rethinking educational change, *Discourse*, 20(2), 235–47.

Kirby, P. C. (2000) *Ministerial review of post compulsory education and training pathways in Victoria* (Melbourne: Department of Education, Employment and Training).

Lamb, S. (1998) Completing school in Australia: trends in the 1990s, *Australian Journal of Education*, 42, 1.

Lasonen, J. and Young, M. (1998) *Strategies for achieving parity of esteem in Eurpoean upper secondary education* (Finland: Institute for Educational Research, University of Jyvaskyla).

Lawn, M. (2001) Borderless education: imagining a european education space in a time of brands and networks, *Discourse*, 22(2), 173–84.

Lee, A., Green, B. and Brennan, M. (2000) Organisational knowledge, professional practice and the professional doctorate at work, in J. Garrick and C. Rhodes (eds) *Research and knowledge at work* (London: Routledge).

Levitas, R. (1998) *The inclusive society? Social exclusion and new labour* (London: Macmillan).

Lusted, D. (1986) Introduction – why pedagogy?, *Screen*, 27, 2–15.

Malley, J., Hill, R., Putland, C., Shah, C. and McKenzie, P. (1999) Trends in the tafe institute workforce and their implications for the training and development of tafe staff, 1998–2008, draft report, Melbourne: Monash University-ACER Centre for the Economics of Education and Training, and Chisholm Centre for Innovation and Research.

Marginson, S. (1997a) *Markets in education* (Cambridge: Cambridge University Press).

Marginson, S. (1997b) *Educating Australia: government, economy and citizen since 1960* (Cambridge: Cambridge University Press).

Marx, K. (1964) *Pre-capitalist economic formations* (New York: International Publishers).

Marx, K. (1976a) *Capital*, Vol. 1 (Harmondsworth: Penguin).

Marx, K. (1976b) Theses on Feuerbach, in *The German ideology* (Moscow: Progress Publishers).

Musgrave, P. (1992) *From humanity to utility: Melbourne University and public examinations 1856–1964* (Melbourne: Australian Council for Educational Research).

National Centre for Vocational Education Research (2002) *Student outcome survey: in summary* (Adelaide: National Centre for Vocational Education Research)

New London Group (1996) A pedagogy for multiliteracies: designing social futures, *Harvard Educational Review*, 66, 60–92.

Nussbaum, M. (1999) A plea for difficulty, in S. M. Okin (ed.) *Is multiculturalism bad for women?* (Princeton, NJ: Princeton University Press).

Robertson, S. (1996) Markets and teacher professionalism: a political economy analysis, *Melbourne Studies in Education*, 37, 23–39.

Rumsey, D. (1997) *Reporting of assessment outcomes within competency-based training and assessment programs under the new apprenticeships* (Brisbane: Australian National Training Authority).

Rumsey, D. (2001) Learning to deal with change in the workplace, Unpublished PhD thesis, Deakin University, Melbourne.

Saul, J. R. (2001) *On equilibrium* (Camberwell: Penguin).

Schofield, K. (2000) *Delivering quality: report of the independent review of the quality of training in Victoria's apprenticeship and traineeship system* (Melbourne: Department of Education, Employment and Training).

Schumpeter, J. (1934) *The theory of economic development* (Cambridge, MA: Harvard University Press).

Seddon, T. (1988) Schooling, state and society: the federation settlement in NSW, 1900s to the 1930s, Unpublished PhD thesis, Macquarie University, Sydney.

Seddon, T. (1993) *Context and beyond: reframing the theory and practice of education* (London: Falmer).

Seddon, T. (1996) Markets and the English: reconceptualising educational restructuring as institutional design, *British Journal of Sociology of Education*, 8, 165–85.

Seddon, T. (2000) Capacity-building: beyond state and market, *Pedagogy, Culture and Society*, 7, 35–53.

Seddon, T. (2001) National curriculum in Australia? A matter of politics, powerful knowledge and the regulation of learning, *Pedagogy, Culture and Society*, 9, 307–32.

Seddon, T. and Cairns, L. (2001) Enhancing knowledge organisations: developing capacity and capability through learning and leadership, in K. Leithwood and P. Hallinger (eds) *Second international handbook of educational leadership and administration* (Dordrecht: Kluwer).

Seddon, T. and Deer, C. E. (1992) *A curriculum for the senior secondary years* (Hawthorn: Australian Council for Educational Research).

Seddon, T. and Malley, J. (1998) *A staff development strategy for supporting research priorities in the state training service* (Melbourne: Office of Training and Further Education).

Sefton, R., Waterhouse, P. and Deakin, R. (1994) *Breathing life into training: a model of integrated training* (Melbourne: Workplace Learning Initiatives).

Sen, A. (1999) *Development as freedom* (Oxford: Oxford University Press).

Sennett, R. (1998) *The corrosion of character: the personal consequences of work in the new capitalism* (New York: Norton).

Shaver, S. (1993) *Gender, citizenship and the labour market: the Australian and Canadian welfare states* (Kensington, NSW: University of New South Wales).

Skeggs, B. (1997) *Formations of class and gender: becoming respectable* (London: Sage Publications).

Stiglitz, J. (2002) *Globalisation and its discontents* (New York: W. W. Norton & Company).

Teese, R. (1981) The social function of private schools, in Sociology Research Group (ed.) *Melbourne working papers* (Melbourne: Melbourne University Press).

Teese, R. (2000) *Academic success and social power* (Melbourne: Melbourne University Press).

Touraine, A. (1981) *The voice and the eye: An analysis of social movements* (Cambridge: Cambridge University Press).

Whitty, G., Power, S. and Halpin, D. (1998) *Devolution and choice in education: the school, the state and the market* (Buckingham: Open University Press).

Yeatman, A. (1994) *Postmodern revisionings of the political* (London: Routledge).

Young, I. M. (1990) *Justice and the politics of difference* (Princeton, NJ: Princeton University Press).

18 Progress at school and school effectiveness

Non-cognitive dispositions and within-class markets

Roy Nash

Massey University College of Education, New Zealand

Source: *Journal of Education Policy*, 16 (2): 89–102, 2001.

What are the characteristics of 'effective' schools? Is it possible to create schools with such characteristics – to assume that they can be discovered – by policy-directed pedagogic action? These questions exercise the minds of educational policy-makers, school administrators and teachers throughout the world. Research into school effects recognizes that a most important aspect of the 'success' and 'failure' of schools can be assessed by the academic attainments of their students. There is now an extensive academic literature on school effectiveness and school improvement but, in the words of a recent review (Harris 2000: 5), 'evidence concerning the outcomes from specific approaches to school improvement... remain in relatively short supply'. The ideal account would show how it is possible, (i) to identify effective schools by statistical techniques able to measure the relationship between 'inputs' and 'outputs' in terms of 'added value'; (ii) to describe the school practices causally responsible for an improvement in students' relative progress, and (iii) to implement programmes of school development competent to improve the efficiency of under-achieving schools. A growing field of educational research is concerned precisely with the creation of such models (Teddlie and Reynolds 2000). The identification of schools where final student attainment is higher or lower than expected on the basis of their levels of intake attainment is undoubtedly the most developed element of this scheme. The research requires large samples, data at individual level, and longitudinal assessment, but the increasingly powerful statistical techniques available in this field provide robust forms of analysis able to discriminate between the effects on attainment due to schools, teachers and students (Patterson and Goldstein 1991). A study from New Zealand, a system with only about 300 secondary schools, might be expected to have only a limited substantive interest to those elsewhere. It is certain that the conditions of urban life in, say, London or Chicago, cannot be compared with those of Auckland or Christchurch. Nevertheless, substantial interest has been shown in New Zealand's market-driven reforms by US and UK based scholars (Lauder and Hughes 1999; Fiske and Ladd 2000), and this contribution may have some interest in that context.

Any study that shows attainment in some schools to be higher than in others, when attainment level on entry to the system is controlled, has thus demonstrated relative academic progress to be associated with particular schools. The Progress at School project was designed as a longitudinal programme to investigate the effectiveness of New Zealand secondary schools. The study was a replication in many respects of influential UK research (Smith and Tomlinson 1989) and was intended to provide information on the impact on student performance of the market-driven reforms to school administration introduced in the late 1980s. An approximately representative sample of 5400 students in 37 secondary schools was followed from intake in year 9 to year 13. Standardized tests of reading comprehension and 'scholastic abilities', which were used to derive a combined 'ability' score, were administered on intake. The reference to 'ability' is adequately theorized: in this context it denotes the scores obtained on specific tests at a particular time, and is not an object of measurement, but an index with known distribution. What relationship, if any, this index has to the various cognitive dispositions of students is not problematic in this context and is not discussed. Most of the sample students attempted School Certificate (usually taken in year 11) and marks were made available for the purposes of this research. Sixth Form Certificate grades (year 12) and University Bursary (year 13) examination marks were also obtained. It will be noted that the research made a five-year longitudinal study employing a sample of about 10% of the year group. The research found some interesting differences between schools in their ability to generate relative academic progress, established that relative academic progress is associated with non-cognitive dispositions, and found evidence of an internal educational market, associated with those elements of cultural capital (Bourdieu *et al.* 1999), within the working class, all of which matters are worth reporting.

It will be useful to begin this presentation with an account of the definitive school effects that were observed. School Certificate means in English, mathematics and science were predicted from the year 9 intake score and used as a criterion of 'output' performance. There were two schools with means in all three core subjects significantly above those expected and three with means below the expected point. In a sample of 37 schools there were thus five that could be identified as adding (or subtracting) value across the core subjects. It proved difficult to reach any testable hypotheses about the causes of relative success and failure in this small set of schools (Nash and Harker 1998). It is not a matter, to anticipate a later argument, of their school composition characteristics. The analysis did reveal, however, some interesting information about the individual characteristics of students who make relative progress at school in academic subjects and those who do not. The positive and negative progress of students – if the jargon is not too unseemly – proved to be much more predictable than that of schools.

Relative progress at school is associated with a set of non-cognitive dispositions revealed by a self-assessment instrument and it will be necessary, therefore, to provide a brief account of the relevant items and their factor structure. A set of 30 items, presented as a *Quality of School Life* instrument and based on a version developed by the Australian Council for Educational Research (Williams and Batten 1981) and employed previously in New Zealand (Wagemaker 1993), was used to extract useful factors on perceptions of teachers, personal status, feelings of being emotionally upset, belief in success at school, and recognition of being able to do better. The majority of students, a total of 3711, completed this questionnaire at the end of year 11. Full details are available in Nash and Harker (1998): the three items most highly loaded on each factor will suffice to illustrate the structure:

Teachers are Fair
Teachers treat me fairly in class.
Teachers give me the marks I deserve.
Teachers are fair and just.

Emotional Response
I sometimes get upset.
I feel depressed.
I get a lot of hassle.

Personal Status
I feel important.
People look up to me.
I know that people think a lot of me.

Academic Self-concept
I learn most things pretty quickly.
I know how to cope with the work.
I know I can do well enough to succeed.

Could do Better
I could do better work if I tried.
I get tired of trying.
I feel restless.

Students were also asked to indicate their expected destination after school and to answer questions about their reading resources and practices. Students' aspirations were coded into a scale (from university to unemployed) using a log transformation in order to deal with its skewed nature (more than a third of the students gave university as their expected destination). Separate non-rotated factor scores were derived from responses on cultural activities with parents and to items on reading. The items most highly loaded on the pupil reading factor were:

Pupil Reading
student enjoys reading
number of books owned
rank given to reading in a list of leisure activities.

The investigation of relative academic progress is not as simple as it might appear. In principle, it is a matter of identifying students who have made positive or negative changes in their relative attainments and analysing the available data to discover what characteristics – that might be involved as causes of gains and losses in this area – distinguish the two groups. The problem is that 'gain scores', as they are called, have some odd properties which, in essence, are caused by the fact that students at the extremes of the distribution can only shift in one direction. Relative progress can be estimated directly, for example, by comparing a student's year 9 performance level, expressed in percentile groups, with his or her year 11 performance. However, it is impossible for students in the highest percentile group to demonstrate relative improvement, no matter how much they actually learn and gain from their education, and students with scores in the lowest percentile cannot decline even if they learn nothing at secondary school. To some extent the technical difficulties associated with this problem can be obviated by focusing the analysis on students in the middle of the ability range because these students have an equal opportunity of making either progress or decline. The analysis reported in this article thus employs a straightforward argument: if students of average ability at year 9 achieve much better or much worse in year 11 examinations than predicted by their intake scores, then any differences in non-cognitive variables associated with relative change in attainment level may be investigated as possible causes of progress or decline at school.

The procedure may be described. The intake ability scores and School Certificate marks in English were divided into nine percentile bands. Relative progress in the three year 9 mid-ability groups was then examined by placing students in three categories by comparison with their relative School Certificate performance; (i) those who remained in the same percentile band or shifted to the one above or below it, (ii) those with School Certificate scores at least two bands higher than their intake ability band, and (iii) those with School Certificate scores at least two bands lower than their intake ability band. The procedure thus generated a group of mid-ability students who have variously remained stable, progressed or declined, in their relative level of attainment in their first three years at secondary school. On this basis, there were 384 (30%) students who progressed, 576 (44.9%) who remained stable, and 322 (25.1%) who declined. The procedure was repeated for mathematics, where the numbers in each group were, respectively, 303 (27.6%), 477 (43.5%), and 316 (28.8%). In English, more boys declined than girls (33.9 and 16.3), and in mathematics more girls declined than boys (32% and 25.4%). It will be noted that the extent of the relative decline in English experienced by boys is greater than the corresponding decline shown by girls in mathematics.

What factors distinguish students in this mid-ability set who either progress or decline? The most appropriate statistic for this purpose is logistic regression. This is a form of regression analysis designed to reveal the variables associated with membership of two groups distinguished by properties of interest. In this case, the two groups are the mid-ability third form students whose School Certificate results show they have (i) progressed or (ii) declined since entry to secondary school. Logistic regression has several useful features; it can handle variables with any form of distribution and it produces results in the form of 'odds', which makes them somewhat easier to understand than conventional multiple regression analysis (Menard 1995). When the mobile groups are entered as an indicator (dummy) dependent variable in a logistic regression analysis the statistically significant discriminating variables prove to be: sex, fourth form aspiration (obtained from responses to a list of options), the 'could do better' factor, academic self-concept, and the reading factor. In other words, if students enter year 9 with the same ability, those who do well in School Certificate are likely to be girls with high ambitions, positive self-concepts, and interested in reading; and those who do poorly are likely to be boys with low aspirations, poor self-concepts and little interest in reading. The chances of being in the progress rather than the decline group, in English, are improved 1.37 times by virtue of being a girl, 0.3 times by holding an ambition to enter university (rather than polytechnic), 0.46 times by virtue of disagreeing that they 'could do better', 0.41 times for a positive self-concept, 0.31 times for a good involvement in reading, and 0.5 times by virtue of being from a professional rather than non-professional household. The odds given for factor scores relate to each standard deviation. The analysis for mathematics shows a similar pattern. It is possible to predict correctly the progress or decline trajectory of almost three out of four mid-ability students from their responses to the fourth form questionnaire, and the pattern is much the same in all ethnic groups. A similar analysis of relative decline by students in the upper third of the ability range includes only sex and aspiration as significant discriminators, and it proves to be rather difficult to identify any characteristics – other than sex for it is evident that the girls do better than the boys – to discriminate between those in the lowest third of the ability range who make some relative progress and those who decline. On some models – the predictions are better for some ethnic groups than others – the prediction of relative progress or decline is correct four times out of five. Compared with our almost complete inability to predict the relative efficiency of schools, this is impressive indeed.

School performance

In the Progress at School sample of 37 secondary schools there were only two that surpassed their expected performance in the core School Certificate subjects, and only three fell that below the expected level (Harker and Nash 1996). The differences between these schools are quite marked. An analysis of variance, controlling for the effects of social class and prior ability, indicates the following effect sizes: English, 0.6; mathematics, 0.26; and science, 0.37. These effect sizes are calculated in the conventional manner by summing the deviations and dividing by the standard deviation: hence, English School Certificate (s.d. 15.5) shows the adjusted covariate means to be 4.98 and −4.33. A student of average ability and social origin could expect to gain 5 School Certificate marks more than the mean for students in that category by attending one of the two most successful schools, and 4 marks less by attending one of the three least successful schools. These statistical results are significant, comparable in range with the findings of overseas research (Teddlie and Reynolds 2000), and indicate definitive school effects. Although it was not possible to carry out observations in these schools it is virtually certain that these positive and negative results were generated by internal school processes. Students in schools that showed a positive effect reported a more satisfactory educational experience than those in the schools that showed a negative effect. In the most successful schools students were significantly more likely to agree with the following items than those in the worst schools:

Teachers give me the marks I deserve.
I learn most things pretty quickly.
I get all the help I need in maths lessons.
I know I can do well enough to succeed.
Nobody bullies me.

They were also more likely to disagree with these items:

I get a lot of hassle.
I keep out of trouble.
I feel depressed.
I get tired of trying.
I have to struggle to keep up.
I sometimes get upset.

All these differences are statistically significant at the <0.01 level with the exception of *I get all the help I need in maths lessons* which is significant at <0.05. It is extremely unlikely that this pattern could occur by chance, and it is reasonable to conclude that there was something about these schools that enhanced or negated their students' sense that they could succeed. Two of these schools were boys' schools and it is interesting to note that there is one in each set. At the school where the boys' made relative progress, 9% gave a negative response to the item *Nobody bullies me*, high enough, perhaps, but in the other school the figure is an astonishing 26%. Even though no fieldwork could be carried out in these schools, some information was received from students in written submissions and in telephone conversations. We have some idea about the standards of teaching, the character of the institutional regime, and so on, that might be involved in creating these differences (Nash and Harker 1998). It is interesting to note, however, that in none of the three underachieving schools was the relative lack of attainment revealed by this analysis observed by the Educational Review Office (ERO) in its public reports for the relevant period. (The Educational Review Office is an office of state independent from the Ministry of Education that inspects New Zealand schools.) These results are highly significant and the pattern of attainment is repeated at other levels. Expressed in round terms, this evidence suggests that the most and least effective 10% of New Zealand secondary schools vary in School Certificate performance by half a standard deviation in English and by more than a quarter of a standard deviation in mathematics and do so largely for reasons within their power to correct. New Zealand educators do not accept that schools lack the capacity to keep bullying under control. It is not, of course, necessarily want of managerial expertise that allows bullying and its associated unhappiness to exist, but an ideological tolerance of the practice ('boys will be boys', 'it's good for them to learn to stand up for themselves', and so on) and a preference for privacy rather than disclosure ('we don't wash our dirty linen in public', 'it's better handled within in the family', and so on). The existence of these discursive positions is only constructed as evidence of 'managerial failure' by a semantic manoeuvre: there are still principals and members of boards of trustees who prefer to run their schools in that way.

One of the most interesting aspects of the Progress at School data, however, is obscured by this analysis of between school differences. It is obvious that there is more variability in examination performance within schools than between them. This finding, incidentally, is consistent with the overseas literature surveyed by Harris (2000: 9), which concluded, 'recent research outlines that variables at classroom level account for greater variance in student outcomes than do variables at the school level'. It is a convention of the school effects literature to compare the most effective 20% of schools with the least effective 20%, and if this is done separately for English and mathematics the effect sizes, calculated in the manner described earlier, are appreciable: English 0.38, and mathematics 0.27. Thus, an 'average' student could expect to gain about 6 marks more in English, and 5 or 6 marks more in mathematics, by attending a school in the upper rather than the lower band of effectiveness. However, to do that this 'average' student would usually have to attend more than one school. It would be necessary to study English in one school and mathematics in another – and in all probability they would be 100 kilometres apart! There are two overlapping schools in the least effective 20% set and only one in the most effective set. It is not possible to detect any pattern in the responses of the students that can account for these within school differences between subjects, but they are presumably attributable to practices of departments and individual teachers rather than to whole school processes. This must make selecting a school on the basis of its comparative examination performance a rather difficult matter. Even if parents were as good as ERO at recognizing under- and over-achieving schools (which is to say not particularly good at all) and could appreciate that neither mean social class nor ability have much effect on relative performance they would still be faced with the problem of having to trade the likelihood of relative success in one core subject against relative failure in another. And even that requires the assumption – a rather large one – that observed levels of school performance remain stable from year to year.

School composition effects

Studies of school effectiveness have frequently identified what is variously referred to as a school composition or school-mix effect. The effect is revealed by a statistically significant association between a relevant indicator of school 'outcomes', usually academic attainment scores of one kind or another, and the average level of social class or ability of the students enrolled, once the statistical effect of the students' individual social class and ability has been controlled. If a positive school composition effect is revealed by statistical analysis then it means, for example, that students of average ability from an average social background are doing better at middle-class schools than at working-class schools. It is still possible to engage in a debate about whether there is or is not a school composition effect. A recent review by Teddlie, Stringfield and Reynolds (2000), although inclined to the view that there is a compositional effect, lists more studies that fail to report an effect than do. This raises a small point of semantics: it seems odd to imply that an effect might exist in studies where none is observed, and the term 'effect' has become ambiguous in this literature, being used to refer both to an actual statistical effect and the school processes supposed to generate it. When these authors suggest that, despite the contradictory results, the overall pattern of data indicate that there *is* a compositional effect, they seem to declare only their belief that some social processes in schools are associated with the proportion of working-class or low-ability students enrolled. Few observers would argue with that proposition. There have been two recent New Zealand studies school competent to reveal school composition effects: the Progress at School project and the Smithfield project (Lauder and Hughes 1999).

The evidence for a school composition effect in these two studies is somewhat weak. The Progress at School data indicate only a moderate school composition effect. The effect is largest in mathematics, where it is about twice the level in other subjects, and amounts to about 0.2 standard deviations for each unit of increment in the school SES composition: this is roughly the mean difference between schools at the second and eighth SES deciles, and as a practical matter an effect of this size might be considered irrelevant. The Smithfield analysis shows several school composition variables to be correlated (many at the relatively low 5% level of significance) with student performance, but the effect sizes are not reported and the results are mixed. 'SES mix', for example, is associated with School Certificate marks in English and science but not in mathematics: one cannot imagine a similar result occurring at the individual level with a sample of any size. Neither aggregate SES nor any aggregate ability variable is associated consistently with School Certificate attainment in each of the three main subjects. The Smithfield analyses have been subjected to detailed criticism in other respects by Gorard and Fitz (1998). It is impossible, of course, to know from the fact that a statistical composition effect is revealed whether it is due to actual processes within the schools or whether it is the result of undetected (or poorly indicated) variables or, as could be so, some combination of both elements.

Thrupp (1997, 1999) has attempted to identify the institutional mechanisms that might create school-mix effects. He argues that the academic achievements of students in predominantly working-class schools is likely to be depressed below the level predicted by their individual level of ability and social origin as a result of social processes within schools. The effective domains of practice include those associated with reference group (peer group), instructional (teaching), and organizational and management. In working-class schools there is, in comparison with middle-class schools, thus more classroom disruption and a lower level of aspiration due to the presence of disproportionately large groups of students indifferent or antagonistic to the institution; fewer opportunities to learn complex and abstract areas of knowledge due to the adoption by teachers of narrow forms of pedagogy; and greater inefficiencies in the mechanisms of social control and the delivery of the curriculum due to special problems faced by the organisation and management of the institution. Thrupp suggests, moreover, drawing on influential theses in the sociology of education, that the principal effective mechanism generating the composition effect is the production by students in low-SES schools of a powerful culture of resistance derived from oppositional elements in traditional working-class culture. The lessons of his fieldwork are so compelling that Thrupp (1999: 122) declares that 'it is hard to see how a school mix effect would not occur'. The evidence from ethnographic work in one working-class school studied extensively as part of the Progress at School study (Nash and Major 1997) lends support to these observations. There probably is more classroom disruption in low-SES than in high-SES schools. Nevertheless, the extent of the difference can be over-emphasized, and what effect it has on student attainment can be no more than a plausible guess. The hypothesis that aspirations are lower in low-SES than in high-SES schools requires a more complex response. Aspiration is largely a function of ability. Scholastically able working-class boys and girls are *almost* as likely to hold high aspirations as scholastically able middle-class boys and girls, and there is little real difference in the aspirations of working-class students associated with school mix or school SES once test scores have been taken into account. Moreover, working-class boys and girls with the same ability scores have similar aspirations whether they attend a high-SES or a low-SES school. The percentage of skilled working-class students, for example, with university aspirations is as follows: SES deciles 1–2, 41.1%; SES deciles 3–4, 31.2%; SES deciles 5–6, 30.3%; deciles 7–8, 26.7%; and decile 10, 53%. The final datum represents two elite schools and only 30 carefully selected students. In fact, aspirations throughout the working class are higher, at least at the age of 14, in low-SES schools than high-SES schools. This is only partly due to the greater proportion of Pacific Island students in low-SES schools, but should be noted. The Pacific Island community is a comparatively recent immigrant group, largely engaged in unskilled labour that looks to the educational system for its collective mobility. As for pedagogy, it is probably true that teachers in low-SES schools tend to remain closer to the concrete and the practical in their discourse than do those in high-SES schools. Once more, however, this contrast can both be over-emphasized and given more causal weight as an influence on school attainment than it properly merits. The argument required to make the theory convincing, rather than merely plausible, would have a complex form. It would need to be demonstrated, for example, that success in the School Certificate examination actually required a level of abstraction and analysis not adequately taught by the typical pedagogy of the working-class school. There must be room for doubt that success in School Certificate – which relies heavily on memory and 'key-word' answer techniques – actually requires a level of abstraction and complexity not adequately taught by any satisfactory modes of instruction. The debate prompted by Bernstein's socio-linguistic theory is relevant in this context. Edwards (1987), for example, sharply disputes, on the basis of sound empirical data, the suggestion that the codes of classroom discourse vary in any relevant respects, or to any significant degree, in middle-class and working-class schools. Moreover, even if Lauder and Hughes' reported findings are taken at face value, the school effect in their study is probably in the order of *one or two School Certificate marks*, which may seem a slight matter to attribute to so fundamental a cause. The final argument, that the working-class school faces special difficulties in the mechanisms of social control and curriculum delivery, would almost certainly be endorsed by any teacher burdened with 'social problems' and with that much less time to teach who has worked in one. It may seem plausible to suppose that students will learn less in low-SES schools than in high-SES schools but, not for the first time, it is necessary to ask whether this account is anything more than intuitively plausible.

Thrupp draws on a 'matched sample' of working-class students of average ability in middle-class and working-class schools. The method is sound: if working-class students of similar ability behave differently in high-SES and low-SES schools there is some foundation for a conclusion. Unfortunately, Thrupp's sample is rather small – five students in one low-SES school compared with eight in three high-SES schools – and relatively little information is actually provided about even these few students. Their academic attainments at school, for example, are not reported and as the entire thesis depends on working-class students at low-SES schools attaining less than those at high-SES schools the omission is all too evident. Nevertheless, the method is interesting and it is possible to replicate the procedure with the Progress at School data. A sample of skilled working-class students with above average intake scores, a rough control for 'ability', may be drawn from the three co-educational state schools with the highest social class mean (Set A, n. 68) and the three with the lowest social class mean (Set B, n. 78). The performance of students in these schools can be compared on a number of respects. The attainments of these groups, Set A and Set B are as follows: ability (presented for the sake of convenience in IQ equivalent form), Set A, 111.0 (n. 68), Set B, 108.9 (n. 78); School Certificate English, Set A 58.7 (n. 21), Set B, 54.2 (28); School Certificate mathematics, Set A, 56.9 (n. 20), Set B, 53.7 (n. 26); Bursary, Set A, 189 (n. 11), Set B, 241 (n. 9). The attainments of these groups of working-class students are not significantly different: the slightly higher School Certificate attainments of those in set A, attending high-SES schools, is entirely accounted for by their slightly higher initial intake score: the year 13 Bursary results for Set B were in some respect the better with all nine successful students gaining at least 200 marks, whereas that level was achieved by only six students in Set A (there is no need for an extended discussion on the Bursary examination: suffice to say that 200 marks will obtain a place in a good university course). It is impossible to gain any sense of a 'school-mix' effect from these results, and even if observational studies were to show – as they almost certainly would – exactly the kind of surface level behaviour by teachers and students noted by Thrupp as characteristic of high-SES and low-SES schools, that would suffice only to show that what is being observed is simply that, surface level 'noise' in both a technical and a literal sense. It is possible that Thrupp has actually reproduced the 'common sense realism' that underpins the decision making of parents as they select the 'best' school on the basis of its class and ethnic composition – a perception notoriously based on unexamined appearances – without paying sufficient attention to more subtle social processes, to be explored here in more detail, generated by social interactions in schools.

Thrupp suggests that a certain 'critical mass of alienated working class students' (Thrupp 1999: 59) is necessary in order for the spectacular explosive celebration of cultural resistance to have a marked effect on the educational progress of students. But there are actually few differences to be observed in the Progress at School data between working-class students attending high-SES and low-SES schools. Compared with working-class students at low-SES schools, those at high-SES schools do report a significantly greater level of involvement with their parents in cultural activities and a higher level of interest in reading, but their academic achievements are not superior. These two differences are evidence, in any case, not of a school effect but of an internal class selection effect: the proportion of working-class students from skilled-manual families is greater in high-SES schools than in low-SES schools (indeed, in a few schools the largest group of 'working-class' students are actually from families where no one is employed). It has already been noted that an ethnic skewing explains the higher level of aspirations in low-SES schools The proportion of students with favourable and unfavourable dispositions towards school, as indicated by *the Quality of School Life* responses, is more or less constant in each school and as a result of this the ratio of working-class students with favourable to unfavourable dispositions is about twice as high in low-SES schools than in high-SES schools. In other words, there are proportionately *more* working-class students with favourable dispositions in low-SES schools than in high-SES schools. This evidence calls into question the 'critical mass' hypothesis – which sees in the large presence of working-class students the conditions for an explosion of class cultural resistance – favoured by Thrupp. The proportion of students who accept the values of the school, or at least do not actively resist them, is approximately the same in high SES and low SES schools, but in the latter institutions working-class students take proportionately *more* of these positions, some of which are *discursive*, and some of which are *actual* in the form of Head Boy and Head Girl, and all the lesser offices, than they do in high-SES schools. There are also indications in the Progress at School data that teachers in low-SES schools – where high levels of ability are perceived as rare – are somewhat more willing to recognize and nurture academic talent in working-class students than those in high-SES schools (Nash 1999).

An internal market within the working class

The evidence that the attainment of working-class students is better at high decile schools than at low decile schools is relatively weak, but if the fact were so then the hypothesis that the school-mix effect so demonstrated is actually caused by school processes would be supported only if the cognitive and non-cognitive attributes of working-class students attending high-SES and low-SES schools proved to be comparable. Some evidence from the Progress at School project that working-class students at high-SES schools have a significantly higher level of involvement in reading and cultural activities has been presented. There is also other New Zealand evidence to suggest that the effective non-cognitive dispositions of working-class students at low-SES and high-SES schools are not identical: indeed, there are some interesting indications of within-class differential selection affecting New Zealand secondary schools.

When families try to avoid low-SES schools, as a good many evidently do, they typically choose an 'adjacent' mid-SES rather than a high-SES school. As Lauder and Hughes (1999) have noted, the practical alternative to a local low-SES school is most likely to be a mid-SES – in some urban areas even another low-SES – rather than a high-SES school. It is probably for this reason that Ministry of Education (1999) data show mid-SES schools to have made the highest rate of improvement on the relevant output indicators. These findings almost certainly reflect processes of differential selection by aspiring families within the broad working class determined to avoid low-SES schools. The data are worth close attention: during the four years inclusive 1995–1998 the number of candidates for the University Bursary examination as a percentage of earlier third form enrolment improved significantly in schools at most SES decile levels (Ministry of Education 1999). On this indicator, SES deciles 1 (11.6%) and 2 (17.4%) schools improved significantly; SES deciles 3 and 4 schools showed no real change; and the mid-decile schools, 5 (10.6%), 6 (3.2%) and 7 (7.6%) showed the strongest average rates of growth. In the highest SES deciles the rates of increase were relatively minor: decile 8 (7.4%), decile 9 (4.1%) and decile 10 (0.6%). This analysis reveals no absolute or relative performance decline in low-SES schools on the crucial indicator of Bursary attainment and is consistent with the thesis of within-class selection. There are some indications that low-SES schools make proportionately greater efforts with the relatively few students of high ability they attract. It is possible to calculate the percentage of students taking four papers at Bursary from the number awarded School Certificate grades 'C' or better. In SES decile 1–3 schools the figure is 17.8%, compared with 13.7% in decile 4–7 schools, and 15.0% in decile 8–10 schools. Rates of access to tertiary education as a percentage of School Certificate candidates awarded 'C' grade or better, are not associated with school SES level.

If within-class selection has a significant effect on within-SES school performance one might expect to find decline in roll, within SES categories, to be associated with a corresponding decline in attainment. The logic is compelling: a school roll declines because families, who might be expected to prefer their local school, decide to send their children (or some of them) elsewhere. That decision-making process will take into account children's individual abilities, interests, and aspirations. In some cases, the decision is managed by parents whose preferences for secondary school may vary according to the perceptions they hold of available schools and of their children's abilities and aspirations. It is not unknown, for example, for parents to prefer an 'academic' school rather than a 'non-academic' school for their most able children, or to have a stronger desire for single-sex schooling for their daughters than for their sons. Even when children are allowed to act on their own preferences, a similar pattern of differential choice may emerge, as a result of friendship patterns and other considerations. Reay's (1998b) account of class differences in the mode and extent of parental involvement in primary schooling provides grounded support for the maintenance of reproductive processes in this area. There is nothing unreasonable in supposing that a market in schools should exist within social classes as well as between them. It is not, of course, always families that make the effective decision. Schools with an enrolment policy may be expected to admit only the most able and committed applicants in as much as the terms of their scheme permit such discrimination. These enrolment decisions, furthermore, are not made only at the point of transition from intermediate to secondary school. On the contrary, some schools make a point of enrolling students with a record of success at fifth form or even later, which generally has a favourable effect on their output indicators. There is also the even more questionable process that sees undesirable students removed from some schools in considerable numbers. Schools that remove students at the end of year 10 – by indefinite suspension for offences to all intents and purposes provoked by the institutional regime – can be detected by statistical analysis and the rejected students usually end up in low decile schools. In short, the hypothesis is that the most able and highly motivated students within a social class are more likely than others to enter a high-SES than a low-SES school whenever they have an effective opportunity. There is a straightforward, if indirect, way to test this hypothesis. If it is correct, then the output indicators of schools with declining rolls will be lower than those of others with stable or expanding rolls. Students who attended schools that expanded in the four years between 1994 and 1998 generally did, in fact, gain higher attainments than those at schools that declined. Ministry of Education (1999) data reveal, for example, that the percentages of students awarded School Certificate and Bursary were, in expanding (and declining) schools respectively: SES decile 1 (lowest), SC 33.1% and Bursary 22.8 (85.9% and 54.4%); SES decile 3, SC 51.7% and Bursary 23.4 (86.6% and 60.0); and SES decile 5 (mid-range), SC 48.8 and Bursary 37.3% (87.4% and 75.4%). The hypothesis is amply confirmed. A similar analysis of 'successful' and 'unsuccessful' schools, defined largely by their roll shift, is reported by Fiske and Ladd (2000). There can be little doubt that this highly significant difference in performance is largely caused by internal selection within the working class. No one imagines that it is exclusively – or even predominantly – middle-class students who have moved into and out of low-SES and mid-SES schools thus causing them to expand or decline in consequence.

Discussion

School development is an applied field informed by research into school practice with little independent knowledge base. The best summary one can give of this literature is that it comes down to appointing the most dynamic principal one can find and giving him or her the necessary resources to do the job! Teddlie and Stringfield (1993: 197), for example, state:

> The careful selection of teachers who are or have the potential to be effective teachers may be the principal's most important activity in moving his school toward effectiveness. Once weaker teachers have been replaced by stronger ones, the faculty will become more stable and the internal socialization process more important.

Other writers, including Gewirtz (1998) and Young (1999), have expressed serious doubt that 'good' management and teaching are responsible for school 'success', and suspect that what is regarded as effective management is characterized as such as a result of its demonstrated success in attracting well-motivated students (who make relatively slight demands on the non-teaching functions of the school), and in appointing and retaining experienced and competent teachers. These models are actually not incompatible and both sets of processes are probably involved.

It is proving very difficult to specify practices within schools that contribute to the relative academic progress of students. As Elliott (1996) has cogently argued, the research in this field typically generates lists, which specify properties of practice in terms that can be uninformative, if not actually tautologous (Myers 1995). The 'effective' school, for example, is said to be characterized by 'purposeful' leadership; staff, student and parental 'involvement'; 'consistency' in areas of teaching and discipline; 'structured' lessons; an 'intellectually challenging' curriculum; a 'work-centred pedagogy'; a 'limited focus' in the presentation of lessons; good record keeping; and a 'maximum' effort on 'communication'. It is possible to have the nagging suspicion that all this is after the fact description, in the concepts of administrators, of what efficient schools are like by definition. If the story is correct, then it seems to tell us that students will learn more from a teacher who presents structured lessons focused on a central topic, who asks questions that stimulate abstract thought, who carries out regular assessments, maintains adequate records, and expects every student to learn at least the fundamental points, than they will from a teacher who puts up an OHP photocopied from a textbook, instructs the class to copy it out, and then spends the lesson time marking a pile of exercise books for another class. This is not surprising: in fact, what is more surprising for those who know their way around secondary schools is that these contrasting pedagogic methods do not seem to result in a much greater variance in learning than seems to be evident. The case of Magnesh Reddy, who was employed with fake credentials as a science teacher in a number of New Zealand secondary schools, has some interesting implications. It was many years before he was exposed and, before it was known that he was unqualified, his performance was officially rated as 'satisfactory' and there is no evidence that his teaching methods differed noticeably from the prevailing norm (New Zealand Herald 2000). The attainments of his students also seem not to have been significantly lower than those in other subjects. As Reddy's knowledge of science proved to be virtually non-existent – he scored 6% in a Bursary examination paper when assessed – it is difficult to resist the conclusion that students in some secondary-school classes have actually learned to teach themselves.

Is the 'added value' efficiency of a school caused by its internal management processes, the organization and surveillance of teachers and so on, or is it more a product of efficiency at the level of attracting the pupils and staff most able to learn and teach? The problems of working-class families and their children in the educational system remain a matter of great concern and, as many writers have argued, among them most recently, Kovach (1998), Thrupp (1998) and Mortimore (1998) there are strategies to be adopted at every level of policy direction. Reay (1998a) has pointed out that one of the ways in which schools respond to the market is by introducing, or re-introducing, ability grouping: there is evidence that this is also happening in New Zealand. There is no dispute between us in these respects about the consequences of a market in education. A little more attention might, however, need to be paid to the existence of an internal market within social classes effectively selecting not only for ability but for the non-cognitive dispositions associated with school success. The relative progress of students at school rests on the capacity of the school to generate positive dispositions towards education and schooling, and these dispositions are, to some extent at least, developed and expressed in social contexts that lie within the control of the school. The contexts of learning and teaching in high-SES and low-SES schools constitute a valid area of investigation that merits the highest standards of empirical research and analytical rigour. A final allusion to Bourdieu (1990) is required: if we can identify the system properties that foster in students the development and expression of dispositions that generate the practices that effect relative progress at school, in high-SES and in low-SES schools alike, then our own chances of making progress in this field may be improved.

References

Bourdieu, P. (1990) *In Other Words: Essays Towards a Reflexive Sociology* (Cambridge: Polity Press).

Bourdieu, P. *et al.* (1999) *The Weight of the World: Social Suffering in Contemporary Society* (Stanford, CA: Stanford University Press).

Edwards, A. D. (1987) Language codes and classroom practice. *Oxford Review of Education*, 13 (3), 237–47.

Elliot, J. (1996) School effectiveness research and its critics: alternative visions of schooling. *Cambridge Journal of Education*, 26 (2), 199–224.

Fiske, E. B. and Ladd, H. F. (2000) *When Schools Compete: A Cautionary Tale* (Washington, DC: Brookings Institute Press).

Gewirtz, S. (1998) Can all schools be successful? An exploration of the determinants of success. *Oxford Review of Education*, 24 (4), 439–57.

Gorard, S. and Fitz, J. (1998) Under starter's orders: the established market, the Cardiff study and the Smithfield project. *International Studies in the Sociology of Education*, 8 (3), 299–314.

Harker, R. K. and Nash, R. (1996) Academic outcomes and school effectiveness: type 'A' and type 'B' effects. *New Zealand Journal of Educational Studies*, 31 (2), 143–70.

Harris, A. (2000) What works in school improvement? Lessons from the field and future directions. *Educational Research*, 42 (1), 1–12.

Kovach, J. A. (1998) Macro ecological reforms as a strategy for reducing educational risks associated with poverty. *Journal of Educational Policy*, 13 (2), 167–78.

Lauder, H. and Hughes, D. (1999) *Trading in Futures: Why Education Markets Don't Work* (Buckingham, UK: Open University Press).

Menard, S. (1995) *Applied Logistic Regression, Sage University Paper, Quantitative Applications in the Social Sciences* (Thousand Oaks, CA: Sage).

Ministry of Education (1999) *Tertiary Education Statistics 1998: Selected Tables Summarising 31 July Student Numbers and Programme Enrolments [Data supplied on disk]* (Wellington: Data Management and Analysis Division, Ministry of Education).

Mortimore, P. (1998) The vital hours: reflecting on research on schools and their effects, in A. Hargreaves, A. Lieberman, M. Fullan and D. Hopkins (eds), *International Handbook of Educational Change* (Dordecht: Kluwer Academic Publications), 85–99.

Myers, K. (1995) (ed.) *School Improvement in Practice: The Schools Make a Difference Project* (London: Falmer).

Nash, R. (1999) *School Learning: Conversations with the Sociology of Education* (Palmerston North: Delta Studies in Education).

Nash, R. and Harker, R. (1998) *Making Progress: Adding Value in Secondary Education* (Palmerston North: ERDC Press).

Nash, R. and Major, S. (1997) *A Year in the Sixth Form* (Palmerston North: ER DC Press).

New Zealand Herald (2000) Bogus teacher jailed, told to repay college, 2 June.

Patterson, L. and Goldstein, H. (1991) New statistical methods of analysing social structures: an introduction to multilevel models. *British Educational Research Journal*, 17 (4), 387–93.

Reay, D. (1998a) Setting the agenda: The growing impact of market forces on pupil grouping in British secondary schools. *Journal of Curriculum Studies*, 30 (3), 545–58.

Reay, D. (1998b) *Class Work: Mothers' Involvement in their Children's Primary Schooling* (London: UCL Press).

Smith, D. and Tomlinson, S. (1989) *The School Effect: A Study of Multi-racial Comprehensives* (London: Institute of Policy Studies).

Teddlie, C. and Reynolds, D. (2000) School effectiveness research and the social and behavioral sciences, in C. Teddlie and D. Reynolds (eds), *The International Handbook of School Effectiveness Research*, (London: Falmer Press), pp. 301–21.

Teddlie, C. and Stringfield, S. (1993) *Schools Make a Difference: Lessons Learned from a 10-year Study of School Effects* (New York: Teachers' College Press).

Teddlie, C., Stringfield, S. and Reynolds, D. (2000) Context issues within school effectiveness research, in C. Teddlie and D. Reynolds (eds), *The International Handbook of School Effectiveness Research* (London and New York: Falmer Press), 160–85.

Thrupp, M. (1997) How school mix shapes school processes: a comprehensive study of New Zealand schools. *New Zealand Journal of Educational Studies*, 33 (2), 53–82.

Thrupp, M. (1998) The art of the possible: organising and managing high and low socio-economic schools. *Journal of Educational Policy*, 13 (2), 197–219.

Thrupp, M. (1999) *Schools Making a Difference: Let's be Realistic! School Mix, School Effectiveness and the Social Limits of Reform* (Buckingham, UK: Open University Press).

Wagemaker, H. (ed.) (1993) *Achievement in Reading Literacy: New Zealand's Future in a National and International Context* (Wellington: Research Section, Ministry of Education).

Williams, T. and Batten, M. (1981) *The Quality of School Life* (Hawthorn, Victoria: ACER Research Monograph No. 12).

Young, D. J. (1999) *The usefulness of value-added research in identifying effective schools.* Paper presented to the Australian Association for Research in Education Conference, Melbourne, Australia.

19 Equity in educational policy

A priority in transformation or in trouble?

Jerry Paquette

University of Western Ontario, London, Ontario, Canada

Source: *Journal of Education Policy*, 13 (1): 41–61, 1998.

The decline of equity?

> So we accept some things and we forget some other things and what we can't forget we learn how to shut out of mind and we adopt the rhetoric that is required of us and we speak of 'quality' or 'excellence' – not justice.
>
> (black principal cited in Kozol 1991: 152)

In this paper I seek to do four things. First, I wish to give a conceptually rich overview of competing concepts of equity in educational policy. Second, I review the fundamental challenge of postmodern thought and values to equity as a serious priority in educational policy. In particular, I want to explore the pitfalls of anti-foundationalism to the possibility of making equity claims and policy in education. Finally, I want to argue that, despite the complex and contested nature of educational equity, despite assaults from both the political right and left on equity as a serious educational policy priority, and despite the implausible obfuscation of 'excellence-for-all' policies, equity remains at the heart of the *raison d'être* of publicly funded education and is here to stay over the long term.

Equity has been a cornerstone of educational policy since the inception of publicly funded mass education systems during the nineteenth century. The concept of equity, of course, is riddled with ambiguities and nuances and weighed down with emotional, conceptual and political baggage. Equity means fairness, but fairness is a two-edged sword. Being fair involves both giving to each according to the common lot (horizontal equity) *and* giving to each according to need and merit (vertical equity). Perhaps in no other public policy domain is the tension between providing horizontal equity and vertical equity more electric and pervasive than in education. Equity, moreover, raises questions of redistribution, of reshaping the way in which resources are allocated, of tampering with the existing economic pie. Equity is not, and has never been, uncontroversial.

Although the term 'equity' has only come into wide use in policy discourse during the current century, the proposition that the state should support a system of universally, or at least very broadly accessible, schools and institutions of learning arose as a political imperative in industrialized nation states during the nineteenth century. The political force of this proposition drew its original energy from basic modernist, liberal political values such as:

1 the importance of an educated populace to social harmony and political stability;
2 the need for literacy to participate meaningfully in the political life of liberal democracies;
3 the link between education and economic contribution to community life as well as to personal and familial self-sufficiency;

and from assumptions about choice and reasonable comparability of services across regional differences. Among the most important of these assumptions were that:

1 left to themselves, many parents might not wish to or be able to choose an adequate quantity, type and quality of education of their children; and
2 only the state could assure a basic level of educational services across the economic, cultural, geographic, demographic and other diversity common to most large nation states.

Both the political values which underpinned public funding of education and the assumptions which politically justified state involvement in its provision, governance and regulation have proven remarkably robust and durable – until recently, perhaps.

On the one hand, equity seems to be alive, well and securely ensconced at the heart of recent educational policy making. Fiscal equity litigation and legislation is a growth sector in American education (Sparkman 1990; Underwood and Verstegen 1990; Fulton and Long 1993; Natapoff 1994). Detracking and destreaming have made the 'levelling' of curriculum an increasingly integral part of educational reform efforts in numerous jurisdictions across North America (Ascher 1992; Wheelock 1992; Argys *et al.* 1995; Ontario Ministry of Education and Training 1995). Mainstrearning of exceptional students continues to gain acceptance as the preferred placement norm even in jurisdictions such as Ontario which have had no formal 'least-restrictive-environment' policy mandate. Overall, at the surface level at least, equity would appear to be an increasingly central pinion of contemporary educational policy.

Yet profound social and economic changes over the last two decades appear to have altered radically much of the value base from which publicly funded education sprang. Changes associated with the socioeconomic upheaval of global population migration, globalization of the economy, pervasive substitution of technology for human labour, the economic marginalization of the young, and more broadly with the postmodern condition in general (Harvey 1989; Bauman 1992), have created new and fundamental challenges to the perceived importance of equity in public-sector education. These challenges are rooted in long-standing ambiguities and contradictions underpinning competing ideas of equity; nonetheless, the new challenges are different in both kind and magnitude from the traditional dilemmas of educational and broader social equity. They are different because they call into question the most fundamental objects of educational equity. Indeed, Bauman lays bare a pervasive ethical dilemma of postmodernism which, by its abandonment of any 'monologic stance' ultimately calls into question *the legitimacy of equity itself as* both a sociopolitical and educational policy objective.

> One may say that the zealous avoidance of the monologic stance leads to consequences strikingly similar to those one wished to stave off [the domination of particularistic moral convictions]. If I consider corporal punishment degrading and bodily mutilations inhuman, letting... others... practice them in the name of their right to choose (or because I cannot believe any more in the universality of moral rules) amounts to the reassertion of my own superiority: 'they may wallow in barbarities I would never put up with... that serves them right, those savages'. The renunciation of the monologic stance does not seem, therefore, an unmixed blessing. The more radical it is, the more it resembles moral relativism in its behavioural incarnation of callous indifference.
>
> (Bauman 1992: xxiii–xxiv)

In an important sense, as Bauman notes, the

> politics of *inequality* and hence of *redistribution* was by far the most dominant type of political conflict and conflict-management [under liberal modernist political conventions]. With the advent of postmodernity it has been displaced from its dominant role, but remains (and in all probability will remain) a constant feature of the postmodern habitat. Indeed, there are no signs that the postmodern condition promises to alleviate the inequalities (and hence the redistributional conflicts) proliferating in modern society... [Instead]... redistributional vindications of our time are focused more often than not on the winning of *human rights* (a code name for the agent's autonomy, for that freedom of choice that constitutes the agency in the postmodern habitat) by categories of population heretofore denied them.
>
> (Bauman 1992: 197–8)

In the moral, aesthetic and intellectual rootlessness of postmodernism, arbiters of value in education, including pace-setting private and élitist public schools and educational institutions are seemingly cast in the position of just the kind of 'callous indifference' Bauman suggests. One can easily imagine even the most multiculturally minded in the best schools muttering with grim satisfaction as they survey the general contemporary landscape of publicly funded education, 'there, but for the grace of God, go I'. The Gordian knot of sameness and difference is particularly difficult to unravel in educational policy.

To call into question the contemporary status and meaning of equity as a public and educational-policy goal is not, of course, to fantasize that equity, however defined, has historically been at the apex of policy priorities. Nor is it to imagine that policies created to foster greater equity, however understood, were markedly successful in achieving their formally announced goals. Neither is it to deny that equity remains an important area of public and educational policymaking. Even less is it an argument that equity in education has been a clear or uncontroversial concept.

As Scheurich (1994) points out, a common theme of postpositivist critique of educational (and other) policymaking is that its greatest utility and most important meaning to policymakers may be as 'symbolic performance' rather than as 'efforts at developing rational [efficacious?] solutions to social problems' (Scheurich 1994: 299). Furthermore, digging deeply into underlying strata of 'social regularities' that sustain and reproduce persistent inequalities does not expose ways of easily reversing inequities, even inequities historically linked to belief systems (e.g. overt racism or sexism) that have ceased to be part of the official ideology of mainstream societies and their policymakers. On the contrary, the policy-archaeology approach Scheurich advocates exposes intractable grids of social regularities rooted in asymmetrical power relationships. These relationships, moreover, involve power that is quite broadly distributed across dominant socioeconomic groups and interests and whose most important prerogative is to arbitrate normalcy and conversely to define characteristics, behaviours and groups that are problematic – a most un-postpositivist enterprise. Here, moreover, as Scheurich emphasizes, policy analysts are key figures in legitimizing dominant ideas of what is problematic and hence worth devaluing and suppressing in society (Scheurich 1994: 311). There has been no golden age of equity from whose pristine moral excellence we have newly fallen.

Since the time of the Coleman (Coleman *et al.* 1966) study debate has raged over the possibility of educational policy interventions changing significantly the overall balance of opportunity, treatment and outcomes in education. Injustices embedded in social regularities persist over time despite quantum changes in the socioeconomic realities of life and despite numerous and costly policy interventions and a series of major reform movements. The persistence of these injustices, moreover, tends to obscure possible fundamental change in both the status and meaning of equity as a goal in public and educational policy.

Foster *et al.* (1996) identify four generic conceptions of educational equity that underpin most equity research and most discourse about equity in education:

> (1) Members of different social categories should be represented in different course types, levels [and qualities] in the same proportion as they are represented in the whole school population.

This 'radical' idea of equity hinges upon two key assumptions; first, as Foster *et al.* point out, that 'ability' is equally distributed across social categories, and second, that members of different social categories should and would desire to participate in different courses and programmes in the same proportion as does the population as a whole. Given the latter assumption, this vision of equity runs directly contrary to the communitarian ideal of local schools responding to local needs, culture and values with local programmes, and is unacceptable to groups whose members believe their cultural survival requires education that is different from that provided to most members of the population as a whole.

> (2) Schools ought to operate so as to distribute students across courses and levels according to *measured* ability.

This version of equity is utilitarian and ostensibly meritocratic. It is also the vision of equity most congruent with the tenets of traditional liberal modernism with its focus on individual autonomy and rights. It also arguably converges with Dewey's idea of a democratic community that balances the importance of shared vision and social harmony with a respect for diversity and difference (Kahne 1996: 33–4). Unfortunately, however, this 'meritocratic' vision of equity conceals difficult underlying questions of cultural bias and community power, especially questions of what will count for valued knowledge and how knowledge and skills will be evaluated.

> (3) Allocation of students to courses and teachers should only take account of ability, not of other factors such as social class or ethnic identity.

This third version of equity is really a variant on the second vision. This variant adds a further restrictive requirement, however, that allocation of students to resources and of resources to students should not be skewed by group affiliation or identity. Short of insisting on 'equal educational outcomes' across lines of demographic difference, this concept of equity imposes the most demanding and restrictive conditions possible on the liberal 'equal opportunity' ethos. Such a vision, of course, like vision No. 1, runs directly counter to 'communitarian' principles of local autonomy and hence is unacceptable to groups that believe their cultural survival demands distinctively different schooling.

> (4) Allocation of students to resources and instruction should take account both of ability *and other relevant factors*, but not group-membership characteristics, such as class and ethnicity, over which students have no control.

This vision of equity allows the possibility that elements in the personal background or make-up of the student can legitimately influence the type of school programme a student experiences – provided group-identity variables are not counted (covertly or otherwise) among them. Unfortunately, this vision still leaves the door open to definitions of 'ability' and 'other relevant factors' that are surrogates, wittingly or unwittingly, for group membership (e.g. culture-specific tests and curricula that define students who lack mainstream 'cultural capital' as academically unable).

Poised, in the current poststructuralist flux, against any of these generic visions of equity are communitarian relativism on the one hand and radical individualism on the other, each profoundly relativistic in its moral, ethical and curricular dimensions. Each in its own way calls into question the appropriateness of focusing public policy and resources on *any* vision of equity, preferring instead to concentrate on empowering individuals and communities as against any general vision of what a common education for the common good ought to look like. Carried to an extreme, either communitarian relativism or radical individualism without any higher commitment to the common good leads in the direction of just the kind of 'callous indifference' toward others that Bauman (1992) decries. As Galbraith has shown with eloquence and insight, moreover, public policy which turns a blind eye to the common good, incuding the right to a decent minimal income for all, risks ultimately the common good of all.

> In the good society all of its citizens must have personal liberty, basic well-being, racial and ethnic equality, the opportunity for a rewarding life. Nothing, it must be recognized, so comprehensively denies the liberties of the individual as a total absence of money. Or so impairs it as too little.
>
> (1996: 4)

What John Kennedy noted in his inaugural address is no less true because we have entered an era of poststructuralist uncertainty: 'If a free society cannot help the many who are poor, it cannot save the few who are rich' (Kennedy 1961). Indeed, given an increasing bifurcation of wealth and income in postindustrial nations, Kennedy's epigram may have particular relevance for our time.

Ultimately 'the good society' cannot avoid issues of equity; neither can any society which aspires to pass on the fruits of its labour, wisdom and strength to rising generations – or even just to survive very long. Moreover, as Galbraith has insisted so pointedly in his last two books, no society can pass on any kind of general wellbeing to its young unless it also offers them broad, generalized access to a reasonably high-quality education. Over the long haul, equity as a central educational policy issue is here to stay. Over the short term, however, it may be in serious trouble.

An increasing concentration of income and wealth in fewer and fewer hands (Rifkin 1995: 170–80; Galbraith 1996: 60) is a palpable sign that few developed nations are currently 'good societies' even in the pragmatic sense of economic and social virtue advanced by Galbraith. Recent evidence assembled by the Luxembourg income study from data provided by OECD member countries suggests, for instance, that income inequality increased during the 1980s in many, although not all, developed countries with the greatest increases in the Netherlands, Sweden, and especially in the UK and the USA which also, by virtually any measure used, have the largest income disparities in absolute terms (Atkinson *et al.* 1995: 58, 80).

The time has surely come to ask some hard questions about the meaning and status of equity as a central goal in educational policy in the 1990s. Has the *meaning and status* of equity as a strategic educational policy priority changed significantly among the principal stakeholders in public education in recent years? Do policy makers on the one hand, and service providers and clients on the other, regard educational equity in more or less the same light as they did a decade or two ago? If, on the contrary, the meaning and status of equity as an educational policy goal have changed, in what respects have they changed and what has driven these changes? What are potential consequences of these changes for educational policymaking and for students, teachers and administrators? Is it premature or unjustified to talk about the death, or displacement, of equity as a serious priority in educational policymaking? Have those with power over resources and policy in education decided, for the foreseeable future, at least, to speak henceforth 'of "quality" or "excellence" – not justice' (Kozol 1991: 152)? Or, alternatively, have politicians and the public simply awakened to intractable limits on the power of public and especially educational policy to change existing distributions of wealth, income, privilege and participation in economic, social and intellectual life?

Equity of what?: the dilemma of postpositivism

The problem of multiple and conflicting conceptions of equity, however, is but one of the basic problems confronting the study and politics of educational equity. The most pervasive and intractable difficulty with sustaining equity as a serious policy goal in education stems from values inherent in postpositivism and from economic neo-conservatism. To the extent that the postmodern condition leads to generalized disagreement about what schools should teach and why, it becomes increasingly difficult to deal at the political and policy level with equity questions – *whatever the underlying vision of equity itself.* However equity is conceived or measured, the question of appropriate equity objects, the *equity-of-what* question becomes less answerable as one moves further from consensus about the mission of schools and educational institutions. In the absence of substantial agreement on what constitutes valued knowledge and skills, in fact, it is impossible even to conceptualize a framework for answering questions of fairness in education. For that reason alone it is not surprising that the apparent importance in education of equity as a central policy priority, even as a nominal, symbolic priority, appears to have slipped considerably of late. Equity discourse is pre-empted when there is no broadly, and increasingly that means inter-culturally, acceptable answer to the 'equity-of-what' question.

The history of equity as a policy priority in education, of course, is not merely one of a growth in policy commitment to equity followed by a decline as postmodern perceptions and ways of understanding have taken hold in developed countries. Such an image would be a serious distortion of a considerably more complex history. Nonetheless, the underlying point remains that postmodern endorsement, celebration even, of heterogeneity of lifestyles and, within certain rather broad limits, of values and mores, makes it less distressing to the general public (and, in particular, the *voting* public) and its elected representatives to accept equity policies unlikely to impact seriously on existing distributions of resources and outcomes in education. The end result is that, even in the USA where judicial challenges to fiscal equity in education have become virtually institutionalized in some states, major inequalities persist in virtually every facet of education worth studying and measuring, and dominant current policy trends (exceptions certainly exist!) may do a better job of concealing and politically sub-limating systemic inequities than of remedying them. Such, Hanushek argues, is the blind alley down which fiscal-equity litigation has taken the USA. Only changing what schools *do* with the resources they have, in particular schools whose students and graduates emerge poorly prepared for life and for work, is likely to make much difference in existing distributions of educational participation and achievement.

> Nothing indicates that more of the same – more spending and more equalized spending – will lead to improvement in the very real problems of our schools without a series of more fundamental changes in perspective and organization. We have developed a system that is geared to mediocrity. We neither reward success nor make much effort to uncover what is successful (Haunshek 1994). When we pursue the pure funding equalization strategy, we observe little in the way of equalization of student outcomes (Downes 1992). What we typically find is that more money is spent without commensurate improvement in student performance.
>
> (Hanushek 1995: 39)

Others (Smith and O'Day 1991) argue for much broader changes in public policy aimed at improved school and life changes for at-risk students. In the Jencks (1972) tradition Smith and O'Day argue that, if the goal were truly to equalize opportunity, it would be necessary not just to ensure that all students have access to 'a high-quality, coherent educational program' (1991: 86) but to assure that all low-income children have adequate health care, nutrition and at least one year of 'rich preschool experience' (p. 87), and to 'expand educational opportunities for low-income and otherwise educationally needy students beyond the school day' (p. 88).

Of course, doing any of these things as a matter of public policy presumes that both the resources and political will are there to do them, an unlikely assumption in the current fiscal and political climate in most of the developed nations. Even more fundamentally, however, doing such things as a matter of public policy presumes that there is sufficient agreement on a shared vision of the educated person and the good life to warrant the resources and effort required. Most developed nations, however, are far indeed from the kind of social consensus that makes the kibbutz possible in Israel.

Gordon cuts to the quick of the underlying dilemma:

> Many of the problems that arise in the attempt to authentically assess the educational outcomes and achievements of populations whose life conditions, experiences, and values differ from those of the hegemonic culture are

> central issues with which the assessment community is struggling in its quest to forge performance-oriented assessments and standards. Increasingly, it is argued that adequate evaluation of progress towards equity is not possible with the standardized tests and procedures currently in use. Concerned educators are striving to create assessment procedures that allow for diverse ways of preparing, expressing, and demonstrating competency as well as allowing for alternatives and choice in the measurement tasks to be performed and the conditions under which probes are engaged.
>
> (Gordon and Bonilla-Bowman 1994: 41)

Yet, and herein lies the crux of the post modernist challenge to equity, if not only *the way in which student performance is assessed* but 'the measurement tasks to be performed and the conditions under which' such measurements are made is to differ from one demographic group to another, what is left of the claim of comparability of results? Is this not but another, albeit more circuitous, route back to the 'different-standards-for-different-people' principle which gained educational progressivism such ill repute among a wide cross-section of powerful non-educators? This time, of course, the different standards would presumably be applied to different demographic groups rather than to students viewed as unique individuals, but the effect on claims to equal, or even comparable, levels and types of learning and skill acquisition can be equally corrosive to development and implementation of policy aimed at equalizing educational outcomes – unless, of course, the policy in question is simply for appearance and political expediency's sake. The only other coherent alternative is to identify and evaluate learning outcomes that can reasonably be compared across cultural and linguistic lines. That is probably the most promising but also most difficult way forward in educational equity.

Ironically, then, at the end of the radically pluralist value commitment of postmodernism may lie a collective conscience considerably softened to gross differences in educational opportunities and outcomes – *especially when policy alternatives are at hand which offer a superficial appearance of substantially greater equality of opportunity.* In particular, the poststructuralist value orientation tends to rule out of order attempts to impose one uniform, uniformly evaluated, curriculum for all. It is no accident that the evaluation community senses acutely the desperation of this state of affairs. Evaluators, after all, wrestle directly with the conundrum of inferring from 'surrogate behavioral expressions' (Gordon and Bonilla-Bowman 1994: 42), often abstract and culture-specific in one way or another, what it is students know and can do. Increasingly, moreover, and not surprisingly, evaluators must work with very vague and confused definitions of what 'all' students should know and be able to do at particular levels of development. In trying to encompass all, curriculum designers often finish by encompassing none.

It is one thing, after all, to assert that room should be made in the curriculum for more than one cultural, artistic, literary or even linguistic tradition. It is quite another to try to build 'a curriculum' around an amorphous mass of inscrutable, empty 'learning outcomes' drawn from no coherent vision of what an educated person ought to known and be able to do. *To the extent that, in the new poststructural social and economic reality, curriculum policy evades any coherent vision of desired knowledge and outcomes, the question of the equity of educational opportunity or outcomes becomes a non-sense.* A curriculum uninformed by some relatively clear vision of what an educated person should know and be able to do *pre-empts equity* as a matter of serious inquiry and policy debate, and of serious reform policy. It is futile to discuss whether individual (or group) A has achieved more or less than individual (or group) B if, in the end, we have no clear idea of what A AND B *should* know and be able to do (due allowances having been made for cultural and linguistic differences). No escape exists from this dilemma. Failure to define a curriculum within fairly clear (not oppressively detailed or narrowly ethnocentric, however) general objectives vitiates equity as a matter of serious policy discourse. And the recent semantic change to the language of 'outcomes' does nothing to change this fundamental dilemma. Either learning outcomes will be sufficiently clear to permit fairly broad agreement on what learning and skills are envisioned, or we need not waste our time discussing (or studying) whether achievement of such outcomes is equitable or even which meaning of equity is more appropriate in the case at hand.

Heterogeneity, progressivism and reaction

Prior to the Second World War, substantial value consensus existed in most developed countries about the purposes, and even about the proper content and dimensions of, and limits to, formal education. Generally education was to serve three main purposes:

- provide basic literacy and numeracy skills to the general population;
- transmit the 'high' cultural, scientific, literary and artistic traditions of Western civilization to a socioeconomic élite; and
- support economic development through research and especially through training in the 'applied sciences'.

Within this broader mandate, secondary education was to play its part, particularly in providing some additional development in basic literacy and numeracy before most students were pushed out of secondary school by stiff academic competition from university-bound classmates and pulled out by employment opportunities that required little or no secondary education. For the majority of secondary dropouts in industrialized countries, these jobs were to be found on and around the assembly-lines which defined the then dominant Fordist approach to industrial production.

Access to secondary education had not yet become a critical social and economic issue for those who did not complete secondary school. Because participation rates in secondary education were much lower than at present, secondary education had not yet attained the status of a viable entry 'filter' for the labour market. While the argument had long been made that education *ought* to be linked to the job market including the general labour market,[1] reality was otherwise. Despite an underlying 'meritocratic' norm that 'those having a greater share of educational benefits merit or deserve a greater share of non-educational social goods' (Green 1980: 43), the pool of secondary graduates remained too small to render the secondary diploma practicable as a general labour-market access credential.[2]

With the prosperity and increasing technical complexity of much work, including much factory work, during the 1960s, developed nations began to adopt policies aimed at raising substantially secondary completion rates (as well as tertiary matriculation rates). As the clientele of secondary schools expanded and diversified, however, traditional academic, subject-centred and driven instruction proved unable to engage much of the enlarged student population in newly created comprehensive or vocational schools. The result was generally a diversification of secondary curriculum that sent students into different tracks or streams according to their perceived abilities and aptness for particular types and levels of education.

It was in this context during the 1960s that educational progressivism gained ascendancy, most notably in the USA and Canada, but also, although with important contextual differences, in Britain. In some ways this wave of educational progressivism during the 1960s and 1970s might be considered one of the first public-policy bellwethers of emergent postmodern consciousness – well in advance of the more recent decline of Fordist modes of production which had epitomized modernist ways of thinking and doing in the private sector. In any case, educational policy was greatly influenced by progressivist ideology during this period, and specifically by the progressivist imperative to individualize learning to the 'needs', interests and abilities of each student. By giving to each according to his or her own ability and 'need', equality of opportunity would be achieved. Equity came to mean accommodating differences in ability and need, differences which, initially at least, were taken uncritically as givens. In economically expansive and generous times, one could afford an expansive, fluid and not-very-demanding definition of equity.

The combined impact of the 1982 recession and the evident and profound challenge to the rest of the developed world of Japanese and German ways of organizing work, production and education, however, fed growing public and business discontent with the content and structure of educational systems widely perceived as rudderless and adrift. Just when secondary graduation rates achieved levels that made the secondary diploma an attractive, readily available credential with which to filter job applicants, employers came to believe that secondary diplomas did not correspond in any consistent way to knowledge, skills, comportment or values. With the squeeze of harder times and the first paroxysms of economic globalization beginning to make themselves felt, full-scale revolt against progressivism was imminent. An equity founded on offering much less academic substance, less (or different) discipline, less (or different) manners and basic culture to some secondary students than to others had been tried and found wanting in the courts of public and establishment opinion. The secondary diploma as a certificate of time-in-school was in imminent danger.

An essentialist revolt: reclaiming a rigorous liberal education

A dangerous educational dry rot was eating away the heart of public education, proclaimed a series of reports on the status of education in the USA and Canada during the 1980s.[3] This softening of standards and truncating of a rigorous liberal curriculum was placing North America at risk in the evolving globalized information economy. A parallel series of perceptions and events in Great Britain (starting, however, much earlier) culminated in a National Curriculum ensconced directly in legislation (Chitty 1988, 1993; Lawton 1996). In England, Prime Minister James Callaghan had, on 18 October 1976, initiated a long and impassioned debate over the merits of a return to a rigorous core curriculum with his 'Ruskin Speech' (Chitty 1988: 41, 1993: 8). In particular, through a series of reports and otherwise, 'the Department of Education and Science championed the idea of a centrally determined non-negotiable curriculum framework while the inspectorate consistently favoured an "entitlement curriculum" – a broad framework representing a synthesis of the vocational, the technical and the academic' (Chitty 1993: 39). In the end, but not until about 1986, Margaret Thatcher, seconded by Education Secretary Kenneth Baker, would decide in favour of a centrally crafted educational programme and eventually embark England on its National Curriculum adventure.

In the USA *The Paideia Proposal* (Adler 1982) and *A Nation at Risk* (National Commission on Excellence in Education 1983) led the charge accompanied by numerous other reports similarly predicting dire consequences unless American education were rapidly reinfused with the rigour of a world-class education system (Boyer 1983; National Science Board Commission on Precollege Education in Mathematics 1983; Task Force on Education for Economic Growth 1983). Sizer (1984) noted not only the problem, but the intractability of some of the situations which perpetuated it. In Canada, the most articulate and influential call for return to rigour and a firm subject base came four years later. The 'Radwanski Report' (1988), a clarion call for return to a traditional, in this case anglo-centric, liberal arts and sciences curriculum, would have an impact totally out of proportion to its strictly Ontario origin and mandate.

The 'first wave' of 1980s school reform in the USA, and to a somewhat lesser extent in Canada, would largely substitute the excellence agenda for the equity agenda. Schools were told to refocus on the real mission of schooling, academic learning of the traditional, subject-based curriculum. No longer should they consider their critical mission to be to provide a 'basic' level of education to all but rather to provide a world-class quality of education to those who could profit from it.

Compensatory measures for at-risk students received almost as little support in this round of reform documents and the policies that flowed from them as did 'individualized' programmes drawn from student needs and tastes. While few went as far as Radwanski in denouncing environmental education, 'multiculturalism' and education about racism as 'stuff' 'litter[ing]' the curriculum (Radwanski 1988: 38), the message to schools was clear – get back to your primary business, fostering excellence in core academic learning. Equity must not be at the price of levelling down the performance of the best and brightest (or most favoured!). The educational-policy agenda of the hour became quality, not equality.

As Thompson (1995: 206–7) points out, however, evidence exists to show that, according to several measures of educational outcomes, both the relative and absolute situation of black students, and to a much lesser extent, Hispanic students (the only two ethnic/racial categories commonly identified in American data), improved considerably during the first wave of school reform in the USA. From these data, Thompson is tempted to the conclusion that the focus on excellence helped disadvantaged minority students differentially more than non-minority students – although he readily concedes that the end result is only a slight narrowing of the achievement gap between majority students and black and Hispanic students (Thompson 1995: 207–8).

An unwritten and unspoken subtext of the first-wave reforms is precisely the message to which only a very-far-right organization such as the Heritage Foundation would dare give voice: educational resources should be reconcentrated on those who have highest potential 'to contribute positively to society', in short, those who bring to school the greatest cultural capital of the type traditionally rewarded by schools and by the social-benefits system linked to school performance and achievement. The first-wave reforms, moreover, Smith and O'Day (1991: 79–84) argue, appear to have had substantially more impact than the more equity-oriented 'restructuring' efforts of the second wave of reform which began in reaction to a sense that a large proportion of students were simply being abandoned in the general rush to raise the quality of education.

Reclaiming equity – sort of

A second wave of reform reports emerged in the USA during the second half of the 1980s. In addition to reports focused on professionalizing teaching and decentralization of school governance (Carnegie Forum on Education and the Economy 1986; Holmes Group 1986), this second wave of reports specifically called for programmes to address the needs of minority and at-risk students (Charles Stewart Mott Foundation 1986; Commission on Minority Participation in Education and American Life 1988). Unfortunately, as Thompson (1995) points out, little changed for the better in the educational situation of minority students as a result of this second-wave report activity and Smith and O'Day (1991: 84–5) point to four reasons why it is unlikely that achievement gaps between blacks and whites, and more generally between at-risk students and others, will continue to close:

- demographic changes (e.g. urbanization of blacks) have already borne their positive fruits; the current challenge includes precisely the rapid development of an intergenerational urban underclass;
- recent declines in college enrolments of young blacks (who are, Smith and O'Day note, future parents) seem likely to slow the effects of increased parental education levels;

- increased poverty, density of poverty, and increased numbers of children born with toxic dependence; and
- likelihood that current educational reforms will come latest and least to those with the greatest need of them.

Regarding the last point, they foresee that:

> Society's push to improve the quality of schooling by changing the character of the instruction and the curriculum makes the task of continuing to reduce the gap even more difficult, both because of the competition for funds and because progressive change will typically come last to the most needy.
>
> (Smith and O'Day 1991: 85)

It takes little imagination to see that most of these trends may have counterparts outside the USA. Given the widespread negative impact of globalization and automation on traditional sources of mass employment, increased poverty and density of poverty along with reduced access to higher education on the part of educationally and economically disadvantaged groups forms a growing part of the socioeconomic backdrop of the most developed countries. There is good reason, then, to be alert to the possibility of a general decline in the equity of educational participation, attainment and achievement in the years to come. But, in the neo-conservative individualism of postmodernity, will anyone, other than the victims, bother to notice?

Meritocracy and excellence (for all?): a final obfuscation

A general reaction against affirmative-action programmes of all types is evident in the neo-conservative politics of, among other places, the USA, Canada, and Britain over the last decade. Broadly speaking, the political right has argued that policies aimed at equalizing opportunity and outcomes for historically disadvantaged categories of persons:

- result in economic inefficiencies associated on the one hand with not hiring best-qualified and most able workers – or, in education, with siphoning resources from the 'most able' students – and, on the other, with the administrative overburden involved in monitoring requirements of such policies;
- fail to take adequate count of individual differences in ability, taste, and motivation; and
- institutionalize the inequity of reverse discrimination.

In the USA, for instance, the Bradley Foundation overtly champions the cause of reconcentrating educational resources on the 'able' through school choice programmes (Miner 1995) and the Heritage Foundation (as cited in Bacharach 1988: 488) misses no opportunity to attack federal compensatory programmes. These are, of course, but two of a growing network of interlinked groups dedicated to a variety of conservative causes but whose interest in education converges on providing quality education to the 'best and the brightest'.

At stake in this debate is more, however, than simply the proportion of available resources going to at-risk as opposed to 'normal' and 'gifted' students. At stake is the fundamental utilitarian principle of social benefits allocated meritocratically, a principle which, in contemporary reality, tends to get translated into 'allocated in accordance with demonstrated educational merit'. Now it is evident that tangible social benefits, especially wealth and income, are not, in any rigorous sense, allocated according to educational attainment or achievement. It is also obvious, however, that educational attainment is, in general and despite notable individual and collective exceptions,[4] increasingly related to such 'tangible; social benefits – as well as to other less tangible quality-of-life benefits. The meritocratic principle favours further tightening of that relationship.

At this point, of course, one enters a particularly vicious and well-known equity circle. If, by definition, those with the cultural capital traditionally valued and reinforced by schools are considered those most likely, and worthy, to benefit from formal education, and if, therefore, resources are concentrated preferentially on these students, others are accordingly blocked out of the education – social benefit – education circuit. It is only when *appropriate and sufficient* resources are made available to those who are outside that circuit that the educationally disadvantaged have a chance of breaking into the meritocratic circle. Indeed, at the heart of some of the most promising contemporary experiments in alternative educational programmes for disadvantaged students is the axiom that students who are behind must be given more if they are to 'catch up' with educationally and culturally advantaged peers. As Levin notes, 'it is obvious intuitively that at-risk students must learn at a faster rate, not at a slower one that drags them farther and farther behind' (1994: 180). The compensatory rationale leads in the opposite direction from simply rewarding educational 'haves' with further resources. Compensatory education, moreover, *provided the educational services offered are efficient and effective with the students to whom they are provided*, can be wise economic investments[5] and respond to a 'meritocratic' norm.

Of course, as numerous critics have pointed out, merely equalizing fiscal resources does not guarantee that these resources will be used in ways that are, at least on average, efficient and effective for the students to whom they are directed. Money *can* matter, but it does not have to – and it will not if it is spent inefficiently or inappropriately (Hanushek 1994, 1995; Hedges *et al.* 1994; Laine *et al.* 1995). No amount of money, in any case, will ensure that *all* students, or all students within a particular demographic category, learn any particular curriculum well, a reality that tends to get lost in much current policy rhetoric. Within every significant demographic category there 'will continue to be a distribution of human capital [and educational attainment and achievement], since different individuals benefit from their schooling investments according to their talents, abilities, and diligence' (Levin 1990: 131).

For those who view the promotion of greater educational equity (however defined) as a legitimate benefit or 'social utility' of public investment in education, the chief problem of providing greater equity resolves itself into finding a combination of beliefs, techniques, organization and pedagogy that is effective in closing achievement and/or attainment gaps between particular 'at-risk' groups of students and the overall, or culturally mainstream, population (and not necessarily by subjecting them to a culturally 'mainstream' curriculum). With the exception of those on the far political right who wish to restrict all educational investment and provision considerations to narrow measures of contribution to economic productivity, something approaching consensus exists that publicly funded schools should *help disadvantaged students approach attainment and achievement levels and distributions associated with the dominant sociocultural group(s)*. Where that consensus dissolves, of course, is in determining just what evidence of what attainments and achievements should count as comparable and to what degree[6] – and how best to raise the performance of identifiable groups with systematically lower-than-average educational attainment and achievement.

Leaving aside for the moment the increasingly insoluble conundrum of competing views about what should count as significant educational attainments and achievement (the equity objects problem), one of the major conceptual stumbling blocks in arriving at agreement on equity measures and policies stems from unequal distribution across populations and sub-populations of characteristics or traits (talent, abilities, motivation, diligence, 'intelligences' and so forth) commonly associated with educational attainment and achievement. In general, such traits, if measured by traditional quantitative indicator(s) (with all of the implied assumptions and limitations) can be shown to be normally distributed across any population sufficiently large. The implications of this 'bell curve' distribution for evaluation of and policy on equity are fundamental. They certainly do *not* include, however, conclusions that certain anti-equity policy groups associate with the normal distribution of such traits (Miner 1995). That variance in the distribution of such traits across time, space and sub-populations is relatively constant does not, in particular, mean that the current means, medians and variance of such 'traits' across different groups within a population are fixed over time. It does not even mean that such characteristics or traits are fixed over time for specific individuals. The sole conclusion possible, given available evidence, is that, on average, over large enough groups and populations, such characteristics, like learning outcome measures, will tend to distribute themselves normally, no more, no less.

Evidence for the malleability of such educationally significant personal characteristics comes from the existing literature on the history of intelligence measures across demographic lines (Jensen 1973; Kamin 1974; Lewontin *et al.* 1984; Plomin 1990) and, more recently, from ambitious compensatory education projects for at-risk students such as Slavin's 'Success for All' programme and Levin's Accelerated Schools (Slavin *et al.* 1993a,b; Levin 1994). While the claim that, 'whenever and wherever we choose' (Slavin *et al.* 1993b) we can assure all students success seems a bit fulsome given current resource realities and escalating poverty among children, such projects leave little doubt that, with redirected and/or greater resources and commitment, especially to preventing early reading failure, chances are promising that at-risk students can experience considerably more school success than at present. The claim that coherent and carefully targeted and rationed interventions such as Success for All might improve the chances that at-risk students experience greater academic achievement and overall school success, however, is a totally different kind of claim from silver-bullet 'excellence-for-all' claims. Even the more modest claim of increased school success must, however, await further longitudinal study to determine whether and to what degree achievement test gains ascribed to programmes such as Success for All translate over the long term into improved educational achievement and successful participation in high-status secondary and post-secondary courses and programmes.[7]

Given the inevitability of a distribution of educational participation, achievement and attainment, no reform, curricular, programatic or structural, will rid schools and school systems of unequal student inputs into education. Students will continue to vary both within and across groups in educationally significant traits and dispositions they bring to school with them, *and would do so even if some sort of universal mandatory day care from earliest infancy largely equalized the 'cultural capital' (Bernstein 1971) they brought to school with them.* Furthermore, it is evident that such variations in educationally significant characteristics and background experiences play a major role in shaping educational outcomes and, in addition, that educational success or failure can influence the development of such characteristics in individuals.

In education, as in the human condition generally, no escape is possible from either a certain degree of determinism, on the one hand, or a certain degree of uncertainty and possibility on the other. To some considerable extent, educational achievement is a collective manifestation of the mystery of determinism and free will in the human situation. We are both free and determined. Students too, are both free and determined. They are free to achieve much more or less than any informed observer would have predicted under the circumstances. But they are also determined, or at least constrained to some degree, by context, experience (including, of course, any compensatory programmes they might receive), and background. It is folly, and leads to wasteful and delusionary policy to pretend otherwise. That is the important germ of truth in the message of the far-right think tanks on the issue.

Nonetheless, from the perspective of those who see the amelioration of educational and social-benefits equity as an indispensable part of the mission of public education, taxpayers, citizens and parents have a right to expect that, to some reasonable degree, publicly funded schools and educational institutions should defy the odds of personal background by narrowing achievement gaps between at-risk students and those from more favoured circumstances. However, unless policymakers and shapers wish to produce mainly disappointment, frustration and destructive and debilitating recriminations and backlash against public educational investment, they cannot afford to demand the impossible from publicly funded schools.

Yet the impossible mandate appearing with increasing frequency in official policy statements and discourse is precisely that schools make all students excellent. Aside from the surrealistic horror of a world of uniformly 'excellent' clones (educationally or otherwise excellent), policy aimed at achieving some sort of absolute equality of outcomes, or even very high minimum performance outcomes, for *all* students is a dangerous and expensive delusion. In the present context of shrinking public-sector funds, ageing populations, and declining consensus on essential learning achievements and outcomes, public education simply cannot afford to foster, or even be complicit in, the myth of a 'Lake Wobegon' educational Utopia where 'all the children are above average'. To do so is, as Biemiller rightly observes, to ensure little more than policy and educational failure and the doublespeak of dissimulation.

> Even if effective compensatory approaches were to eliminate SES/minority differences, there would still be a substantial range of performance among children of the same age. When we confront teachers and school systems with expectations that all children should be performing at or above age-normed 'grade level,' we ensure 'failure' for a significant proportion of children or teachers....When we set unrealistic expectations, we create an atmosphere in which teachers, principals, and board officials may respond with practices that obscure the truth.
>
> (1993: 9)

The key equity policy issue is not whether *all* students will be excellent – in reading, writing, mathematics, science, integrated humanities, or anything else. The notion that all students can be excellent in anything, much less in everything, is a dangerous nonsense. The key equity policy issue is whether some groups in society have levels and distributions of educational attainment and achievement that are significantly below population-wide norms – and what can be done to help such groups more closely approach norms of attainment and achievement associated with the overall population or with the dominant socioeconomic reference group(s). Given this limitation on equity policy and possibilities, a central concern becomes when and how and in what context students should begin to be differentiated in the programmes, curricula and pedagogy they receive.

Not until quite recently, however, was the inevitability of a distribution of educationally significant characteristics challenged. Until recently neither policymaker nor politician would have thought of raising his or her voice to insist that schools make *all* students excellent students. Arguments focused rather on appropriate ages and methods for sorting students into different subject concentrations and levels of difficulty. Only within the last decade has the audacious language and oxymoronic policy of 'excellence for all' made its way into the educational policy arena. If the goal of secondary completion rates approaching the 100% level is suspect on pragmatic, economic, pedagogic and common-sense grounds (Green 1983; Allison 1984; Seidman 1996), the goal of 'excellence for all', is, in so far as such an oxymoron has any meaning at all, a policy battle of Sisyphus-like proportions against the intractable reality of variation in human ability, motivation, intelligences and so forth. Doing battle with aspects of the human condition that could only be changed by politically and morally grotesque social and human genetic engineering makes, need it be said, for bad policy!

When seriously and overtly tried, it also elicits some fast reality therapy and quick policy reversals. A particularly disingenuous example comes from Jim Dinning, then Alberta Minister of Education, who, in November of 1990 announced a reform project rooted deeply in the idea of 'excellence for all students' (Alberta Education 1991). The Alberta government and ministry took this goal sufficiently literally to attempt to set one sole 'standard of excellence' criterion for all students in provincial subject exams. Predictably, students stubbornly refused to redistribute their exam performance with sufficient skew so as to place a majority of students above a credible 'standard of excellence' threshold level in this Albertan Lake Wobegon. Alberta rapidly reinvented the double standard, an 'acceptable standard' (a sort of pass level performance) and a 'standard of excellence' for superior performance. When one tries to use educational policy to change summarily one of the deepest givens of the human situation, individual variability – and when one advertises that fact clearly in language everyone can understand – hasty retreat is the only politically viable option.

Few governments, however, have shown Jim Dinning's audacity or disingenuousness. Much current policy discourse on equity in education, and considerable formal policy, however, is mired in a similar Utopian project. *It is one thing, and an entirely worthy liberal democratic policy objective, to work to reduce significant inter group differences in the level and distribution of educational performance by improving the performance of low performing groups and to improve overall levels of performance; it is quite another, and hardly a sensible investment of scarce educational resources, to try to eliminate variation in educational achievement and related human traits – and this is true even though these traits are unfixed and relatively malleable.* Significant variation will persist. Human beings are different – and that matters (despite the arguments put forth by Slavin under the provocative title 'Students differ: so what?' [Slavin 1993]). No reason exists to believe that some Utopia of near-absolute educational outcome equality will reward perseverance in destreaming, detracking and curricular homogenization – or in the curriculum meltdown of radical subject integration. While space does not allow full critical discussion of the complex issues surrounding currently fashionable interpretations of the existing research literature in these areas, sufficient reason exists to be very circumspect about increasingly frequent invocation of such policies as magic-bullet solutions to the problem of achieving greater educational equity.

The ultimate equity policy question, in any case, remains what schools can do to reduce invidious differences in the type, level and variance of achievement across demographic lines of difference, just as the ultimate quality question is what schools can do that improves mean and median performance levels without negatively impacting on certain segments of society. If the kernel of the equity policy question is equalization of outcomes across lines of demographic difference, then what is needed appears to be three related courses of action:

1. experimentation with interventions aimed at improving the *long-term* educational participation, achievement and attainment of the disadvantaged;
2. longitudinal monitoring of long-term impact (especially at the senior secondary level and beyond) on achievement, but also on:
   (a) participation in particular course types and sequences,
   (b) at particular levels of difficulty; and
3. more demographically detailed and sensitive analyses of patterns of achievement and course and programme routes.

The price of current equity policy obfuscation may be very high – especially for those trapped in the worst socioeconomic situations and schools. On the one hand, the silver-bullet rhetoric of detracking our way to 'excellence for all' provides an impression that greater equity will be a natural by-product of renewed focus on increasing the quality of education. There is grave reason to doubt this logic and serious reason also to suspect that the end result of the current economic and educational-reform conjuncture will be reversal of equity gains made during the 1970s and early 1980s (Smith and O'Day 1991).

Equity, a policy priority in peril?

Oddly enough, the flowering of poststructuralist uncertainty and individualist neoconservative politics in the early 1980s coincided with a wave of reform aimed at renewing the quality of education by returning it to a clear focus on the contemporary vision of a broad liberal arts and sciences education. Just as North American and some European societies were becoming more fully aware and tolerant of their internal differences, a strong reform movement emerged which sought to reclaim the heritage of rigour associated with academic excellence and élitism – and to reclaim lost economic competitiveness into the bargain.

The political and economic conjuncture at the moment does not bode well at least for the short-term future of equity as a serious, rather than a nominal or symbolic, educational policy priority. Resurgent neo-conservatism, government revenues sapped by global restructuring and galloping automation, and greying populations whose political attention is focused more on health care and security than on education, none of these favour the equality agenda in publicly funded education. Neither does a poststructuralist social value system that leads to pervasive doubt about the knowledge, skills, values and commitments students from different backgrounds should share.

Schools cannot equalize social benefits, not completely, not directly, a fact which has been widely acknowledged since at least the time Jencks (1972) published his reassessment of the Coleman (1966) data. Schools can, however, make a difference in the knowledge, skills, values and engagements students bring to further education, the workplace, and their civic and private lives.

Schools have, perhaps, a better chance of making a difference when in-school programmes are combined and coordinated with community, municipal and other efforts that contribute to the intellectual, emotional, linguistic and learning-readiness development of children. Reports associated with the so-called third wave of reform in the USA have recommended comprehensive measures to capitalize on this potential including health care for infants, parenting, health care and nutritional guidance, quality child care and preschools programmes, support systems within schools that include health services, nutritional guidance and counselling, and more (Committee for Economic Development 1987; National Governors' Association 1990; National Commission on Children 1991). French experience with pre-kindergarten supports the long-term benefits of pre-school education in reduced retention to grade (McMahan 1992) and France has been experimenting with integrating services for children at the municipal level for close to a decade. In Ontario, a recent Royal Commission on Learning made extensive recommendations for integrated and community-based services to children (Royal Commission on Learning 1995: 43–9).

Neglecting or obfuscating the equity imperative of public education will not make it go away. Moreover, unless publicly funded education can demonstrate its capacity to foster at least some relative improvement in the educational and life chances of the disadvantaged, it seems increasingly probable that it will be found wanting in the court of public opinion. Unfortunately the task both of doing so, and being seen to do so, has arguably never been more difficult than at present. Disarmed by postmodern divergence on what should constitute a base of knowledge, skills, values and commitments the overwhelming majority of the young should share, both the political left and right seem alarmingly susceptible to empty euphemisms of excellence for all and to the facile and largely symbolic policymaking they engender. Equity in educational policymaking appears to be in trouble in the short term and, optimistically, in fundamental transition over the longer term.

Notes

1 Coulter cites a particularly poignant line from Bott (1920) who recommended that for young people 'a causal connection between school record and industrial status, which does not now exist, must be deliberately created and impressed upon them' (1991: 31).

2 Seidman (1996: 5–9) presents formal arguments on limiting cases of possible correlation between educational and social benefits and liabilities.

3 While some Canadian reports, in particular the Sullivan commission report in British Columbia, took quite a different stance, what the politicians eventually construed such reports to mean was inevitably a call for increased rigour and higher standards. In this respect, Crawley's commentary of the fate of the Sullivan report is particularly telling (1995).

4 Analysis of employment income by age cohort, for instance, shows that in Canada over the last three census periods, the employment-income advantage of *young* secondary graduates over dropouts has been dwarfed by the loss in real-dollar employment income the young have experienced (Paquette 1994, 1995).

5 Levin (1990) examines in depth the question of the social utility of promoting both economic efficiency and productivity on the one hand and equity on the other. In the

same piece, he provides a relatively exhaustive inventory of the economic benefits associated with promoting higher levels of achievement on the part of disadvantaged students.

6 Another major source of disagreement is the particular restraining conditions that should be attached to the norm of equal opportunity or outcomes (see discussion above on pp. 337–8).

7 Slavin *et al.* note that their Success for All programme has shown substantial positive effects on reading performance of all students in grades 1–3 (1993a, especially p. 15, 1993b), and on reductions in grade retentions and special education placements (however, one of the conditions of the programme is that special education placements be used only for serious disabilities). Slavin and his colleagues point out, however, that these effects cannot be considered 'maintenance' (residual, after-programme) effects, however, because the programme continues through the elementary grades (although one-on-one tutoring becomes very rare after grade 1) (1993a, especially p. 15).

References

Adler, M., 1982, *The Paideia Proposal: An Educational Manifesto* (New York: MacMillan).

Alberta Education, 1991, *Vision for the Nineties: A Plan of Action* (Edmonton: Alberta Education).

Allison, D. J., 1984, The limitations of secondary schooling and the problem of secondary education. *Teacher Education* (24), 18–37.

Argys, L. M., Rees, D. I. and Brewer, D. J., 1995, *Detracking America's Schools: Equity at Zero Cost* (9501) (Denver: Center for Research on Economic and Social Policy).

Ascher, C., 1992, *Successful Detracking in Middle and Senior High Schools* (Washington, DC: Office of Educational Research and Improvement [ED]).

Atkinson, A., Rainwater, L. and Smeeding, T., 1995, *Income Distribution in OECD Countries: Evidence from the Luxembourg Income Study* (Paris: OECD).

Bacharach, S. B., 1988, Four themes of reform: an editorial essay. *Educational Administration Quarterly*, 24(4), 484–96.

Bauman, Z., 1992, *Intimations of Postmodernity* (London: Routledge).

Bernstein, B., 1971, Class, Codes and Control, Vol. I (London: Routledge & Kegan Paul).

Biemiller, A., 1993, Lake Wobegon revisited: on diversity and education. *Educational Researcher*, 22(9), 7–12.

Bott, E., 1920, Juvenile employment in relation to public schools and industries in Toronto, in *Studies in Industrial Psychology*, Vol. IV (Toronto: University of Toronto).

Boyer, E., 1983, *High School: A Report on Secondary Education in America* (New York: Harper & Row).

Carnegie Forum on Education and the Economy, 1986, *A Nation Prepared: Teachers for the 21st Century* (New York: Carnegie Corporation).

Charles Stewart Mott Foundation, 1986, *America's Shame, America's Hope: Twelve Million Youth at Risk* (New York: Author).

Chitty, C., 1988, Two models of a National Curriculum origins and interpretation, in D. Lawton and C. Chitty (eds), *The National Curriculum* (London: Institute of Education, University of London), 34–48.

Chitty, C., 1993, The school curriculum: from teacher autonomy to central control, in C. Chitty (ed.), *The National Curriculum: Is it Working* (Harlow, Essex: Longman), 1–25.

Coleman, J., Campbell, E. Q., McPartland, J., Mood, A. M., Weinfield, F. D. and York, R. L., 1966, *Equality of Educational Opportunity* (Washington, DC: US Department of Health, Education and Welfare).

Commission on Minority Participation in Education and American Life, 1988, *One-third of a Nation* (Washington, DC: American Council on Education).

Committee for Economic Development, 1987, *Children in Need: Investment Strategy for the Educationally Disadvantaged* (New York: Author).

Coulter, R., 1991, Persistent themes: some reflections on the history of schooling and work, in D. Allison and J. Paquette (eds), Reform and Relevance in Schooling: Dropouts, Destreaming, and the Common Curriculum (Toronto: OISE Press), 28–38.

Crawley, M., 1995, *Schoolyard Bullies: Messing with British Columbia's Education System* (Victoria, BC: Orca).

Downes, T., 1992, Evaluating the impact of school finance reform on the provision of public education: the California case. *National Tax Journal*, 45, 405–19.

Foster, P., Gomm, R. and Hammersley, M., 1996, *Constructing Educational Inequality: An Assessment of Research on School Processes* (London: Falmer Press).

Fulton, M. and Long, D., 1993, *School Financial Litigation: A Historical Summary* (Denver: Education Commission of the States).

Galbraith, J. K., 1996, *The Good Society: The Humane Agenda* (New York: Houghton Mifflin).

Gordon, E. and Bonilla-Bowman, C., 1994, Equity and social justice in educational achievement, in R. Berne and L. Picus (eds), *Outcome Equity in Education* (Thousand Oaks, CA: Corwin Press), 24–44.

Green, T., 1980, *Predicting the Behavior of the Educational System* (Syracuse: Syracuse University Press).

Green, T., 1983, Excellence, equity, and equality, in L. Shulman and G. Sykes (eds), *Handbook of Teaching and Policy* (New York: Longman) 318–41.

Hanushek, E., 1994, Money might matter somewhere: a response to Hedges, Laine, and Greenwald. *Educational Researcher*, 23(4), 5–8.

Hanushek, E., 1995, The quest for equalized mediocrity: school finance reform without consideration of school performance, in L. Picus and J. Wattenbarger (eds), *Where Does the Money Go:? Resource Allocation in Elementary and Secondary Schools* (Thousand Oaks, CA: Corwin Press), 20–43.

Harvey, D., 1989, *The Condition of Postmodemity* (Oxford: Basil Blackwell).

Hedges, L., Laine, R. and Greenwald, R., 1994, Does money matter?: A meta-analysis of studies of the effects of differential school inputs on student outcomes. *Educational Researcher*, 23(3), 5–14.

Holmes Group, 1986, *Tomorrow's Teachers* (East Lansing, MI: Author).

Jencks, C., 1972, *Inequality: A Reassessment of the Effect of Family and Schooling in America* (Harmondsworth: Penguin).

Jensen, A. R., 1973, *Educability and Group Differences*, 1st US edn (New York: Harper & Row).

Kahne, J., 1996, *Reframing Educational Policy: Democracy, Community, and the Individuals*, Vol. 10 (New York: Teachers College Press).

Kamin, L., 1974, *The Science and Politics of IQ* (New York: Halsted Press).

Kennedy, J., 1961, Inaugural address, Washington, DC.

Kozol, J., 1991, *Savage Inequalities: Children in American Schools* (New York: Crown).

Laine, R. D., Greenwald, R. and Hedges, L. V., 1995, Money does matter: a research synthesis of a new universe of education production function studies, in L. Picus and J. Wattenbarger (eds), *Where Does the Money Go?: Reource Allocation in Elementary and Secondary Schools* (Thousand Oaks, CA: Corwin Press), 44–70.

Lawton, D., 1996, Comparisons with English 'reforms', 1979–1995, in G. Milbum (ed.), *'Ring some alarm bells in Ontario': Reactions to the Report of the Royal Commission on Learning* (London, ONT: Althouse Press), 15–24.

Levin, H., 1990, The economics of justice in education, in D. Verstegen and G. Ward (eds), *Spheres of Justice in Education* (New York: Harper Business), 129–47.

Levin, H., 1994, The necessary and sufficient conditions for achieving educational equity, in R. Berne and L. Picus (eds), *Outcome Equity in Education* (Thousand Oaks, CA: Corwin Press), 167–90.

Lewontin, R., Rose, S. and Kamin, L., 1984, *Not in our Genes: Biology, Ideology, and Human Nature* (New York: Pantheon Books).

McMahan, I., 1992, Public preschool from the age of two: the Ecole Matemelle in France. *Young Children* (July) 22–5.

Miner, B., 1995, Who is backing 'The Bell Curve'? *Educational Leadership*, 52(7), 80–1.

Natapoff, A., 1994, 1993: the year of living dangerously: state courts expand the right to education. *West's Education Law Quarterly*, 3(4), 639–71.

National Commission on Children, 1991, *Beyond Rhetoric: A new American Agenda for Children and Families* (Washington, DC: Author).

National Commission on Excellence in Education, 1983, *A Nation at Risk* (Washington, DC: Government Printing Office).

National Governors' Association, 1990, *Educating America: State Strategies for Achieving the National Education Goals* (Washington, DC: Author).

National Science Board (U.S.). Commission on Precollege Education In Mathematics, Science and Technology (1983), *Educating Americans for the 21st Century: A plan of action for improving mathematics, science, and technology education for all American elementary and secondary students so that their achievement is the best in the world by 1995: A report to the American people and the National Science Board* (Washington, DC: National Science Board Commission on Precollege Education in Mathematics, Sciences, and Technology).

Ontario Ministry of Education and Training, 1995, *The Common Curriculum: Policies and Outcomes, Grades 1–9* (Toronto: Ontario Ministry of Education and Training).

Paquette, J., 1994, *Publicly Supported Education in Post-Modern Canada: An Imploding Universe* (Toronto: Our Schools/Our Selves Education Foundation).

Paquette, J., 1995, Universal education: meanings, challenges, and options in the third millennium. *Curriculum Inquiry*, 25(1), 23–56.

Plomin, R., 1990, *Behavioral Genetics: A Primer*, 2nd edn (New York: W. H. Freeman).

Radwanski, G., 1988, *Ontario Study of the Relevance of Education, and the Issue of Dropouts* (Toronto: Ministry of Education).

Rifkin, J., 1995, *The End of Work: The Decline of the Global Labor Force and the Dawn of the Post-market Era* (New York: G. P. Putnam's Sons).

Royal Commission on Learning, 1995, *For the Love of Learning: Report of The Royal Commission on Learning*, Vol. IV (Toronto: Ontario Royal Commission on Learning).

Scheurich, J., 1994, Policy archaeology: a new policy studies methodology. *Journal of Education Policy*, 9(4), 297–316.

Seidman, R., 1996, National education 'Goals 2000': some disastrous unintended consequences. *Education Policy Analysis Archives*, 4(1), 1–39.

Sizer, T., 1984, *Horace's Compromise: The Dilemma of the American High School* (Boston: Houghton Mifflin).

Slavin, R. E., 1993, Students differ: so what? *Educational Researcher*, 22(9), 13–14.

Slavin, R. E., Karweit, N. L. and Wasik, B. A., 1993a, Preventing early school failure: what works? *Educational Leadership*, 50(4), 10–18.

Slavin, R. E., Madden, N., Dolan, L., Wasik, B., Ross, S. and Smith, L., 1993b, *'Whenever and wherever we choose . . . '* The replication of Success for All. Paper presented at the a meeting of the American Educational Research Association, Atlanta.

Smith, M. and O'day, J., 1991, Educational equality: 1966 and now, in D. Verstegen and J. Ward (eds), *Spheres of Justice in Education* (New York: Harper Business).

Sparkman, W. E., 1990, School finance challenges in state courts, in J. K. Underwood and D. A. Verstegen (eds), *The Impacts of Litigation and Legislation on Public School Finance* (Grand Rapids: Ballinger Division, Harper & Row).

Task Force on Education for Economic Growth, 1983, *Action for Excellence: A Comprehensive Plan to Improve our Nations Schools* (Washington, DC: Education Commission of the States).

Thompson, T., 1995, Minorities and educational reform: a question of equity and excellence, in R. Ginsberg and D. Plank (eds), *Commissions, Reports, Reforms, and Educational Policy* (Westport, CT: Praeger).

Underwood, J. K. and Verstegen, D. A., 1990, School finance challenges in federal courts: changing equal protection analysis, in J. K. Underwood and D. A. Verstegen (eds), *The Impacts of Litigation and Legislation on Public School Finance* (Grand Rapids: Ballinger Division, Harper & Row).

Wheelock, A., 1992, *Crossing the Tracks: How 'Untracking' can Save America's Schools* (New York: New Press).

Index

A library at your fingertips!

eBooks are electronic versions of printed books. You can store them on your PC/laptop or browse them online.

They have advantages for anyone needing rapid access to a wide variety of published, copyright information.

eBooks can help your research by enabling you to bookmark chapters, annotate text and use instant searches to find specific words or phrases. Several eBook files would fit on even a small laptop or PDA.

NEW: Save money by eSubscribing: cheap, online access to any eBook for as long as you need it.

Annual subscription packages

We now offer special low-cost bulk subscriptions to packages of eBooks in certain subject areas. These are available to libraries or to individuals.

For more information please contact webmaster.ebooks@tandf.co.uk

We're continually developing the eBook concept, so keep up to date by visiting the website.

www.eBookstore.tandf.co.uk

UNIVERSITY OF WALES, NEWPORT
LIBRARY
AND
INFORMATION
SERVICES
CAERLEON